Hysteresis

Speculative Realism

Series Editor: Graham Harman

Editorial Advisory Board
Jane Bennett, Levi Bryant, Patricia Clough, Iain Hamilton Grant, Myra Hird, Adrian Johnston, Eileen A. Joy

Books available

Onto-Cartography: An Ontology of Machines and Media, Levi R. Bryant
Form and Object: A Treatise on Things, Tristan Garcia, translated by Mark Allan Ohm and Jon Cogburn
Adventures in Transcendental Materialism: Dialogues with Contemporary Thinkers, Adrian Johnston
The End of Phenomenology: Metaphysics and the New Realism, Tom Sparrow
Fields of Sense: A New Realist Ontology, Markus Gabriel
Quentin Meillassoux: Philosophy in the Making Second Edition, Graham Harman
Assemblage Theory, Manuel DeLanda
Romantic Realities: Speculative Realism and British Romanticism, Evan Gottlieb
Garcian Meditations: The Dialectics of Persistence in Form and Object, Jon Cogburn
Speculative Realism and Science Fiction, Brian Willems
Speculative Empiricism: Revisiting Whitehead, Didier Debaise, translated by Tomas Weber
Letting Be Volume I: The Life Intense: A Modern Obsession, Tristan Garcia, translated by Abigail RayAlexander, Christopher RayAlexander and Jon Cogburn
Against Continuity: Gilles Deleuze's Speculative Realism, Arjen Kleinherenbrink
Speculative Grammatology: Deconstruction and the New Materialism, Deborah Goldgaber
Letting Be Volume II: We Ourselves: The Politics of Us, Tristan Garcia, translated by Abigail RayAlexander, Christopher RayAlexander and Jon Cogburn
New Ecological Realisms: Post-Apocalyptic Fiction and Contemporary Theory, Monika Kaup
Indexicalism: Realism and the Metaphysics of Paradox, Hilan Bensusan
Hysteresis: The External World, Maurizio Ferraris, edited and translated by Sarah De Sanctis

Forthcoming books

Letting Be Volume III: Let Be and Make Powerful, Tristan Garcia, translated by Christopher RayAlexander, Abigail RayAlexander and Jon Cogburn
Infrastructure, Graham Harman

Visit the Speculative Realism website at: edinburghuniversitypress.com/series-speculative-realism.html

Hysteresis

The External World

Maurizio Ferraris

Edited and translated by Sarah De Sanctis

Edinburgh University Press is one of the leading university presses in the UK. We publish academic books and journals in our selected subject areas across the humanities and social sciences, combining cutting-edge scholarship with high editorial and production values to produce academic works of lasting importance. For more information visit our website: edinburghuniversitypress.com

© Maurizio Ferraris, 2024

English translation © Sarah De Sanctis, 2024

Edinburgh University Press Ltd
The Tun – Holyrood Road
12(2f) Jackson's Entry
Edinburgh EH8 8PJ

Typeset in 11/13 Adobe Sabon by
Cheshire Typesetting Ltd, Cuddington, Cheshire
printed and bound in Great Britain

A CIP record for this book is available from the British Library

ISBN 978 1 4744 7847 2 (hardback)
ISBN 978 1 4744 7848 9 (paperback)
ISBN 978 1 4744 7850 2 (webready PDF)
ISBN 978 1 4744 7849 6 (epub)

The right of Maurizio Ferraris to be identified as the author of this work has been asserted in accordance with the Copyright, Designs and Patents Act 1988, and the Copyright and Related Rights Regulations 2003 (SI No. 2498).

Contents

Series Editor's Preface	viii

ONE. MEDITATION

TWO. OBSERVATION

Introduction: Ontology and Ecology	9
1. The Problem Is Not the Platypus. It's Kant	17
Naturalisation of Physics	17
Aesthetics	21
Space	23
Time	28
Phenomena	31
Logic	37
Deduction	37
Schematism	43
Principles	54
Farewell to the Transcendental	65
2. What Is It Like to Be a Slipper?	68
Epistemology/Ontology	68
The Slipper Argument	68
Ontological Constraints	70
Unamendability	75
First Distinction: Science/Experience	84
Schemes	85
Concepts	108
Science	115
Experience	127

vi   Contents

    Second Distinction: Truth/Reality   132
    Third Distinction: Internal World/External World   142
        Autonomy of Aesthetics from Logic   144
        Antinomy between Aesthetics and Logic   149
        Autonomy of the World from Conceptual and
          Perceptual Schemes   158

THREE. SPECULATION

0. Where Do We Come From?   173
    0.1 In the Beginning Was the Web   173
    0.2 Coming to Light   175
    0.3 Pleroma, Pentecost, Emergence   179

1. What Is Hysteresis?   181
    1.1 Questions   181
    1.2 Metaphysics   187
    1.3 Matter and Memory   193
    1.4 The Common Root   200
    1.5 Difference   206

2. Recording   215
    2.1 Ontology   216
    2.2 Resistance   220
    2.3 Resilience   226
    2.4 Emergence   234
    2.5 Reference   242

3. Iteration   247
    3.1 Technology   250
    3.2 Repetition   257
    3.3 Remembrance   261
    3.4 Re-elaboration   268
    3.5 Verification   276

4. Alteration   282
    4.1 Epistemology   283
    4.2 Truth Bearers   286
    4.3 Forms of Life   289
    4.4 *Logos*   295

5. Interruption   299
   5.1 Teleology   300
   5.2 Direction   303
   5.3 Meaning   304
   5.4 Truth Users   312

FOUR. RECOLLECTION

Notes   327
Bibliography   346
Index   357

Series Editor's Preface

The Speculative Realism series at Edinburgh University Press would never have been complete without a book by Maurizio Ferraris, long-time Professor of Philosophy in Turin – the city where he was born in 1956. Amidst the ongoing resurgence of realism in continental philosophy, it is worth recalling that Ferraris has a good claim to be the first full-blown realist in the continental tradition since Nicolai Hartmann, a now-distant contemporary of Martin Heidegger. Given that the education of the young Ferraris was closely linked with the famed anti-realists Jacques Derrida and Gianni Vattimo, one would expect him to place the question of reality in sceptical quotation marks, or even ridicule it outright. Instead, Ferraris had sufficient courage to walk an initially lonely path towards the realist ontology he defends today. A stunningly prolific figure, Ferraris has authored somewhere on the order of seventy books, of which eleven are available in English translation at the time of this writing. Yet far from being a reclusive scholar, this book-writing machine of a man is also a socially dynamic organiser, a hero to Italian notaries due to his book *Documentality*, and someone who crosses the proverbial analytic–continental divide as easily as if he held a diplomatic passport.[1] He is the driving force behind Labont (Turin's Centre for Ontology), and as affable a dinner companion as one could hope to meet. Along with the German philosopher Markus Gabriel of Bonn (whose own book *Fields of Sense* appeared previously in this series), Ferraris spearheads the New Realism movement in philosophy.[2] No matter how grim the challenges still faced here and there by realist philosophy, Ferraris always appears to be in high spirits and never ceases working. Even a chance encounter with him at a conference often leads one to receive valuable news and to be drafted into two or three future projects.

As Ferraris tells us at the beginning of his book, its two main parts, 'Observation' and 'Speculation' (renumbered as Two and Three to make room for a fresh introductory passage), were written twenty-one years apart. This helps us understand at least two things about the book. First, it demonstrates the consistency of Ferraris's philosophy since the occurrence of his realist turn. Nothing in the first part of the book feels dated, for the simple reason that Ferraris has not changed his basic views on the topics discussed there. He is still a rather pointed critic of Immanuel Kant's critical/transcendental philosophy, as advertised bluntly in the title of his 2013 book, *Goodbye, Kant!*[3] Much of the early portion of the present book develops his critique of Kant in detail. Perhaps the culmination of these pages is the amusing section entitled 'What Is It Like to Be a Slipper?', an obvious riff on Thomas Nagel's famous article on the experience of bats.[4] Whatever the different cultural categories of various human beings encountering a slipper on the floor, they do not create it *ex nihilo* with their minds, but must come to terms with the autonomous reality of the slipper itself. Ferraris goes on to consider the various cases of dogs, worms and ivy meeting the slipper, and although such a thing as a 'slipper' exists hardly or not at all in the very different life-worlds of these creatures, for all of them it is an independent force with which they must reckon. On the basis of this thought experiment, Ferraris proceeds to unmask a variety of philosophical fallacies. In so doing, he draws on the encyclopaedic knowledge and gift for clear presentation that have made him such a powerful voice in the still-young realist tradition in continental philosophy, a current of thought unfortunately nurtured on Edmund Husserl's and Martin Heidegger's view that the realism/anti-realism dispute is nothing more than a 'pseudo-problem'.

Second, the long gap between the composition of the two main parts of the book helps explain why its very title, *Hysteresis*, does not occur until the second of these parts. The concept of 'hysteresis', which Ferraris defines in his opening pages as 'the ability of effects to survive even when their causes have ceased to exist', is the culminating notion of this book. Readers familiar with Ferraris's theory of documents will immediately notice a connection here, since a document is nothing other than a recording of causes that eventually pass away: we can still research wedding records from the eighteenth century and census registries from the nineteenth, though all of the humans to which they refer are long since dead.

The usual philosophical term for this is 'emergence'; the radical argument of this book is that emergence is best understood as *produced* by recording. Against the usual arguments about whether epistemology has priority over ontology or the reverse, it turns out that recording is prior to both of these.

To say any more in this Preface would spoil much of the fun for the reader. But needless to say, Ferraris's central thesis is that recording is the primary feature of reality. Adopting an 'emergent' point of view over what he calls a 'Pentecostal' one, Ferraris treats essence and appearance as equally fundamental: there is simply no being without appearing. As he puts it, 'Recording has the metaphysical property of transforming passivity into activity, event into object, case into law.'[5] I mentioned earlier that he is a celebrated figure among Italian notaries; indeed, they sometimes even regale him with fancy meals and wines, as I once saw for myself. The reason should now be clear: in the wake of Ferraris's philosophy, the notary's transformation of acts into documents begins to take on nothing less than metaphysical significance. Far from being a pesky minor bureaucrat, the notary mimics the very moment of Creation, preserving while transforming whatever material they encounter. If there be a God, then God is a notary. That is simply the most amusing metaphysical consequence of hysteresis, a concept whose implications are profound.

Graham Harman
Long Beach, California
September 2022

One

Meditation

Twenty-one years have passed between the two main parts of this book, 'Observation' and 'Speculation': the gaze on what there is and the attempt to reflect on the conditions of possibility of what there is. So what unites them, you might ask, if not the rather loose thread of the author's identity? Rest assured, there is more; or at least I hope you will think so after reading. But before I leave you to it, I would like to say a couple of words that may make things easier to follow.

At the end of the twentieth century, when I wrote 'Observation' (which came out in Italian in 2001 under the title *Il mondo esterno* (The External World), my concern was to relaunch realism – or more precisely the critical force of the real – in a context where both analytic and continental philosophers seemed persuaded that reality was not a matter for philosophy, which was supposed to deal either with reasoning (for the analytics) or ideology (for the continentals). Both kinds of philosophers were living under the weight of the Kantian saying 'intuitions without concepts are blind'; therefore, to be a philosopher means to deal with concepts, whether to analyse them (as analytics did) or deconstruct them (as continentals did). Thus, both sides forgot about the other side of Kant's saying: namely that concepts without intuitions are empty. Above all, they both overlooked the fact that intuitions often tend to disprove concepts, expectations and rules.

The notion of 'Unamendability', which lies at the heart of 'Observation', underlines precisely this point. Intuitions may be blind, but most of the time they are more than sufficient for our being in the world, with or without concepts. I do not need to know Newton's laws to ride a bike, and I do not need to have read Keynes to use money. This is demonstrated not only by the most banal observation of human life, but also by the fact that if concepts played any constitutive role in the construction of reality, then they would be able to change reality, too: not just in the epistemological sense of what we know or believe we know, but in the ontological sense of what there is.

Now, one of the very few things we can assert with total certainty, even more so than 'Ego cogito, ego sum', is that the Tyrannosaurus Rex never knew it had this name, and that this did not prevent it from being exactly what it was. Similarly, turning to our everyday world, we can very well know that there are both a rabbit and a duck in the famous rabbit-duck illusion, but we can still only see one of them at a time: the eye is not the docile servant of the brain. And this is just a silly example. The important thing is that this feeble resistance of perception harbours the enormous resistance of the world, which was there before us and will remain there after us, perfectly indifferent to our concepts.

Ten years after 'Observation', I contributed to launching the movement called New Realism by making explicit, in a public and not strictly philosophical sense, the theses I had set forth in 2001. The stage had been set in a book I had published back in 1997, a broad historical-theoretical investigation that was far too long to be translated. That book was *Estetica razionale* (Rational Aesthetics), in which I argued for considering aesthetics not as a philosophy of art, but primarily as the philosophy of perception: of *aisthesis*, or of feeling as that which comes before thinking. New Realism became part of a wider constellation made up of other similar views, such as Graham Harman's Object-Oriented Ontology or Quentin Meillassoux's Speculative Materialism. At the end of the present book you will find an article of mine that appeared in 2014 and discusses the history and prehistory of the movement, ending with a commitment that I hope to have honoured with 'Speculation'.

This brings me to the second part of this book, which is the result of my most recent work. As I was saying, in the 2010s my purpose was to build a transcendental realism (which in fact was the title of an article I published in *The Monist* in 2015). What does 'transcendental' mean here? A return to Kant? Not at all, although Kant has always been a model to me, whether in a negative or positive light, setting the standard for how philosophy should be done. The problem for me was not the Kantian epistemological question of the transcendental as the condition of possibility of experience (which for Kant, and especially for idealists, quickly become the possibilities of knowledge). Instead, the problem was ontological, concerning the conditions of possibility of the existence of objects. In short, why is there something rather than nothing?

In *Documentality: Why It Is Necessary to Leave Traces* (published in Italian in 2009), I had given a response to this question that was limited to the social world. Social objects, such as debts, credit, marriages and wars, exist because they are recorded acts, whether in people's heads or – even better (it is safer to say) – in documents. Recording is therefore the great hidden force that makes the social world possible. Just think of a wedding between amnesiacs, without documents or witnesses: it would amount to very little. And its unprecedented and underestimated power is demonstrated by the fact that the boom in technical recording capabilities produced by the Internet has completely revolutionised our world, with a force even greater than that of the industrial revolution.

My conclusion, then, was that the controversial phrase made famous by the great philosopher Jacques Derrida (for me a master) – 'there is nothing outside the text' – was obviously false. There are countless things outside the text, even if the text is expanding (5G is just that, the attempt to make a map of the empire on a 1:1 scale). Instead, claiming that 'there is nothing social outside the text' is a solid truth to which not enough attention is paid. Conversely, all that can become text, or more precisely all that can be recorded – like our heartbeats, our purchases, our online interactions – is social, and can be bought and sold, accumulated, exchanged.

Now, in my *Manifesto of New Realism* (2012) I had argued for the independence of ontology from epistemology, denied by what I call the 'transcendental fallacy', i.e. the confusion between the conditions of possibility of knowledge and the conditions of possibility of existence. In the social world it may seem that the transcendental fallacy applies, yet it does not. Indeed, recording is not the same as knowing (Funes from Borges's novel knows something about this) and the Internet is more reminiscent of the Library of Babel than the transparent Infosphere or Collective Intelligence that is often talked about. Besides, as I was saying before, I don't need to know the laws of economics to pay for a beer; what matters is that the payment is recorded, at least in the bartender's mind (and mine, because otherwise I would risk paying twice).

Let me clarify. Social objects, such as a cartoon about a Tyrannosaurus Rex or the table in front of a judge, exist perfectly well without concepts as long as they are recorded (in the cartoon and in the chancellery proceedings recording the judge's decisions). In the cases of both natural and social objects, concepts and knowledge are very useful, and having spent my whole life studying, I would be the last one to deny it. However, they are not ontologically constitutive. The judge's table also exists for those who ignore its existence, and one can very well be condemned for reasons one does not understand or even know about ('Someone must have slandered Joseph K'). What is ontologically constitutive, at least as far as social objects are concerned, is recording. So what about the other kinds of objects?

In order to answer this question, in the part of the book called 'Speculation', with Kant and against him, I have decided to indulge the fate of reason that pushes it to venture beyond the limits of experience. In the social world it can be seen from experience that recording constitutes objects, and, as I was saying, the Web has amplified this law on a gigantic scale. But what about the natural world? Experience gives us evidence that does not contradict the role of recording in the constitution of objects in general: if there were no permanence in time, and thus a continuation of the effects even after their causes have disappeared (in this case, the carpenter's work), the table in front of me could fall apart. That is why the table is solid and has the properties it does. Is this enough to say that recording ontologically constitutes the table? Of course not. One still needs wood and a carpenter.

Let's take a step back from the conditioned (the table) to the unconditional, or rather to its condition of possibility. Another philosopher who enjoyed talking about tables, in his *Timaeus*, describes the action of a demiurge (a craftsman) who makes the world starting from ideas. Ideas are the form, which is added to matter so as to give life to objects. But how do you go from form to matter? Plato tells us about the *chora*, a third genus – an intermediate kind between form and matter – and describes it as an ability to record. It's really true: recording is what form and matter have in common, and this is acknowledged not only by Plato or Bergson, but also by contemporary physics, which tells us about a Big Bang, an explosion in which a very concentrated memory exploded, giving life to matter, to space and time. Without recording, that explosion would be long forgotten and would have left no traces.

Although when I am ill I see a doctor and not a philosopher, in the case of the *chora* or the Big Bang I can see that they are both speculative hypotheses, which start from things of which we have experience and make considerations from there, assuming the regularity of nature ('natura non facit saltus'). In my case, what unites Observation and Speculation – the two parts of this book but also the two poles of my philosophical work – is what I propose to call 'Hysteresis', i.e. the ability of effects to survive even when their causes have ceased to exist. This notion is used in many fields, ranging from physics to sociology. I have preferred it to that of 'recording' because it allows me to unite under a single term both recording in the proper sense (something remains) and iteration (something repeats itself); both alteration (in repeating itself, something undergoes a change) and interruption (sooner or later everything will end in total stasis, the thermal death of the universe, which will mark the final victory of recording over everything and everyone).

'You mean then, just like Derrida, that there is nothing outside the text? Is this what you mean by saying that there is nothing without hysteresis, and that nothing itself, as the end of all things, is an effect of hysteresis?' Of course not. A text comes with meaning, intelligence, or at least an author; otherwise the term is only used as a metaphor. Instead, in hysteresis there is no author, no meaning, no intelligence, but just a lot of time and a lot of space in which, at certain times and in certain areas (as far as we know), meaning, intelligence and even authors have emerged. Whether these authors have written meaningful or intelligent things is for the reader to decide, and it is in this spirit, not without fear, that I conclude this premise.

Turin
15 August 2020

Two

Observation

To Paolo Bozzi

Ex te ipso excede: in exteriore homine habitat res

Introduction: Ontology and Ecology[1]

I remember one morning in 1979, in Milan, at the office of the journal *Alfabeta*. Gianni Sassi – not a voracious philosophical reader but a very intelligent man, who unfortunately left us too soon – was reprimanding an editor for cheekily inserting a review of his own book in the journal's next issue: 'You cannot do that!' shouted Sassi, 'It's a question of ontology!' – of course, he meant deontology. Those were the years when people started saying 'epochal' instead of 'important', and 'ontology' – a philosophical specialisation – was becoming an everyday term, in the wake of Heidegger's popularity.

Heidegger's idea was that the beings we encounter in the world hide a more fundamental Being that makes them possible, determining them through conceptual schemes (that is, concretely speaking, through the books we have read and the language we speak). He also thought that this encounter with Being – stratified in tales, traditions and libraries – constitutes a sort of duty, replacing those of religion and morality. In this sense, Sassi wasn't wrong, after all, in mistaking ontology for deontology. This duty, for Heidegger, concerns not only people, but also beings: if they really want to be what they are, they have to be confronted with the more fundamental Being.

This idea doesn't seem too far-fetched, either. The Aristotelian notion that experience comes before science, Leibniz's reference to the principle of a sufficient reason for everything, and – finally and mostly – Kant's transcendental argument that everything that can become science has to become science (just like every person must become moral), all point in the same direction. The fact that *Being and Time* was a piece of transcendental philosophy was fairly obvious to Löwith when he proofread the text for his professor.

For a long time I agreed with all of these views; then I developed some perplexities about them. On 28 September 1999 I was in Mexico City and had just begun work on this part of the book, which is a criticism of the abuse of conceptual schemes and transcendental arguments in ontology. Suddenly, the external world hit me: the room started shaking. At first I thought I was hallucinating – I had never experienced an earthquake before. Now, if the earthquake in Lisbon in the eighteenth century could constitute a serious objection to the philosophy of history and theodicy, that of Mexico City could indeed be the counterproof of the identification between ontology and the 'Meaning of Existence': I didn't know much about earthquakes, wasn't expecting anything of the sort, and yet things went the way they did for me as well as for the other 25 million people around me. I know this argument will sound suspicious, since Lenin already used it against Mach's empirical criticism. However, that morning in 1999, the world was encountered: unforeseen and discordant, but not hallucinatory. So the seismic event offered another version of the attack in Thomas Mann's *Buddenbrooks*, when little Antoine, in response to her grandfather's request, lists the entities that make up creation: 'I believe that God made me ... and all creatures ... including clothes and shoes, meat and drink, hearth and home, wife and child, fields and cattle.'[2] Creation is an external world that we encounter, in which things are what they were before we were born and will stay that way after we die. Which of the two versions of ontology – Sassi-Heidegger or Earthquake-Antoine – is the right one?

A little history could be useful here. Ontology is part of metaphysics, and if Aristotle had never spoken of metaphysics he would never have talked about ontology (although, of course, he never used the term 'ontology' as such). Many centuries later, Avicenna (980–1037) clarified that the subject of metaphysics is being as such; later, Francisco Suarez (1548–1617) ordered the subject matter, dividing it into general metaphysics (which deals with being as such) and special metaphysics (dedicated to rational psychology, theology and cosmology); soon after, in 1613, the term ontology appeared in the works of two authors of philosophical encyclopaedias: Rudolf Goeckel's *Lexicon philosophicum* and Jacob Lorhard's *Theatrum philosophicum*. Finally, in the first half of the following century, Christian Wolff (1679–1754) wrote a treatise on it that marked a breakthrough.[3]

However, the glory of this NovAntiqua was short-lived, and in §33 of his *Encyclopaedia* (1817) Hegel already referred to Wolff's treatise as an old scholastic, nominalistic and inconclusive work. The reason for this sudden obsolescence is fairly obvious: about forty years earlier, in his *Critique of Pure Reason* (1781), Kant suggested founding metaphysics as a science. Since the paradigmatic science, for him just as for us, was physics, metaphysics appeared to be the vocabulary of a dead language: what is the point of talking about *ens quatenus est ens*, when we can learn the fundamental laws of matter? If there is still room for philosophy, the latter must exist in a close relationship with physics. This was marked by the idea of transcendental philosophy, which gives ontological depth to epistemology.

Physics collects and relates facts; metaphysics has to prove that they rest on some laws: if the world is mathematisable, it is because our senses and our intellect are naturally mathematical, and the task of philosophy, on its way to becoming philosophy of knowledge, is to naturalise physics. That is, philosophy has to show that the mathematised science of nature is not merely a historical contingency that might or might not have happened, but a constitutive endowment of human nature. As a consequence, the world is not what we encounter through experience but – at a deeper level – it is the world as explained by physics.

Despite appearances, the situation ends up being vaguely paradoxical: precisely when experience is identified with physics, the latter moves further away from our perceptual data, telling us about a world in which even Newton's physics is the exception to laws that go beyond any experience we might have. Indeed, it is one thing to learn that the Earth revolves around the Sun, but quite another to try to cook in a space like that described by Minkowski. Of course, the first formulation of atoms and the conceptual schemes required to know the world date back to the age of Democritus, but at that time it was still possible to posit an almost perfect overlap between the sensible cosmos and the intelligible cosmos. The latter was roughly the world of tables and chairs, only more minute; water atoms flowed more gently than earth atoms, while atoms of air were thinner and thus able to fly around, while the lightest atoms were those of fire. The world of ideas ended up being the same as the sublunary world, arousing the embarrassing debate about whether fingernail dirt also has a corresponding idea. At that time, the universe of science – compared to that of experience – appeared roughly like the afterlife dreamed of by the daughters in Giuseppe di Lampedusa's *The Leopard*: 'identical with this life, all complete with judges, cooks and convents'.[4] But now this is no longer the case, and as soon as Kant assimilated experience and physics, the latter was already exceeding into the microscopic and the macroscopic.

It is easy to understand why, with *Being and Time*, Heidegger wanted to reconnect ontology to the sphere of experience, that is, to everyday life. However, there is something fake about this move. For instance, Heidegger suggested that maybe we still haven't started thinking, which sounds like an oncologist stating there is no cure for cancer, yet. According to Heidegger, it seems, if we sharpen our mind and rub our eyes we'll be able to see the world as it really is. If this is so, then what about the relationship between ontology and everyday life? The best answer is probably a question: 'So what have we been doing so far? Haven't we been thinking? Have we just thought we were thinking, like a wizard trying to cure rheumatism with a frog-based potion?'

While questioning our thinking, Heidegger would never have dared to suggest, for instance, that we haven't started feeling yet: he knew very well that he would have been taken no more seriously than a magician. The difference between being and entity, between the apparent phenomenon and the deep reality that affects it, takes on a bizarre quality when transposed into the sphere of human and ecological interactions. What would you say to someone claiming that the chicken on your plate is not really a chicken, it's not a chicken *als solches*, because the real chicken is elsewhere? Perhaps you'd think you've come across a lover of organic, free-range chicken, but you would certainly never consider that he means your chicken is merely apparent.

Indeed, there is an obvious difference of value in – say – a physicist claiming 'this table doesn't exist, what exists are the subatomic particles that make it up', and someone making a similar claim to a police officer to prevent him from confiscating their furniture. In the first case we have a scientific and fully legitimate statement; in the second we have a witty sophism which would probably not have worked anyway, as the police officer would still have confiscated that particular aggregation of subatomic particles and not another one.

Reductionism is usually ascribed to positivists, but the claim that being is not the entity's being also hides a reductionism of its own, coming from the tradition of the sciences of the spirit that, faced with the mathematising reduction of the phenomenon proposed by natural scientists, have merely set against Descartes' mechanism the conceptual schemes derived from Leibniz's criticism[5] that one should not only consider causal and mechanical links, but also final ones: purpose, meaning, value, etc. By taking that road, ontology becomes a peculiar form of epistemology, and the paths of analytic and continental philosophy are thus able to meet at a crossroads.

Take the famous American philosopher Willard van Orman Quine: for him, ultimately – with a very traditional view – there is only one science, the Paradigmatic Science, which has its core in physics, logic and mathematics. A significant consequence of such an approach is that there is also only one object: the physical world as it can be accessed by the mathematised science of nature. So far, so good: we all know that Quine is like that. But let's take Gadamer: he proclaims himself the champion of 'extramethodical experiences of truth', that is, of art and history, and thinks his views are different from Quine's. And yet, upon closer inspection, they are not: not only *de facto*, as Gadamer uses aeroplanes and trains instead of horses or sedan chairs, but also *de jure*. In fact, he also talks – albeit critically – about one single method of Science. He sets his discourse within a philosophy of history – that is, a process of universal development – which stands to humanistic disciplines in the same relation as scientific teleology to other spheres.

Once they have posited the axiom, continental philosophers choose their options according to the context: if they are ill they go see a doctor instead of reading Rilke, believing that the best thing to do is to resort to the mathematised science of nature; if they are simply nervous or upset they go for Rilke and not for a doctor, claiming that when it comes to the practical sphere of our decisions and aspirations, science is not everything. In fact, science represents the iteration of non-inventive protocols, whereas art and similar experiences create 'openings' in the world endowed with the same power of innovation that analytic philosophers ascribe to science. That is to say, ontology is a *dépendance* of epistemology, whether it be physicalist or anti-physicalist, and the overcoming of metaphysics offers a romantic version of physicalist reductionism.

Being and Time came out in 1927. Around the same time, two Berlin Gestalt thinkers, Otto Lipmann and Helmuth Bogen, published *Naïve Physik*.⁶ Their basic idea was not that the world of appearance should be traced back to its deeper, true essence: in everyday experience we are under the impression that the world is made up of solid and determined things, not images and chimeras. It is little use to know that colours are chromatic waves and that the Earth is round if we want a dress of a given colour or are building a house – in the end, it is also little use to wonder if we have or have not started thinking yet. *De facto* and *de jure* are two different and often opposed levels; the rational is not necessarily the same as the real, nor should it be. Physics does not have the final word on everything. At most, it has the final word when objecting to unlikely statements on the world, such as those expressed by a sceptic ('this table only appears such to me') or a nihilist ('this table doesn't exist').

The fundamental differences on which I am basing this book – between ontology and epistemology, experience and science, naive physics and expert physics – is crucial here: the fact that there are unamendable experiences is a powerful objection to the thesis that conceptual schemes are omnipotent. It is not true that thought is exclusively destined to achieve the ultimate truth of things: one can learn a specialised language and become a professor of the theory of probability, but this will not prevent one from making common mistakes outside the university.⁷ Sight is not at the service of thought, because I can know as many things as I please, but I'll still see things as they appear. In order to object to reductionism, one must start from here: the way things appear to us cannot be amended by resorting to a more fundamental level of matter or spirit. Our experiences are not primarily aimed at implementing theories, nor do the latter constitute our second nature; rather, they are the outcome of historical contingency in a given cultural context, which has given rise to a specific science (whereas other cultural contexts either didn't think about it or had no interest in it).

The thinker who is mainly responsible for reductionism or, if you will, epistemological inflation, is Kant – the chief supporter of transcendental philosophy. In fact, if we claim that experience represents the prehistory of science, we assume that if something is there it is because it has to be there. This attitude leads one to curse the stars like one of Metastasio's characters, because then the world would be often unjust, inexplicable, senseless, full of optical illusions and things that don't add up. Why not wonder if the problem lies elsewhere? Maybe our senses are not necessarily predisposed for science – and therefore they do not lie to us, as they are not made to establish the truth – but are rather intended to guarantee a behaviour that is fit for the environment.

In order to mark the difference between seeing and thinking, experience and science, one should wonder whether the real field of ontology – of what there is, of what we are confronted with in everyday life – is truly that of conceptual schemes (that is, the conceptual a priori of epistemology as hermeneutics and of hermeneutics as epistemology). Rather, the sphere of ontology is that of the external world, that is, something that one cannot explain or interpret or change: it is like a solid rock, which one comes across and breaks one's spade upon.[8] Ontology is not like a sour goblet we have to drink unwillingly, but is rather related to the fact that beyond a certain threshold – given by our life, our environment, our time – doubting, interpreting and transforming (as well as the belief that we are doubting, interpreting and transforming) lose meaning.

There are different levels of reality, mainly distinguishable for their duration: the physical world and its transformations are lost in endless time, whereas people change over observable time, and every day scientific articles often deny theories published a few weeks earlier. In between, there are astronomical ages, geological and zoological eras, Egyptian dynasties and (as Gadda put it) Hegiras. It seems futile to regulate the transformations of our mood based on cosmic ages (astrology doesn't have a very good reputation); there are many scientific interpretations of colours, and yet if we go to Greece we can all witness what Homer aptly described as the 'wine-dark sea'.

This is the immense atavism of the senses, which suggests something that is little thought of: the real Platonism is that of perception. Choosing the transcendental path, on the contrary, one generates a world upside down: one postulates a universe that could not work without conceptual schemes and conditions of possibility, just like without students and professors there would be no universities. If I see a table, I can very well say that in a million years – provided science and humankind still exist – research will still go on; but I cannot really claim that I need categories to put a book on the table. If I do claim that (and people have done so), I produce epistemological inflation. What I want to propose here instead is a deflation, based on two reasons.

The first is the following: things go the way they go, but there is no reason why they should go that way. A fact is not a law, and therefore logical categories have only a limited scope. The point is not to offer alternatives, but rather to articulate a typology in which 'if it can, it must' is only one option, next to 'it can, but it doesn't necessarily have to' and 'it cannot'. The second reason is that, to this day, there is not a single proof that what is founded on the transcendental couldn't be equally well founded without it: the claim that experiences are necessarily mediated by conceptual schemes cannot be proven, as it would presuppose an observer with no experience.[9] This is factually impossible, much more so than an attempt to place a huge sheet of paper behind the Moon to make it look grey rather than white.

The fact that such an experiment – which cannot be done by resorting to children raised by wolves, blind people healed by computerised vision goggles, etc. – proves to be unfeasible is not only an argument against direct perception. It also gives us a counterargument that, by demonstrating the unfalsifiable character of indirect perception, shows us that the latter is a dogma and a working hypothesis rather than a verifiable truth. Experience might require the 'here' and the 'now', but can anyone seriously prove or deny that to perceive an object one also requires 3,857 unconscious categories? Conversely, is it true that in order to say 'here', 'there', 'this', 'now', we really need a very complex apparatus? And mostly, how can one prove that we think in terms of 'here', 'there', 'this', 'now', when we are not talking?

The use of categories is rather akin to the impossibility of an *ars oblivionalis*, so that, once you think of a pink elephant, you cannot get it out of your head. Usually, at this point, one specifies that the transcendental is not constitutive but regulative. Nevertheless, if the transcendental does not constitute things, I really cannot see what one should do with it, at least in ontology. In short, the problem is not the platypus – the difficulty of the a priori system in dealing with some empirical knowledge – but rather Kant: the transcendental setting that has affected thought until very recent times.

So let's see how things work with the transcendental and how they work without it, in the world external to conceptual schemes.

I

The Problem Is Not the Platypus. It's Kant

Naturalisation of Physics

Analytic and ontology. In the *Critique of Pure Reason*,[10] the relationship between Analytic and Dialectic corresponds to that between general metaphysics and special metaphysics in Suarez's partition. This can be verified with the following table.

Therefore, in the Analytic, Kant is proposing his ontology. He doesn't draw it directly from Suarez, but rather from Baumgarten's *Metaphysics*, which he adopted in class as a textbook. Again, a table comes in handy here.

Again, the Analytic/Dialectic relationship in the *Critique of Pure Reason* reflects exactly the traditional partition, as shown by a third table.

From logic to physics. So far, we have been dealing with simple structural correspondences which, however, reveal a crucial

Table 1. General Metaphysics and Special Metaphysics. Epistemological Versions

Suarez	General metaphysics	Special metaphysics
	being as being (ontology)	Cosmology Psychology Theology
Kant	Analytic	Dialectic
	Cosmology and Psychology (everything that can be accessed through Newtonian physics and Cartesian introspection)	Theology, and everything that – in Cosmology and Psychology – cannot be accessed through Newtonian physics and Cartesian introspection)

Table 2. Baumgarten's *Metaphysics* in Its Fundamental Articulations

Ontology	Internal	External
(Predicates of being)	External or relative	Identical and different
		Simultaneous and successive
		Cause and caused
		Signum and *signatum*

Cosmology
Psychology
Theology

Table 3. Analytic and Dialectic in the *Critique* of Pure Reason

Ontology	Of concepts	Judgments and categories
(Predicates of being)	Of principles (limited to analogies of experience, for reasons I will clarify)	Substance
		Reciprocal action
		Cause

Cosmology
Psychology
Theology

point, namely that the Analytic is Kant's ontology. But there is one important difference. Suarez, and even more Baumgarten (going though Leibniz and Wolff), assume that the object of ontology consists of everything that is not logically contradictory: a mountain made of gold falls within ontology, but a square circle doesn't. This situation – which depends on the primacy of the principle of reason – is not one Kant was happy with: in line with an idea that was relatively popular in his day, he excluded the possible from the sphere of ontology, thereby also expelling from it mountains made of gold, hippogriffs and telepathy (which are not motivated by the characteristics of this world). Essentially, he restricts the field of ontology to the real, which means ultimately to the sensible – 100 real talers are ready at hand – as opposed to the possible. For this very reason the principle of non-contradiction is only a norm for analytical judgments, which have nothing to do with reality, but only with formal properties of the intellect. The supreme principle of all synthetic judgments becomes the agreement between intuition and the internal sense, that is, a version of the intellect's *adaequatio* to the thing, which is also the distinction between formal and transcendental logic. But what does Kant mean by 'real'? When circumscribing ontology, he is also forced to exhibit the criteria by which it is determined that something is real, and his answer is that the real is the object of physics. The dependence of ontology on logic is transformed into a new subordination.

Hence another consequence: Newtonian physics is a mathematical physics, and therefore mathematics, pushed out the door through the critique of rationalism, comes back in through the window by means of the adoption of physicalism. Such subordination, barely disguised, opens a breach for all the prejudices of modern philosophy: Kant draws on the Cartesian assumption that what is in us is more certain than what is out there; from such an axiom, he obtains the result that we only really know what we have produced ourselves, which explains the insistence on the Copernican Revolution and on the schematism. And to mitigate the aura of arbitrariness surrounding subjectivity, he turns the bland Platonism of the empiricists – who treat ideas as psychological productions – into a stronger Platonism, for which ideas are in our heads but at the same time ensure the true bone-structure of the real, which is made up of triangles, cubes and icosahedrons. The point is not to re-propose the fantastic cosmogony of *Timaeus*, but to apply Newton's (anything but fantastic) cosmology: space is geometry, time is arithmetic, our senses are natural meters and thermometers; and everything that is not mathematisable is not, or in any case is less than all the rest.

At first glance this may not be obvious, since Kant does not say that we are innate physicists and mathematicians, that is, he does not claim that we apply Newton's laws every time we throw a stone in the air and move away so it won't fall on our heads. However, his discourse implies that if we really knew what we were doing, then we would realise that indeed an infinite number of calculations take place in our head whenever we throw a stone. So, a way to describe what happens in our heads and in the world is transformed into the true nature of what happens in our heads and in the world, in which that head exists by sheer chance. Kant proceeds to a mathematisation of experience, which is another way of saying 'a naturalisation of physics': Newton's laws are assumed as necessities of human nature, valid for us and for beings like us; physics is not history but nature, and the latter is a book written in mathematical characters. The lever of naturalisation is the revolution, implemented on the 'model' of geometers and physicists: mathematics works extraordinarily well for the description of the physical world, but its efficacy appears mainly factual; metaphysics must show that the fact is based on a law.

Profit and loss. This solution makes room for metaphysics, but doesn't come without problems:

1. *Physics and metaphysics.* Where does physics end and metaphysics begin? Kant saw how hard it is to distinguish metaphysics from the other sciences based on its higher degree of universality, since, as he says himself (B XXII), it seems trivial to claim that the concept of 'extension' belongs to metaphysics and so does that of 'body'. But some serious problems would arise by wondering if the concept of 'fluid body' falls within metaphysics, because at this rate everything would be 'metaphysical'.

Recognising the disease is not the same as treating it, and in fact the moral of the story is not hard to find: just take a step back from physics, and you'll have metaphysics, which would then be a somewhat weaker and blurred version of physics. Metaphysics begins when you half-close your eyes, according to a division of labour which is based precisely on the distinction – that Kant considers unlikely – between general principles and special principles. On its own, all that is left to metaphysics is the domain of questions that have either no answer or too many answers – no longer a matter of Analytic but rather of Dialectic.

2. *Analytic and dialectic.* But is the lack of response eternal or temporary? And if it is only transitory, where does the analytic end and the dialectic begin? Nietzsche already presented the theme of the beginning or eternity of the world as far from undecidable: on the one hand, there is the scientific hypothesis of the heat death of the universe that therefore – because it will end – must have had a beginning in time; on the other hand, there is the hypothesis – which Nietzsche advances as genuinely scientific, and defends for that very reason – of the eternal return. This argument could be extended: progress in genetics may not have solved the theological problem, contrary to what former President Clinton optimistically suggested when he argued that the Human Genome Project has revealed the 'language of God'. However, it has certainly falsified the assertion that not even a future Newton could have explained the mere development of a blade of grass.[11] It is not an empirical problem but a conceptual one, since everything in the dialectic that appears undecidable for reasons of law may only be undecidable for factual reasons.

3. *Empirical and transcendental.* The problem has a broader impact: where does the empirical end and the transcendental begin? As we have seen, the distinction between metaphysics and science proper does not lie in their objects – general in the first, particular in the second – but in their method, because mathematics and other sciences directly deriving from it examine the universal in the particular, whereas metaphysics grasps the particular in the universal. However, as the sphere of the particular and decidable is indeterminate, metaphysics appears as labile and provisional, because physics is constantly moving forward.

4. *The boundless conceptual.* So, if we embrace the Copernican Revolution, we get the opposite of the certainties we hoped to obtain: we will only ever know knowledge. Therefore, properly speaking, we will have no knowledge but mere tautologies, confirmations of conceptual schemes, which on the other hand are constitutively unstable. And what would the benefit be? To be able to explain literally everything, because the transcendental machine is no different from the fictions of the psychology of faculties, which explained sleep through the *virtus dormitiva*. This can be seen in Table 4, which constitutes the outline of my reading of Kant.

Aesthetics

Mathematics and ecology. Here is the premise that ensures the boundless transcendental. Kant explains an apparent paradox: it is not that we see things and then derive space from their position and time from their movement; on the contrary, without space and time as pure sensible intuitions there would be no experience of objects. This paradox is willingly accepted as it goes hand in hand with common sense, according to which we see things in a certain way and not another because our sense organs are made in a certain way.

Compared to conventional wisdom, however, Kant polemically adds a challenging element: our organs are naturally mathematical, that is, they are structured by what had been the unconquerable fortress for empiricism, as it appears difficult to make mathematics depend on habit. This idea may seem bizarre, if one doesn't consider the controversy that motivates Kant's choice, not only because experience bears very little resemblance to mathematics,

Table 4. Transcendental Aesthetics and Analytic as the Naturalisation of Physics

Aesthetics	Mathematics	Time (arithmetic)	
		Space (geometry)	
		Phenomena (physics)	
Analytic	Logic	Judgments and categories	
		Deduction	
		Schematism	
	Physics	Systems of principles	Postulates of empirical thought in general
			Axioms of intuition
			Anticipations of perception
			Analogies of experience — Substance / Cause / Reciprocal action
Dialectic		Antinomies: what physics doesn't know and therefore metaphysics doesn't speak of	

but above all because if perceptual processes have a salient feature compared to logical ones, it is precisely the fact that the former generally do not observe the principles of economics that govern the ideal of thought and are subject to the traditional epistemological election of mathematics.[12] In short, Kant does not seem to consider that what is defined by transcendental aesthetics is a real environment and not a sheet of paper in a laboratory. The best way to grasp the flaws of this description is to compare the Kantian perspective with an ecological approach: Kant wants to demonstrate that space makes experience possible, but thinks that to do so it is sufficient to claim that space allows for the application of geometry to experience.

Space

1. *Euclidean and non-Euclidean.* For Kant there is only Euclidean geometry, which conforms to our perception, except for marginal cases. Accusing him of not considering non-Euclidean geometries appears anachronistic, but the biggest problem is that our perceptual performances are oversized and undersized compared to Euclidean geometry, so that the overlap on which he bases the entire transcendental aesthetics does not hold: the perceptual fact does not correspond to a mathematical law, unless one claims that the Supreme Being has messed up his calculations, or is actually an Evil Genius who enjoys fooling us.

(a) *Incongruent opposites.* In short, things do not add up either by excess or by defect. On the one hand, and Kant realised this in the case of incongruent opposites, there are figures – like the right hand and the left, the spirals of two shells or two hop plants – which we easily perceive to be symmetrical, and this would not be possible if we were only using Euclidean geometry. Thus, we are able to grasp the symmetry of triangles traced on opposite hemispheres, as in the figure below, something for which the geometry of linear dimensions is insufficient.

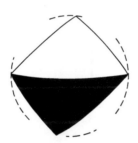

Our naive geometry even includes some elements of topology, since we are able to handle holes of all sorts; likewise, we can use a chess board without difficulty despite the fact that the hypotenuse, unlike in Euclidean geometry, is three boxes long just as the catheti. This circumstance may appear trivial, and has traditionally been applied in painting: for example, the way in which the window is reflected in the mirror of the Arnolfini Portrait is a case of non-Euclidean geometry. And yet if Kant was right in every way, van Eyck's image should appear ominous and inexplicable.

(b) *Sloppy geometry.* On the other hand, there are figures like the following, implausible even in terms of Euclidean geometry, which instead we consider very plausible indeed – proving our sloppy geometrical skills.[13]

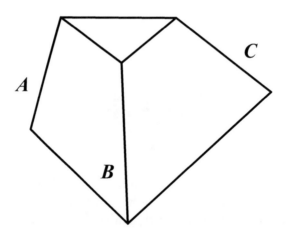

And consider how Signorelli's Dante and Virgil would appear if indeed they resembled their shadow[14] (while, when looking at the picture, we do not pay too much attention to it).

These observations bear witness to the fact that our perception of space does not naturally conform to Euclidean geometry; these contrasts, although not huge, are enough to refute the hypothesis of a harmonious correspondence between the phenomenal and the Euclidean (that is, for Kant, the 'geometrical' tout court). However, one can understand why Kant found it necessary to play the card of complete reversibility: he wanted to keep perception safe from its alleged contingency, while responding to the empiricist attempts to bring habit and experience into geometry: for example, in the constitution of depth.

Nevertheless, by betting on an equation without residues between geometry and space, Kant would be in serious trouble in motivating phenomena like perceptual constancy, for which a person four metres away does not seem half as tall as when she's two metres away – Berkeley easily explained this as habit. Moreover, it is not necessarily true that space is intuition and not concept. Indeed, one can safely say that the opposite is true, because there are different spaces exactly as there are numerous different pens or dogs.[15] Let's verify this claim.

2. *Air space and ground space.* This multiplicity is obvious from an ecological point of view, for example in relation to the differences between air and ground space. There's a big difference between walking up and down in a room, flying a drone and thinking about cosmic distances; Kant instead assumes that all those spaces are the homogeneous parts of a single continuum. On closer inspection, the problem is not empirical, and rather involves the idea that even if a lion could speak, we would not understand it. Between galactic and ecological spaces there is such a great difference that it is impossible to think of them as part of the same intuition. On the other hand, nothing prevents one from tracing all those cases back to the same concept, just as a stool, a stuffed chair, a leather recliner chair and a car seat can be summarised under the generic concept of 'seat'.

3. *Open space and closed space.* Moreover, still at the ecological level, there is a difference between open and closed space. Kant is thinking about outer space – the plains or the sea – which seems to be more like physical space; but this is different from inner space. Think of the cloister of a monastery: there is a garden, which perhaps can be considered as a small plain; but then there is the space behind the columns, with shadows and lights. Is it really the same space, ecologically speaking? And most importantly, if the infinite space that annihilates us when we think about it and the reassuring space of our room are both called 'space', perhaps it is because, as usual, there is a unifying concept that – after performing an abstraction that neglects many important aspects – brings together significantly heterogeneous realities.

4. *Other animals.* Third, in the Kantian perspective, spatial intuitions would be valid for us as well as for beings like us. Here there are at least two problems.

(a) *Flies, frogs, cats.* Consider beings that are quite dissimilar to us in shape or size, like various animal species. Going by what we can observe from the behaviour of a fly or a frog, there is space for them, too. Wondering what space might be for a fly or a frog is not the same as asking whether we would understand them if they could talk, nor is it similar to wondering what space might be for an angel. Communicating with a cat can be very difficult indeed. Picture this scenario: you are in bed and don't want to play with the cat, but he bites your big toe; you push him away, but he believes it's part of the game, and bites you again. Then you throw him off the bed and he jumps back up: for him it is still part of the game. This might go on for a long time: he does not speak English or any other language, and you cannot just say 'I don't want to play now'. That, however, does not mean that the bed is something significantly different for you compared to what it is for him, as well as for frogs and flies. Conversely, according to Kant, the world of cats, flies and the frogs that eventually eat the flies, is something completely inaccessible to our examination, and two similar acts – a man taking a stick, a dog taking a stick – have absolutely nothing in common, since the former would be a shared appearance and the second would be an event inaccessible in its true essence.

(b) *Men and women.* And now consider beings conspicuously similar to us: women if one is a man, or men if one is a woman. It is observationally obvious that men and women have a different sense of direction, and here common sense is corroborated by experimental data. Likewise, experimental evidence shows that there are patients with parietal lesions that omit the whole right side of space. And since the time of Husserl and Piaget it has been known that space – as a whole, and not only in depth, as in Berkeley – can change with the evolution of the person. Again, if space is subject to involution or evolution, and varies between males and females, in what sense would it be a pure sensible intuition?

5. *Distal and proximal.* Finally, sticking to us humans, it has been experimentally demonstrated that one can distinguish between distal and proximal perceptual space, a premotor area and a representative space. Such spaces are in turn organised both in relation to the subject (egocentric) and in relation to the environment (allocentric); all these subspaces – which at least in the egocentric/allocentric opposition represent two different solutions adopted by Kant, but which he conceived as alternative[16] – constitute not limitations of a single absolute space, but elementary spaces. Even in this case, the a priori and intuitive character of space is questionable to say the least.

6. *Mental and real.* Moreover, it is far from obvious that space is simply external: mnemonics and spatial reasoning use a mental space, such as apartments and streets in which to place loci. If it is stated that such a space is analogue, why shouldn't this also

hold for the pure sensible intuition of space compared to what we actually consider space? And if instead it is argued that it is an imaginary space, the argument also applies against Kant, because mental images have almost none of the properties of the thing represented.

7. *The Earth*. Obviously, all the differences between ground and air space, open and closed space, egocentric and allocentric systems, etc., do not prevent me from going from a closed space to an open one, from the Earth to the sky, from the sky to space, and even from this life to the beyond: absolute space is Husserl's Promised Land, absolute time measures the becoming of that land as a changing whole. However, if the Earth is ontological, then mathematics has nothing to do with it. Conversely, if it is identified with the Newtonian spacetime, then it is the Earth that has to bow out because this view does not consider that the Earth was there before the invention of mathematics.

Time

As for time, assimilated to elementary arithmetic (for Kant, the origin of number lies in the fingers) just as space is assimilated to Euclidean geometry, the epistemological intention is even more marked: space has to be absorbed in time in the internal sense, just as geometry can be transcribed in mathematical terms. This is why – given that the internal sense is also the synthetic unity of apperception – it is possible to subdue the external world to judgments, categories and principles, which make up the transcendental logic, thanks to the mediation of schemes, which are forms of time.

1. *Soul*. Now, if we called the borscht 'pizza', we could easily state that pizza is a traditional Russian dish. Likewise, if we call 'time' dawn and sunset, boredom and anxiety, mental contents and even spatial representations, it will be an easy consequence that time is everywhere. Of course, this is the case with the Cogito: if the synthetic unity of apperception must accompany all my representations, if every time something happens to me that thing happens to me, it is not difficult to conclude that I am everywhere. However, in this case, it just means that I am where I am if and when I am there, but not that time is everywhere. However, it is difficult to find an argument to fully show the (even just formal) equivalence between space and the external sense, or between time

and the internal sense: how do we regulate the apparent similarities between things as different as the I-think, the Cogito, the soul, the wait, memory, the movement of the stars, train times, and generally between what we seem to have inside and what we see out there?

For all we know, there may be no analogy whatsoever: it may simply seem to be that way. And yet, the greatest strength of time lies in its hypothetical identification with the Cogito, which oils the transcendental machine and its joints: thinking of something is not the same as knowing it, but knowing it means thinking of it. Mostly, encountering something – at least *de jure*, if the world went as it should – is a cognitive act. Nevertheless, the thesis that time truly has an all-encompassing function only works if one assumes that the Cogito is somehow all the beings it knows. But what if it didn't know them? Or at least if it didn't know them all?

One could rightly object that the synthetic unity of apperception cannot be psychologically accessed. In so doing, though, one would wield a double-edged weapon: if the synthetic unity of apperception has nothing to do with the psyche, then one wonders what on earth it is related to. Furthermore, this constitutes a purely formal if not even nominal solution: saying that time mediates between inside and outside because it is an insensible sensible is like saying that a green glass mediates between a green leaf and the transparent air. In all likelihood, a Kantian would reply that any other way would ultimately hand us over to empiricist induction and then to scepticism. But this answer is far from satisfactory, because it is like saying that the only way to avoid going to the dentist, sooner or later, is to have a beak rather than teeth.

2. *Land, sea, sky.* One might object: time is not sufficient for the occurrence of something, but it is necessary for it to present itself – if something appeared and disappeared without any temporal regularity, even if it were resistant, would we be willing to consider it a substance? Permanence in time thus seems to be a necessary condition for the ascription of reality to any object.

Conversely, doesn't denying time ultimately mean acquiring an eternalist perspective, with all the difficulties that ensue? However, for Kant there is at least one case in which time is a sufficient as well as a necessary condition: the 'I think' as self-affection and as temporal flow. On the other hand, to deny the omnipresence of time is not to argue that time is not there. Mostly, eternalists do not deny time: they say it is an appearance and then reduce appearance to movement. However, what I have in mind is nothing of the sort: the shadows or objects that appear and disappear are cases of becoming, starting from which we speak of 'temporality'; otherwise we would not do so. If one saw the same scene for a lifetime one would not conclude that that was a 'very strong substance': one would not have the idea of substance, and therefore of time. Kant's thesis is true for a theory of science, since without 'yesterday', 'tomorrow', 'a year ago', 'two hundred years from now', science would not be possible. However, this does not hold for a theory of experience, where the a priori and transcendental character of time is, if possible, even more doubtful than that of space.

(a) *A priori*. As concerns the a priori character, if it is hard to think of a colourless space, it is equally hard to think of a time without at least some movement, inside or outside the soul. In both cases, the fact that the counterarguments are psychological does not save Kant, as they appear as responses to his own arguments, which therefore turn out to be derived from an introspective examination. And when psychology comes into play, there are endless exceptions to the unitary and a priori character of time; suffice it to say that people very often have very different experiences of temporality, to the point of exasperating each other.

(b) *Transcendental*. As to the transcendental character of time, is a table truly in time? Even if it were, it would still be in space much more than it is in time. Even what happens to the table over time – wear and tear – seems to actually take place in space: time, if anything, is what comes out by thinking that all those things didn't happen simultaneously. Of course, a piece of paper falling to the ground from that same table seems to be more in time, but that's because it's an event. On the contrary, I can very well state that the book you're holding is present; the fact that it is in the present doesn't add much. I can also claim that when you close the book and put it on the shelf (or in the fireplace) the book will be absent: does it make sense to say that it will then be in the past, and that it was in the future before you started reading it? I don't find it hard to predict that the book, like all things, will sooner or later cease to exist, and nothing will be left of it.

Once upon a time people thought that disappearance is the work of Chronos, who generates and eats his children, but this is a myth and a saying, because Chronos creates just as much as he destroys. In fact, the disappearance of the book means that the book has ended up elsewhere in space (in the drawer, in the fireplace) or that it has deteriorated due to things that exist in space like humidity, or fire. In short, referring to time is just a way of saying that in space there is a spirit that contemplates what happens in it.

Phenomena

Most obviously, Kant does not pay sufficient attention to the crucial difference between a representation in us, which only exists if we think of it, and something outside of us, which exists even if we do not think about it. Here we run into a forest of problems.

1. *Consciousness*. When I look at a table, I do not merely contemplate a representation in my mind: the thought of it is one thing, perception is another. I may think the Pythagorean Theorem is in my mind, but not that behind my eyes, under my hair, and between my ears, there are also my toothache and the pen on the table. I distinguish a thing from a representation, and I know I can point at a thing to another person and expect them to give it to me even though they have many categories and knowledge different from my own. Likewise, I move my head, and yet I feel that the world stays still, unlike what happens if I move my eye with a finger. It is true that this does not yet prove that the world as an intentional object is the result of an integration of representations. The eye moves but the rest of the body doesn't, my self-perception does not change, I know that I'm moving my eye, while if I were under hypnosis and someone were moving it with electrical stimuli things would be different and the world would move. However, under the profile of experience, the stability of the world as I move my head is similar to colour constancy, which means that things tend to retain their colour even under different lighting. Indeed, here I am not dealing with a representation, but rather with a three-dimensional world – the table on which everything is at stake. This does not happen when you look at a picture or revel in a fantasy in your head.

2. *Photography*. However, for Kant a photo and the world are the same, and this basically also holds for the table seen and the one that is remembered. Consider the classification (B 376–7/A 320) according to which 'representation' is the general term indicating perception as representation with consciousness (note that Kant does not consider the possibility of unconscious representations, as they would go against the omnipresence of the

synthetic unity of apperception). In turn, this is distinguished into sensation as subjective representation and knowledge as objective representation, which includes empirical and pure concepts that, if non-deducible, are ideas. Now, it is little use to recall – against Leibniz's continuism – that sensations originate in the senses and thought in the intellect, if the conclusion is that they both lay out on the neat sheet of representation. The fact that some representations are three-dimensional doesn't seem a significant argument for Kant. Likewise, he doesn't seem concerned with the fact that these representations are not only – like the other ones – in our minds but refer to the world and are therefore real, that is, unamendable. Their unamendability means that they are as resistant and solid as mathematics, the anti-empiricist unconquerable bastion. Yet Kant didn't notice it, sharing Hume's idea that experience is the basis of science, perception is contingent, and therefore science is uncertain unless you ground it on metaperceptual foundations.

3. *Sensation and perception.* Nevertheless, perception has nothing to do with the mental images of things, but with tables, chairs, people and rainbows, which we cannot change as we like: the object of perception is always separate from the act of perception. 'Did you hear that ring?' You hear it in the phone, not in the ear or in the air: you tend to locate the sound, immediately and wrongly, in your mobile phone. 'See that house?' You see it there, not in your eye. Perception certainly involves an iconic memory, which is the basis of attention (I try to recognise something, and I find it: I have an apple in mind, and I find one on the table). However, I rarely mistake my representation with the apple on the table. On the contrary, Kant's representationalist framework makes room for the unlikely thesis that I first formulate subjective judgments of sensation and then objective judgments of perception. This is false. In normal conditions – which are never 'normal conditions of observation' – we don't say 'it seems to me that the sky is blue', but 'the sky is blue'. Normally – not when I am myself à la Schiller, but simply when I am not engaging with science – I formulate, with or without categories, objective judgments of perception. When in doubt, with sceptical – that is, proto-scientific – caution, I may formulate subjective judgments of perception ('it seems to me that'). Anyway, the determination of an objective judgment ('it is intersubjectively true that . . .') in a scientific sense is a whole other story. In short, it is not difficult

to see an asymmetry between sentences like: (i) 'Take that pen on the table'; (ii) 'It seems to me that there is a pen on the table in the other room'; (iii) 'It seems to me that there is a pen on the table in this room.' The third sentence is placed at a different level, and in fact – unlike the others – I could pronounce it if I had taken mescaline.

4. *Appearance.* So if everything is OK, I think there is a thing in front of me. Moving to perception and sensation (the receptors) is a sceptical gesture motivated by some disturbance or hitch in reality, for example when we wonder if there is a gas leak, or if we are just hearing our ears ring. In addition, we do not doubt the existence of the world, but only small portions of it ('Did you see that or is just me?'). Instead, Kant and many other philosophers believe that the two separate questions, whether there is an outside world and whether that world is just as I represent it, constitute one and the same question. The idea that there might be something merely encountered in the world – a reflection of an opening window, a rustling behind us, the vibration of a ship's anchor, an elephant – that is not accompanied by a cognitive act, is not taken into account. However, in ontological terms, I may doubt the veracity of all my experiences, but not the fact that there is something in general. The fact that I do not have a theory, or that my theory proves to be wrong, is not necessarily a handicap.

This is rather ironic: experimentally, the supposed certainty of sensation as opposed to the uncertainty of perception is sharply denied, as there is much greater accord on perceptions than on sensations. On the contrary, a physicalist epistemology can only ever produce a phenomenalistic ontology. All that Kant obtains from his transcendental aesthetics is an inflation of appearances, with an outcome opposed to that of sense certainty. For Kant, the phenomenon is only what is gnoseologically accessible, without exhausting the totality of ontology. Defining something as an 'appearance', albeit a necessary one, means assuming that it is transitory: *de jure*, if things went as they should, it shouldn't exist. This goes hand in hand with Kant's definition (A 101) of the phenomenon as a simple play of our representations. Ultimately, this means that there is no difference, in principle, between a phenomenon and the imagination. However, the chickens are coming home to roost when we are told (B 70) that appearance is not a predicate of the object, but of the object in relation to the subject that perceives it as a phenomenon.

5. *The rose in itself.* Now one might observe: if red doesn't belong to the rose in itself, what does it belong to? Is the colour red in the eye and not in the thing? Claiming that red is the outcome of the interaction between the rose and the eye doesn't mean much: there has to be a moment when this interaction is on the side of the eye or on that of the rose. In the former case, one falls into perfect subjectivism and red is pure appearance; if the decision takes place in the eye, why should there be a red rose and not, say, a yellow potato?

Thus, the underlying problem of the concept of 'phenomenon' is: why should what we see not be what it is? At the basis of this, there is the idea that appearances deceive us because perception is contingent. However, Kant does not oppose *onta* and *phainomena*, like Plato, nor does he consider phenomenology as a doctrine of appearance as something between truth and falsehood, like Lambert.[17] Rather, he gives phenomena full legality; so one does indeed wonder: why call them 'phenomena', setting them against the things themselves? After all, speaking of 'things in themselves' is superfluous, come to think of it: who would ever truly speak of 'things in themselves' or 'things for me'? A thing is really for me only to the extent that it is also in itself. This shows that 'noumenon' or 'thing in itself' for Kant means rather something like: the thing as it would be if our senses were as reliable as our scientific knowledge; or, even better, the thing as it would be if we could know it without the entire, aesthetic and logical, apparatus of subjectivity. On the other hand, Kant's idea is that we only know the outside of things, never the inside (B 321–2/A 265–6): if we cut a potato in two, we will still find a surface, and the same happens when peeling an onion. If so, then why speak of 'phenomena' and not surfaces? Strictly speaking, maintaining that the thing in itself is unknowable means claiming that it has no relationship to the phenomenon, whereas Kant assumes that the noumenon has with the phenomenon at least a causal relationship.

6. *The rainbow and Saturn.* Here we recognise the action of epistemological scruples, which can be easily verified and accounts for the entire transcendental aesthetic. At one point (B 63/A 45), Kant argues that the rainbow is a second-level phenomenon, almost an optical illusion, where the real phenomenon would be made up by rain and light. In other words, for him rainbows are not really part of the world; which, strictly speaking, contains causes

before things, so that the reality of a rainbow is slightly higher than that of the alleged pots of gold to be found at their end. And if one looks up to the sky, equipped with a telescope, one will find other second-level phenomena: that is, again, a kind of optical illusion. This is the case, for example, with the rings of Saturn (B 70). Those rings – according to Kant – do not exist: deceiving ourselves, we mistakenly take them for real. Yet, their shadows are exactly like all the others: we see them just like the shadow of our house, we don't merely think of them, as we do with the orbits of the planets. Kant's attitude towards the rings of Saturn has at least one ancestor: the 1698 English translation of Huygens's *Cosmotheoros*, where the engraver, misled by his habits and especially by the assumption that the rings are non-things, corrected the original artwork by erasing the rings' shadows, so as to retain only the planet's.[18]

7. *The stimulus error.* Here is the mental cramp I referred to when talking about 'epistemological scruples': Kant shows a marked tendency to make the stimulus error, that is, to mistake phenomena for their explanations. However, as Wertheimer noted, whenever I see a house, some trees and the sky, I could also say that I have 327 levels of brightness and colour tones. But what I see is not that: what I see are the sky, the trees and a house. From the phenomenological standpoint, a similar confusion involves anything but legitimate operations, a confusion which can be summed up as tracing the observed back to the measured, and reducing the first to 'optical illusion' whenever there is not a perfect parallelism.[19] The temptation to confuse cause and effect, that is, the explanation and the phenomenon to be explained, is as strong as it is groundless. In the final analysis it is absurd, because the cause is usually temporally separated from the effect (A causes B, at least according to Kant's scheme of causality), and if there is the effect there is not the cause. And even in cases where the cause persists together with the effect (for example, fire and heat), it is understood that the cause is one thing and the effect is another, and that the same effect can follow from very heterogeneous causes, since I can laugh at a joke, because someone is tickling me, or because I smoked hashish. This is such an obvious consideration that it does not deserve to be emphasised too much. Yet many times the confusion takes place nonetheless.

8. *The privileges of logic.* Why give in to such a mistake? For centuries people have accepted that there must be a world of ideas,

and few have complained about it, whereas we are reluctant to consider the world of phenomena as something other than a transient appearance to be explained by going back to its causes. Yet when I see a white light, it doesn't matter all that much to determine whether it is sunlight or artificial light, or if I see it because I've banged my head. The latter are the causes, not a phenomenon, and stating that I see a white light because I've banged my head doesn't mean I don't see it. Similarly, the perception of green is not green, just as the death of a loved one does not make us hate them, even if it is a cause of pain. The fact that a Bloody Mary is prepared with a mixer and not a shaker demonstrates that it is not irrelevant whether there is more or less air in a cocktail when it comes to determining its taste. Likewise, hot and cold water are both H_2O, but have a very different perceptual renderings: we don't like our soup cold or our water warm. And yet, the attitude towards logic seems very different from that reserved to aesthetics.

(a) *Genetics and logic.* Even critics of the *topos noetòs* are willing to support those who affirm that the world of logic cannot be explained in any way through genetic studies on why we think in a given way. Now, already on the second aspect there is much to be discussed. Thought, it is argued, should be separated from the thinking subject, otherwise logic would be a mere individual psychology; for apparently similar reasons, it is asserted that logic is not at all explained by genetic studies. Meanwhile, it should be noted that the identification between psychology and individuality is not equivalent to the appeal to the genetic reason. Also, one can legitimately argue that logic is to thought what perception is to physics: namely, a small part. Reasoning based on the calculation of propositions is nothing more than an application of the theory of mental models, which is based on representations of the true, supplemented by representations of the false, so as to obtain the matrix of the calculation. Then, by separating thought from those who think, we do not get individual psychology, but rather invariants of the phenomenology of thought processes.

(b) *Genetics and aesthetics.* It is still curious that we are so quick to jump from what we perceive to its causes. The reason is probably the following: the logical level of causes seems to be the final *telos* of research (and it is, in a theory of science), the goal to achieve by amending our perceptual experience; whereas the phenomenal level is taken as nothing but the starting point – it has everything to gain if it is brought back to a world of causes and reasons behind the phenomena. Which, again, from the perspective of a theory of science, seems difficult to contest (we would hardly be willing to pay a doctor who considers only what we can see ourselves with the naked eye, or listen to an astronomer describing what we see during an eclipse instead of explaining the reasons behind it), but it does not constitute a description of experience.

Logic

Deduction

Sensation as input. So Kant moves from aesthetics to logic, which is discursive and not intuitive. Just as in aesthetics he identified intuition with mathematics, here his basic idea is that logical categories are not to be drawn from experience, but rather from thought. This is the ideal of a general logic, purified of any extrinsic and therefore uncertain element – Kant disagrees with the 'modern logics' that have built pieces of psychology and theory of science into the discipline – because logic must not serve as a research tool, but rather as the canon of thought, which reveals mistakes but does not contribute to producing new knowledge. Logic, however, does not deal only with itself: as transcendental logic, it must also work as the condition of possibility of experience, and here its sphere appears reduced compared to general logic, since experience concerns the real and not the possible.

This leads to further problems. While it may well be true that there are twelve categories of experience, it remains to be explained why experience really needs them. The only way to do so, strictly speaking, would be to say that the world itself is a mess, and that whatever order it has comes precisely from logic. However, Kant does not fully embrace the chaos hypothesis, since even a seemingly minimalist statement like 'in bare succession existence is always vanishing and recommencing, and never has the least magnitude' (B 226/A 183) admits that there is a succession independent from thought; so he claims that sensation is an essential input for knowledge. Nevertheless, once it is granted that knowledge begins with sensation, continues with concepts and ends with ideas, it will be difficult to attribute the order of experience to the role of the categories. In short, this is a chicken-and-egg problem that would be resolved fairly easily simply by declaring that experience itself is ordered, and that the categories are only operative in science. Instead, Kant complicates things by arguing that experience is first 'in time', but that, if we think about it, categories were already there to order it.

However, especially in the version of 1781, Kant's way of deducing the legitimacy of categories for experience is in every way a justification of their usefulness to science. Sensation is impressed on the soul, recorded in memory and rationally identified: I see a branch, my working memory fixes the image, I say to myself 'it is a branch' (and not a snake). Then the impression is stabilised and passes from the working memory to a more durable storage, such as my long-term memory, communication to someone nearby, an article, a book, etc. So far, so good, except that this is a movement in which memory, from 'preservation of sensation', imperceptibly turns into possibility of sensation, so that an epistemological attribute is used retrospectively as a condition of possibility on the ontological level.[20] At least two elements are in play here: on the one hand, the psychologically observable fact that if one does not remember A one cannot detect a change when B occurs; on the other, the mixture between a form of retention that is not very self-aware and a voluntary and conscious memory. However, the two planes can hardly overlap: think about how well we remember faces seen once while we really struggle to connect them with names, and, above all, think of how we often realise only halfway through a film that we have already seen it.

Now, back to the branch, Kant cannot help observing that it was already there, with all its characteristics, before I saw it and independently of my categories. Indeed, despite fearing it might be a snake, I am forced to admit that it is a branch. Also, Kant programmatically states that all knowledge begins with sensation, regardless of the damage this does to the idea of 'Copernican Revolution'. After all, he could have claimed that nothing at all begins with sensation apart from experience, which is not necessarily the origin of all science. However, once committed to the opposite statement, he could have ended up in pure empiricism and claimed that experience does not produce science in the classic sense (that is, certain and evident knowledge) but only likelihood. To avoid this, he opts for an intermediate solution: sensation is first in time, but categories intervene right afterward, ensuring science, without which – Kant ends up arguing – experience itself would be impossible. And yet, if the world is ordered as it is, what is the point of the subject? Conversely, if it is not, how can one claim that the subject orders it? Now, there are two possibilities: either sensation is a generic input, from which, depending on the activated categories, will emerge a rabbit, a hat, or a magician (and then one argues that all knowledge beginning with sensation means nothing); or sensation is already formed (and then one wonders what the point of our categorical grid is at the ontological level).

The chaos hypothesis. Let's say that the world is a mess. If it is interwoven with bits of green, brown, rough, solid, etc. sensations, it seems illogical to think that there is something given in experience (a tree, a star, a potato) and that the data is independent from our expectations, past experience and the conceptual schemes with which we view the world. On the contrary, the inevitable argument will be that the assumption that there is something given in experience does not go without saying, but follows from the application of the conceptual scheme of objectivity.

1. *Flow and regularity.* However, if experience really started as a chaotic stream, how could it happen that this floating world is stabilised and becomes the environment familiar to us, furnished with people who do not change their faces, trees that lose their leaves in autumn, nice objects and ugly objects, whole or broken things? Also, many people (regardless of their knowledge, beliefs or opinions) and many animals (no matter how small or simple) relate to things, avoid obstacles, grab objects, eat, fight and mate – and all of this seems to happen without the application of a conceptual scheme understood as a system of beliefs or a set of epistemological assumptions. Of course there could be subconscious endowments, but that is a whole other story: Kant, instead, believes that the endowments in question are all accessible through reflection without any need for empirical research.

2. *Vortices.* Also, if the world is made of vortices arranged at a later time by the senses and the intellect, why is it that every so often we see swirls, squiggles, phosphenes? Or, to put it otherwise, if the world is woven of sense data, why are pointillism, impressionism and divisionism historically recognised pictorial movements, rather than the rule of human vision? If the world truly depended on the order of knowledge, and the latter was a flow – as Kant admits by hypothesising the synthetic unit of apperception as

temporal flow – then why should there be such different states, like the waking and dreaming states? And why would so many things stand still instead of continuously moving or flowing? If you think about it, it is all quite hard to explain.

3. *The stable world*. If Kant had merely tried to account from an epistemological standpoint for the internal organisation of the world, then it is unclear how he could have thought to have built an ontology. Once you speak of ontology, it is hard to dodge the contradiction between transcendentalism and realism. In the end, the latter prevails, and it is best to acknowledge that the world is stable: it has its laws and enforces them. Of course, one could object that the fact that reality is like this and not otherwise could also be traced back to a law. This is true, and science works precisely on the assumption that everything happens for a reason and eventually we will probably find the reason for all things. However, one has to admit that this is in no way equivalent to positing the need of a categorial grid for experience.

The order hypothesis. But then, we have admitted that the world has an order. And if sensation is the beginning, then what I get when drinking coffee is a dark and warm liquid, a specific smell and taste, etc. Everything I may add later is ontologically poor, yet this is where Kant focuses his attention, because he wants to demonstrate how many intuitions and categories are needed to drink a cup of coffee. It would be much easier if he claimed that many intuitions and categories are needed to describe the act of drinking coffee, but he chooses not to do so in order to avoid empirical issues of physiology. In any case, it is easy to see the many contradictions, in Kant's Transcendental Deduction, between the epistemological assumption that categories make experience possible and the phenomenological fact that experience is an organised whole before and regardless of the categories.

1. *Synopsis of sense*. Kant speaks of a 'synopsis of sense', meaning that each representation is connected with all the others even before knowledge orders them (A 97–8). It is hard to disagree, although the wording seems a bit extremist and far-fetched: if science can legitimately set itself the goal of building a theory of everything, it is because the world is hypothetically an interconnected organism and, in the long run, it will turn out that my dripping sink has something to do with the orbit of Pluto. And yet, in our experience we mainly deal with sinks and their surroundings

rather than with Pluto, and in this scenario things have internal and external properties independent of our categories. The synopsis here is a given structured set that offers itself to our senses; it is not hard to think that, in such a world, everything is already there: quantity, quality, cause and – why not? – reciprocal action. There are likely no postulates of empirical thought in general, as this is not a conscious *cosmotheoros*. However, this does not affect the full consistency of the scene – just as in this series of spots, devoid of meaning, but not of stability, shape, colour, size and spatial relationships.

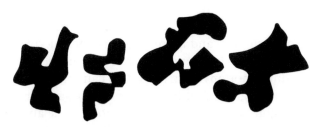

After all, Kant could have said that before the three epistemological syntheses (perception, imagination and the concept), there are essential distinctions – say, figure/ground – which make it so that an object is such and presents those features that we'll find once we begin to study it, with marginal exceptions in which the observation intervenes on the observed. Nevertheless, if this is the case, then there is no consistency with the principle that, without a retentive power, experience would be impossible and there would be no world (A 99). In the first case there is an ontological circumstance: there is something, ordered, structured in such and such a way, etc.; the second, instead, is about science, where that 'something' is recorded and stowed in imagination, and finally transposed into the concept. And yet, there is an important point here. From the standpoint of epistemology one can and must claim that 'there is nothing outside the text', that nothing escapes conceptual schemes. However, when it comes to ontology, things are different: something exceeds the text, and for that very reason it can be distinguished from mere imagination and give rise to knowledge.

2. *Cinnabar.* Concluding the Deduction (A 125), Kant also writes that we are the ones who introduce order and regularity into the phenomena we call 'nature'. The passage appears to be in sharp contradiction with what he said a few pages earlier (A 100–1), namely that without constancy and norm in the

phenomena – if, say, the cinnabar were sometimes red and sometimes black, sometimes light and sometimes heavy – 'no empirical synthesis of reproduction could take place'. The case of the cinnabar disproves the Transcendental Deduction: I can provide all the meanings I want, but the organisation I find is already given, encountered, stable and regular.

3. *Imagination.* Not even Kant could seriously think that the transcendental is the only thing that gives the world some order. This is eloquently confirmed by his appeal to the reproductive imagination, when he claims that 'the reproductive synthesis of the imagination belongs among the transcendental actions of the mind'.[21] If you think about it, it is strange to attribute the transcendental to sensibility, and if you speak of 'productive imagination', things don't really change all that much: we can imagine almost everything, not anything at all (we can imagine something 'bleen', in between green and blue, but not a square circle – we'll picture an octagon, or the rapid succession of a circle and a square, or something like that). This is only possible, though, because we take up and re-assemble the data of sensibility, that is, of the things we encounter in the world. Moreover, the definition of imagination in B 151–2 does not differ from the definition of reproductive imagination in A, except that in 1787, with a purely nominal operation, Kant differentiates between reproductive imagination and another unspecified imagination, which would be productive. However, he doesn't say what this productivity really is – one can only speculate. If we remove any determined content from imagination, we can postulate something – which could be productive, but only if we agree with Kant that all facts have their condition of possibility in a law. However, if this is the case, then it really is true that reproductive imagination should be counted among the transcendental actions of the mind, because experience is actually an organised whole.

4. *Association of ideas.* But then, why should reproductive imagination be considered transcendental, and the association of ideas purely empirical? One answer is that associations are always determined, whereas the faculty to play is a formal character that makes them possible. However, there is no reason not to call 'association' the general form authorising particular associations, and then we would get something analogous to reproductive imagination. Kant is suspicious of association because he considers it dangerously related to scepticism, but perhaps this

is not the right path to follow. The point is not to claim that all associations are subjective and relative, but rather to note that: (i) the likelihood of this being the case is far from negligible, and the choice is not between necessary and likely, but between very likely and highly unlikely; and (ii) not all associations are alike. Some are objective and valid for all (the thunder follows the lightning) and some are purely subjective and idiosyncratic (a madeleine reminds me of Combray). Keeping (ii) in mind, we will realise that there is no difference between the objective side of associations and reproductive imagination as a transcendental faculty of the mind. If there's association in the mind, it is because there is normality in the world, whereas Kant treats regularity as contingent, while resorting to association to explain certain perceptual attitudes, as if the stances that induce habits did not count, and what mattered was rather the supposed power of the spirit to produce regularity.

Schematism

How the scheme works. The burden of the proof of transcendentalism thus moves from the Deduction to the Schematism, that is, from the general law to the single cases. The scheme works roughly as follows: we have categories, which obviously work in general and abstractedly, and we get perceptions that, instead, are particular and concrete. However, perceptions turn out to be preventively domesticated and potentially homogenised, as they present the form of space and time. So, perception and category reveal a common trait: the first may be small or big, hot or cold, bright red or pale pink, permanent or transitory, prior or subsequent to another and so forth; the second has the notions of number, degree, substance, cause, reciprocal action, etc. Nevertheless, how does one put the common elements together? One traditional answer is offered by the category of number: mathematics formally homogenises what we have in our head and what is in the world, or connects two worlds, one of ideas and the other of objects. However, Kant needs to explain the ontological reasons for the application of the categories to sensibility, so he cannot be satisfied with a formal correspondence. It is difficult to claim that numbers are actually in us: it seems to be a hypothesis like any other, and not even a very reliable one, because it seems that infants are only able to distinguish up to seven items, which does not prevent them from seeing many more. And yet, something along those lines can be said of time: if I decided to count to 60 to roughly calculate a minute, what I would sense in me would not be the number 60, but rather the time going by as I count. Moreover, the course of time would not be purely subjective, because while I was counting, a minute would go by even outside of me (for instance, my bread would get toasted, etc.). So, Kant decrees that the schemes are forms of time. How these forms act as mediators, though, is not clear, and the abstract principle appears as the reverse mirror image of the double transcription made by Cartesian science, so that the observable quality is reduced to quality, and the latter is translated into quantity. In the schematism, the categories are transposed into numbers, and then arithmetic results in geometry, i.e., in observable quantities. Let us examine the two moments of the transition from digital to analogue.

1. *The number.*

(a) *Operations.* Categories provide us with purely intellectual syntheses, acting as the fundamental arithmetical operations. Therefore, we have $7 + 5 = 12$; $12 - 5 = 7$; $7 \times 5 = 35$; $35 : 7 = 5$. Only, at a categorial level, operations are rather obvious as regards quantity and quality but not so much as regards relation (the substances would be the numbers 7 and 5, according to the other paradigm of synthetic a priori judgment, the permanence of substance); reciprocal action would be the fact that if I do not insert the 'plus' between 7 and 5, they will stay unchanged; causality would be that if I do insert the 'plus' I'll get 12. Modality seems really hard to conceive. So, the only two pure principles Kant feels like committing to and actually using in order to demonstrate the transcendental character of categories are substance and cause: you can see this in the chapter on schematism, and verify it (I'll dwell on it later) in the system of principles. Kant also restates it in the transcendental doctrine of method (B 795/A 767), where he says that experience is anticipated by causality and by the principle of permanence of substance. Given that here it is still and always a question of mathematics, time comes in and assures naturalisation. The idea is that we do not simply deal with numbers – which can be applied to objects or events just as one may use a meter or a watch – but rather with a real flow, which is present inside me, intuitively, as internal sense, and which is also operating outside of me. All Kant has to do is argue that when a leaf falls, in the world, in an empirically real form, then in addition to the leaf, the tree, the air and the soil, there is also a pure sensible intuition called 'time'. Which is like saying that if there are four books on the table there must also be the number four as such, hidden somewhere.

(b) *The operator*. The weakness of time is also its strength: you can't see it, and therefore it gives no consistency to intellectual synthesis. So, the transition process from the categories to substance, cause, reciprocal action, quantity and degree – that is, to tables, pots of boiling water, squirrels, submarines, etc. – still lacks an essential element, and Kant got stuck on this point for quite some time. Then in the late 1770s, based on Tetens's psychology, he came up with the trick of imagination, to which he gave an unprecedented mission in the history of philosophy: retaining the present as it passes, imagination establishes temporality. Kant now has an operator that serves to unify categories and time, and also counts as the means capable of ensuring the transition from digital to analogue, from the intellectual synthesis to the figurative synthesis, colouring, sensibilising and particularising the categories. The schematism is based on these ingredients; however, it is easy to notice that the standardisation of disparate elements is possible only on the basis of a somewhat equivocal use of words, similar to the multiple meanings of 'temporality', and that under the trappings of naturalisation the *naturalisandum* continues to shine through. Just note that Kant – unlike Locke, who explained the passage from the particular to the universal through the implausible theory of general ideas – says that the scheme is a 'construction method' and, again, gives the example of number: 5 would be the method of construction of a picture like *****. So, despite the many claims that the scheme is independent of mathematical construction,[22] and that metaphysics is independent of physics, it is easy to note that the scheme exists in continuity with both.

2. *The line*. The example of number 5 as the construction method of ***** is significant. It is certainly for the sake of simplicity that Kant didn't use as an image, say, £££££, @@@@@ or $$$$$. However, this is also due to the traditional idea that time is made up of instants developed in a flow, just like space is made up of points that form lines, in a mysterious passage from the discrete to the continuous. Now, on closer inspection, this conception underlies the whole schematism: the model-scheme, the only one that illustrates the possibility of representing time through a

line, as if to phenomenologically confirm that arithmetic has a geometrical counterpart. Kant refers to it five times. Let's briefly go through them, keeping in mind that here Kant believes himself to have shown, with these examples, the possibility of the transition from thought to extension.

(a) *Spatialisation*. The first circumstance is found in the transcendental aesthetics (B 49–50/A 33). As a form of internal space, time has no figure but is represented through space as a line, which has all the characters of time except for the fact that all parts are simultaneous in the spatial line, while being successive in time. In Kant's presentation, this seems to be a psychological matter, but there's more to it: it reveals that time can be compared to space and therefore is not a mere concept, but a sensible a priori intuition. For Kant, this parallelism is the key, if not to the unreasonable efficaciousness of mathematics, at least to how the mind can adhere to the world.

(b) *The object*. The line appears again in a passage of the Deduction (B 49–50/A 34) where Kant wants to prove that the pure laws of thought can legitimately refer to experience: seeing something in space does not amount to knowing it. For this to happen, it is necessary that the object – in this case, the line – is synthesised so as to delimit a space. In this way, in addition to describing a figure, the line will also circumscribe the unity of consciousness in the knowledge of the object in question, reflecting the fact that the conditions of possibility of consciousness also ensure the possibility of knowledge.

(c) *Thought*. Reciprocally, the spatialisation of time is also what sensitises the synthetic unity of apperception, which as such is not perceived and is only thinkable, exactly as we do not perceive the electrical activity of the brain. This is stated in §24 of the Deduction (B 153–4): no wonder, writes Kant, that we intuit ourselves as phenomena and not as things in themselves, because even when we think of a line we cannot help representing it in thought. Therefore, the line with which the soul first constructed the object is also the line with which the subject is constituted as an object for its own self-representation.

(d) *Consciousness*. This is restated in another occurrence of the line, soon after (B 156). Here Kant is arguing that we only know ourselves as phenomena and never as noumena: time can also be represented only as a line, which is thus equal to consciousness, as time is the form of internal sense.

(e) *Geometry*. The last occurrence, after the schematism, can be found in the system of principles, specifically in the axioms of intuition (B 203/A 163–4). In it we find one of the clearest expositions of the Kantian theory of mathematics and its role in the constitution of the possibility of experience. Kant's idea is that extensive qualities are produced by the addition of points. Productive imagination can ensure such additions, and geometry is based on this possibility of transit. In short, therefore, the figure below is a polyvalent line that can be equally called Geometry, Consciousness, or Object, based on the power attributed to time ever since Aristotle's *Physics*: to move from the discrete to the continuous, from the *stigmè* to the *gramme*.

Why it doesn't work. No wonder schemes lack both the fine grain of experience and the characters of objects, but would we recognise things in a mono-coloured world made of pure geometrical shapes? Wouldn't we mistake sheets of paper for steel sheets, doors for curtains, small windows for big focaccias? This is the consequence of abusing the concept of 'representation', and it is no coincidence that schemes lack other requirements, such as the third dimension and movement, essential for the recognition of many objects. Imagine a person in a dark room with little lights upon her – only movement would make it clear that she is indeed a human being (many predators in fact only recognise their prey by their movement). It also implicitly follows that schemes are not even useful for subsumption, but only for the formalisation and numbering of an experience that can fully take place without schemes. If I so wish, I can very well go from a dog to his picture, and hence to his quality and quantity – with the picture I can even recognise the dog. However, quality and quantity are of no use to me – more precisely, they are only useful in an abstract sense. Let us verify this.

1. *How does the line bend?* To put it in its simplest and most decisive terms, the issue of the passage from concept to scheme, from scheme to figure, and from figure to thing is like asking: how can one bend the line?

48   Hysteresis

And then, having traced the silhouette, how does one apply colour? And if colours are already ordered in the world, what's the use of the scheme? Or else – in the less ambitious version of the scheme as subsumption – how to unify the different points in the line, if they are not already ordered and unified in the world? The only way that comes to mind is akin to 'connect the dots' games in puzzle magazines.

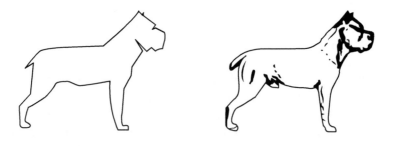

2. *Is France truly purple?* To support the theory of the line, Kant specifies that the scheme is a monogram and not an image. But what exactly is a monogram? Kant explicitly claims that it is like the physiognomists' silhouette, able to outline the features of a person in a few traits. However, this is not a method of constitution but a system for recognising something already known. This is the manifest inconsistency between the two schemes mentioned by Kant: on the one hand, the model of the line as an external representation in time; on the other, the scheme of an object already encountered in the world. Let's admit that I recognise pure geometrical a priori shapes in objects I experience; however, if the schematism is a system for recognising elementary geometrical shapes (say, bananas and telephones), what is the use of the schemes of substance, cause and reciprocal action? This would

lead once again to the Platonic problem of how to get from ideas to things. In fact, the scheme of the Turin–Milan motorway (unlike the real thing) is not 126 km long and doesn't take two hours, so the mental image lacks precisely space and time. Why should a character that is not in the image be made possible by the image itself? The same goes for recognition. Take the following conversation:

'I had a dream about my mother.'
'Are you sure it was your mother and not someone who looks like her?'

What would it mean? From an epistemological standpoint, we don't care whether France is purple or Paris is square, and so forth. It would only matter if one confused cartography with phenomenology.

Kant's idea, instead, is to extend the principle to the whole of reality and ultimately give secondary importance to the difference between the map of France and the territory to which it refers. We can admit that very different things can work for certain purposes: we have all used maps, and boards to play games, distinguishing both from the table. The problem is that we know how to use a map, whereas schemes are much trickier: we don't really know what they are or, mostly, how they refer to the world. Take an aggregation that is partly brown (or green, or white), partly transparent, and separate from a wall: how is this recognised as a window and distinguished from what we see through it? How is it subsumed under the category of substance? To take another example: how do I find a pen if I need to write something down? Kant would say it is thanks to schemes of empirical concepts, which do not concern him.

However, considering that – apart from the ideas of reason – everything in the Kantian world can be the object of a possible experience, the role of schemes turns out to be quite superfluous. The most merciful interpretation is to see the scheme as a Gestalt quality, which as such, however, does not require the application of concepts or an apparatus of pure forms of sensibility, because figural qualities could very well adhere to the objects with no need to insert them into a transcendental aesthetics. Upon closer inspection, the fundamental problem is that Kant doesn't offer alternatives: on the one hand there is thinking as a logical function, on the other there is knowledge following from the union of thought and what is given. This is actually equivalent to saying that there is either consciousness or science, because every time the former approaches a given there is science, at least potentially. And yet Jonah ended up inside the whale mistaking it for a fish, and things wouldn't have changed had he known it was a mammal.

3. *The scheme of dog.* No wonder it is hard to find the scheme of dog – let alone that of platypus. Not only are schemes just numbers in disguise but – provided schemes have a meaning – it is really unclear how they perform their supposed function of transit from extension to thought. In the end, this is the iceberg that sinks the ship of the schematism: so far we haven't found a single proof of the particularisation of the category that Kant speaks of, and one is led to think we'll never find any if, as Kant claims, schemes concern the pure concepts of the intellect and not the empirical ones. The big hue and cry whipped up by categories, time and imagination does not change the fact that experience is not made up of pure concepts, but of objects starting from which one can formulate empirical concepts. So the aporias of general ideas return in the schematism as a method of construction, which Kant does not seem to notice, minimising the very serious issue of the relationship between pure and empirical concepts. The problem appears at the beginning of the chapter on schematism: the thing is, it is not solved – in fact, it is not even perceived as a problem.

(a) *The plate and the circle.* In a first case we have the simple illustration of an abstractive process upon a very simple object: in the empirical concept of plate I think of roundness, whereas in the geometrical concept I intuit that same roundness (B 203/A 163–4). However, it is this elementarity that allows Kant to disregard a crucial problem: the relationship between pure and empirical concepts. It does not take much to go from a plate to a circle and the other way around; but try to imagine the complex architecture of geons needed for the Cathedral of Amiens or even a tree.

(b) *The image and the scheme.* Elsewhere (B 180/A 140–1), Kant underlines the difference between images – always inadequate as general ideas – and schemes, which are construction methods (so that one can draw a triangle without copying it from a street sign). This merely repeats Thales's idea of construction – further proof of the fact that Kant is actually thinking of geometrical construction. Based on that, we should naturally be able to do what Thales failed to do – that is, construct a tree or a spike a priori, instead of a triangle. The objection that this is not construction but subsumption is too accommodating: if one takes subsumption to the letter, one will find a pure empirical derivation, and the response to scepticism will go to hell.

(c) *Quadrupeds in general.* In a third instance, finally, Kant touches on a huge problem – at least as big as a dog. In fact, he speaks of what happens when applying to experience the scheme of a 'quadruped in general'. What on earth would that be? How is it supposed to let me recognise a dog and not just any other quadruped, including a table, a chair, a portable heater on wheels and a baby crawling? That is, once again, how does one go from pure concepts to empirical concepts? The recognition of the scheme of dog can probably be applied only in one specific situation: I see a dog, look up in the sky, and choose to call a constellation 'dog' by linking the dots of the stars with imaginary lines.

4. Real figures and recognitions. The world is not truly made up of lines. Should we conclude that experience introduces flaws and imprecision notwithstanding epistemological normality? And how would these imprecisions make it through? Resorting to fractals and the evolution of geometry after Kant doesn't help, because the problem is at the source – that is, in the assumption that geometry is an indispensable ingredient for experience as such (and not just for the scientific description of experience). As for the scheme of dog, there are only two viable solutions: either it is an example – as Kant later said in the *Critique of Judgment* – and has nothing to do with construction; or it is a process that is far from conceptual and has nothing to do with mathematics. To recognise a dog is not to identify a well-defined figure. The point is not, as in the case of general ideas, to think that, by coalescence, a Poodle, a Chihuahua, a German Shepherd, a Great Dane and a Doberman end up unified in a single figure, both large and small, light and dark, and valid not only for dogs, but also for beavers and a number of other entities. Apart from the impossibility of imagining a Dog In General, we should have an a priori unifying rule of the empirical concept of dog, which would allow us to distinguish the essential from the accidental. Clearly, though, it is not so: the road is always open to an encyclopaedia à la Borges that would put dogs under two categories, those belonging to the Emperor and all the others, though assimilated to suckling pigs. In addition, at the basis of such a hypothesis one should assume that to see a dog and behave accordingly one should have the concept of dog; but then it is unclear why cats run away from dogs despite presumably not having that concept. Thus, the recognition happens through movement, the rhythm of their walk, which is obtained by confusing the gaits of different dogs. It is not excluded that a similar configuration ultimately constitutes the revival of a theory of abstraction, but I would point out two circumstances: first, it is clear that here we are not dealing with the image of a dog in general, but with the collection of details common to several dogs – which, moreover, is far from resembling the figure of a dog – so as to avoid the objection with respect to general ideas; second, the abstraction does not appear to be in any way oriented by a concept of dog.

If a child were to ask us what a dog is, we would say that it has four legs, a tail, a black wet nose, long or short hair, that it barks, that it smells if it gets wet, that it is used to keep guard or for hunting. If we wanted to provide a zoological definition, even roughly, we would say that it is a mammal, omnivorous, related to wolves and jackals, etc. And in all cases we would be using concepts, while it would be weird to explain what a dog is by saying that it moves in a certain way. In short, here we are confronted with a fairly indeterminate sphere, which properly has to do with a primary experience, or rather with something that we cannot even call 'experience' if, with that term, we mean an organised whole. In any case, it surely does not constitute a neutral amorphous background which we shape as we like according to our concepts.

If I first see a confused green patch and, getting closer, realise that it is a number of elms and beeches, it is because they are elms and beeches, and not because in the meantime I have learned from a manual of botany the differences between elms and beeches. Then, distinct from the primary and fundamental layer, there is an area of redescriptions: the expert one, given not by the pure concepts of the intellect (which are still insufficient) but by scientifically grounded empirical concepts; and the pragmatic one, which comes from recognising examples. In other words: one can schematise with or without concepts, but the primary layer of experience probably needs no diagrams or examples, operating through Gestalt structures that require no conceptualisation – or rather, whose conceptualisation would be extremely abstract and sophisticated: think of the challenges entailed by a full theory of the figure–ground relationship, which is a structure that is already perfectly accessible to several animals.

Indeed, the fact that the stereotype's characteristics do not exhaust the content of the concept, provided by an essential object reference, is an internal component of our concepts of natural kind. The object reference thus appears independent from, and more important than, its known characteristics because of the non-conceptual nature of the recognition and the re-identification that I'm stressing. In any case, if I see a small white car and then a big black car, I do not deny that the second is a car because the first – the one that my dad had once shown me saying 'this is a car' – was different. I recognise a concept (or, rather, a name) in two aspects that I see as very different. And if this is not a proof of non-conceptual content, I wonder what could be.

5. *Insensible sensibles*. One last problem. As I mentioned earlier, if we ask what is the mediation between extended and unextended, and between sensible and intelligible, one would be inclined to suggest: 'it is number'. Kant, however, says 'it is time'. But it is not difficult to note that what appears to be the only way for mediation could be replaced by many other functions already in the *Critique of Pure Reason*, because Kant repeats for imagination and diagrams what he says of time as an insensible sensible. Now, with

a little patience, one can find loads of insensible sensibles: the Platonic *chora*, light, music, fantasy, almost everything ... In fact, it seems that 'insensible' is taken by Kant as a synonym for 'intangible'. So, all that is felt with some sense, or just with the imagination, but cannot be touched with your hands, becomes an insensible sensible. At this rate, though, the song 'O sole mio' can very well be considered an insensible sensible too, as one can hear the music but only touch and see the guitar or the gondolier. Here I am obviously suggesting a reductio ad absurdum, to which one could reply that 'insensible sensible' is only something mediating between something logical and something aesthetic, which doesn't hold for 'O sole mio'. However, it is not trivial to establish how the insensible sensibles offered by tradition truly perform their mediating function. And faced with the disheartening vagueness of the answers, one should conclude that 'O sole mio' is not an insensible sensible, but neither are time, *chora* or anything else. Also, to what end should one posit these implausible sensibles when there is already one that works just fine: number? This line of reasoning seems convincing, except that then there would be no need for a transcendental philosophy. It would suffice, if you like, to have an epistemology – which, however, should confess its state of total subordination to physics.

Principles

Talleyrand used to say: 'Les principes, c'est bien, ça n'engage personne.' This is certainly not the case with Kant: the burden to prove naturalisation went from the Transcendental Aesthetic to the Deduction, and then to the Schematism. So, the game played on the field of principles seems like the last resort of transcendentalism. Principles aim to demonstrate the intimately numerical character of experience. Allegedly, these are measurement tools that play an increasingly decisive role, to the point of becoming – in the analogies of experience – a veritable condition of possibility.

Table 5. Kant's Principles Compared with Some Normal Measuring Instruments

Postulates	Clock
Axioms	Ruler
Anticipations	Thermometer, photometer
Analogies	Abacus

1. *Postulates of empirical thought in general.* These come last, but it is worth looking at them first, since Kant explicitly admits that they have not an ontological but an epistemological function, regarding the relationship between the knowing subject and the object. The idea is that if something can be in time, it is possible; if it is in time, it is real; if it is at all times, it is necessary. So we have to do with inherently modal principles, which relate to our ability to know – i.e. to describe – objects, and not to objects as such; and since for Kant there is only the real, we can safely acquit them in our investigation.

2. *Axioms of intuition.* These are numerical principles that coincide with the category of quantity. Kant's idea is that every intuition has a number; that is, it is big or small. If I have a table in front of me, I can measure it with a yardstick or with a thermometer by using it as a ruler. We have already seen that this performance, useful for the re-description of the experience, appears far from necessary for the constitution of experience, so I will not repeat myself here.

3. *Anticipations of perceptions.* These are numeric principles, too, but they concern quality. Kant's idea is that every perception has a degree, that is, it is strong or weak: the table in front of me can be white, black or brown, warm or cold, etc. I will grasp the chromatic intensity (with a photometer) and the heat (with the more banal thermometer) at once, not little by little as in axioms. Again, this is more often useful to the re-description than to the constitution of experience.

4. *Analogies of experience.* The only principles with a possible ontological scope are the analogies of experience, which indeed derive directly from the schematism, since the only schemes Kant refers to are substance as permanence and cause as succession. I will speak briefly of reciprocal action, as it is a rather superfluous principle, whereas we could legitimately state that we wouldn't experience substances or causes without the corresponding principles. In a way, in the analogies we find the birthplace of the Copernican Revolution: objecting to Hume that experience does not teach us causality and substance but that, on the contrary, the latter are what makes it possible.

Substance. The substratum of any change is the metaphysical transcription of the physical principle of the permanence of substance.[23] So, what really is synthetic in the principle is the idea that substance is something permanent in time and, as a corollary, that there is a difference between substance and accidents, which for Kant is essentially a distinction between the physical and the phenomenal. Now, this line of reasoning is quite suspicious, and for more than one reason: we have widely seen how indecisive temporality is from an ontological standpoint; one might add that, in this case, the distinction between analytic and synthetic, as well as that between empirical and transcendental, appears highly problematic. The idea that permanence in time is a synthetic attribute of matter – whereas extension in space is an analytical property – seems questionable. Indeed, it is as questionable as the idea – defended by Kant when distinguishing between analytic and synthetic – that 'this body is extended' is an analytical judgment, while 'this body is heavy' is synthetic a priori (that is, derived from experience). In fact, it is as hard to conceive a body without weight as it is to conceive a body without extension or colour. In other words, to follow Kant, a hallucination would fully satisfy the analytical characters of matter. This is all the more absurd because, as we have seen, the principles that for Kant are undoubtedly synthetic a priori – such as the axioms of intuition and the anticipations of perception – would only be the transcription of what, in the version we are examining, corresponds to an analytical judgment (extension, quantity) and an a posteriori synthetic principle (degree, quality). Furthermore, the synthetic a priori principle of substance, that is to say permanence in time (while extension in space would be the analytic a priori principle, and weight the synthetic a posteriori principle) becomes an unreliable guide from an ontological point of view. And it is even more so if we ask not whether it is really impossible to experience substances in the absence of an ad hoc category, but rather what would happen if we were really to consider substance as permanence in time, with no other specifications.

1. *Physical characters.* Let's start with the difficulties entailed by the Kantian characterisations.

(a) *Permanence in time.* The first element seems innocuous: if we apply to the letter the conception of substance as the permanence of something in time, we will find that many things are, indeed, substances, contrary to what Kant himself would say. (i) Space and time, for instance, are substances, together with light and many other things, including music played in lifts. (ii) Holes, shadows, reflexes and consecutive images are also included on the list,[24] as they do persist for a relatively long time, cannot be destroyed, and are endowed with identity ('it is the shadow of that chair', 'it is the hole of that cheese', etc.). (iii) The same goes for toothaches, obsessions, forced memories, names, theorems and all ideal objects, which would be fine for Plato and for Russell, but not for Kant. (iv) Finally, the fame of Homer, the Roman Empire and Iago's malice should easily be part of the family. Thus, the notion of 'substance' as it is defined by Kant authorises a doctrine of ghosts, since there is no criterion for distinguishing a real object from an ideal object, nor a hallucination from a phenomenon. See for yourself: you will surely recall Kant's unconvincing argument to refute idealism, which fails to demonstrate the existence of a general external world (the internal flow of time does not prove that there is a still space outside: there could very well be two times, one fast and one slow) and to discriminate reality from dream and hallucination. In the end, everything that persists in time is supposedly a substance, including Pegasus, iron wood and magic, and Kant's ontology is even more welcoming than Clauberg's or Quine's.

(b) *What does it mean to 'persist'?* Also, what does it mean to 'persist'? Not to move? Obviously not: a dog, in Kant's too generic sense, is a substance. Not to change? Not this either: chameleons are made up of substances. It is posited that permanence depends on an internal composition, so that if I change an atom in a table, that table is no longer the same substance. And yet this doesn't seem to be a problem for Kant (after all, permanence in time says nothing about the internal composition of the substance). However, if we make substance depend on permanence, we end up seeking a phenomenal attribute with alleged non-explicit inner properties – to the point that a person would not be a substance, because she changes character and cells over time. What is particularly confused is the assimilation between substances and individuals: a person, like a knife or a memo, is an individual that in turn is made up of various substances; the latter as such are physical and chemical, not phenomenal. But then why do we need the scheme of substance to recognise a person? When we recognise someone, we do not submit them to a physical-chemical test, but merely perceive them phenomenally. After all, Kant himself insists on this point many times, when he claims that we first know the outside of things and only later the inside.

(c) *For how long?* There is a third element, which is less obvious but more awkward: how long does something have to last for it to be a substance? Is a sneeze not a substance because it happens fast or for some other reason? Is an instant a substance? In a way it is, because it has to be something; in another way it is not, because it is gone immediately, never staying still. And if a note is not a substance, is a symphony? What about a pop song? If you assume that an instant, as short as it may be, has to persist – or it would not be an instant – then the note, too, has to persist (and also has an identity, as C is certainly different from G). Therefore, a melody should be a substance as well. And yet if we change all the notes and keep the ratios between them, the melody maintains its identity, therefore there are two individuals qualified as the same but made up of entirely different substances. This circumstance should not be underestimated, as the question 'for how long?' reveals a vicious circle concerning the assumption that every bit of time is time. This is all the more relevant if we assume, with Kant, that time is intuition and not concept, so that the smallest fraction of time is every bit as much time as are eternity or a fortnight: infinite permanence does not establish an analogical relationship – say, a mobile image of eternity – as would happen if we considered time to be a concept. Therefore, if things are as Kant says, not only substances but also accidents turn out to be permanent in time, and the definition of substance appears completely void.

Kant fails to notice this for at least three reasons: first, he does not consider the 'how long' issue and relies too much on commonsensical assumptions. Second, he fully embraces the distinction between substance and accident. Finally, he does not consider the terrible consequences of the thesis that 'everything is in time'. Furthermore, considering phenomena as appearances – albeit necessary – he doesn't notice that they can very well be substrates, according to his definition. And then, what about the ship of Theseus, which retains its shape while being made up of entirely different parts from its initial components? Similarly, if I look at the Sun setting on the sea, I see a band of light coming towards me; but if I asked someone fifty metres to my left 'can you see that strip of light?', they would answer 'yes', while actually referring to another strip: one that is directed towards them. The problem concerns what Chisholm typically calls *entia successiva*:[25] what is the true being of a wave, water, or its shape? Chisholm's solution is to distinguish a wide and popular sense in which waves persist over time, and a narrow sense in which only primary entities persist, i.e. mereological aggregates and people, but not plants and artefacts – let alone waves, rainbows and the like. Kant fails to see the problem and, if anything, would define a wave as a false appearance like a rainbow or the rings of Saturn; this is because he has established that 'substance' is what is inherent in the elementary structures of a thing, and not in its phenomenal properties.

2. *Ecological characters.* Kant provides physical characterisations, but does not consider that he is tacitly adopting ecological criteria. As a consequence, though, the number of problems increases. This is because of the fundamental misunderstanding underlying his work. Of course we could easily recognise objects without the category of 'substance', as the latter concerns chemists and physicists, but Kant fails to note this precisely because he takes us to act like chemists and physicists instead of animals in an environment – which is what we really are.

(a) *Substances or objects?* In our experience we rarely come across substances, but rather objects that are long or short, thick or thin, smooth or rough, transparent or opaque. And the same arguments that can be used to show that the notion of substance, as the permanence of something in time, cannot be learned by experience alone, can be applied to the categories of 'rough', 'translucent' or 'hairy', since it does not seem illegitimate to claim that without the idea of 'hairy' we could not subsume beards or dogs. The fact that Kant doesn't make this claim does not depend on a peculiar distinction between 'substance' and 'hairy', but on the fact that 'hairy' only concerns certain substances – or better, objects. Anything can become a category if one so wishes, and, by multiplying entities, one can demonstrate that it is a priori, or even transcendental: can we rule out that without the 'hairy' category one could still see beards and dogs?

(b) *Duration in time or hard objects?* Our ontological insights seem relatively impermeable to the indiscriminate application of the principle that 'substance' is the permanence of something in time. This is quite clear – if one can say so – in the case of the shadows. Kant tacitly assumes that the criterion for determining the substance is impenetrability along with certain physical characteristics, but he explicitly states that it is permanence in time. If he expressed his thought – in line with a phenomenological rather than physicochemical perspective – in terms of things, non-things and quasi-things, he would be authorised to attribute the character of substance to shadows and to distinguish between shadow (which Kurt Koffka classifies as a non-thing) and shade (which Koffka classifies as a quasi-thing). This would take place within a naive framework corresponding to our fundamental intuitions, which struggle to admit that shade is a substance and yet recognise that it is something, which can be obtained with hats and umbrellas. Yet, one wonders which is the true naivety. In particular, there is still a question to be answered: suppose Kant did not mean that the shadow is a substance, but rather failed to consider all the consequences of his thesis. Should one conclude that we cannot recognise shadows? Technically, that should be the case, because Kant mentioned the scheme of substance, but no schemes of appearances or accidents. Again, he did not think about this because he only cared about what could found a science, probably supposing that appearances were false and that, by subtracting accidents, one could easily come to the root of substance.

(c) *Events*. Third, consider that in our experience, we encounter not only substances but also events, which do persist in time and therefore could be considered substances according to Kantian parameters. And then there are event-objects like rainbows, waterfalls, rivers, slaps, sunsets and smiles. Nevertheless, as we have seen, for Kant rainbows would be second-degree phenomena of rain, the same way as rivers, waterfalls and sunsets. Instead, a slap and a smile would probably be nothing (but then how is it that we recognise them?).

(d) *Accidents or qualities?* Finally, even if one does not dogmatise the distinction between primary, secondary and tertiary qualities – because without the category of 'niceness' or 'gloominess' many aspects of experience would be excluded from consideration – categories can still number more than twelve, and can also be different from the Kantian ones. Mostly, they are not necessarily required for experience to take place. In short, one could very well argue that we find substantial things, green and rough, without any logical category, because our aesthetic structures are enough to make us do so – especially because cucumbers are indeed green and a little rough.

Cause. With causality, Kant shows he has several strings to his bow: if I push a piece of chalk with a pencil, the chalk moves; if I lacked an a priori concept of 'cause', it is doubtful whether I could learn this out of mere habit. Therefore, at least in this case, science appears necessarily to be presupposed by experience – a certain science, being a priori. And yet this statement does not stand up to a less superficial examination. To understand this, it suffices to think of the many meanings of the word 'cause': a pencil causes chalk to move in a very different way from how smoking causes lung cancer or ignorance causes injustice. If we try to discriminate perceived causality and thought causality, as well as epistemic causality and phenomenal causality, we will realise how unreliable it is to claim the a priori necessity of causality for experience, and we will also understand that the last bastion of transcendental philosophy proves to be anything but unconquerable.

1. *Perceived causality and thought causality.* Here I would like to demonstrate that perceiving causality is not the same as thinking its category, because we experience causality even when it goes against what we think. Let's admit, with Kant, that thinking of something does not mean knowing it, and therefore nothing prevents us from experiencing false causality; but then it is hard to see what the Copernican Revolution was for. If instead it did help dispel the sceptical argument, then the mere fact that I experience a cause I would never think of, contradicting what I know, disproves Kant's claim that cause is a priori compared to experience.

(a) *Metzger's toilet flush.* Let's begin with an obvious case of perceived and unthought-of causality. In 1943–4, the perceptologist Wolfgang Metzger was doing his military service in Cassino, central Italy. One day he went to the lavatory and, when he was done, flushed the toilet. At that precise moment, a grenade hit the building, and Metzger thought he was the one who, by operating the flush, had caused the disaster. Now, Metzger saw the causality, at least in terms of subjective description; to be neutral, let's say he perceived it. The point indeed is that he saw, he did not think: 'it seems extremely unlikely that flushing a toilet would be enough to cause a building to explode'. On the other hand, Metzger had such a vivid and incontestable impression – endowed with the evidence typical of sensible perception – that he struggled to understand that what he perceived was actually impossible. Indeed, he struggled to stop feeling guilty. Metzger had therefore experienced an unlikely causality; also, he had experienced a false causality, because the flush had nothing to do with it – contrary to what happens in *Once Upon a Time in America*, where a man is blown up after flushing the toilet in a restaurant. At least in the fictional story the causality was real – the flushing triggered a detonator – even though still not likely. In short, Metzger's perception of causality cannot be explained either in terms of empiricism or in terms of rationalism: if experience truly happened through unconscious judgments comparing what happens with previous experience, or with the sovereign light of reason, Metzger should not have immediately intuited a causality. Therefore, one can also intuit causality without always resorting to intellectual – that is, for Kant, epistemological – functions.

(b) *Hemingway's ceiling light*. Causality is neither learned through habit, nor thought a priori, but rather encountered before any thought or cognition. Let us compare Metzger's case with two other stories, to point out the 'encountered' nature of unlikely causality. In the 1920s, in Paris, Hemingway flushed the toilet and the ceiling light fell on his head; he was probably surprised, but not as much as Metzger. Another time, the latter was walking with a colleague in Berlin, at twilight. At one point, he gave his companion a pat on the shoulder and suddenly the street lamps went on. Again, he had the strange feeling of causality – not that of hearing the water after flushing the toilet, but that of having the light fall on your head after doing the same thing. The moral of the story is that Hemingway's case appears statistically unlikely but true, whereas the pat on the shoulder and the grenade are unreasonable and unlikely, and yet they are all given with the same evidence. What is encountered, in these anecdotes, has nothing to do with knowledge or truth.

(c) *A stranger in Irpinia*. One may object that Metzger was particularly sensitive to such things, and that they could only happen to him, since he was probably biased by his shady perceptological interests. This argument, though, appears questionable, as similar things have happened to people who knew nothing of perceptology. During the earthquake in Irpinia, for example, a man with no background in perceptology (and probably no theoretical interest in it or in pseudo-causality) was playing cards; he put down an ace with no particular vehemence, and ended up on the floor below. He, too, struggled to understand that he had not been the cause of this, given the event he encountered. False causality, after all, is similar to Beta movement, where the temporal sequence of two light sources is perceived as the linear translation of the same light. What Metzger encountered here is something that one does not think or infer, but sees – as a causality, which thus appears not to be simply thought.

2. *Epistemic causality and phenomenal causality.* One could claim that this casuistry ends up supporting pre-comprehension: (i) it happens all the time that an event B takes place right after an event A; but (ii) when we feel that some conditions are met (like physical contact between A and B), then we perceive causality; however (iii) we do not perceive it but think it, thanks to the unconscious work of habit, memory and culture. Yet if this were the case, now that we no longer consider action at a distance as magic, we should interpret any event in the world as possibly implied in some causal interaction. Instead we do not do so, but merely isolate some phenomena as causally qualified events and, in some rare and somewhat laughable cases like Metzger's, perceive a causality that responds to Aristotelian rather than Newtonian physics. Therefore, this has nothing to do with cultural pre-comprehension or the action of the principles of pure intellect – rather, what's at work here is a perceptive modality that might very well be mistaken, but which certainly does not depend on the intellect.

In fact, pseudo-causality à la Metzger cannot be amended, unlike what happens with thought causality. In some cases, there are thought causalities that are not even perceived: no one has seen universal gravitation, and when the tide rises it seems to be a cause drenching the clothes left too close to the shore, rather than an effect of lunar attraction. But we just need someone to explain the phenomenon to us, and we will be ready to recognise effects where we previously saw causes. Similarly, we can very well give up belief in certain causes that prove to be wrong explanations. You can easily confirm this: since we cannot see microorganisms with the naked eye, for a long time there was talk of spontaneous generation from the corruption of rotting bodies. Here thinking causality rather than seeing it was no guarantee, as it led to conceiving an invisible causality that was certainly plausible, but false. In science there are many cases in which an unlikely causality, which contrasts with habits and expectations, proves to be true: it appears unlikely that one could become anaemic from eating a lot of pasta, but for those allergic to gluten it is true; just as it seems likely, and not only for alchemists, that red wine could give you energy and remedy anaemia – but again, it is not true. However, the common feature of such 'causes' that turn out to be wrong explanations lies in the fact that we can abandon them when we want to. Unlike phenomenal causality, epistemic causality is not encountered. But Kant confuses them in his system, having identified ontology with epistemology.

Reciprocal action. According to Kant, to be able to see a house from the roof to the foundations or from the foundations to the roof, I must have a category that allows me to consider that experience as a related organism in which everything conspires with everything else (*tout se tient*) – this Leibnizian statement has been especially popular in old-school detective stories, where every detail is present in the story for a reason. Also, this same category, for Kant, authorises me to think (in this case) that the link does not exert any appreciable action, since the operation can be repeated several times and in any way, whereas if I look at a boat going down the river I cannot reverse the direction of the observation, and in the meantime the boat will sail away. The general form of reciprocal action is the norm of a universal connection of experience, which would require the representation of a necessary connection of all representations. Kant sets out this principle with the tranquillity with which a historian would argue that the notion of universal history is implied by any particular story, but obviously is not the case. Perhaps I would not begin any scientific investigation without hoping to reach, sooner or later, a theory of everything. This, however, does not prevent me from experiencing very minute and determined things, with no glimpse of their connection – sometimes not even of their very causes.

Instead Kant assumes that, to look at our table, we need what Einstein vainly sought for much of his life: in fact, Kant mistakes the epistemological precept according to which knowledge begins when we establish relationships between phenomena, with the encountered fact that something may very well happen to us without appearing to be part of a previous frame, and without everything in the world being interconnected. One should therefore multiply entities beyond necessity to the point where one is forced to assume reciprocal action, so as to explain why it is that – despite being intimately linked and subjected to the synthetic unity of apperception – things sometimes appear as if they were completely disjointed, perhaps because their secret conspiracies are so hidden as to remain secret.

One could obviously object that Kant was not talking about pens, laptops and lamps, but rather about universal gravitation. But what has gravity to do with our ecological experience, which Kant also wants to address? It is not forbidden to claim that, from God's standpoint, everything is present and connected. It is also legitimate to hope that, when science is realised as absolute knowledge, we will indeed be like God. However, what Kant does is claim that if we do not know everything about something then we know nothing, indeed we do not even experience it – and this is a far-fetched statement. A child throws a stone up in the air and then moves to dodge it. The stone's motion is probably explainable (by grownups and depending on the historical age) in terms of Aristotelian or Newtonian physics, but what the kid does is based on experience, not on the theory of natural places or gravity. Furthermore, grownups are usually not professional physicists, so their justification systems are more likely based on contingent common sense – the same that makes us rely sometimes on Aristotle, sometimes on Newton, and at other times on Einstein. What follows is that, in both cases, experience takes place outside of science.

It is surely legitimate to note that, in the phenomenal world, the absence of dependence relations is the rule, not the exception:[26] that the world is written in mathematical (or any other) language is a hypothesis pertaining to science, not experience. If one argues that perhaps the figure/background partition constitutes a 'character' of this book, together with mathematical quantities, one will have to admit that it is difficult to write 'character' without quotation marks to show the misuse of a term. Attributing meaning, that is, weaving connections, is no rule. Dr Watson misses half of the interrelations recorded by Sherlock Holmes, but this doesn't prevent him from enjoying life, or practising medicine – when, no doubt, he notices more interrelations than he does at dinner.

Farewell to the Transcendental

The first to notice that something did not add up was Kant: the development of his thought in the productive years from 1781 to 1790 appears as a way to address the problem inherited from the previous decade. The problem with ontological transcendentalism was this: given a system of categories and forms of sensibility, how can concepts refer to percepts, determine and subsume them? The problem was never solved, other than by unlikely solutions appealing to the common roots of sensibility and intellect (B 29/A 15) or to the mysteries of the human soul (B 180–1/A 141), in an attempt to cut the knot that Kant couldn't undo. On the one hand Kant merely accumulates seemingly irrefutable arguments for the constitutive role of intellect over sensibility; on the other, the relation between sensibility and intellect remains obscure. There is no way forward, so in the *Critique of Judgment* Kant takes a step back.

1. *Reflective judgment.* The determinant judgment is discarded, replaced – not flanked – by the reflective judgment. The official version is that objects are first determined by the intellect, but then the subject reflects on them. However, the compromise would hold only if Kant had shown that things are just like that; but he did not, hinting instead that they are otherwise, and that there is really no ontological need for the transcendental, since objects are self-determined. If we stick to reflective judgment alone, the fundamental question of the first *Critique* – whether synthetic a priori judgments are possible – is abandoned. As an epistemological assumption and not an ontological constitution, the reflective judgment must be content with reconstructing retrospectively a necessity that is natural, and that would be such even outside of the transcendental horizon. In short, the transcendental does not intervene when I see something that looks like a stick but could also be a snake, but rather when (without its phenomenal appearance having changed) I decide it was just a stick. And there are many things I can do with this stick: as a practical man, use it to scare away a real snake; as a botanist, consider to what plant it belongs; as a craftsman, use it to manufacture a walking stick in the shape of a snake. In the end, I may wonder if the handle looks rather like the muzzle of an otter or a marten, or if the stick recalls certain Neolithic tools or rococo coils, but it is clear that I have now crossed a threshold – which is surely legitimate, but not so important.

2. *Schematising without a concept.* Schematism is no longer there: while the scheme is for a real determination, symbolism simply ensures an analogy. It is not that the physical world to which mathematics applies appears necessary and stable because our senses and our intellect are made in a certain way; rather, it helps to think that the world may have some teleological order so that physics and the other sciences can find their scope. Which is

like saying that the whole of science is fully contingent with respect to reality. The schemes openly become epistemological functions and, at most, heuristic ones (suffice it to say that in §59 of the *Critique of Judgment*, 'substance' and 'cause' are considered metaphorical expressions), abdicating any claim to ensuring a genuine relationship between extension and thought. On the one hand, with the critique of the aesthetic judgment, Kant deals with non-conceptual contents, which – in his view – are not related to the faculty of knowledge, but rather to that of pleasure or displeasure. On the other hand, all of the critique of the teleological judgment is rather like a thematisation of the conceptual schemes we use – at a scientific level, and regardless of any internal finality of nature – to give meaning to the world when describing our experience. In short, in the *Critique of Judgment*, the Analytic, in open contrast with the *Critique of Pure Reason*, is composed of non-conceptual content; while the Dialectic becomes instead, specifically, the sphere of an epistemological principle which states that to understand nature one should assume that it has a final structure. The issue is therefore how to formulate working hypotheses in laboratories, and not how we see things.

3. *Non-conceptual content*. So it is no longer true that intuitions without concepts are blind; or rather, it is only true at the epistemological level, and has no further ambition. The link between thought and extension takes place ideally and not really – only in science. In other words, here there is no schematism homogenising inside and outside, but rather a theory of science promising that – in an infinite time needed to find the truth – every difference between nature and mathematics will cease to exist.

4. *Ontology without the transcendental*. There is much more to say – in line with a long and respected tradition – about Kantian epistemology. However, since my goal is to outline the characteristics of an ontology, I will have to follow a different strategy. The question I want to answer is: If we follow the transcendental, we admit that schemes determine experience; at most, with some post-Kantian liberalism, we can say that schemes can also be taken as paradigms that mark the different ages of physics. And yet, is this true? A plumber who fails in a procedure should iterate it many times, displeasing his customers, until . . . Well, until when, exactly? Could it be that, as in the Mexican earthquake, the outside world can turn up without waiting for our conceptual schemes to be ready for it?

2

What Is It Like to Be a Slipper?

Epistemology/Ontology

Essential distinctions. One can do without the transcendental if one acknowledges the fundamental differences between ontology and epistemology. They are listed in the table below.

The Slipper Argument

Before proceeding to the articulation of these distinctions, I would like to explain the background of my reasoning.

1. *People.* Take a man looking at a carpet with a slipper on it; if he asks another to pass him the slipper, the other, usually, does so without significant difficulty. This is a trivial phenomenon of interaction, but it shows very well how, if the outside world indeed depended even a little not so much on interpretations and conceptual schemes but on neurons, then the fact that the two

Table 6. The Differentiation between Epistemology and Ontology

EPISTEMOLOGY Amendable	ONTOLOGY Unamendable
Science: linguistic, historical, free, infinite, teleological	**Experience:** not necessarily linguistic, non-historical, necessary, finite, not necessarily teleological
Truth: not coming from experience, but teleologically oriented towards it	**Reality:** not naturally oriented towards science
Internal world (internal to conceptual schemes) Paradigm: the conceptual scheme. It is in the head and speaks of the world, therefore it can be amended	**External world** (external to conceptual schemes) Paradigm: all things unamendable. It is in the world and it cannot be changed with thought

people do not have the same neurons should make the sharing of the slipper impossible. It might be objected that the neurons do not have to be exactly identical in number, position or connections. This, however, not only weakens the argument, but contradicts evidence that is difficult to refute: the fact that differences in past experiences, culture, brain structures and capacities may lead to significant divergences at a certain level (does the Spirit proceed from the Father and the Son, or only from the Father? What do we mean by 'freedom'?) is common knowledge, and it is the reason why there are disputes between different opinions. But the slipper on the carpet is another thing: it is external and separate from us and our opinions, and it is therefore provided with an existence that is qualitatively different from the kind we tackle, say, when discussing issues such as euthanasia. In other words, the sphere of facts is not so inextricably interwoven with that of interpretations. Even in this very simple thought experiment, we are dealing with a world external to our conceptual schemes.

2. *Dogs*. Now let's take a dog that has been trained. He is told, 'Bring me the slipper.' And, again, he does so without encountering any difficulties, just like the man above, even though the differences between his brain and the man's are enormous and his understanding of 'Bring me the slipper' may not seem comparable to that of a human. In fact, the dog does not ask himself whether the man is really asking him to bring the slipper or if he is quoting the sentence or using it in an ironic sense – while it is likely that at least some people would.

3. *Worms*. Now let's take a worm. It has no brain, nor ears; it has no eyes; it is far smaller than the slipper and only has the sense of touch, whatever such an obscure sense may mean. So we cannot say to it, 'Bring me the slipper.' However, crawling on the carpet, if it meets the slipper it has a choice between two strategies: either go around it or climb over it. In both cases, it encounters the slipper, although not quite in the same way that I encounter it.

4. *Ivy*. Then let's take ivy. It has no eyes, it has nothing whatsoever, but it climbs (or at least we describe it this way, treating it as an animal and attributing a deliberate strategy to it) up the walls as if it were seeing them, or moves slowly away if it finds sources of heat that annoy it. The ivy will either bypass the slipper or climb over it, not unlike the way a man would do in front of an obstacle of larger size, but with neither eyes nor conceptual schemes.

5. *Slipper*. Finally, take a slipper. It is even more insensitive than ivy. But if we throw a slipper onto another slipper, it encounters it, much as happens to the ivy, the worm, the dog and the man. So it is really hard to understand in what sense even the most reasonable and minimalist thesis about the intervention of the perceiver upon the perceived can make some kind of ontological claim, let alone a strong one. Also – and this is the core of ontology – one could very well not take another slipper but simply imagine that the first one is there, in the absence of any animal observer or a vegetable or another slipper interacting with it. Would there be no slipper on the carpet, then? If the slipper is really there, then it must be there even if no one sees it, as is logically implied by the sentence 'There is a slipper' – otherwise one could say, 'It seems to me that there is a slipper' or, even more correctly, 'I have in me the representation of a slipper', if not even, 'I have the impression that I have in me the representation of a slipper.' Consider that making the existence of things depend on the resources of my sense organs is per se not at all different from having them depend on my imagination, and when I argue that there is a slipper only because I see it I am actually confessing to having an hallucination.

Ontological Constraints

The slipper experiment is useful to distinguish the cognitive relationships that can – and often should – be established with the world and the ontological relationships that occur in the absence of those relationships.

1. *Subjects and objects*. One could object: 'Why stick to worms and slippers? If the huge colourless rough thing encountered by the worm is the same slipper that I see, then why exclude the possibility that there are beings able to see protons? In any case, in a dark room we can only recognise the passage of photons, and yet you include light in your ontology while excluding photons. This means that your ontology of medium-level objects is, at most, an ecology and perhaps the lexicography of a rather ignorant common sense.' This objection, though, only holds to an extent: without the environment, the psyche, my very life, the things I deal with while I'm alive in an environment would be the same, whereas my conceptual schemes would be gone. Suppose that, reviving an old-fashioned punishment, they decided to stick a nail in my head: at first I would feel terrible pain, then nothing,

and in the end I would cease to be, along with my memories, my expectations, my conceptual schemes. Yet the effectiveness of the nail would not have changed, determining first the pain, then the dementia, and eventually my death. If it had changed, if – say – the nail had disappeared when I stopped feeling it or thinking of it, maybe I would have been OK; but then it would have been an imaginary nail.

2. *The pragmatist fallacy.* This is why the world is not at the interpreter's disposal: I can grab a handle to open the door, but only if the handle is actually there and is solid enough; I can use a Mont Blanc fountain pen as a filter to watch a solar eclipse, but I just cannot do the same with a silver Sheaffer. My room for manoeuvre is not limitless, because the material conditions of the object must be such as to allow for the function. Now, the properties that can induce me to make use of higher-order performances are based on lower-order resources applying to beings that have no idea of what a handle, a pen or an eclipse might be, like a worm crawling on the Mont Blanc using it as a locomotor support.

(a) *Grasping.* The fallacy of pragmatism is often to believe that any object can come in handy for an agent who wants to use it as a tool, without regard for the fact that a spade can also serve as a bat, but not the other way around. So, the ontological constraints imposed by the object reveal a sharp independence of our conceptual schemes, setting an insuperable barrier to any conventionalism. It does not seem illegitimate to state: 'Anything can serve as a currency'; at first, given that currency is very much related to convention, the statement seems reasonable. However, it only holds up to a point: apart from pieces of metal and paper, currency has been made up of bags of salt or shells, but never tables or cows, as they are not easy to handle (cows should also be taken care of) – we might as well switch to bartering, where you can recycle old coins as buttons for Tyrolean clothing. Similarly, one cannot use soap bubbles or pieces of burned paper, and the same goes for grains of sand, atoms and fresh meat. Ontological constraints are closely intertwined with ecological constraints: at the North Pole a pound of fresh meat could well count as currency, but there would still be restrictions related to its size: a cube with a side longer than 15 cm is difficult to transport, and suggests the use of a handle, turning into something like a beauty case. Obviously, if one does not use lipstick, blush and cleansing milk, one has no use for a beauty case; however, even if one needed cosmetics, one would tend to discard a 150 cm x 150 cm beauty case, maybe even without a handle.

(b) *Avoiding*. The greatest limit of pragmatism, though, is not its neglect of these trivial and yet decisive facts, but rather its overturning of our natural attitude. According to pragmatism, most of the time we should be grasping objects or people – that is, engaging in intentional or deliberate actions – and the rest should be a shadowy, almost non-existent blur. Here, apart from the fact that in this way pragmatism implicitly incorporates a theory of sense data, it is the description of experience that is baffling. In fact, most of the time, we do not reach out to objects; we rather avoid or dodge flies, trams and annoying individuals. And to do so, it is not enough to consider them non-existent *eide* or bundles of sense data created by an evil demon. Just as surprise (we will see shortly) refutes the hypothesis of the universality of interpretation, so avoiding ensures an essential limit to the ontological claim of pragmatism, which turns out to be a second-level description: interpretation may or may not be there, and is exercised on an ontologically solid basis.

3. *Things and their descriptions*. Indeed, it is something different from the pragmatist fallacy to claim that ontologically constant structures bear epistemologically different descriptions.

(a) *Descriptions*. Take the Moon: for Xenophon it was a frosted glass lamp, for Heraclitus a bowl with the concave part turned towards us, and even Galileo had to hang a spherical mirror on a wall to prove it was not itself a mirror – in that case the Sun's light would focus in one point – but an opaque body. And then there are those who think the Moon is made of cheese. In any case, Xenophon, Heraclitus, Galileo and those who think the Moon is made of cheese all refer to that disk, appearing in that way and not another. Even someone with a dairy-related conception of the Moon will think of a round cheese, like a Camembert or a whole Parmesan – at least on certain nights (those in which Quevedo wrote about the 'sangrienta Luna') – or a Dutch cheese; but they would never think of provolone. That the same object may bear such a wide variety of descriptions does not decompose it, but defines it: the disc in the sky remains the same, what changes are the conceptual schemes and interpretations regarding its true nature; and it does not help to confuse the two levels – we can truly end up on different planets. For example, if I am an

Assyrian, I see Hesperus and then I see Phosphorus (i.e., Venus). Later it turns out that they were the same star; then it turns out that it was not a star, but rather a planet. Nevertheless, what we see has not changed: all that has changed is what we think, and this is the characteristic of science. The latter may – but does not necessarily – extend to experience, because knowing that a ball is made of stone or papier-mâché will modify my behaviour, but knowing that the Earth revolves around the Sun really doesn't. It can certainly be argued that accepting the existence of atomic particles is similar to accepting the existence of the Homeric gods. Now, at the epistemological level, this is literally true, as those are interpretive schemes; what matters is not to conclude that the Homeric gods were considered by the Greeks as natural events rather than as the explanation of natural events: Achilles sees lightning, exactly as we see it, and tells Patroclus that it is a thunderbolt from Zeus. Likewise, neither Bohr nor Homer, upon the appearance of lightning, would simply assume that they were seeing lightning. Or rather, maybe Homer would, but for a different reason: being blind, he would infer from hearing the thunder that a lightning flash followed. Interpretative schemes, and therefore science, are typically considered provisional, because they are made in view of reaching the truth.

(b) *Perceptive renditions.* However, none of this affects what there is. From this point of view, the Necker cube appears enlightening. Let's make use of an explicit version of it:

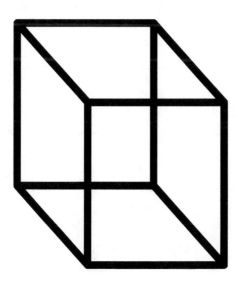

74 Hysteresis

The figure has six possible renditions:

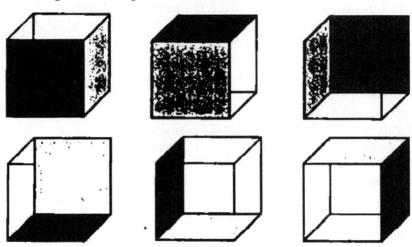

There is only one figure, and there are six perceptual renditions, which are mutually exclusive (when I see one, I do not see the others) but can follow each other in time; whereas if we identified ontology and epistemology we should claim that the six renditions are as many different objects, to be multiplied by all their interpretations (a box, a frame, a wire, etc.). But it is not so, since I know I am always seeing that cube, and in any case I am not seeing a duck (at most, I might take it as a symbol used by some people to designate ducks). Some argue that the possible renditions are seven, including also the view of the cube as a plane figure, but it is not so easy to see it that way. Yet this result is achieved without difficulty if I change the figure:

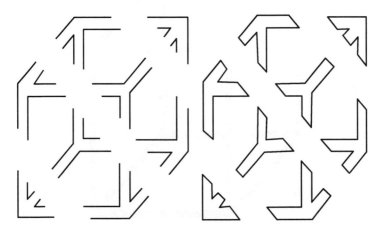

Note that in the second version I cannot even see a cube: I can only think it.

4. *Futile sciences.* And now, from factual situations, let's turn to an issue that concerns the right, i.e. the legitimacy, to posit, at least in principle, that all areas of experience turn into science. Magazines used to have (and still have) etiquette columns; there are guides to the best hotels and restaurants; but above all there are people who are rightly proud to be connoisseurs in the field. In the Place de Clichy, in Paris, there is a fairly solemn place, with glass and mirrors, called Académie de billard (Pool Academy). Documentaries about animals often show us scenes that are described as the apprenticeship of a beast, such as a lioness teaching her cubs how to hunt. Why is it hard to take these things seriously as scientific projects? Why is it that the lioness is not like a professor? Not because what she teaches is irrelevant (is it more important to spend years studying a single beetle, as can happen to an entomologist?), but because we think that here there is no essential relationship with knowledge as infinite amendability. Scientific knowledge is not just hopefully true now; it is the promise of future wisdom: what we know now may be completely false, but in the long run, by following this path, we shall find the truth. Of course one could object that the laws of atoms and galaxies are as unamendable as those of perception, and that what changes is our ability to reconstruct them adequately. Fair enough, but we still perceive tables and chairs without knowing laws, or knowing wrong laws, whereas without laws we'd know absolutely nothing of atoms and galaxies.

Unamendability

Starting from what I have said so far, I would like to make a general point: the weapons of an anti-transcendental strategy are the same as those used to differentiate ontology from epistemology. Let us examine this issue.

1. *The encountered.* Let's start with a trait common to all the cases listed in the Slipper Argument: the encounter with something that was there regardless of its being understood, thought or represented. Following the classification provided by Metzger, this time as a theoretician,[27] it is useful to distinguish between a physical reality (that of the natural sciences, which is not the object of experience) and a phenomenal reality, which we deal with in life.

Think of Metzger's case: even though he knew very well that flushing the toilet cannot cause an explosion, he thought it did. Here the great distinction is not between true and false, but between encountered (the building exploding) and represented (the building as we think of it, remember it, imagine it, and when we conclude that the flush couldn't have caused the explosion). In this reality we come across things that are not there and appear contradictory (nothingness, for instance: we say nothingness doesn't exist, and yet when we say there is nothing on the wall we feel like we are saying something, and other people seem to understand us) and we fail to encounter things that we know to be there (for instance, the electrical processes in our brain). Furthermore, we distinguish sunshine and rain from a rainbow, an umbrella from a shadow, a boat from its reflection in the water. In short, we encounter everything apart from science, though neither without method nor without reasons; indeed, in a much more stable way: I encounter the world today, tomorrow or in a thousand years in the same way, because it cannot be amended.

2. *The unamendable.* 'Amendability' and 'unamendability' are crucial concepts in my discourse. It has been said that death is the treasure-chest of life, the condition of possibility of life, etc., but this fails to consider that, if death can take on all that value, it is essentially because it cannot be fixed or amended, just as we cannot correct those propositions that Wittgenstein called 'grammatical'. The sphere of irreversibility appears much wider than that: if a pair of Clarks shoes is brown, we can't wear them with trousers with which we would match a pair of beige Clarks, i.e. we can't expect those who look at us to think they are one colour rather than another.

Here's the point: some things, after all, are more difficult to correct than others. I refer to those things that, more so than others, appear independent or even indifferent to conceptual schemes as a means of progressive amendment; the colour system in which certain combinations appear to us as more harmonious than others is largely influenced by taste and history, but the colours themselves are not – and to confuse the two levels is a gross mistake. Furthermore, one can distinguish between 'content' and 'object', noting that one can very well think of non-existent objects, in which case the thought would have content, but not an object.[28] However, the object is the discriminating factor: we can review a scientific theory just as we might imagine a winged horse, but we cannot see a red pen where there is a white rabbit; and the fact that the scientific theory differs from the imagination of a winged horse depends, ultimately, on the inability to see the red pen in place of the white rabbit, while we can say that some bachelors are married and that 2 + 2 = 5. Of course, I cannot exclude in principle the possibility that one day, maybe after a summer storm, ontology might become amendable; but there is not a single act of my life that justifies the hope of such an occurrence, although there are some who have had their bodies cryogenically preserved in the hope of being revived in a hundred years.

It is also conceivable that, in an infinite time, we will know everything about everything, and then all the propositions of science will be Perfect and Adequate Concepts. Between that time and the initial one, which originated in history and marks the birth of science, one may imagine endless corrections to our conceptual schemes. I do not so much care to know that in 10,000 years, perhaps, we will see things differently, than to know for sure that 2,500 years ago the Greeks saw them as we do. Similarly, one can reasonably assume that the day will come when polar bears will have fins instead of legs, but no one would claim that at the present state of our knowledge polar bears have fins. However, if amendability fully embraces the argument that 'you can, therefore you must', in the sphere of the unamendable we find more complicated typologies which disregard this rule: in short, it's not true that you always can, and above all, power does not always equal duty.

(a) *Why it is not true that we always can.* This sphere has two subsets, which I'll describe in greater detail at the end of this part of the book: non-perceptive unamendables and mostly, paradigmatically, perceptive ones. The former include tautological propositions, those that cannot be amended in the light of new information nor be falsified, those that cannot be decomposed any further or modified by imagining alternative worlds; that is, on the whole, the 'grammatical' propositions in Wittgenstein's sense. As we will see, there is a wider sphere of analytical judgments, incorporating the fact that it is grammatical to assume that I have a brain – while you could imagine that a box is empty – whereas it is not grammatical to assume that I might not be wearing underwear.

In any case, funding research to determine if what we call 'blue' should, more shrewdly, be designated as 'red' does not seem smarter than financing a study to decide if it is really true that no bachelor is married. The cases of grammatical unamendability seem to reflect – even if in a non-genetic way – a more general condition, which applies not only to those who understand what 'bachelor' means, but also to dogs and worms that understand little, or to slippers that understand nothing: if my suitcase is too heavy to take into the plane's cabin, I cannot just wish for it to weigh less, but have to leave it as hold luggage; if I have lost my keys, I have to call a locksmith; if I see a door that appears to be open but is actually very clean glass I'll slam into it – I have not amended a perception, I have just felt. If I see a camel in the Sahara walking in mid-air, I may rub my eyes and say it's a mirage and that it only seems to me that the camel is strolling in the air, but the fact remains that I see it in mid-air. On the contrary, once I'm told that America was discovered in 1492, it no longer makes sense for me to assume it was discovered in 1592. I no longer think that, or it becomes for me a false proposition. Likewise, it is much easier to believe that smoking kills than to quit smoking – just try not seeing a cigarette if one is there in front of you.

(b) *Why we shouldn't.* If I'm asked 'Do you take XY to be your lawful bride?' and answer 'I do', I'm not acknowledging that I indeed want to marry XY: I am performing an act endowed with legal value, which cannot be amended, but can be abrogated. Also, it is possible to make statements without making science: if someone claims to have seen a ghost they are not making a scientific statement, unless they produce arguments to support that thesis. If making a reference is just a function like any other – such as giving an order, making up a story, cracking a joke, translating, thanking or greeting – then it seems obvious that the scope of science and its conceptual schemes, starting from the reference to the truth, is smaller than one might think. There are many fields of our experience that stay unconceptualised, often forever, despite being conceptualisable in principle and therefore not appearing chimerical: if I move, open a box, dial a number or put a vinyl LP on the stereo I am not having conceptual experiences. Conceptualisation would happen if someone asked me what I'm doing, and the point would then be to clarify if my answer is right or wrong – that is, if my description is scientifically accurate. Likewise, the description of the actions I performed yesterday only turns into a series of amendable concepts if, say, the police ask me to account for them in order to verify an alibi; in this case telling the truth becomes important. Instead, it seems hard to claim that I have 'made' the truth the day before.[29] Rather, I will have done many things that I perceived as neither true nor false: does it make sense to wonder if I truly made a coffee when it comes out of my coffee pot? If anything, if the coffee doesn't come out, I might wonder if I forgot to put the water in. The same goes for many other questions – 'Did I lock the door?' 'Did I take the keys?'; all of this, however, is far from constituting the totality of experience even for the most obsessive person. Finally, it seems clear that there are contents that can never be conceptualised: why do we like Vermeer's yellow wall? What does this mean? There are no concepts here, at most there are hypotheses, whereas we can have many clear, distinct and falsifiable notions about the life and work of Vermeer. Nevertheless, when describing perception and speaking of 'pre-categoriality', Kant implies that what is given, say, sensibly is destined to become a category, and if it doesn't become one it is only provisionally, for reasons of time, attention or similar: *de jure*, the world can be considered archaeologically logical because it is ideologically such, since, with the hyperbole of the transcendental, the final meaning of activity must already be entirely enclosed in the original passivity. Therefore, the question of non-conceptual content is misplaced, because ever since its formulation it has assumed that the natural destiny of the content of an experience is to become a concept. On the contrary, it very often simply provides the basis for fictional or emotional reactions, which will hardly be transposed into concepts and, in some cases, may also turn out to be non-conceptualisable. This is what Kant correctly classified under the title of 'aconceptual' rather than 'preconceptual', claiming that 'the beautiful is what is liked universally without a concept'; but this consideration can be extended well beyond the sole sphere of the feeling of pleasure or displeasure: the aconceptual has nothing to say (what does a sunset say to us if we look at it neutrally, not as professional or amateur meteorologists, physicists, or people without a GPS looking for the west?). In other words, it doesn't have 'informational states' and never will have any, by definition, because its teleology isn't oriented that way.

(c) *Why we don't necessarily have to.* As I recalled earlier, the motto 'you can, therefore you must' holds not only in morality, but also in science: if you can amend a concept, then you must amend it, if not now then later. However, in experience, the fact that I can get up and leave a room doesn't mean that I have to, nor that all non-conceptual contents, thanks to our second nature (but what second nature? Philosophy or the prohibition of incest? Cuisine or the burial of the dead?), are obviously destined to become amendable concepts. The fine grain of experience can prove disadvantageous in the conceptualisation of science, focused on countability and iterability, but it can be an advantage in other fields, since food hard to describe can be good to eat, and a complex painting can be beautiful. To be teleological, one should either deplore the squandering of faculties which takes place in perception, or argue that just such a surplus shows that experience does not necessarily appear directed towards science.

More simply, it would be useful to observe that there is no forced transit between the two spheres, so that the abstractive abilities present in experience should not be ascribed to conceptualisation, not even teleologically. I can describe a toothache as a piece of information about the state of my teeth, which I will be able to verify by going to the dentist; but when the tooth aches, it does not want to tell me anything. Thus, there is a whole sphere of action – even a complex one – that certainly can be amended without having to be so: posting a letter, tying your shoes, making a sandwich, taking the train or driving a car, listening to a concert, looking at a painting, reading a book. For a great part of our lives we do not behave as scientists, entertaining any special relationship with the truth or with the ideal of amendability. Sometimes, the futility of a shoe-tying science can be disguised by a tenacious epistemophilia: there are advertisements exhibiting 'scientifically tested' toothpastes, with men in white coats performing demonstrations on the subject. What kind of scientific tests are the toothpastes subjected to? We are accustomed to thinking that for every field of experience there is a corresponding science – or, at least, that there should be – but it's not true. Not only because there are imposing perceptual phenomena – like the consecutive image – to which very few pay attention, but also because there is no such thing as, say, an infinite science of making knots.

3. *You learn from experience.* Or do you? Of course, one can say that you learn from experience, as it seemingly presents a strong character of amendability, albeit referred to analogous cases recurring more than once. However, one only learns from experience in the sense of often learning wrong things of which one ignores the principles. And when the mistake becomes evident, do we understand why? Often we don't, and yet we are aware we have made a mistake. After all, once we've acknowledged the mistake, what truly changes? It is little use to write treatises on the passions if what we want to do is amend them, whereas it makes more sense to amend the intellect: indeed, as we shall see, the definition of

'concept' as the exclusive attribute of science and that of 'amendability' come to coincide. Of course, even in experience we spend much time recognising causal connections: if the sky is cloudy, we take the umbrella. However, this causation is neither necessary nor always true. After the first couple of sneezes I might very well think to myself 'I probably have a cold'; but if I keep on sneezing and nothing else happens, then that annoying experience stops being a symptom: it is just a nuisance and is telling me nothing. It would be bizarre to consider every attitude towards sneezes as a case of folk or medical semiotics, turning the observable data into symptoms; in this case, it is hard to understand why one should say 'sneeze' and not 'cold', 'allergy', 'neurosis' or anything else our relative cognitions could suggest. These considerations can be specified in two ways.

(a) *Repetition*. Experience is mostly what happens, and when we say that we learn from experience we usually mean bad experiences. Therefore, it seems fairly clear that learning isn't what experience is for, but that it is rather a collateral and mostly unwanted effect. Since in experience we only learn based on what has already happened, the intimately innovative scope of knowledge would appear inexplicable. Indeed, take this description suggested by experience; it comes from Colonel George Hanger, a British veteran, and dates back to 1814:

> A soldier's musket, if not exceedingly ill bored, will strike the figure of a man at 80 yards; it may even at 100; but a soldier must be very unfortunate indeed who shall be wounded ... at 150 yards, provided his antagonist aims at him; I do maintain ... no man was ever killed at 200 yards, by a common soldier's musket by the person who aimed at him.[30]

As a result, some went so far as to repurpose the bow, following an infallible reasoning based on simple experience.

(b) *Innovation*. Things are different in science, where experience proper is generally left to guinea pigs and not to the researcher, while one of the truest features of what is properly called 'experience' is that the experiences of others are useless. Science has learning and the assessment of truth as its primary purpose, in accordance with a process that is meant to be cumulative and infinite, that is, directed at the future and capable of innovation. No matter how many images of science there have been, no matter how deep the epistemological fractures decreeing the distinction of chemistry from alchemy, it must be assumed that what remains unchanged between Paracelsus and Lavoisier is the idea of progress, which may call into question, or even rule out, any previous acquisition or even the idea of 'science' historically given until then. What stays unchanged, though, is the idea that – even if it be through a radical questioning – we have taken a step forward. Indeed, in science we would hardly speak of 'going back to tradition'. Also, experience and science share the possibility of saving what has been learned in memory. However, experience lacks two other aspects that, instead, are constitutive of science: the transmutation of knowledge and traditionalisation to allow for the cumulative idea of progress. After all, what I'm trying to say can be easily illustrated by the different tasks and expectations of an employee and a researcher.

4. *Amending the intellect and sharpening the senses.* At the core of the matter, as usual, we find amendability. One can be short-sighted, astigmatic or deaf, and a far-sighted person – by virtue of her own natural endowment – may perhaps become a sniper, but would not necessarily be a better ichthyologist than a myopic or an astigmatic. An ichthyologist, a child and a pike see the same perch, even if only the first knows its scientific name and classification. If at first it doesn't seem unmotivated to expect the ichthyologist to see more things than the child, this is only because we tend to attribute to seeing the characteristics of thinking: the ichthyologist 'sees' that the perch is a perch, that it is or it isn't developed, that its colour is normal or abnormal, that it has an organ where the child only sees scales, etc.; in each of these cases, though, it might more properly be argued that the ichthyologist thinks that is a perch, that it is developed, and so on.

However, as grownups in this day and age, we are convinced that science is the best conceptual scheme. In practice, we go to the doctor rather than the shaman; at most, and it is a vaguely problematic case, we give our children Oscillococcinum, despite our suspicions about homeopathy; and in extremis there are those who go to Lourdes despite not believing in the Resurrection. All this implies an ideal of the unlimited growth of knowledge, and of the infinite amendability of concepts. Nevertheless, is it truly the case that this ideal can and must affect every sphere of experience? If it were so, then someone who says 'I'll come down to Turin from Cuneo' should be reminded that they are actually coming up, if you look at the map, or that they are going neither up nor down, if you look at the cosmic scale. The expression should be considered wrong. Why isn't it so? What court can judge, in this case? Is it a purely irrational expression? Then why does it not seem meaningless like 'abracadabra' or contradictory like 'square circle'? It seems quite obvious that these are heterogeneous environments, where an ecological factor is decisive.

If while strolling on a clear night I look at the Moon, I'm not playing the astronomer, and would not do so even if, with the discomfort caused by my space suit, I looked at the Earth from the Moon. My ecological sphere can vary, but my ontology can never incorporate performances that systematically require the intervention of instruments lying outside of it. Here, too, we recognise the role of unamendability. Even Vittorio Benussi, who claimed to be able, with exercise, to neutralise various optical illusions, could not see the Earth as round, and in any case he kept defining them as 'inadequate presentations', not as 'illusions', because there is a discrepancy between presentation and belief that in some cases, through repetition, exercise and a change in point of view, may be cancelled. There is also the case of Josephson, winner of the Nobel Prize for Physics (as well as in-patient in a psychiatric hospital for a while), who claimed to be able to see with the naked eye the passage of a single photon in a dark room, after appropriate training. However, these are surely borderline cases: first of all, the photon really existed, unlike scientific opinions, which can be inconsistent; and second, relying on this case would be like trying to learn normal human behaviour from a professional athlete, or from a fakir able to bend spoons with the power of thought (and it is a fact that he really bends them, even though the case appears very different from the previous ones). Finally, suppose it becomes fairly frequent one turns into a werewolf and acquires extraordinary powers of smell and hearing: in this case, hearing dog whistles would become an obvious part of our ontology, like smelling the smell of vodka from five metres away, as happens to Michelle Pfeiffer in *Wolf*. The hypothesis is quite seductive, but false: if one uses a dog whistle and asks a friend 'Did you hear something?' the other will say, 'no, I haven't heard anything' – the operation that would be required to hear the dog whistle would be quite different from that needed to answer the phone.

Now that the preliminary observations have been made, let's move on to some essential distinctions: science/experience, truth/reality, internal world/external world.

First Distinction: Science/Experience

Epistemological deflation. Epistemological inflation arises from the assumption that without theories we would not have empirical reality. The fact that a mental inspection should be presupposed as a constituent part and a condition of possibility of experience is usually demonstrated by considerations that, in their apparent non-opposability, share the dubious philosophical career of the stick that, partially immersed in water, seems bent. Here is a famous case: wax seems sometimes solid and perfumed, sometimes liquid and odourless; how do I know that it is the same substance, if not because what I see depends on what I think? Those who propose this argument fail to consider that, if I see the wax as it melts, I need no reasoning, and that if it doesn't – until I get an explanation – no reasoning will allow me to establish the continuity between the two phenomena until the liquid wax, solidifying again, shows me what has happened (in the eighteenth century, the King of Siam thought that ice had nothing to do with water, never having seen it in his country). Another famous case is the following: I open the window, see hats and cloaks down in the street, and I know that they are people; if only perception counted, I would see hats and cloaks, and nothing else. Here too, I am simply remembering something I've seen before, therefore I am not thinking, so much so that even a dog recognises his master with or without a hat and coat, just as he recognises the hare if it's running, still, or lying skinned in the kitchen. Likewise, when I look at Jastrow's figure I can see a rabbit or a duck, but never both of them simultaneously, despite the fact that I have the concept of both.

Even in the face of such obvious evidence, the first pan-epistemological assumption is that only a naive person would think that when we see we are mainly seeing. The first step in science would be to understand that when the mind looks beyond what appears immediately, its findings cannot be attributed to the senses, and then, with a hyperbole that is little justified, that when we see we are actually thinking, otherwise we wouldn't manage to get by in life. The fallout is that, once such an axiom is held, you are forced to postulate unconscious inferences, occult qualities and other obscure perceptological manoeuvres even in the most innocent acts. I close my eyes so as not to let a gnat in? This is due to a rapid inference that has connected many complex concepts, dictionaries and encyclopaedias, all in a flash. A book falls on my head and I faint? Another lightning-fast inference, at the end of which I conclude I must faint – and I do. This doesn't make any sense. Do we really always need a concept to have experience, normality, anything at all? Or are we using 'concept' and 'conceptual scheme' in such a broad sense that they will appear fictitiously ubiquitous?

It is obvious that, when we see the hats and cloaks, we do not carry out inferences like 'I see a hat that is moving, but hats are not self-propelled, so there has to be a man walking underneath it'; therefore the cognitive faculties that are surely involved in perception do not access an explicit formulation. But then why speak of 'concepts' and 'conceptual schemes' given that we are not aware of those concepts; that is, that we do not use them in the same way as a scientist applies a theory? Isn't it worth stopping the squander of this limitless conceptual sphere? This is what I would like to do by (i) delimiting the notion of 'conceptual scheme', (ii) circumscribing the sphere that belongs to concepts, and (iii) showing when it is legitimate to speak of science. Finally, (iv) I will outline the sphere of experience as not necessarily overlapping with science.

Schemes

Explicit theories and unconscious instructions. Actual science is limited to excluding false interpretative schemes while corroborating the true ones. It does not cultivate ontological interests, as it ultimately only answers to something that can be redescribed as 'ontology', that is, to the external world. Epistemology, however, is a different thing, although it may be shared by scientists when they talk about what they do: it is the ontologising translation of science, based on which the kitchen table is made up of subatomic particles, as void as the surrounding air, etc. Compared to real science, epistemology presents significant defects. First, it tends to accredit a synecdoche, where 'science' would be physics as the fundamental knowledge from which other forms of knowledge spread out as from a root or an inverted pyramid. And the positivist view, based on an equation between science, nature and mathematics, is not guaranteed (there is more mathematics in economics than biology), and yet it is reassuring, confirming that what we encounter in nature is experience. The latter then, when properly organised, becomes science. Hence, as usual, the hyperbole that (i) without unconscious instructions – which would imperceptibly turn into conscious theories – we wouldn't have experience; and (ii) a similar set of instructions and theories appears necessary since the world, by itself, is devoid of order.

Now, on the one hand, denying that when we see a book we also think it is a book seems to be just a stubborn bias, just as it seems implausible to claim that when I hear Italian I only recognise a sequence of sounds and not words belonging to a language I speak. It is plausible that thinking and previous experience, as well as memory and imagination, play a constitutive role in perception; perhaps in many cases, but not all. Mostly we do not know the extent of the internal world and that of the external. To go back to the example of language, I can very well record a complex sequence of words without understanding their meaning, which proves that interpretation is not originary. First I hear or listen to a sentence, only later do I understand it; therefore, it was perceived before it was understood. If something isn't clear, or I wonder what my interlocutor meant, then I can properly speak of interpretation. Nevertheless, in most cases we do not seem to apply conceptual schemes, but rather to perceive or think of things that are just so and not otherwise. Certainly, when I was expecting to see a man and found a mannequin instead, it was not the conceptual scheme that corrected my assumption. In the same way, it is not a conceptual scheme that arouses a slight sense of unreality in some scenes of *Pearl Harbour*, or when I see for the first time an object I didn't know existed. Of course I can say that what led me to recognise a mannequin instead of a man depends on my assumptions related, respectively, to the concepts of 'man' and 'mannequin': it didn't move, it didn't breathe, it was made of plastic, and therefore it was a mannequin.

The limitation of such an approach is that it works too well, since it may also apply to crows, which would therefore have concepts as soon as they are no longer afraid of the scarecrow. Also, if we apply it to the letter, it produces manifestly implausible outcomes. Suppose someone doesn't dance and sees a couple dancing the tango: they should suppose that he unconsciously has awareness of the tango. Therefore, in a world built by our conceptual schemes with an infinite allowance of bricks, we should never be disappointed or surprised. But to what extent do schemes matter? Take a barrel rolling down an incline without having any theory of falling bodies; if I put Atilius Regulus in it, it would roll exactly as if it contained a lot of inert potatoes, or a bear, and the process would not be disordered. In accordance with the Slipper Argument, dogs, worms, ivies and slippers are beings with very different schemes from ours, or even no schemes at all, and yet they share a world. Now, why do things have such admirable stability regardless of our opinions and our concepts, and why is the world a set of interactions in which animals with six or eight legs, or no legs, with or without eyes, or with completely different eyes, and people with profoundly diverse cultures, can come together as in one world? It appears risky, to say the least, to postulate that a Supreme Being holds the world together through continuous operations that ensure the ordered flow of events, or that a series of potentially scientific instructions are given to animals as an implicit endowment (instinct, nature) and then to people as an explicit one (language, culture, science: the second nature). And note that the second hypothesis, that of an unconscious or conscious instruction, is even more adventurous than the explanation through divine intervention, because we all know how many differences of opinion characterise our education, and vice versa how much harmony underlies our perception. In fact, conceptual discussion can go on until exhaustion, whereas inter-observation tends to find a point of convergence rather soon.

Now, what first strikes one most sharply in the hypothesis of boundless conceptuality is its circularity: one has to posit a world of vortices, of sense data, of wild anomalies, of crooked sticks, and claim that this impossible world turns into our habitat thanks to our mediations, and that the fact that such mediations take place is demonstrated by the admirable normality of the world, as anyone can see – in fact, we all know that, if we want to, we can tell other people what happened to us, that is, our experience, thereby proving conclusively that there are mediated experiences. Nevertheless, 'mediation' means many things, and two things especially, which are often assimilated and then quietly assumed as corresponding dogmas.

1. *The cultural filter.* The first meaning is that of a cultural filter that supposedly affects perception in a totally decisive way and cannot be received as such because it is devoid of any foundation. Of course, one can note that there are many ways of making sense of the world and that these influence our re-descriptions of experience and even our physiological reactions, but this is a different story. If I order rabbit at a restaurant and, after eating it, find out it was a cat, I feel disgust, unlike a Korean; but if I order a glass of water and they bring me a glass of vodka, my reactions will mainly be affected by the amount of alcohol taken, and not just by the disappointment that my request was not granted. People usually can distinguish between cultural and natural mediation, so much so that when this distinction isn't so clear – as in the placebo effect – these cases are studied as interesting oddities. Many observations can be made, and rightly so: finding it nicer to eat crabs rather than spiders comes from a cultural prejudice, which is very sharp in the crab/spider case, less so in the snail/worm case. But nothing in the world would make us like the *garus*, that sort of Worcestershire sauce tasting like rotten fish that the Romans used to put on everything. However, if you grow up eating *garus*, worms, spiders or human flesh, you'll develop a taste for them, no less stable than the taste of those who eat crabs and snails, and be able to distinguish – say – between fresh and not so fresh spiders, etc.

Nevertheless, it should be noted that habit, i.e. mediation, selects worldly cycles, not randomness, and if the Chinese can die from eating cheese – because they haven't developed the right enzymes given that they don't eat fermented milk for cultural reasons – it's not as if the French like every single kind of cheese. Furthermore, we should also note that the Greeks corrected their columns by making them slightly convex so as to counterbalance the eye's tendency to see them as concave – a trick that still works for us today. This mediation, which has nothing cultural about it, is infinitely stronger than the previous ones I mentioned.

2. *The natural filter.* The second sense of 'mediation' is that a set of categories and pure forms of sensibility determines the world as we perceive it, which in itself could very well be made up of chaos and vortices. Now, if the first sense seems obviously

adiaphorous in an ontological study, the second isn't all that inevitable either, and it seems to draw its patents of nobility not from real usefulness, but rather from a long cultural stratification and from the benefits of Lazy Reason. There is only one way in which the mediation appears really inevitable, and that is in terms of the epistemological value of conceptual schemes: when we look at something as scientists we are testing assumptions which we are aware of, and there is no doubt that at a similar level there are mediations, the kind that have led us to the laboratory. However, why should those or other mediations intervene when we see a table, hear a whistle or eat a sandwich? And why, unlike in the first case, do we not even notice this mediation? It is one thing to say that, based on the hypothesis that 'the butler did it', or that there is a gene responsible for a predisposition to nicotine addiction, crime, or both, we select and organise clues that seem conclusive. It is a very different thing to argue that without a system of categories – which, moreover, are independent from experience, because otherwise they would fall due to the criticism of induction – we could not experience the world.

It might help to limit the term 'theory' to scientific theories, otherwise one is exposed to the heavy retaliation that every category is a theory, which is manifestly untrue: theories and concepts are just epistemological, so you can very well find beings who live without theories or concepts (other people, animals, ourselves in more than one circumstance, indeed, *katà poly*). Conversely, categories do not constitute the prelude of science, as they could be mistaken for heuristic or explanatory schemes while working well as classification methods. Also, their origin may very well be rooted in our perceptual equipment, or in earthly regularities, or in our convenience, which have nothing to do with knowledge. In short, there is no reason to be indulgent and see the ubiquitous intervention of conceptual schemes, although in many cases, but not all, what we experience is conceptualisable.

Interpretations. We usually distinguish what we do intentionally, following schemes of action and interpretation, and what we do without thinking. 'I wasn't thinking' is generally accepted as an excuse, but no one would say that happily in the field of science – so much so that the causality of the discovery of penicillin takes some credit away from Fleming. The generic term 'conceptual scheme' means many things that are not necessarily related: (i) a conscious and amendable interpretation, such as the Ptolemaic or Copernican view; (ii) a conscious but unamendable norm, such as the rules of poker: if we changed them, it would become another game; (iii) the application of consciously learned instructions based on a stimulus–response process: I see that the street light is red and I stop; (iv) the application of subconsciously learned instructions based on a stimulus–response process, like the syntax of my native language; (v) the application of norms that fall within my natural endowment, such as the figure/ground distinction, the opposable thumb, etc. On closer inspection, only the mixture between meaning (i) and all the other meanings motivates the argument that there are no facts, only interpretations: that is, the strongest dogma in favour of boundless conceptuality.

Let's now look at Nietzsche's argument in favour of interpretations:

> Against positivism, which halts at phenomena – 'There are only facts' – I would say: No, facts is precisely what there is not, only interpretations. We cannot establish any fact 'in itself': perhaps it is folly to want to do such a thing.
>
> 'Everything is subjective', you say; but even this is interpretation. The 'subject' is not something given, it is something added and invented and projected behind what there is. – Finally, is it necessary to posit an interpreter behind the interpretation? Even this is invention, hypothesis.
>
> In so far as the word 'knowledge' has any meaning, the world is knowable; but it is interpretable otherwise, it has no meaning behind it, but countless meanings. – 'Perspectivism'.
>
> It is our needs that interpret the world; our drives and their For and Against. Every drive is a kind of lust to rule; each one has its perspective that it would like to compel all the other drives to accept as a norm.[31]

And now let's look at the counterargument provided by Achille Campanile:

> – So – said the old Carl'Alberto to the bleached blond gentleman, taking up a subject that the sudden appearance of some superb lobsters had momentarily interrupted – so you were telling me you won a million at the roulette.

– Indeed.
– Lucky you! How long ago?
The bleached blond gentleman made a quick mental calculation and said:
– It will be a year at Easter.
– A year!
– After all – went on the blond, after thinking for a minute – it's still a year till Easter.
– It's true – noted the old man – how come?
– It's very simple. The thing happened seven days ago or, to put it better, just yesterday. What am I saying? This morning! It happened this morning. No later than this morning. Actually, a minute ago. Actually, it is happening now as we speak.
– As we speak?
The blond was lost in remembrance.
– To be more precise – he said – I'll tell you more, I can tell you everything anyway: the thing is yet to happen.
[...]
– And when should it happen, more or less? – the old Carl'Alberto asked the bleached blond gentleman, after a pause.
– What? – said he with a full mouth.
– What you were talking about. Winning a million.
– This coming week I believe. I believe, let's be clear.
– You're not sure?
– Quite the opposite: I'm sure it will never happen. Also because I have never won at cards.
– Of course – noted the old man with a wink – you must be lucky in love.
– No – said the bleached blond gloomily – there's another reason, and only I know it.
He went quiet, as if talking about this matter were painful for him. But the old man insisted:
– If I am not indiscreet – he said – may I ask you what this reason is?
– Please, do.
– So: what is this reason?
– I have never played.[32]

1. *Infinite interpretations?* The bleached blond gentlemen will never win, because he has omitted an act that will never be a fact, and no interpretation can ever fix that. After all, the idea of infinite interpretations clashes with several deep intuitions, and

is reminiscent of the artifice of Don Ferrante reading Feyerabend: there are infinite explanations (are there?), and therefore the thing doesn't exist. At the basis of all this is a rather simple chain of elements: all things are traced back to institutions (fantasy football, universities and marriages), and then, because none of these things can be seen, it is concluded that there is nothing in the world apart from interpretations. First of all, it is unclear why interpretations should be the one thing to survive the reductionist wrath. Of course, one could say that those who speak of conceptual schemes do not necessarily do so to claim that there are no facts, only schemes. Likewise, scrupulous transcendentalists and moderate constructivists merely say that certain conceptual schemes are needed in order to experience the world. However, either these statements say really too little (what we see might be related to what we think: who has ever questioned that?), or they claim way too much. Every day I happen to stumble into something Bare and Brutal – that is, precisely what I should never encounter according to the theoreticians of universal interpretations – by experiencing obscure pain, impressions, fleeting glimpses. I also find better defined things, but I don't feel like I am finding the outcome of conceptual schemes, as they are apparently just as sharp for beings with conceptual schemes that differ from mine. This, indeed, is what determines our values. If we could transport bodies as easily as we do thoughts, probably all our values would be different; if we only lived for thirty seconds, our values would be entirely different, or non-existent; the same would probably happen if we were immortal. So, if the notion of 'fact' were obscure enough to be useless, confirming or denying the subsistence of a fact should be roughly equivalent choices, whereas it seems very easy to grasp the difference between a fact that did happen and one that did not.

(a) *True facts*. It is absolutely obvious that there are true facts. Indeed, it is almost redundant, because a false fact is not a fact. Anyway, this is a page: would you deny it? Would you deny that France won the Euro Cup in 2000? I could go on till morning listing true facts.

(b) *False facts*. It is also obvious that – to use a purposely redundant terminology – there are false facts, that is, non-subsistent facts. If I claimed that Nietzsche lived in Piazza Castello 13 in Milan, I would be saying something false. Similarly, I found out

that a picture of Nietzsche used in a monograph I published a while ago was actually a picture of King Umberto I.

This was a proper mistake, one that Nietzsche himself would have surely recognised as such. This doesn't happen with old, somehow consolidated mistakes: we don't find it strange if somebody says 'I got your invite', even though we know 'invite' is actually a verb and has become accepted as synonymous with 'invitation' through common use; but even in a thousand years our descendants will hardly claim that the picture represents Nietzsche and not Umberto I (provided they know this is the case). Hence the manifest unsustainability of the thesis that the truth is but an old mistake whose origin got forgotten: it could well be a very ancient truth, and nothing would change. Besides, here one can see a crucial limit in Nietzsche's thesis that holds not only in ontology but – given its extremism – also in epistemology: there is no serious theory of truth and knowledge that can do without accounting for mistakes, whereas the thesis that facts are just interpretations seems constitutively unable to justify this possibility.

(c) *Factoids and things you would not believe.* There is also a more interesting aspect. After the list of true facts and false facts – namely non-facts or other facts – I could produce another one of factoids and things you would not believe: for instance, the train tilts and gasps, and for a moment it feels like you are levitating in the absence of gravity; is there even a single passenger who believes that it is truly so? Would anyone worry or even be surprised? Would anyone question the fact of being on a train and thinking gravity had been suspended (which would mean they are in orbit)? And above all, would we really consider our unreflected exclusion of factoids as an interpretation?

(d) *Strange but true*. Reciprocally, there are several facts that seem false but that, if explained, we are willing to take for real. The idea that the Swedish national dish – cabbage rolls – is descended from the Turkish national dish, grape leaf rolls, may seem a hoax, like the idea that Mexican and Chinese are the same language. But it is indeed the case – dating back to the time when, after the battle of Poltava, Charles XII of Sweden found shelter in Turkey. Actually, we do not encounter any particular difficulty in believing that spaghetti came from China, and yet it seems it is not literally true, since there was at least the intermediary of the Arabs. In other words, the improbable may very well be true, but if facts were fully subject to interpretations it should not be so.

(e) *Interpretable facts*. If, then, there is a very extensive list of facts – from sunset to the result of a football match – that do not require interpretation (you can say that the Sun does not actually set, or that it was the referee's fault, but this is a completely different matter), there is also a list, rather more succinct, of facts that (can) require interpretation: a doodle, a flourish, a cloud, some battles (Borodino, not Marengo) allow for interpretation; an X-ray or a Rorschach blot demand it; but not everything is a doodle. Consider this figure:

Here the play of interpretations can take on the frivolous freedom of the dialogue between Hamlet and Polonius: Is it a cigar? A flying saucer? The upper part of a mushroom cloud? A badly drawn coin seen from the side (ish)? A piece of Parmesan, again from the side and badly drawn? A magnifying glass? Or, simply, an elliptical shape? You can think and interpret, but only because the figure looks poor, and all our interpretations add meaning, without actually enriching it. So much so that a trifling addition is enough to stabilise a doodle:

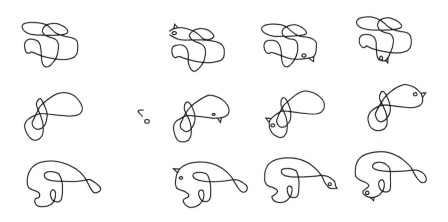

One could object that things aren't always this simple, but focus on 'not always' as opposed to 'there are no facts, only interpretations'. If taken seriously, Nietzsche's thesis is that there are no facts, and this is the most absurd thing one could come up with. If instead one takes it to mean 'sometimes what appears to be a fact is indeed a matter of interpretation', then one is faced with a solid obviousness, which surely isn't enough to create a philosopher's reputation.

(f) *Inconsistent logical relations*. Finally, there are logical relations between states of affairs that may be inconsistent: if you have never played roulette, you will hardly have won a million; in this case what is inconsistent is the relationship *even if I do not play roulette I can win a million*; or rather what is not there is a modal property of the relationship *it is possible that even if I do not play roulette I may win a million*. Likewise, witty as it may seem, it is impossible to go back in time and kill oneself by killing one's grandfather, because another fact – that I am here thinking about murdering grandpa – proves that I didn't go back in time, and surely did not kill my grandfather.

2. *Curbing interpretations.* In other words, one has to curb one's interpretations. If someone asks me what the time is and I say it's quarter to five, there isn't much to interpret (provided it is indeed a quarter to five), and whether I mean a.m. or p.m. seems rather easy to establish provided I'm not in a cave. However, if I said it was quarter to five when it was actually a quarter to six, my interlocutor would be entitled to ask relatively psychological questions ('Is he just wrong?' 'Did he do it on purpose?' 'But why?'). As for me, I can wonder whether they really wanted to know the time or just wanted to chat me up. Interpretation does not apply everywhere, but only in doubtful cases, which are rather rare in everyday experience but happen all the time in science, because of its very nature. It is easy to see that the thesis of the universality of interpretation arises from a verbal and conceptual abuse of 'facts', 'interpretations' and even 'facts and interpretations'.

(a) *Facts.* As concerns facts, it is true that if I say 'it is a fact that snow is white', I am just saying that snow is white: it is a matter of truth, and here it is right to claim that facts are intratheoretical. Nevertheless – along with the deflation I'm proposing – it seems an exaggeration to say that all facts are intratheoretical. Things would be different for a statement like 'snow is white and reminds me of the good old days', not to mention the problems that would arise with orders, prayers and phatic enunciations: 'Shut the door', 'Please God, let me win a million dollars at the lottery', 'Hello, who is it?' Note that there are things in these sentences: the door, a million dollars, maybe even God, but there are no facts (apart maybe from the lottery, which is an institution that as such can explain why the word fact is ambiguous here). 'Fact' can sometimes refer to things, as in the snow example, but not always: 'the lottery' is an institution made up of tickets, of licences and money, but there is no such thing as 'the lottery' in itself. Nevertheless, that the lottery cannot be strictly reduced to a thing doesn't mean it is a simple interpretation, so much so that the process by which the one who has the chosen ticket gets the prize is anything but arbitrary.

(b) *Interpretations.* Let's now move on to interpretations. Those who argue, correctly, that the notion of 'fact' is a bit obscure[33] will have to admit, even more so, that the notion of 'interpretation' does not seem too clear either, and that indeed its ambiguity is what gives rise to the thesis that there are no facts, only interpretations. Ontological universalisation rests on the many senses in which one can speak of 'interpretation': (i) as linguistic expression (the sense of *Peri hermeneias*); (ii) as interpreting; (iii) as artistic execution; (iv) as clarification of an obscure meaning; (v) as understanding (empathetic transposition in another age and another person: Schleiermacher–Dilthey); (vi) as unmasking (Nietzsche–Freud–Marx); (vii) as the sum of all the above – 'there are no facts, only interpretations'. In any case, unless one claims that everything is interpretation, the latter is not a natural attitude – so much so that we notice when we are interpreting, or rather, most of the time, we try not to interpret but to stick to how things really are. Which means that when we do not realise it, when we are not expressly asked to, when we are not forced to because there is something that is not clear, we do not interpret – at most, we involuntarily misunderstand. Likewise, there are professional interpreters, which wouldn't be the case if interpreting was natural.

(c) *Facts and interpretations.* Finally, as for the syntagm facts-and-interpretations, let's compare some statements that will give us the key to seeing the fallacy underlying universalisation: (i) 'there are no witches, but only persecuted women'; (ii) 'there is no phlogiston, but only a process of oxidation'; (iii) 'there is no water, but only H_2O'; (iv) 'there are no facts, but only interpretations'; (v) 'there are no cats, but only interpretations'. It is easy to see that these affirmations are not equivalent: (i) and (ii) are fully legitimate epistemological statements, (iii) is a risky transfer of epistemology into ontology (and seems to be a translation mistake), (v) is simply absurd; (iv) instead is such a widespread and shared thesis that it appears as a platitude, and yet it is not only ontologically false, but also one of the most direct causes of the confusion between ontology and epistemology. The claimed omnipresence of interpretations is reduced abruptly, revealing itself as an essentially epistemological function: first I see a white thing, then I realise it's a man, then that he is the son of Callias, then I think that he is a fool, then that he also reminds me of his father, etc. Interpretation comes in only later. If then one wants to say that it is possible to add schemes and interpretations to what we encounter in experience, well, it's obvious. However, it isn't granted, nor does it mean that every act of comprehension is an act of interpretation just because it can be reconstructed thusly ('speaking about what one sees or thinks'). Likewise, it is not the case that every interpretation is historically biased – provided that understanding has a meaning beyond the limits of an introspective psychology, since it is very common to believe we understand something while being completely wrong.

Intuitions and concepts.
1. *Are intuitions without concepts blind?* From the extremist thesis that facts do not exist we come to a seemingly more moderate claim: that intuitions without concepts are blind. The catalogue of interpretations is anything but infinite, and essentially boils down to four senses – of course, the four senses of writing.

(a) *Literal sense.* 'Without concepts you wouldn't perceive anything.' This seems absurd, and no one would ever defend such a statement – or if one did, it would be on the same level as the Trinity, or the *credo quia absurdum*. Actually, there is a way to justify such a claim: by dogmatically assuming the non-subsistence of any layer of experience that doesn't find its real condition of possibility in science, given that without conceptual schemes there would be no perceptions. It is clear that this condition could only hold for very simple tools, like a ruler or a compass, which do not have eyes or ears to begin with.

(b) *Allegorical sense.* 'Without concepts you do perceive, but in such a confused way that it's like not perceiving.' This claim sounds less bizarre, but one should still clarify that 'like'. 'Like not perceiving' means suffering from perceptual agnosia? Or, conversely: if the order of perceptions comes from concepts, should we conclude that what we see (or would see: note the non-falsifiability of the argument, which calls for a typical impossible experiment) are vortices, bundles of sense data, colours and the like, which only become tables, chairs and people thanks to concepts? If that were the case, there would be some quirky consequences: if I see a picture of a car, and I recognise the brand, colour, licence plate etc., then it means that the concepts are related to the percepts; but if I run into an arabesque of which I cannot decipher the meaning, I am authorised to conclude that it is not objectively a doodle or an encrypted image, but that it is maybe the same picture as before, except that the concepts have not clung so well. Let's face it, it does not work.

(c) *Moral sense.* 'Without concepts you do perceive, in a distinct and clear way, but you wouldn't understand anything.' Here of course the only element that needs clarification is the verb 'understand'. It is actually hard to understand what 'understand' should mean here. The problem doesn't lie in an ineradicable ambiguity of the verb 'to understand', but rather in its specific occurrence in the sentence 'Without concepts you perceive, in a distinct and clear way, but you wouldn't understand anything.' The sentence doesn't mean anything more than 'Without concepts you do perceive, but in such a confused way that it's like not perceiving'; it is just more prudish or reticent.

(d) *Anagogic sense*. Therefore, we are left with the weakest sense: 'Without concepts you do perceive, in a distinct and clear way, but you lack paradigms – scientific or otherwise – to insert what you perceive within our belief systems.' Indeed. The next obvious step for this interpretation – which almost appears futile or trivial – is prosopagnosia (I see someone I know, but due to a brain deficit I do not recognise them) or even simple ignorance (I see someone I don't know and I do not recognise them). Which means that this most profound sentence is but a tautology: 'If I don't know something, then I don't know something.' Still, there might be people unaware of the meaning of 'dog', but this wouldn't prevent them from encountering a dog and interacting with it.

2. *Counterexamples*. In any case, it is not difficult to falsify all these allegories by showing that:

(a) *Concepts are blind*; meaning that you cannot see with concepts alone, as in mimetism or equal triangles with a different orientation.

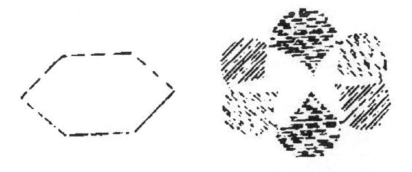

The hexagon disappears, even though I can think of it.

100 Hysteresis

The triangles are equal in shape and disposition, but the different background orientation makes it hard to grasp their equality.

(b) *We can see, but without concepts*; that is, we struggle to comprehend what is seen.

We see the waterfall, but we do not understand how it can work. Similarly, in the Moebius strip and the Klein bottle, the interior and the exterior are intertwined in a way that is not immediately understandable, but this doesn't mean that we cannot see them.

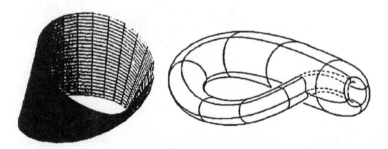

3. *Recognising objects*. The idea that an intuition should require a concept derives from a confusion between cause and effect that is reminiscent of the misinterpretation I highlighted about the omnipresence of interpretations. Think of Cook seeing a platypus for the first time. Given that he is a human being and not a beaver, he is inclined to make hypotheses formulated in terms of knowledge and that, in this case, would prove wrong. However, this doesn't demonstrate that intuitions without concepts are blind: rather, it demonstrates the opposite. If I don't know what it is I'm seeing, it's not that my intuitions are blind: they seem blind only when I start formulating, based on concepts, erroneous hypotheses. In any case, if I see a platypus, I can say 'I don't know what it is, but it's surely not a dog'; I certainly wouldn't say 'It is nothing.' I am likely to think that it's an animal and not a plant, a rock or a mechanical part. On the other hand, if I had seen a drawing of a platypus in an Australian textbook and knew nothing more, I could very well say 'this is a platypus' and be fully certain of it, despite being ignorant of the properties of platypuses, or having wrong information that led me to attribute to them the features of mongooses, or to believe that they are made up of bits of other animals, etc. Finally, I might have read a whole treatise on the sex life of platypuses and still be unable to recognise one.

I can very well subsume an object without having its concept, or I can have a concept and be unable to apply it.[34] One might object: subsume under what? Speaking of subsumption seems to imply the existence of a concept. Maybe it means that I can recognise an object without knowing the corresponding word; however, lacking the word does not entail lacking the concept, and even if it were possible to recognise objects without concepts it would still be unclear why 'recognition' should be assimilated to 'subsumption'. My response is: how can I possibly have a concept of an animal I do not know? What sort of concept would it be? Here the use of 'concept' becomes too broad to be significant: I can maybe see someone that looks familiar, wave, wonder who it was and finally remember it was the newsagent. Referring to concepts here and claiming that thanks to them I wave at the newsagent and not at his bike means using 'concept' in a risky way. Likewise, it seems really hard to say that an experience described in erroneous terms is not an experience: Columbus landed in America thinking he was in India, but he still experienced sailing and landing.

On the other hand, the fact that one can recognise parts of

objects goes against the idea that you should always presuppose a concept for any percept. Suppose we see on TV a mysterious object, a piece of something, like a detail of the hose of a vacuum cleaner. We see a succession of black rings; therefore we recognise shapes and colours, but we cannot say that we have a concept (the indication that is offered is purely negative: 'What you see is not a whole but a part'). Having a concept, though, means more than one thing, and in a very strong sense it means 'knowing the essence'. Yet, one certainly need not know the essence to see a piece of a vacuum cleaner. We see very well and, if we have epistemologically inadequate concepts ('series of rings'), we do not know what it is – but we still see it. Then the frame widens, and now we see the whole vacuum cleaner. Only the Iroquois chief of the third *Critique* – the one who only appreciated delis in Paris – would still be perplexed despite seeing the whole thing; had he read Kafka, he might believe he's met the Odradek. Any other (grownup) person of our age, though, would see a vacuum cleaner and know what to do with it in at least two senses: they would know how to use it and could teach the chief what a vacuum cleaner is. Now, in these two cases – which are not equivalent – we have a concept that, however, does not determine the possibility of perceiving the object through its essence, but that of using it as a tool and as an example. This is even clearer in the case of a false recognition: suppose I do not know the Greek alphabet and see the effigy of Alexander the Great on a 100 drachma coin. I might think it is Sylvester Stallone: would I really have a concept? I would, in the sense that I wouldn't only have a percept. In other words, Kant's thesis surely has a meaning, but only an epistemological one. If I see a chair, point it out to someone else, and they tell me with seemingly persuasive arguments that it isn't a chair, I can very well reply: 'If that isn't a chair, then I haven't got the faintest idea what it may be.' It is only in this situation – which indicates epistemological perplexity – that intuitions without concepts are blind.

The Kantian statement therefore means: (i) one cannot do science without concepts, and (ii) if concepts are wrong, we might be perplexed. However, neither of those facts implies that without the concept of 'chair' we'd just see a hole instead of a chair, or that we wouldn't be able to distinguish it from the floor, the wall and the table. If, then, non-conceptualisability ruled out objectivity, we'd also struggle with tertiary qualities: we couldn't explain the phenomenon of VIPs, the fact that some bottles of Barbaresco are worth £400, and things like restaurant guides. Likewise, it would be unclear why one guide is more reliable than another: if all matters of taste are subjective, what would be the point? Sure, objectivity might not be the right word here, as it recalls measurability, but it is obvious that secondary and tertiary qualities are not as easy to measure as the primary ones. The point would rather be to state that tertiary qualities are real and not mental – that is, that beauty is not entirely a subjective matter. To explain everything away in terms of persuasion, advertising and conspiracy theories is rather convoluted and, again, no less problematic than the hypothesis of pre-established harmony – not to mention that the choice of a young beautiful woman instead of a cantankerous-looking old man for a commercial is probably due to a reason, certainly not as strict as 2 + 2 = 4, but not fully arbitrary either.

4. *Intuitions without concept are naked*. Emil Lask proposed to reformulate the Kantian saying as follows: form without content is empty, content without form is naked.[35] This means that without concepts – in fact, Lask more cautiously speaks about 'forms', weakening Kant's hyper-epistemological setup – there can still be a world that is fully equipped and determined, only without a logical 'robe'. Nakedness must have attracted the attention of Husserl, who years later in *Experience and Judgment*,[36] trying to highlight the essence and the origin of the predicative judgment, wrote that judgment is a robe of ideas thrown onto the world of intuition. So, the object must be evident in its self-givenness, in which no predicative form is included: the grammar of seeing, hearing and touching is different from that of thinking. Little by little, though, the relationship between the predicative layer and the ante-predicative one acquires a teleological dimension and the grammar of feeling is originally oriented towards the grammar of thinking so that, in short, continuity prevails over separation. The reason is easily explained: Husserl starts from the assumption that judgment is originated in the ante-predicative sphere, not in the very plausible sense that judgments are not nice and ready in our minds when we are born, but in the traditional – and, I think, less plausible – sense that judgments are originated from sensations. The autonomy of the ante-predicative state thus appears as a mere postulation, because ever since its appearance it gets meaning from its teleological orientation towards the predicative. Which is to say that the world is there but we know nothing about it, and therefore it's unclear why we should be interested in it: the original autonomy of the ante-predicative depends on its final dependence on the predicative.

Lask and Husserl manifest a dissatisfaction with the Kantian idea that logic has a constitutive role with regards to aesthetics, especially when it comes to primary nakedness, and they insist that the robe only comes in later. Yet they picture the robe as a kind of prosthesis roughly determined by the anatomy of the naked body, and the metaphor fits perfectly: Plato compares knowledge to a robe that can be kept in the wardrobe, in an inactual way, or that can be worn in an actual way.[37] In other words, these thinkers bring back Leibniz's *lex continui*: from night to midday, going through dawn – which is like saying, once again, from fact to law. Therefore, as for the matter of nakedness and the robe, my attempt is to show that there is absolutely nothing in the world that pre-constitutes the logical form creating its genetic artefact, as you can wear a redingote, a sweat suit, a toga or a peplum, which only share the one function of responding to the needs of the naked body, depending on the circumstances and climates. The bond, as you can see, is teleological and not archaeological, because a redingote, a sweat suit, a gown and a peplum do not strictly fit the needs of a human body: a gorilla could wear them too, or we could hang them in a wardrobe or fold them into a bag.

Previous experience. Now let's come to the minimalism of conceptual schemes: the idea that previous experience interferes significantly with the current one. Previous experience can mean many things: (i) a person's set of experiences, especially repeated ones, so that people with different lives would have considerably different experiences; (ii) the historical presuppositions of experience, that is, concretely, the culture of those who see a table or a tree (and, if reading counted decisively, perhaps only very devoted Muslims who only read the Koran could count on some degree of stability); (iii) the stages of learning, like learning to use a tool (but it is clear that a violinist doesn't only see violins everywhere); (iv) even a consecutive image should be considered a previous experience (and here you can see the problem, because an afterimage is effective insofar as it is not a previous experience, in the proper sense, but a present one); (v) finally, in its most canonical and ubiquitous form, previous experience resonates as follows: 'any current experience is conditioned by previous experiences, which work as minimal conceptual schemes'. Now, this family of arguments, though seemingly convincing, demonstrates exactly the opposite of what is claimed by its supporters. In particular:

1. *It is not a universal mechanism.* In the doctrine of previous experience, it is assumed that experience is never something merely passive, as it always entails a margin of activity. However, this image works for talking about something that has happened to us, but not for something as it happens: if we stumble into a piece of furniture and see stars we swear long before we realise that we had miscalculated the distance. Also, we usually notice when previous experience is at work, which proves that upon all other occasions (which are the majority) there is no previous experience involved. Besides, if it truly was a universal mechanism then there would be the problem of the first time, which can only be solved by resorting to a system of innate ideas that goes against one of the presuppositions of previous experience.

2. *It is not ontologically efficient*: it only works at a psychological level. We notice we have previous experience precisely when our expectations of present experience are not met, like when we feel slightly nauseous on a broken escalator. Surprise, in general, is an attitude born out of seeing previous experience denied by the current one: something that wasn't supposed to happen occurs; a place turns out to be slightly different from what we remembered or imagined, etc. This fact is usually evoked to prove that expectations matter a lot in perception, but if this really were the case, then they should never be denied. And yet we do happen to be surprised, and in surprise the inferential chain is abruptly broken: there is an external world, endowed with its own characters, that does not demand interpretation. If we assume that we see the world through conceptual schemes within us, how could we explain this fact? What would the first experience be like? And note that even our most recent experience could surprise us, and it does – the same goes for all the experiences in between. If one has never been to Bologna, no matter how many photographs one has seen of it, when one gets there one will see a number of things one hasn't thought of and yet are very trivial (streets, houses, chairs, etc.). Here is an experience, which is always unexpected to an extent, to the point that we protect ourselves through rituals, anxiety and so forth. On the other hand, I'm unlikely to be surprised by my representations or memories: at most, I may be surprised by remembering or not remembering something. Let alone my interpretations: they never surprise me – at most, I'm shocked by other people's interpretations. Surprise – which manifests itself from our very first days of life – shows that the mind has an intrinsically predictive

attitude (we expect normality) but not a constructive one (we do not see regularities: we see what is there, which can surprise us). The same goes for boredom, the opposite of surprise: if we truly were always interpreting the world, we'd never be bored – or we'd always be, as we'd already know the answer.

3. *It doesn't work as it should*. Also, when it does apply, previous experience does not act as it should to support the thesis that it constitutes present experience. On the contrary, if I repeatedly show you two disks, the right one being slightly bigger than the other, and then show you two perfectly identical disks, you'll think that the left one is bigger. Sure, one can say that expectations affect what we see, but it would be more correct to say that they affect what we pay attention to. Consider the following experiment: you see a film in which three basketball players in black play against three dressed in white. The task is to count how many times the players in white exchange the ball. While counting, 75 per cent of people (including myself) fail to notice that in the meantime a man dressed as a gorilla comes onto the court and does everything he can to get noticed. This experiment concerns attention but, ontologically, it doesn't prove anything: if the task were to watch the players in black, if the gorilla were red, or if I were actually in the room, I would end up encountering the gorilla. The moral of the story is that I simply do not pay attention to the gorilla. Therefore, claiming that we isolate what we need from an indistinct background seems risky to say the least: if that were the case, when I'm feeling hungry I should be able to cut out a ham sandwich from a primordial *chora*, but I couldn't do so when I'm feeling full – rather, I'd have negative hallucinations. Things are different with aversions: once I was sick after eating oysters and now I no longer eat them – but I still see them, and avoid them. One must cultivate a pathological subjectivism to confuse the two cases; and that our needs interpret the world does not yet mean that they determine it, otherwise we would live in perpetual conflict, or would be responsible for all sorts of disasters.

For the most part, the argument of previous experience starts from the indisputable fact that perception mixes expectations and judgments to conclude that perception wouldn't exist without them; clearly this is not so, since people with different cultures see the same things. Also, if it were the case, one should postulate concepts to explain animal behaviour. Furthermore, the mixture as such is obscure: all that we actually experience, on many occasions, is the simultaneity between some percepts and some mental contents – which, as in Kanizsa's famous image, do not prevent us from seeing things that openly contrast with everything we know about the world.

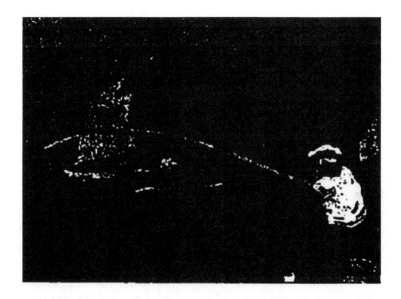

I have never seen a fishing line go behind a sail, but I can see it in this image.

Likewise, no island would suddenly emerge from the sea, full of birds, and yet that seems to be the case here.

Now let's move on to the deflation of the concept of 'concept', which I propose to restrict to science as an amendable project.

Concepts

Conceptual and non-conceptual. Suppose one wants to say what a concept is. It could be a good idea to distinguish it from the percept as the non-conceptual; however, it is far from simple to do so, and the traditionally proposed criteria do not seem to be decisive.

1. *Clarity and distinctness.* As we have seen, the fact that something can be conceptualised doesn't mean it has to be, be it *de facto* (there is no time to do so) or *de jure* (it's not worth it). If this is true, then it is far from obvious that, even in processes and experiences in front of everyone's eyes, the conceptual should be inextricably intertwined with the non-conceptual and vice versa. That this may seem implausible depends precisely on the transformation of a possibility – the potential conceptualisation – into a necessity and a duty, as such valid only in science. Of course, roughly speaking, a concept can be a name, an obscure and confused idea, a clear and distinct idea, and many other things. It is easy to imagine that, if we reserved the label 'concept' for clear and distinct ideas, then we would find lots of non-conceptual contents even in science and up in the logical space of reason; in fact, a lift would then be a non-conceptual content for everyone except a lift technician, or its designer. However, if the conceptual sphere also includes obscure and confused ideas – which Leibnizians wrongly conceived as characteristic of sensibility – then we would be simply denying the existence of percepts, trivially confusing sensibility and intellect. The reference to obscurity or clarity, confusion or distinction, is not at all a distinctive criterion for recognising concepts and differentiating them from percepts, since there can be clear and distinct concepts or obscure and confused concepts, and the same goes for percepts. Leibniz probably thought that concepts are clear and distinct because usually what we call a concept is just that, and we are ashamed to use obscure and confused concepts. However, the fact that concepts appear unpresentable or empty doesn't mean that they shouldn't be considered concepts, sticking to a distinction with which I personally disagree. Otherwise names like 'Volyn', 'Lausitz', 'Courland' would constitute, for most

people, as many percepts, with the aggravating circumstance that the conceptual or perceptual nature of something would come to depend on the lexical competence of the speaker. In any case, speaking of 'concepts' without defining them – as if everyone knew very well what they are – really doesn't seem to be the right move: 'concept' isn't clearly different from 'idea', and every remembered percept could become a concept, so that finding non-conceptual concepts should be very hard. Of course, every percept as reported, i.e. put into words and said to us or to others, can become a concept; but this does not imply that the percept has become a concept, or that the perception requires a linguistic form, which is perceived as distinct from the perception.

2. *Activity and passivity.* Often, with a Kantian reference, 'conceptual' is understood as active and 'non-conceptual' as passive; however, this distinction appears suspicious and controversial. Speaking of 'activity' is a gnoseologically postulatory assumption; in fact, it assumes that we are free agents, which even for Kant is nothing more than a postulate to be set in the intelligible world to ensure the possibility of moral action. Conversely, for all we know about ourselves and the world, we could very well be puppets in the hands of blind fate. In addition, and keeping an eye on the phenomenal layer, the active/passive distinction appears essentially psychological: at its root, there is something like the idea that it is one thing to remember the Sun at midnight, another to see it at midday. Here we witness primarily the fact that I cannot voluntarily perceive the colour 'yellow' unless there's a yellow thing in front of me, whereas I can think of yellow whenever I want, just as I can think if and when I want about the Pythagorean Theorem or the Trinity.

Based on this – which, again, does not specify if what I am dealing with is a word or a thing, if it belongs in a dictionary or an encyclopaedia, or if I can just remember the name 'Trinity' or if I also have to know what it is – it is decided that all that can be evoked at will is a 'concept', and the rest is a 'percept'. Nevertheless, there are unpleasant memories we'd rather not have, with respect to which we are passive;[38] we cannot break the laws of logic with impunity; if I could not remember a concept and a demonstration, or even just a name, I should conclude that they are percepts, to the point that each memory lapse should fall under the chapter of sensibility. In short, to postulate that concepts are active and percepts passive, identifying sensibility with receptivity and intellect with spontaneity, is a widely accepted argument that is nonetheless rather suspicious, because it is fundamentally genetic, that is to say causal, and is therefore electively tilted in favour of the concept.

It is a strange way to see things, because if that were the case then anytime we are not thinking of the non-contradiction principle, or perhaps even if we enunciate it without thinking, it would be a percept. Not to mention when we have a name on the tip of our tongue and yet can't remember it. Is it a percept, too? In addition to aporetic arguments there is a positive one: consensus and negation are not a prerogative of judgments, as they already appear in a-conceptual experience, such as the negation of a perceptive expectation, the feeling of repulsion for an object, and the like.

3. *Judgment.* One may object that the problem lies elsewhere and is inherent in the issue of judgment; to put it in Kantian terms: the senses do not think and therefore are neither true nor false, whereas the intellect judges and can reject or accept what it passively receives from the senses. Nevertheless – again due to the inscrutable question of freedom – here we get into hot water, because we have no evidence that the intellect's rejection or acceptance should be considered an argument for spontaneity. Maybe we accept or reject what comes from the senses because we are programmed to do so, and we only believe ourselves to be acting freely whereas the real freedom lies in the senses that, regardless of our judgment, keep presenting us with the same phenomena. And yet we fail to notice this, and think we are free in our intellect, whereas we are actually free in our senses. Take the Müller-Lyer illusion:

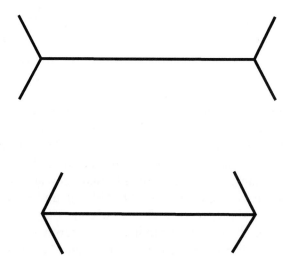

We very often read that this allegedly proves the spontaneity of the intellect, because the passive and gullible senses fall into the trap, while the savvy, critical and spontaneous intellect is able to see through it. And yet I would say that the very demonstrandum is being used as a proof. After all, there is a perfect balance here: we always see A and always think B. So why should B be spontaneous and A passive? One could very well also claim that we are forced to reject A in the name of B, whereas the senses – being very active indeed – persist regardless of the intellect in reproposing A. Albeit reformulated by appealing to judgment, the thesis about the spontaneity of the intellect and the passivity of the senses appears as a hypothesis in which there lies the possibility of science, because if we truly could do nothing to amend the intellect, 'science' would be an empty word.

4. *Abstract and concrete.* It is far from obvious that a good distinction between concepts and percepts should follow from the idea that the first are abstract and the second concrete. On the one hand, 'abstraction' is a very vague term, which can designate both the ability to grasp generalities (the triangle, the chair) and the ability to retain aspects of what is perceived (the colour of this triangle, the shape of this chair). Aristotle noted that first principles are as evident as sensations for this very reason,[39] therefore evidence cannot necessarily be attributed to logic. Also, it is difficult to argue that the figure/ground distinction isn't abstract; however, it is no less hard to claim that it is conceptual. The fact that percepts normally have a finer grain than concepts doesn't exclude the possibility that they might be abstract. Indeed, the idea that only concepts are abstract results from several confusions.

(a) *Categorising.* 'Abstracting' is mistaken for 'categorising'. A category is a form of classification: there are professional categories, boxes into which I can categorise – say – old shoes, and so on. The term 'category' is extremely vague, because its distinctive trait is neither its format (as there are both perceptive and mental categories), nor its extension ('colour' and 'red' can both be categories), nor its content (there are mental categories, real ones, etc.) Apart from that, the decisive point is that I can abstract without categorising: for example, pull something out of one box without placing it in another. Conversely, take a bloodhound that at a three-way junction sniffs two of the roads, rejects them, and takes the third without having to sniff. Has it made an inference? Or take a fox that, walking on ice and hearing the sound of water, changes direction because the ice is too thin. Has it performed a syllogism? The distinction is not between concrete sensibility and abstract intelligibility, but rather between what can be defined, if necessary, and what is recognised (even abstractly) without definitions or categories: a cat can fall asleep on a bench, or a carpet, or a chair without resorting to a categorisation – which would be mistaken if it subsumed all of the above under the concept of 'chair'. Mostly, if the categorisation were formalised, it would refer to something much more abstract than 'chair', like 'surface' or something similar.

(b) *Naming*. 'Abstracting' is mistaken for 'naming', with a loose use of the concept in which giving a name and being able to repeat it to another person is taken to be synonymous with conceptualising it. In such a liberal sense, every word would be abstract and should be considered a concept. At least two problems arise here. First, if every concept is a name, not every name is necessarily a concept – think of proper names, which do not describe any feature of the person or pet. Second, there may very well be abstract functions that exist without being somehow christened: when I set the table, I don't do so by naming the plates and the cutlery, and my action – usually performed absent-mindedly – does not depend on a set of words.

(c) *Ideas*. 'Concept' is mistaken for 'idea' or even 'memory'. Claiming that abstraction is the exclusive property of the concept would mean that anything removed from its here and now would be abstract (in this case, 'subtracted'), and thus conceptual. Now, Kant is right when he argues that red is not an idea, as clearly as it may appear to us – that is, as easy as it is to distinguish it from other colours, even though it would be very hard to list all its characteristics. The fact that there can be a concept of 'red', just as there can be a concept of 'percept', doesn't mean that red and percept are concepts. I can make inferences starting from 'red' (if a metal is glowing red it will burn me), I can distinguish it from 'green', and I know it is a colour and so forth, but this doesn't mean at all that red things are conceptual. Saying the opposite, one falls into a vicious circle in which all that can be conceptualised is conceptual, thereby asserting the omnipresence of the conceptual and of reason. And yet, the excitement that red seems to arouse in bulls doesn't depend on a recognition of the concept of red, but rather on seeing a muleta waved by a bizarrely dressed fellow. Things are no different with humans: the way in which red excites and green tranquilises activates very different mechanisms from those related to politically connoted colours; therefore, trivially, what acts are objects and not concepts, sometimes along with something discursive, sometimes without any such thing.

(d) *Actual and potential*. 'Actual' is mistaken for 'potential'. By prioritising the transcendental and the mistaken inference that, because something can be conceptualised, it is conceptual, it follows that the non-conceptual is nothing more than a conceptual unexpressed. This is the most delicate point.

5. *Form and matter.* One could also say: the senses grasp matter, the intellect grasps the form. But is it true? Even from an Aristotelian perspective, irredeemably marked by a distinction between matter and form, the strongest abstraction, which leaves out matter to grasp only the form (not only when I think of an apple but also when I perceive it, the apple does not physically enter my brain through my eyes and hands), comes from perception, not from the active intellect.[40] If the senses grasp shapes without matter, if the eye doesn't see the apple or the tree, how can one rely on this distinction to separate sensibility and intellect if not by claiming that matter is the predecessor of the form, sense the precursor of intellect, experience the archaeology of knowledge, and therefore all forms derived from the senses represent as many matters for the intellect? On the other hand, one might wonder: why should there not be abstract percepts? Instead of identifying abstraction with 'concept', in a move that raises the problems enumerated here, does it not make sense instead to hypothesise two spheres, concepts and percepts, each of which has autonomous powers of abstraction, only differentiated because the conceptual sphere, unlike the perceptual, is amendable? As usual, this would refer to the distinction between what the object of science is and what the object of experience is.

6. *Concept and science.* A definition of 'concept' has to follow an alternative route: in the concept an 'ought' is implicit, which is born from its reference to science and amendability; no one ever dreamed of amending their own shadow, but one can, and indeed should, amend one's concepts – otherwise they wouldn't be concepts but, in the best-case scenario, prejudices. As we have seen, the fact that we learn (or rather can learn) from experience is not a necessary character of the latter, contrary to science: here we only learn when we find connections and ascribe them to real causes, whereas we can very well have experiences – positive or

negative – without having the faintest clue as to what happened or how. One may nevertheless claim, according to an externalistic theory, that concepts are no less unamendable than percepts. The concept of 'water' has never changed, on Earth, from the Babylonians to Bill Clinton: water is the substance found in rivers and seas, a substance we drink, etc. The properties of being in rivers, being in seas, being drunk, strictly speaking, do not fall within the concept of 'water' but are part of the knowledge thanks to which we establish the content of the concept – that is, water. And it is precisely the immutability of the concept that allows us to explain the cognitive process, the transformation of beliefs about water, so that what is amendable are the beliefs, not the concepts. However, this is an abuse of concepts akin to that of interpretations, since there is no reason for debating 'concepts' where one could speak of 'names'. When I say 'coil ignition', I am not necessarily covering its internal properties, as I have little to amend. The point is not the format of a certain mental content – for example discursive/non-discursive – but rather the fact that there is some perfectible knowledge connected to the word. So, anxiety is not a concept, because there is nothing amendable about it: nothing is added to the concept, nor is anything changed about it; again, what we call concepts are simply names, which, compared to percepts, only have the feature of being thought-of without losing any essential characteristic.

Having the concept of 'finger' is nothing more than being able to see fingers and having the word finger in one's vocabulary along with its grammatical instructions: it's not like the concept of finger has existed since the dawn of humanity, like actual fingers. At some point, people started talking about 'fingers' (some have hypothesised it was the very first word of humankind: 'tik'), but they haven't deliberately set out to amend the word, because there wasn't much to be gained from it. This doesn't mean one couldn't do so or that it hasn't happened ('tik' at first designated both the finger and the act of pointing), only that the process has taken place over such long and remote ages that no one has noticed. The history of languages and translations shows the transformation of commonly used concepts, the reference of certain words and certain linguistic usages: the metonymy with which we indicate the way humans speak, 'language', is 'lip' in the Bible's Aramaic; the Italian 'gola' (throat) comes from the Latin 'gula', which means 'cheek', and is also found in part in the French 'gueule' for 'face'. Nevertheless, we wouldn't consider such transformations as amendments, because this is not a progressive teleology like that of science. Also, there are words – like 'barma' in Piedmont dialect, meaning 'a rocky shelter from the rain' – that date back to the Neolithic: no one has ever amended the word; rather, at some point the umbrella was invented. Conversely, 'atom' has indicated fairly different things, but always denoted a common essence to which it was adapted: the concept of something indivisible, which has led to the identification of subatomic particles.

Now, after circumscribing schemes and concepts, let's come to the third step of the deflation: the delimitation of science, which is not a natural character of the human being but rather something that appears at a given moment, provided there are *logos*, history, freedom, infinity and teleology. Obviously, similar requirements appear necessary but not sufficient, since one could organise voodoo rites in line with them. So, to avoid circularity ('science is everything that makes use of concepts') and conventionalism ('science is everything that is taught at the university'), I propose the following definition: 'Science is all that explains (= finds the causes of) something visible through something invisible, but in such a way that, at least *idealiter* and in an infinite time, the invisible will be appropriate to the visible.' According to this definition, physics and teleology are sciences, but mysticism isn't. What I wish to highlight is (i) that here science appears as a deferral of experience, contrary to the (Aristotelian and empiricist) vision that sees it as an extension of experience; and that (ii) deferred experience has to account for reality, which is the object of ontology, but doesn't take it as a universally reliable source for its theorisations. I will show this by explaining the antinomies between aesthetics and logic.

Science

Logos. Science establishes relations, i.e. *logoi*, that are both linguistic and mathematical.

1. *Language.* One can legitimately argue that linguistic communication appears necessary for the processes of abstraction and the awareness of the conditions of the truth of a thought, which are what identifies its contents. This may seem like an argument for language, but it actually narrows and clarifies the sphere of science: even with the best of intentions, it seems difficult to admit

that language organises experience, and therefore maybe orders the Pacific Ocean. As usual, the supposed universality of language is confused with the fact that many things have absolutely nothing to do with language, even though they can be described in words. California or Julius Caesar are not just language, and if they were they wouldn't matter to us. Likewise, it is fairly obvious that a statement like 'Sacramento is the capital city of California' wouldn't be conceivable without language. But if I call a tooth the 'left second premolar', isolating it from other teeth, from the jaw or the head, it is undisputed that there are reasons for this, and in fact no one asks me 'why do you call it premolar and not "incisor"?' On the other hand, a child is likely to be surprised that the capital of California is not Los Angeles. Clearly, the thesis of the primacy of language wants to turn the world into a sphere that can be subject to scientific investigation (or to an investigation made by the Oprah Winfrey Show, or the Aristotelian Society) rather than ordering a shapeless matter.

Now, you can be in a lab or a library, attending a seminar. You are using concepts – you speak or write, even though this is a necessary but not sufficient condition; concepts are amended throughout the research or discussion, and the norm of amendment is that they are either right or wrong in the light of our present knowledge. One could discuss infinitely, according to a teleology oriented by truth; no one truly has the final word, because today's truth may be tomorrow's phlogiston. This, though, doesn't mean that there aren't things outside of language – nor does it exclude that one might have silent and yet complex and organised experiences. It could be argued that those experiences can be expressed in various circumstances more or less adequately in language ('The train arrived at 15:30' is different from 'I felt indescribable pain'), which, however, does not imply that they are linguistic.

I can see a dog in his kennel and a man coming home, and assume that, unlike the dog, the man – at least in most cases – can tell himself and others what he is doing; which, at an ontological level, doesn't seem too relevant. I can also see a man and a dog nervously walking around, in apparent aimlessness and both looking worried (suppose the dog is a bulldog), but it seems futile to posit that the dog is thinking about his troubles. If, however, the man could not tell me what he was thinking about, I'd have every right to believe that he was simply walking around aimlessly, just like the bulldog. The latter, still, would not truly be nervous, both because it appears inscrutable what it means for a bulldog to be nervous, and because he is unlikely to be always nervous, as he apparently would be if we attributed a human facial expression to him. Also, every time there is thought there is language (at least potentially), as shown by the examples I have given; however, when there is language there is not always thought: I can read a whole page and then wonder what I have been reading, or answer mechanically, or make a Freudian slip.

Next to these general considerations, I'd like to add a negative argument: could one transmit the third antinomy telepathically? And if so, would it still count as science? I doubt it, because it would lack the element of language: intuitive knowledge and infused knowledge are a mystical dream, but no one would give a Nobel Prize to God, since everything he knows he acquired without language, which is to say without work or merit. Likewise, deaf mutes add up two deficiencies which are not comparable, even though they present the same origin: deafness is, so to speak, an ontological limit, whereas mutism is an epistemological defect. The first inhibits experience, the latter can pose a limit – which can be compensated for through writing or gestures – to the transmission and socialisation of experience, and therefore also to science. Finally, the deaf-blind suffer more serious ontological amputations than the deaf-mute, even though from the epistemological point of view they are virtually coplanar – provided they learn to read and write. In fact, no one could say that a blind person or a deaf-blind person does not think, just as no one would claim that they can see – which proves the obvious difference between seeing and thinking.

Now let's consider the matter from the other side. As we discuss something during the seminar, the chair on which we are sitting is uncomfortable, there's a light bothering us, we scratch our head. In the library we feel like sneezing, or we leave the lab because we need a coffee. These are all experiences, which we don't dare correct – and often we don't even communicate them to others. Sometimes we struggle to notice them ourselves (that dull pain that then turned into a toothache – when did it start?). So, experience is eminently non-linguistic (we hardly formally think of what we're doing as we're doing it), non-conceptual and unamendable (I do not amend my idea of uncomfortable, but sit elsewhere). So, the epistemological deflation corresponds to a rarefaction of the omnipresence of language: the Hopi surely feel pain if they fall, even if their vocabulary doesn't include a notion of 'substance'. Instead, it is easily conceivable that the Hopi might think $2 + 2 = 4$ – even if it is still unclear in what sense. Likewise, we are willing to attribute sensations, memory, imagination, beliefs, technical skills, dreams, depression, suffering, friendship, love, parental care and communication to some animals, because their behaviour often seems similar to ours: this is enough to constitute an experience – what Leibnizians called 'analogon rationis' – and yet is not enough for science. The moral is that all an animal needs to be human is the idea of an infinite amendability, namely the concept and the teleology of science and history, and of science as history: that is, reason in the Leibnizian sense. Note, though, that these characteristics are lacking in many humans, too, as there are societies without history and without science; also, they are less active than one might think even in the most diligent and honest scientists.

It is also clear that the experience requested by science, amendable and inextricably imbued with conceptualism, along with the daily practice in which we seek to exploit our naive observations, do not constitute the whole of experience. In fact, you can certainly not accuse a beaver – not necessarily because it is far-fetched, but rather because it is inscrutable and futile – of lacking perfectible concepts, nor can you claim that its industriousness represents a form of imperfect science. On the contrary, you can easily say that the beaver makes use of its experiences, which for it perhaps act as memories, so that it no longer builds a dam on a creek that has previously proven unsuitable. Surely one wouldn't say that its perception is also inextricably interwoven with concepts. Note that the example is hyperbolic, describing an attitude that, translated into anthropomorphic terms, can be understood as technological and project-like.

Let's turn to a classical and very simple case: a dog that has been beaten in the past flees at the sight of a stick. Is he using concepts? One wouldn't say so, if anything because the millennial debate on animal intelligence has cyclically come to a halt faced with the hardly controvertible evidence that dogs do not speak but bark. So let us take the symmetric case of a human who, having been bitten before, flees at the sight of a dog: by analogy with the former, we should say that there is no proof of the use of concepts here. This, in a way, is dramatically true: the man would hardly flee based on concepts, but will instead use them to explain – to himself and others – the reasons why he ran away. The dog may never use them. This is clearly another example of the fact that, in many obvious situations – a dog running or a man fleeing are not evanescent and inconsistent sense data – there are non-conceptual concepts, and that our experience is far from being inextricably interwoven with activity and passivity. It is plausible that one may not empirically solve problems related to mental models, and that one may conclude that a dog has a model of its master's mind, just like a chimpanzee has a model of the mind of the bigger monkey it is hiding from. However, it is a very different thing to claim that the dog acts based on concepts than to claim that my reader does. As far as we know, the beings that we too generically call 'animals' have non-conceptual experience, just like humans, and humans have access to the concept not because of their occult quality – different in humans compared to animals – but because the former, endowed with language, are also endowed with the objectification and discussion of contents.

2. *Mathematics.* What has been said of language is also true of mathematics: the donkey goes straight to the hay knowing nothing of Euclid; Euclid can axiomatise, but is not doing the same as the donkey, who will never understand those axiomatisations. In general, for humans things go otherwise, not when they walk but when they reflect on their actions: they can learn Greek and read Euclid, so as to find a correspondence between an axiom and their behaviour, and then they are induced to identify the action with the axiomatisation – but this is a fallacy. At a geometrical level, they can mistake seeing with thinking in points, lines, triangles and generally everything that goes under the title of evidence. In some cases, sensing a dissonance may likely seem equivalent to noting a calculation mistake. But based on such assumptions it is concluded that mathematics is everywhere – which is a thesis coextensive with the one about the ubiquity of language. The same immanence of the mathematical science is a consequence of the link between science and language, since mathematics sees relationships, but is not science, just as language, alone, is not science. Here, too, it is reasonable to suggest deflation.

(a) *Observed and measured.* We could say that if we had no concept of 'point' we could not make the judgment 'this is a point', but I doubt that in order to see the point one needs the concept of 'point', nor that to see the point one has to make the rapid and unconscious judgment 'this is a point'. A dog probably does not do that, and we probably do not do it either, because there are several situations where we experience but do not formulate judgments; anyhow, it seems unlikely that we are all natural scientists, logicians and geometricians, knowing from birth what we are supposed to learn at school (and often struggle to). This is even more obvious when it comes to measures: the distinction between observed and measured is mostly clear, and yet observation entails the recognition of physical characteristics: hence the legitimate inference that perception is abstract even without arithmetic or geometry.

When I look at the starry sky or a speckled hen, I do not need to count the stars or the spots to see what I see, just as it is difficult to count the fingers of one hand in peripheral vision whereas even infinitesimally small movements of the same finger are clearly detectable. Conversely, I can very easily think of a chiliagon, i.e. a 1,000-sided polygon, but I struggle to picture it, just as I struggle to imagine a square circle: even if I saw one, I could not tell at a glance whether it was different from a 999-sided polygon. Then I put a chiliagon alongside an 837-sided polygon: perhaps I would recognise the difference, but not because I'd be counting the sides. Similarly, if I am driving a car and overtake a truck, I do not lean to the right to see how many centimetres separate my left side mirror from it; if I did so, I'd probably go off the road. In reality, I can easily keep talking to whomever is next to me while overtaking a truck, without paying too much attention to what I'm doing.

(b) *Constructing and re-describing*. One might object that the point is not to use mathematics to constitute experience, but rather to note that it can redescribe the whole of reality. However, this isn't necessarily true either – Kepler thought that God had built the universe according to mathematical laws, but some celestial bodies can behave in a wholly unpredictable way. Therefore, the convergence is nothing but an explanatory scheme full of holes that gives teleological meaning to science – not a matter of fact.

(c) *Limited ubiquity*. Ultimately, mathematics is believed to be ubiquitous for the same reasons I have examined in relation to language: every time we scientifically organise something, operating at the level of a re-description, a mathematisation can follow. For instance, the transformation of the linear signal into the retinal image and then into a three-dimensional image is a physiological process that can be mathematically re-described, but this does not imply that it is mathematical, let alone that to implement it one must have knowledge of mathematics.

History. It is also obvious that only the possibility of inscription (albeit in the minimal version of oral traditionalisation) can allow for historicisation, and that therefore societies without writing or tradition do not have a history – which doesn't mean only 'handed down old customs' but also 'science'. A doctor today is nothing like a doctor of the nineteenth century, and is supposed to possess knowledge closer to the truth compared with the earlier doctor. Therefore, there is a claim of absoluteness guiding our choice to go see them. However, if we could go to consult a doctor of the year 2216 we would, because this absoluteness is related to a historical development configured as infinite progress. Conversely, we wouldn't mind living in a nineteenth-century house, provided it is in good condition. So, historicity is immanent in science and its method: when a researcher protests against the limits imposed on biotechnology, he or she usually refers to the fact that you cannot stop the clock. This is a historicity that settles in conceptual schemes and in the method, which is the most historical thing imaginable, while you can very well have experiences without history.

Freedom. When speaking of the concept of 'concept', we have seen how problematic the idea of freedom is. However, as long as we keep this notion, we can say that science is free, while experience isn't. Nobel Prizes and Fields Medals are not assigned at random; not even the Nobel Prize for Literature. Nobody gets a prize for being hit in the head by a brick, unless he or she volunteered as a guinea pig for an experiment; we do not praise the apple instead of Newton and – apart from Judge Schreber and The Man Who Mistook His Wife for a Hat – it is easier to become famous as a doctor than as a patient. Now, freedom is not natural: indeed, it seems necessary to postulate that it is transcendent. Suppose a scientist manages to prove that there is no freedom because elementary particles move in a necessary fashion. This is certainly a great discovery, so he receives the Nobel Prize – but then they should take the prize back, because if freedom doesn't exist, then he didn't really deserve it. Suppose another scientist manages to prove that, instead, freedom does exist, because elementary particles move at random. The discovery is even bigger, so he receives the Nobel Prize – but then they should take the prize back, because if he discovered it by chance, he didn't really deserve it.

The only way out of this conundrum is to claim that the object of the discovery – be it necessity or freedom – does not directly affect the discoverer, or better, it does so in ways so tortuous that they are inscrutable. However, this argument holds for necessity and not for freedom, so the theoretician of necessity would appear as an impostor, and the supporter of chance as someone who made it by a miracle. Anyhow, science is not simply knowledge (as dogs are able to find their kennels and horses their stalls even without human help), but rather knowledge that is shareable, communicable and freely amendable. Which is roughly what is done in academia. Now, academic research may or may not be disinterested. The fact that it might have ulterior goals, though, doesn't prove anything: one may be disinterested in studying the structure of matter, probably not so much in studying finance. However, when one is disinterested, it's the sign of a scientific approach. Nevertheless, if we are not free but just cogs in a great mechanism, then Newton discovered his laws by necessity, just as a meteorite crashes into the Moon; and then we could only say that what seems to be science is actually not, but is simply nature. As for falsifiability, the theme of freedom should be tackled as follows: only one who is free can be wrong. A stone hitting someone in the head is not wrong; those who throw the stone are. Ultimately, the point is this: if we want science to be possible, then we have to hypothesise a sphere of amendable concepts in an ideally infinite progress. There is a potentially interesting consequence: if freedom is not extrinsic to science but partly constitutes it, then science – unlike experience – is a purely hypothetical construct, because we don't know if there is something like 'freedom'. One might very well believe one is doing science and not in fact be doing it, just as it is possible that science never existed. However, it would be senseless to claim that there has never been experience on Earth. To deny that there ever was a sensation it is necessary to appeal to a *Malin Génie*.

Infinite. When, within the sphere of experience, I see a cat, I do not think that it is me seeing it, nor do I wonder immediately if I am truly seeing it or if it is indeed a cat. Things are different in communication: 'I have seen a cat', 'I think I've seen a cat', 'It is indeed a cat', and so on. Instead, science conceives of the present only as the outcome of past assumptions projected towards an unlimited future implicit in every single moment of the investigation, so as to make it intimately relative and constantly subject to further falsifications. One is free to go to physics class, to play pool, or to play heads or tails: in the first case, there is a virtually infinite progress; in the second, a finite progress; in the third, no progress, as there is no such thing as the world champion of 'heads or tails' – that's the only difference.

Science is an activity whose aim is the transformation of the subjective and occasional into the objective and necessary, and this is supposed to happen sooner or later, even in an infinite time. Typically, Husserl's idea is that the subjective and the occasional will never become objective and necessary in all respects, but that, *de jure*, we must take the teleological perspective, so as not to set limits to the infinity of reason.[41] Now, it is not difficult to see that such an assumption is not at all implausible in epistemology. However, let's transpose it into life: the world would overflow with people who do not know what they do or what they say, because their every action or statement would be a step on an infinite ladder. Then let's transpose it into perception: we would be dwelling in a world of false appearances, with respect to which Plato's cave would be a miracle of stability. Let's articulate this contrast.

1. *Perspectivism and inter-observation.* Would it make sense to say that I see an absolute wall? It is obvious that I see it only from one side or the other, and hardly in all its extension. But it is also clear that this happens precisely because it is a true wall, not a flat projection, so that partiality and reality coincide, whereas a partial truth is never satisfactory, and a half-truth is what is usually known as a lie. Perspectivism wasn't initially born as relativism (the fact that you can see a town from different perspectives means that it's real; the fact that a hand-made bed – unlike a bed in a painting – has more than one aspect is an argument for its reality). Likewise, the fact that people with such heterogeneous world images, with conflicting cultures and educations, and even with different senses (diabetics can lose the sense of smell, and then there are the deaf and the blind, but also the bald and those who have a sixth sense, that is, are very intuitive) recognise themselves as belonging to a shared world, constitutes a good reason to think that there is a world independent of our senses and our ideas or sciences. The argument can also be extended to inter-observation: if indeed any perspective constituted an irreducible singularity, it would be unclear why people can correct each other and integrate

their comments on anything whatsoever, or why we tell someone to come and stand next to us if we want them to see something that can only be seen from where we are. Then, the fact that only eighty out of 100 observers see a particular phenomenon may be a well-founded reason for epistemological scepticism, but doesn't hold in ontology: a judge would conclude that the phenomenon did occur.

2. *Infinity*. From an epistemological point of view, it may very well be argued that we will never reach the end of a subatomic analysis of a pen; but claiming that the pen, even with the observing conditions varying considerably, can also be described in infinite ways at the phenomenal level is quite unheard of. Moreover, it is true that I'll never know if the person who stands before me is sincere or not – because, ultimately, they may not know either: *individuum est ineffabile*. Nevertheless, if I ask them to pass me the pen they will understand what I mean, and this doesn't appear at all miraculous. Now, there's nothing scandalous about arguing that science is an endless process, but the interpretation of experience has a beginning, a lower threshold (perception or following a rule) and an end, or a higher threshold (decision), and the rock that stops our spade from digging further is ontology precisely insofar as it sets a limit to our hermeneutics. Similarly, records in the 100 metre dash are continuously broken, and it is a matter of fractions of a second; you are not supposed to take steroids and anabolics, that is, it is necessary to respect the characteristics of the species. One wonders when the progress will end (surely no one will beat the record of 300,000 km per second), or if, in the long run, we will not just get tired of trying. In any case, the sentence 'this morning I could have run five miles in five minutes' is as absurd today as it was in 1912, when Moore used it to indicate the type-case for something impossible. Likewise, we can build smaller and smaller laptops, but there is still an objective limit related to the fact that while chips can get smaller, our hands can't. In physics and biology things go otherwise, in mathematics there is an inflation of theorems, and in general it does not seem legitimate in principle to set a limit to the infinity of reason.

3. *Incompleteness*. Infinity, though, is different from incompleteness, which isn't the same as relativity. Again, perspectivism claims that we can see something under different profiles and points of view and that therefore, in most cases, each of its presentations is partial. This, though, doesn't preclude the possibility of

having a relation with the object, as you can stumble against one side of the table without seeing the other. Nor does it imply that the simple relation with the outside of things is sufficient, as you can drive a car without knowing much about its internal components and functioning. Phenomena are incomplete because things are full of minute details, hidden faces, hidden gears; but then, it is not even worth talking about phenomena, precisely because it is not clear what there could be beyond them.

4. *Opening*. One last consideration. One could rightly note that the infinite doesn't exist, as it's a limit-concept used in mathematics to homogenise and simplify calculations, but totally adiaphorous outside of a formal concept. It would follow that amendability, as a character of science, cannot be infinite, but is itself indefinite or open, so that the difference between infinite and indefinite, by which I'm trying to distinguish science and experience, loses all value. However, you'll admit that – at an ecological or mesoscopic level – science appears to have a much longer duration than experience, to the point that it doesn't share any measurement with it. From the point of view of the user's convenience, although not from that of her estate, buying a house or renting it for a hundred years – as often happens in England – are equal; and the custom, evoked in *Turandot*, to marry only for a thousand years is not a sign of the particular inconstancy of the Japanese, and is equivalent to the formula 'until death do us part'. No one would seriously argue that, from a logical point of view, the Japanese commitment seems stronger than the Western, because no one has ever lived for a thousand years. And from the epistemological point of view the two contracts are equivalent, as they are both liable to the open character of induction.

Teleology. There is a further delimitation: science, ultimately, has to deal with experience, even if the point is not always clear. Precisely because they are empiricists, scientists do not operate in a laboratory in the same way as two monkeys groom at the zoo, or as a Greek prays with the rosary: they are looking for something, and they do so with a conceptual scheme, so that experience is naturally considered the prehistory of science. Here, though, lies another delicate point. In fact, experience is what constitutes the teleology of science, which, as such, appears to be necessarily teleological and not accidentally so. In its infinite progress, science has increasingly targeted the world, and it is in view of the world that it amends its concepts: trivially, there must be, albeit in a purely ideal form, the ability to compare the theory with something – no matter if this results in a Kantian idea or in showing up at Fort Knox asking for the equivalent in gold of a 20 dollar bill. I can measure the segments of the Müller-Lyer illusion and observe that, despite appearances, they are of equal length; but this verification, carried out with ruler in hand, is not mental: I see – and do not just think – that the two segments are both the same length, say, 10 cm. Above all, the possibility of describing a world either as a set of independent objects or as a system of constituted facts does not justify a Solomonic balance of the two alternatives. Indeed, this agrees with naive realism, because I can describe a tree as a childhood memory, as a preconception, as a construction of my senses or concepts, etc., yet the tree is there, and if anybody denied it we wouldn't believe them, because knowing (or believing ourselves to know) the cause or genesis of something doesn't affect what is observed.

So here's the meta-philosophical core of the deflation I've proposed thus far. It is fully natural that, if one goes to military school then the aim is to become a second lieutenant, then a colonel and finally a general; it is equally natural that those who do a PhD, or go into a convent as a novice or a gardener or a philosopher disappointed by the *Tractatus*, or work for a company as a lawyer, do not do so to become generals. As for the finite and the infinite, it seems fairly obvious that science, by definition, has no end, while experience does. Between science and experience, then, there is the domain of technology, which is perfectible, but only up to a certain point: you cannot really improve a spoon, nor can you assume infinite perfectibility in the art of tying one's shoes. And certain techniques, such as astrology, are justified not by appealing to an endless progress, but rather to an immemorial tradition with persisting traces: Babylonian astrology does not seem less advanced than ours, and yet it does not seem legitimate to speak of science here – which is not a form of depreciation, since Babylonian art appears no worse than ours either. Ancient art in general is not deemed inferior to the modern; the introduction of perspective increased the likeness of representations but not the artistry of the paintings. Conversely, the way in which communion under both kinds (i.e. with both the consecrated bread and wine) disappeared from Catholic religious services is considerably different from the way in which phrenology was abandoned. Likewise, even at the age of forty, we are unlikely to have mastered the art of tying a necktie any more than at twenty. In many cases of the field of experience the scheme of perfectibility hardly applies: we miss snow as it used to be, food as it used to be, films as they used to be, but we hardly miss laptops as they were five or ten years ago.

Thus, the second nature, more exactly, and sticking to epistemology, has a historical origin: there was a time when it arose. Therefore not only was there a time when it was not there, but there were (and are) people who had (and have) not known it for a long time. Some are still – that is, for the moment, at this stage of a teleological becoming – excluded from it (for example, in what seems to be so obviously the Internet age, many still don't have a smartphone); others only vaguely know about it; others know it very well but most times don't resort to it. Now, can we really say that the 'others' (Gypsies, the endogamous, Brahmins, Dalits, but also English who know nothing of Locke, or Germans who know nothing of Einstein, and then again Locke and Einstein before they studied) are simply wrong, and know not what they do or say? Even more so, it would be difficult to argue that when the Indians and the Chinese (whose cultures are for Husserl subsidiary and secondary compared to the Western idea of *episteme*) see a colour, prepare food or comment on a text, they are simply sketching the outlines of a truth written elsewhere – and not even in Europe. If, however, we consider the notion of culture in a more determined way, i.e. as European science and philosophy, then even among scientists there would be, in 99 per cent of their experience, nothing more than nature and habit. The opposite is also true: if you take the notion of second nature too broadly, as any kind of capitalisation of experience, deliberate or not, then you'll have to admit that crows have it too, when they learn to no longer fear the scarecrow.

And now, after reducing schemes, concepts and science to their sphere of competence, let's talk about experience.

Experience

Ecology and mesoscopy. The sphere of experience is ecological,[42] and defines the field of ontology not positively, but negatively: as if to say that ontology is not nature, but that which sets a limit and an end to technology and science.

Already in the eighteenth century, a Swabian pastor, Johann Christian Oetinger, had criticised the microscope and the supposed uncertainty of secondary qualities: his argument was that if God had wanted us to see micro-organisms, he would have given us the appropriate senses; and it was absurd to say, like Leibniz, that God didn't see colours. I do not intend to resurrect old apologetics (if only because they amount to the abuse of a transcendental argument: our senses are structured so and so because they have to be so and so). Instead I wish to draw attention to the fact that the ecological and mesoscopic dimension, which evolves a lot more slowly than our science and technology, provides the definition of the average concept of reality. In other words, the point is not to postulate a natural level of human functions, nor to delegitimise any prosthesis, from the laptop to the smartphone. Rather, the point is to consider that if certain prostheses have worked better than others that existed for some time before them, it is because human life as we know it is more compatible with spectacles and mobile phones than with microscopes or telescopes. Why then is it relatively hard to accept that using a phone is qualitatively different from looking at the sky through a telescope?

Our experience is steeped in technology: we are continuously dealing not only with computers, aeroplanes and elevators, but also with sticks, knives and wheels; and technology, just like science, appears linguistic, historical, free, amendable and infinite. But it only seems so: the spoon and the wheel do not evolve. Other things do, like laws for the protection of the environment; not to mention the conservatism of sensibility: the injunction to 'sharpen the senses' is different – first of all because it is much more constrained – from the injunction to 'amend the concepts' and 'change the paradigms'.

1. *Tools*. To illustrate this briefly, it will be handy to use a table articulating a primary consideration: there is a crucial difference between putting on a pair of glasses or contact lenses and mounting a telescope or a microscope on your eyes. Glasses – including sunglasses, as long as they are used on a bright day or under a spotlight – as well as contact lenses restore a necessary function for a human being in the world. The other tools are used by scientists and are harmful outside the library or laboratory: try driving with a microscope on your eye; and above all, try to behave by identifying the world with the conceptual schemes that you have of it. Conversely, have a coffee with a pygmy, go on vacation with a Hopi, watch a football game with an Eskimo; in my opinion, not much will change, but if the theory of the action of conceptual

schemes on the world were true, then there should be huge conceptual gaps, and those experiences would likely be doomed to failure. To prove this, try speaking of cosmology with a pygmy, a Hopi and an Eskimo, with your newspaper vendor and with a professional cosmologist: you'll be in for a treat.

So, there are ontological tools, built for experience and its prosthesis in technology, and epistemological tools which are only good for science.

One might object: if ontology is supposed to speak of what there is, then your approach is wrong, since it denies the existence of things that we know to be there – like quarks – or even all that we presently do not perceive. Conversely, your approach affirms the existence of things we know do not exist, like stars exploded millions of years ago, hallucinations in delirium tremens, and the like.

2. *Objects.* However, consider that the ontological discontinuities typical of ontology do not appear interesting – and are even somehow inaccessible – from the point of view of physics simply because they do not play an important role in the causal structure of the world, regardless of their intervention in perception. They are a way in which physical reality presents itself that is only relevant in relation to the activity of a given perceptual system, but does not depend at all on our perceptions and beliefs nor, a fortiori, on our

Table 7. Ontological Tools and Epistemological Tools

Experience	Eyes Spectacles Sunglasses	They do not increase a function, but correct a dysfunction with respect to an environmental structure
Technology	Spyglasses Marine Binoculars Opera glasses Magnifying lenses Jewellers' monocles	They do not restore a natural function (except maybe opera glasses), and do not promise an infinite progress. They allow us to see what would still be ecologically accessible from another vantage point. So, they do not visualize.
Science	Microscopes Telescopes	Being of no use in the environment, they do not restore a function. They serve the development of an endless knowledge. They visualize.

Table 8. Ontological Objects and Epistemological Objects

−1	Epistemology	Charms, quarks, atoms, molecules, C-fibers and enzymatic reactions
Borderline	?	Viruses, mites, unconscious
1	Ontology	Tables, chairs, mountains, nervousness, getting sunburnt, 2 + 2 = 4, metres, kilometres, minutes, days, sounds between 20 and 16,000 Hz
Borderline	?	Venus
+ 1	Epistemology	Galaxy

languages or theories. It is the sense of unamendability, and the definition of the dimension of ontology, that produces ontological and epistemological objects, as in the following table.

The ontological dimension concerns objects that are neither too large nor too small, and that are commensurate with the scope of our senses in ecological conditions and with the average duration of human life. I should note that this constitutes neither a marginal domain, nor a banal field, both negatively and positively: negatively, there is not one criticism of eliminativism or reductionism that does not appeal, even implicitly, to a mesoscopic size; positively, there is not one legal decision, fair or general/universal, that can prescind from the sphere of ontology, even if taken as a popular psychology. However, one could object that, in this way, the difference between ontology and epistemology would depend on perceptive thresholds (haven't I just shown this with the table about the relative scale of ontology?), so that metres and kilometres concern ontology, while cosmic distances or microscopic dimensions and geological eras concern epistemology, to the point that a mite would be an epistemological and not an ontological object. And, finally, the link between ontology and ecology is nothing but a version of pragmatism, based on which – against all evidence – things only exist for our needs and purposes. This way, taking it a bit further, there would be an identification between ontology and epistemology in which things would simply depend not on science but on technology, and the world would only belong to man and – with a touch of extra liberalism – a few animals of similar size. However, I've never said (at least not here)[43] that ontology is naive physics. The latter does not tell us the truth about things, but merely gives us a powerful tool to falsify the idea of an archaeological identity between science and experience; it doesn't give us an account of ontology, but indicates the layer in which ontological assumptions take place. Secondly, if there is a potential misunderstanding, it rather concerns ecology, which seems to positively define an environment to identify it with ontology. Nevertheless, ontology harbours the conviction that what there is was there before me and will be there after me, which by definition cannot hold from an ecological perspective, where the environment is born with its inhabitants. Here's the limit of the ecological view: reducing the environment to something accessible to the animal, instead of thinking of the world as what exists regardless of any animal.

3. *The world*. What we encounter exists in a world that is not an object, but rather the sum of all objects – in the same way for humans, worms and slippers. The real characteristic of the encountered is that you may or may not encounter it (the worm does not encounter Kanizsa's triangle because it doesn't see it, like we do not encounter protons). However, if theories about what we encounter can be amended at will, the encountered cannot be amended once we've encountered it: it is like this and not otherwise. The concept of world is indeed based on the idea of an unamendable encountered: the world transcends the environment, where you can still note that the reference to the encountered doesn't have a purely psychological, ecological or phenomenological value. Note this: if I say 'the world as I know it', or at most 'the world as I encounter it', I can refer to sensible and conceptual schemes; but if I say 'the world as I have encountered it',[44] I am referring to something else – the world as it was before I knew it and as it will be when I stop knowing it, outside of my conceptual or sensible schemes. It is the world as it is before my birth and after my death, therefore outside any psychology, ecology or phenomenology, but not without them, as their function is that of a differential providing a range of levels of reality.

Denying the omnipresence of schemes, concepts and science (and, especially, their teleological concatenation), but not the significance of natural mental structures and skills in making up experience, certainly comes out in favour of the fact that our perceptual experience is not conceptually or inferentially mediated. However, this is no argument for the existence of the objects of our experience independently of our mental skills. Therefore, a further step is required to corroborate the Slipper Argument: to mark the difference between epistemological truth and ontological reality, explaining in what sense naive realism shouldn't be mistaken for empiricism, phenomenology or philosophy of ordinary language, which maintain a genetic link, albeit a weak one, between ontology and epistemology.

Second Distinction: Truth/Reality

Empiricism. It isn't true that the alternative to transcendentalism is empiricism. These are actually two sides of the same coin, on both of which the transcendental argument fully works. For transcendentalism, there is never direct experience, so that one has to transcribe the theories of experience within a framework of theories of science allowing for experience. If such a thesis – which is paradoxical to say the least – is often assumed with no reticence, it is because transcendentalism is parasitical on empiricism, sharing its principle of reversibility without residue between science and experience. The case of Kant is paradigmatic because, behind the decision to identify the real with mathematical physics, there is the idea that the world is essentially contingent, that is, unable to provide certain knowledge. Now, this isn't enough to justify radical scepticism, though Kant thought otherwise: between 100 per cent certainty and 99 per cent likelihood there is an abyss, much deeper than the difference between 99 per cent likelihood and 1 per cent probability. The fact that the latter case seems very implausible and the former very likely didn't matter for Kant.

It would be wrong to claim that, in order to speak, one must know the essence of what one is referring to, and that to manifest pain or use a tool one should know, with physiological or technological competence, their causes and functioning. Likewise, life would be impossible if we couldn't generalise inductively based on a number of instances (however small). Saying that no induction is legitimate unless one has examined every case or at least proven that the contrary is false would leave us paralysed. I am indeed proceeding by induction when I say that the Adriatic is salty, the Baltic is salty, the Caspian is salty, and therefore that all seas are salty; if I then find out that the Baikal isn't salty, I'd conclude that all seas are salty apart from the Baikal – that is, the Baikal is not a sea. The supposed unknown fact doesn't disturb the previous induction at all. It is not so for Kant, however: experience can give no certainty, if the certainty we want is the one ensured by mathematics (immediately) and science (in an infinite amount of time, so never *de facto* but always *de jure*). For a system based on pure experience and in need of geometrical certainty, the sceptical dissolution is inevitable: we are certain that we exist, but have reason to doubt everything else, even the way in which we represent ourselves to ourselves.

The problem, as usual, is conceiving experience as the precursor of science and not as an autonomous sphere, and this is a traditional difficulty. The Aristotelian image of experience,[45] for which the flight of sensations, like a scattered retreating army, suddenly stops when a soldier stops running and reassures his companions, so that the phalanx gets back together, fails to explain the critical point: at a certain point, no one knows how or why, the stampede of sensations stops and is organised into a coherent structure. But why should it do so, if it did not already have an internal organisation? A similar conception is perhaps the best distributed thing worldwide, as it also holds in Platonic representations of the birth of science: the opening scene of *2001: A Space Odyssey*, in which – after geometry has fallen from the sky in the form of black and smooth monolith – the ape tosses a bone that's suddenly become a club and then turns into a spaceship, translates a fundamental discontinuity in terms of continuity. Clubs are used by apes, by the Aborigines, by ourselves under certain circumstances, and in no way represent the imperfect ancestors of spaceships, whereas the theories of the Presocratics are indeed the rudimentary precursors of contemporary physics. So, clubs and poems *Péri physeos* can only be assimilated if one conceives of experience as teleologically projected towards science, which has important consequences: especially the thought that most humans, apart from a few cutting-edge scientists, do not have a world but just sketchy prejudices, incomplete theories, unlikely doctrines, so that life would be a tale told by an idiot signifying nothing.

Both versions, the Aristotelian and the Platonic, should be revised, as they describe two different things: on the one hand, a doctrine of freedom, where (at least in theory and according to some descriptions) they can work; on the other, a phenomenology of reality, where they can hardly apply. The act by which a fleeing army gets back together is purely aleatory, seemingly not conditioned by the nature of things and their relations, so it is unclear why our experiences, on the contrary, are so consistent. Mostly it is unclear why – if experience doesn't carry out its investigations every time, but only re-examines all beliefs at once – there can be a time when one chooses to begin this revision. This time could either never come or depends on the arbitrary decision of the subject, and the apparent self-organisation of data – such as when we write our autobiography or sum up a situation – is only possible because we have to make a decision or formulate a verdict on ourselves. In other words, it happens under the pressure coming from the outside world. As for the Platonic version, if geometry did fall from above, that is, if it began one sunny day thanks to a proto-geometrician – be he Thales or whoever else (in this case, an ape), but in any case a single individual – then it would still not be true that experience is the precursor of science, because only some apes have arrived at spaceships while others are still stuck with clubs.

If these descriptions do not work, it is because they put reality at the origin of truth, while the opposite is true: the truth is not archaeologically founded in reality, it is teleologically ordered towards it. Astronomers no longer look at the stars, but the stars, observable to the naked eye on a clear night, continue to be the object of astronomy. The distinction between *de facto* and *de jure* is a norm, but it harbours the idea that the two, over a relatively long time, might find correspondence. The possibility of correspondence with the ostensible and perceived reality is thus immanent to the truth, but truth is not identified with reality, as experience can take place regardless of knowledge. Anyone who makes a feast of salted anchovies in the evening faces the concrete possibility of suffering a restless night's sleep due to indigestion and thirst. Since Aristotle (the first thinker – to my knowledge – whose thought on this has been preserved, which does not exclude the possibility that there might be some related papyrus from the fourth dynasty) there have been various naturalistic classifications of anchovies, salt and its properties that have been organised and explained in many ways; the physiology of sleep and wakefulness has been subjected to a large number of scientific descriptions; there have been many theories of dreams, etc. Yet even today, if before going to bed I eat a can of salted anchovies, I will very likely be subject to restless sleep, whether I know the current status of ichthyology, chemistry and physiology, or their history, or know absolutely nothing about anchovies, not even from personal experience (if it's the first time I've eaten them or seen them).

Phenomenology. However, ontology is not identified with phenomenology, because to speak of phenomena means to refer to that which by definition is a transitional moment, destined to find its truth elsewhere. Instead, it is unclear why things should be different from what they appear, or why one should be content with having *eide* in knowledge when, in real life, one has to do with cars and flies and not *eide*.

This is the innermost weakness of phenomenology. For Husserl, unlike for positivism, the point is not to recognise the only reality in the world investigated by the natural sciences; and unlike historicism, it is not a question of isolating a parallel field, the world of the spirit, as opposed to the physical world. Rather, the point is to investigate reality, both physical and psychic, in an attempt to establish necessary laws that are higher than natural ones. In fact, the latter are more exact than historical ones – as history repeats itself more approximately than nature – but are also more decisively and insidiously conjectural. While the world of the spirit – not of that of Julius Caesar, but of all of us when observing – appears undoubtedly present, that of nature is out there, it seems to be there, but we know nothing about it, so that everything the natural sciences say could be radically false. One could object (and indeed it has been objected) that it seems absurd to claim to know givenness without dealing with experience. If Husserl couldn't go along with this, it's because he identified experience with science, so that any reference to data would seem a failure in the face of physics, which led him to argue that when the eidetic knowledge contrasts with experience, you have to correct the latter, unlike what happens with the laws of nature.

Still – and this is my main point – this is clearly not the case. Natural science cares fairly little that a square of a given colour inevitably appears lighter or darker depending on the background against which it is perceived; but anyone who wants to analyse the properties of the external world cares about it indeed – just think of the importance of colour-matching in fashion, visual art, etc. Only, there is no reason to speak of 'phenomena': the appeal to the immanence of consciousness that characterises transcendental phenomenology doesn't seem to correspond to the way in which we relate to things in the world. Reciprocally, it seems to assume that the approach of science consists in a direct contact with reality, which, obviously, is taken as the natural presupposition of our theories: the natural attitude, here, is the *naturaliter* scientific attitude.

136 Hysteresis

Thus, when one suspends or brackets existence, one is taking off a decisive piece for ontology, even though the representation might be epistemologically more appropriate, just as a map might be more useful than a photograph, and the latter easier to handle than a thing. The *epoché* regards thought, not existence, but then one might as well explicitly orient it towards a realist ontology.

Philosophy of ordinary language. If this is the problem, though, why not resort to philosophy of ordinary language? Now, it is true that one theorises at one's desk, or on the couch, whereas ordinary language is like the wheel or the spoon, sedimenting habits stratified over generations. Nevertheless, at a desk or on the couch one can also use ordinary language to say, maybe even believing it, that the Moon is made of cheese, or to come up with absurd and harmful therapies. Language, as an intentional and conceptual activity, is indeed the manifestation of a belief, as it can very well voice a proto-science or a pseudo-science. Also, it appears to be unstable, as it is subject to the linguistic consciousness of the speaker, even in the lexicon of perception, while a sniper does not have a significantly different visual experience from a short-sighted person, who sees things more blurred, though not smaller or more distant, of a different colour, a different shape, etc. Then it is very easy to object that natural language is more important *de facto* but not *de jure*, so that it cannot be considered sacrosanct. Thus, I'd first like to sketch a defence of the relative validity of ordinary language, and then show that, if this defence if possible, it is because the main reference of an ontology is not linguistic.

1. *Local revision and global revision.* Within his interpretation of Husserl's life-world, Barry Smith rightly speaks of the difference between local revision, to which one can subject commonsense experience, and global revision, which the latter escapes by definition.[46] This goes along with the abovementioned hypothesis that science (more amendable) is confronted with experience (less amendable). This is a peripheral variability not of experiences but of beliefs about experiences in front of the general stability of the system that supports them. In language itself there is more than one sphere that has nothing to do with science: not only the scope of the performative, but also a large number of expressions that cannot find a scientific translation. Witches and angels can easily be sidelined in a reductionist approach, but the lexicon of popular psychology cannot. There is a sense in which 'I hurt my foot',

'I'm sad', or even 'it gets on my nerves', cannot be transcribed in scientific terms any more than 'you'll excite your C-fibres' translates into 'you'll get burnt', or any more than 'you just had a difficult childhood' – said by a hypothetical therapist to Hitler – challenges our fundamental moral intuitions. Also, epistemology – which we can access through conceptual schemes – speaks of atoms and galaxies; likewise, one can study enzymatic reactions of the brains of people as well as dogs and horses. But no one has ever sued dogs or horses, or atoms or galaxies, just as the forms of naive psychology that govern our behaviour and judgments about others' behaviour ('I'd like a glass of water', 'he was rude') cannot be reduced to enzymatic reactions. Therefore, at this level, the conceptual schemes of epistemology do not hold, or intervene only in special and problematic circumstances, like when you summon psychiatric experts in court. Finally: who would ever amend *Crime and Punishment*? And yet this is the realm of ordinary language, which in the case of literature seems able to create unamendable objects just like houses and tables, thereby enriching ontology.

2. *Witches may come back*. There is a second argument: are we sure that witches cannot come back? After all, the criticism of ordinary language rests on the assumption that perception and the language based on it are contingent, whereas science is definitive. Indeed, it is easy to see that, at least very often, the opposite is true. Historically, one can easily verify this. Science has increased not certainty but scepticism, not for contingent reasons but for reasons immanent to the concept of science as the infinite search of truth. Today water is H_2O, tomorrow who knows, and all I know is that I can drink water, turn it into ice, boil it, use it to clean stuff, etc. – all things that could be attributable to a liquid with the same properties but a different molecular composition compared to water. Also, views of the past can change, perhaps not as quickly as the Soviet encyclopaedia, but almost. Things are different in experience. We never say 'Today it's a chair, tomorrow who knows', or 'now it's a finger, one day it'll be something completely different', or 'it is gold but it could turn into lead'. If this is the case, though, then the epistemological setting blatantly fails to rebuke scepticism. Making science the best paradigm of experience or, more roughly, assuming that experience is just the popular name for science, is indeed like saying about water 'today it is H_2O, tomorrow we'll see'. Which means at least two things: from the reference point of view, it gives rise to problems that start

in the past (is what Archimedes called *chrysos* really our gold?), continue in the present (when Putnam says, 'elms', what is he talking about, as he confesses to not knowing how to distinguish them from beech trees?), and are projected into the future (what will multiple sclerosis mean in a hundred years?). From the point of view of ontology, the problems appear to be even more serious, giving a new energy, in spite of themselves, to the claim of absolute knowledge: if you don't know everything about one thing and its relationships, if you don't know everything about everything, it's as if you knew nothing. Nevertheless, even disregarding this hyperbole – which is immanent to the discourse of the unreliability of induction related to the problem of infinity – the fact remains that a scientific approach entails a world upside down in which what is manifested sensibly is appearance, because the truth lies in numbers, molecules, atoms, quarks, etc. In other words, just as – according to the theory that art is but the sensible appearance of an idea – the visitor to an art gallery sees the vestiges and reminders of the artists' concepts, so those who systematically extend the hypothesis of science as the best paradigm should admit that chairs and steaks are just incomplete appearances, and after all mere abbreviations of more complex definitions, as if they were popular sayings or proverbs.

3. *Legal truth*. A third argument shows that there are public spheres of experience in which physics does not apply as the best conceptual scheme. I am not speaking of voodoo rituals, but rather of courts. Let us assume that an incorrectly installed water pipe causes flooding downstairs. Everyone will admit that this is a case of a water leak, and at most the point is to determine whether the blame should be attributed to the plumber, to the owner who had not closed a faucet, or maybe (which is less likely, in light not only of Newton, but also Aristotle and Aesop) to the tenant downstairs. Anyone called to testify would say: there was a water leak. Imagine instead that someone applies the norm that the only truth is that of physics. They would say 'some H_2O has filtered downstairs', but they couldn't say so with certainty. In fact, not only can it not be excluded that it was a liquid with all the phenomenal appearances of water, but with a different chemical composition – let's say it was XYZ, as in Putnam's Twin Earths: you need to summon an expert to confirm it – but above all, no one could argue that water is actually H_2O; it is so now, in the light of what science says, but in the light of what science says, we cannot rule out that sooner

or later it will be rebaptised and known in a different way. So, in the end, not even the expert could really swear that there was some H_2O: he could only assert that there was what in the current state of knowledge is called so, not excluding the possibility that a further development of science may prove that it was something else. For this reason, in court, it sometimes happens that the truth is legally determined, otherwise the evidence could be tampered with, not by the witnesses or defendants, but by scientists who are elsewhere formulating new laws. In other words, if the ultimate ascertainment of reality always depended on science, not only would there be paradoxical results, but it would be like sending out an invoice destined never to be paid, because research never ends. Also, the criteria used in court often have little or nothing to do with essence, and often regard form or function: the prohibition of access to motorcycles also holds, extensively, for vehicles without combustion engines, or using pillows instead of wheels, or sleighs pulled by reindeer, etc. In short, the problem of Twin Earths only arises for an Anti-Adulteration Squad, constituting the exception, not the rule. Of course, Muslims have a strictly nominalistic way of getting around the prohibition on drinking alcohol: it only specifies not drinking wine or beer, so they drink spirits instead. One could say that such petty ways of deceiving the Almighty do not rely on phenomenal appearances but rather on essential properties. I do not think this is a good counterargument, because the extension of the prohibition to beverages not mentioned in the Koran depends on the – phenomenologically easy to spot – identity of their effects.

4. *Bad moods, anxiety and excuses.* Also, it has been legitimately noted[47] that the structure of excuses offers a powerful arsenal of ontological assumptions that are given – rightly or wrongly – fundamental plausibility, and this line of reasoning can be extended to the whole sphere of 'likelihood'. When making excuses, it is acceptable to say things like: 'I wasn't thinking', 'I was in a bad mood', 'I didn't know', 'I thought that . . .'. And this is no minor thing. On the one hand, there are epistemological excuses, which are historically conditioned: today, in court, it wouldn't be admissible to say 'an alien forced me to steal the wallet' (although one day maybe it will be) or 'an inner daemon ordered me not to escape the trial and consequent judgment' (but there was a time when this was plausible); while there have been cases in which the defence has invoked the theory of multiple

personalities. On the other hand, there are ontological excuses referring to a grammatical role of pop psychology, therefore escaping historical revision in observable times: 'I thought about it, then I slapped you' doesn't sound like an excuse, but more like a deliberate admission of responsibility, just like saying 'I knew very well that pressing that button would cause a catastrophe, so I pressed it' is the best way to end up in jail, and something like 'I wasn't in a bad mood, I just chose to be rude' is a provocation. Of course, things are not straightforward, as the world of experience is filled with all sorts of objects: notions of science that have filtered into common speech ('Alzheimer's' instead of 'dotage'), expressions that are hard to translate scientifically ('bad mood', 'it gets on my nerves'), common sense theories as to how we do and should think, and finally ways to perceive the world regardless of what we know about it. And it's not all the same, because we can amend parts of common sense (maybe not 'bad mood' but certainly 'dotage') just as we correct beliefs about spontaneous generation or the fall of bodies, but we cannot see the roundness of the Earth, nor can we, in everyday reasoning, ensure that the *modus tollens* seems as clear as the *modus ponens*.

5. *'It hurts here'*. Recourse to ordinary language is not a mistake when dealing with experience itself, but rather when claiming to make, with no recognised competence, assertions with some scientific value. In the world of experience, the restrictions related to the essence, as the internal composition of the thing, do not follow an indiscriminate course (it is one thing to check that no components are missing from a car, another to check that there are no atoms missing). In a normal communicative context, it doesn't make sense to say 'I see the thirteenth mirror of the telescope', instead of 'I see Sirius', or to specify 'I think' in every statement, including in answer to the question 'what time is it?' Furthermore, suppose I said: 'Hand me that pen that I think is blue on the table I think is brown'. Faced with such a request, my interlocutor would wonder what I'm talking about and what pen of what colour he's supposed to find on what table, not to mention whether what I think is a pen is indeed a pen. My interlocutor is likely to wonder if I'm OK. Again, the claim to grasp essences – fully legitimate as such – in the wrong context does not give greater certainty but rather supports relativism. The same goes for the claim to make the effect irrelevant by reducing it to its cause: in the case of essence it seems legitimate to hope for consensus, at least in a

homogeneous culture; but in the world of causes dissent may also prove to be significant among the experts – a headache can have various causes, and it would be really embarrassing if I could not just say I have a headache and were forced to make a diagnosis. If, going along with my pessimism, I said 'I have brain cancer', some would probably say 'no you don't', others would make different diagnoses, and in the worst case scenario some would say I'm right. After all, it seems a lot more reasonable to cut it short and just say I have a headache. And note that, at least in the case of 'brain cancer', I had a credible reference, whereas the patient going to the doctor because she thinks she has arthritis in her thigh (raising the question of what she is referring to, as you cannot have arthritis in your thigh) would have been better off pointing at the sore bit and saying 'it hurts here'.

Naive realism. Descartes ironised on the fact that common sense seems to be far from common. However, common sense is generally suitable for its purposes not due to some special access to things – which would place it in a better position than science, thereby making the latter pointless and unnecessarily complicated – but because it is ecologically adequate. However, if good sense applies to what is perceived directly, it means that this sphere is not too rough or too subtle: on the contrary, it is public and stable, only vanishing in the horizon of science. The same can be said of perception: it is devoid of inferential processes, innate, fast, immediate, inevitable, structured as a whole, and tends to postulate that information is always sufficient, that is, doesn't need integrations,[48] if only because it is not electively knowledge-oriented. Of course, we can qualify our relation with things in terms of beliefs (I thought the pot was cold, but now I've burnt myself) but this is already a second-level description. As I was about to touch the pot I wasn't believing anything at all, I was just about to touch the pot; most of all, when I'm draining the pasta and some hot water splashes on me, I am not believing that the water burns: it just burns. Likewise, walking around without thinking that the Earth is round is not the same as believing that human sacrifices are legitimate for ritual purposes. This point is crucial: the difference between seeing and thinking ensures the passage from common sense to naive realism.

By thinking that there are tables, chairs and colours manifesting their properties and constants independently of what I say or know or even of how much I think of them, I am certainly not being a transcendentalist. However, I'm not being an empiricist either, verifying whether such properties are sufficient to establish a law. Nor am I stating a belief: to my knowledge, no one has ever ventured to found perceptological religions, where believers would worship some optical illusion or kneel in front of a colour. As Wittgenstein rightly noted in his criticism of Moore, in *On Certainty* but already in *Philosophical Investigations*, it makes no sense to argue that a sentence such as 'I have two hands' constitutes a truth – it is rather a truism and a reality which doesn't want to be treated as science or as the basis for knowledge, even though it procures the teleology of each science whenever it must deal with the world. If an Islamic judge sentences a thief to have one hand cut off, it's not science that justifies his belief that the thief has at least one hand, because 'I know people have two hands' is not like 'I know Napoleon was born in 1769'.[49] I cannot amend the hand, I can only cut it off, whereas I can correct someone if they say that Napoleon was born in 1768. Likewise, it doesn't make sense to order 'half a pint of *real* lager', unless they have given me a bitter ale instead.[50] So, naive realism is not the origin of science, nor is it a 'fundamental knowledge' from which all theories start, but rather something that science must teleologically address without being based on it. Unlike Moore, I have no wish to list all the things that are evident for me. I am more interested in the thresholds that neither you nor I can ever cross: the lack of harmony between the encountered world and the thought-of world is the rock resisting conceptual schemes, but not the rock on which to build a castle of alternative theories.

Third Distinction: Internal World/External World

Autonomies and antinomies. Hence the paradigmatic value of naive physics, showing how the Copernican world does not necessarily represent the truth of the Ptolemaic one, and how the latter constitutes a level of reality which even a Copernican has to deal with. It is only in this sense that naive physics has a normative value for theories: as a *telos* and a stumbling block for knowledge rather than an autonomous layer of truth. If naive physics were the starting assumption of our theories, it would have to be either false or true. If it were false, we'd fall into the typical situation where experience is the inadequate precursor of science, filled with optical and auditory illusions. If it were true, we'd be forced to swear on geocentrism, on the spontaneous generation of butterflies from the deterioration of the flesh, and on the fact that heavier things fall faster, as well as that the spoked wheels of Jaguars rotate in the opposite direction to the direction of travel. But physics is not a storeroom of truths, but rather of falsifications of the hypothesis of a teleological continuism between experience and science. Thus, what naive physics says to philosophy and science is only that the *telos* is not necessarily in the *physis*. Taking naive physics as a stumbling block, one can find three important distinctions between the internal world and the external world.

1. *Aesthetics is autonomous from logic.* That is, perception is independent of conceptual schemes or, positively, non-conceptual contents do exist. After noting the ontological inconsistency of the thesis that intuitions without concepts are blind, I want to demonstrate that the idea that perception is contingent follows from the undue transposition of epistemology into ontology, such that the contingency of non-perceptive laws drawn from perception is dogmatised in the contingency of perception.

2. *Aesthetics is antinomical with respect to logic.* Rather than considering the constancies of the observed world as the substrates of logic and science (regarding supposed irregularities as perceptual illusions), I want to demonstrate that the charges set against perception represent a hyperbolic form of the assumption that perception is but the dark background of knowledge; you can see this by examining in how many cases thinking is different from seeing. Thus, although the appeal to antinomy may seem redundant, it is critical: it is not enough to say that perceptual schemes are independent of conceptual schemes, because then it could be argued that the former are the preliminary form of the latter, while the asymmetries between seeing and thinking become relevant precisely to call into question the legitimacy of teleology.

3. *The world is autonomous from conceptual and perceptive schemes.* This has been my point from the very beginning. And I intend to prove that recognising the autonomous character of the world cannot come from the immanent/transcendent opposition nor from an outside as opposed to an inside – if it is assumed as a topological polarity – but from recognising something external to conceptual and perceptive schemes: something external as essentially unamendable. To clarify what I mean to do by referring to autonomy and antinomy, let's take the following image:

It is a moving scene. A man in his fifties, looking a bit tired, affectionately greets some young men in uniform who are looking rather run down. The man looks at them with fondness, and any observer would be moved by the scene. This doesn't happen, though, because anyone today will recognise it as a picture of Adolf Hitler meeting a unit of the Hitlerjugend destined to defend Berlin. Therefore, here we (i) see a person; (ii) feel something; (iii) censor what we feel based on what we know of that person. At this highly culturalised level we can already find a contrast between seeing and thinking – let alone when we see the Earth as flat despite knowing that it is round.

Autonomy of Aesthetics from Logic

Criticism of the transcendental. Let's start with the claim of the autonomy of aesthetics from logic, which does not qualify as a manifesto on behalf of the senses – as on many occasions I may have reason to doubt them – but rather as an attempt to disprove the transcendental. This attempt is articulated into three moves: 1) disproving its presupposition, namely the idea that concepts are necessary for percepts; 2) showing the fallacy of switching from 'can' to 'ought' in every field of experience; and 3) underlining that the world can very well do without the transcendental.

1. *The presupposition*. Let's start from the underlying reason why, against all evidence, we are inclined to exclude the possibility that aesthetics may exist without logic, and perhaps to establish the equivalence aesthetic = irrational, which is as widely attested as it is fundamentally unjustified. That is to say, let's start from the idea that perception is contingent. This hypothesis, assumed as a dogma, comes from the *metabasis eis allo genos* we have seen in the empiricist abuse of induction. The fact that I cannot formulate a universally valid law starting from induction is amplified and deformed into an argument against the reliability of perception. The 'likely' character of induction, then, is assimilated to the idea that the senses deceive. And if it is argued that intuitions without concepts are blind, then any difference between perceiving and formulating an inductive law falls. However, the argument does not hold, unless you demand from perception something that does not pertain to it: if I turn on the light a hundred times, the hundred and first time it might not work because the bulb has burned out – as shown by perception, which is not at all responsible for the fact that the law is wrong, since it has nothing to do with it. Thus, the supposed contingency of perception is only the contingency of laws that transcend perception, based on non-perceptual inferences that can be drawn. With perception I can formulate the law: 'When I turn the light on I see colours, when I turn it off I don't', but not the law 'Every time I press the switch the light comes on.' This misunderstanding is based on many factors.

(a) *Aleatory character*. The aleatory character of perception would depend on the circumstance that no one can bathe twice in the same river; that is, that perceptions are transient or apparent as much as the physical reality to which they refer. During her state visit to Italy in the autumn of 2000, Queen Elizabeth II demanded English mineral water branded 'Malvern'; good luck telling her that no one bathes twice in the same river. Indeed, one can very well do so, unless one ends up in the wrong river: what may be significant at the molecular level (water flows) ceases to be so geographically (the Po does not become Po-Ticino after Pavia, nor 'Po-Ticino-Adige' after Verona). Of course, one could simply object that with the river and the mineral water I've simply been playing with words, given that 'same' river or 'same' water have a coarser grain than what Heraclitus meant. This is true, but still, herein lies the problem: 'river' is a geographical entity with certain macroscopic characteristics, in which you can bathe as often as you want, as long as it's there; the water flow does not compromise its ontological integrity, just as the Danube, the Donau and the Ister are not three different rivers.

(b) *The law*. As for the law, in experience something is true until it is proven false (after all, the Aristotelian *katà poly* assumes that even a given number of counterexamples is no decisive argument against the reliability of a practical norm). In science, instead, something is false until it is proven true. Claiming that all knowledge is certain and evident, and that doubting takes you no closer to truth than never doubting, seems a substantially unmotivated claim from the ontological point of view. One can legitimately object that someone who has many figures, examples and notions – however vague – of many things, etc., knows more, practically speaking, than someone who has never seen them, so long as they're aware that those are not things, but images. Now, what is vague is not necessarily inexistent, nor is it merely aleatory, but then clarity does not analytically coincide with distinction.[51] We can have clear but confused knowledge, because we are unable to recognise the known characteristic inherent to a colour, for instance the exact chromatic intensity or, more simply, the components of a red flower. And before having clear knowledge, we have a lot of unclear knowledge, which nevertheless is still something: if I hit my head against something I feel dull pain, and ignoring what caused it doesn't make it better. Now, an epistemology that is not clear and distinct is not much use; it is not even an epistemology. But indistinct clarity is still something. That is to say, it has ontological value: I see something white 1,000 metres away, I see a man 100 metres away, I see Callias's son 10 metres away, etc.

(c) *Objectivity*. As for the misunderstanding about objectivity, there is the case of colours. According to the argument that if you turn off the light, everything becomes black, some have concluded that colours are contingent, which is to say that if in one case red and blue both appear black, then it's a case of simple anomy (absence of laws). However, if I switch off the light I'll always see everything black, and when I turn it back on the colours will reappear. At most, one could say that colour logically depends on extension; but nothing prevents one from claiming the opposite, that is, that all extensions have at least one colour. The colour-blind see fewer colours, just us we do when we watch a film in black and white; nevertheless, just like at the cinema we do not see sometimes the positive and sometimes the negative, as if one time we see blue, then yellow, then grey, because a causal action can produce a variety of perceptual outcomes that may be simplified, but are structurally constant. Similarly, individuals with the disorder known as protanopia stop at the traffic light because they see the light at the top go on, not because they discriminate the red; that is, they still recognise the constants. People insist on the fine grain of perception: not only do the colourblind see colours differently, but the same colour – in normal circumstances – can be seen as blue, turquoise or green by three different subjects; this, though, is due to the fine grain, not to subjectivity, because the next day A still sees it as blue, B as turquoise and C as green.

Finally, one could make the case that textile workers grasp more colour shades, and sommeliers refine their perception of flavours. However, it is assumed that the nuances really exist, and that the experts merely taste or see them better, otherwise they would not be connoisseurs, but rather visionaries. However, the fact that a blind man does not see, or that a colourblind person does not discriminate certain colours, does not constitute an argument for the claim that colours do not exist, or that they are subjective or inter-subjective, or even cultural. Otherwise, it would make no sense to send out invitations requiring a black tie, or to note that someone was wearing a blue jacket or that the car that ran over you was red. Apartheid was based on the possibility of discriminating between white and black people, in a far from aleatory way, whereas it would be quite difficult to discriminate based on one's blood group; we play chess without confusion between the pawns; in earlier times, armies were differentiated by colours, whereas modern armies – still through the use of colours – try to blend in with the environment and so on.

2. *The fallacy.* If the passage from perceptive constants to meta-perceptive inferences has appeared so obvious, it is, once again, because of the transcendental argument: if it is so, it must be so. Now I'd like to note how many times the opposite is true: a) even if it is so, it might be otherwise (either in any way or in some other ways); b) even if it is so and not otherwise, the law might only apply to the environment in which it originated; c) the fact that sometimes the transcendental argument does hold doesn't make it a universally valid principle.

(a) *It is so but it could be otherwise.* The graph of the chaotic motions of matter might be so complicated as to appear like a sort of story, so that the principle that *natura non facit saltus* is not an observational datum, but rather a precept, similar to the requirement of perfection in reading comprehension, to define a field in which there can be exceptions. On the other hand, maybe things cannot be just any other way, but just some other ways. Take the Gestalt laws (figure and background, closure, directionality, good form and so on). They are ascertainable, and do not appear to be purely subjective – usually it's not as if some recognise a background where others isolate a figure, and the fact that this can sometimes happen is no objection, in a sphere in which one does not seek universally valid laws – even though they often compete with one another and appear fully abstract without being conceptual. The fact that, for instance, the laws of structural coherence and significance (against the expectations of Gestaltists) are not always realised does not mean that everyone sees the world as they wish: it means, if you will, that meteorology is less predictively effective than theoretical physics. Also, the fact that laws compete against one another doesn't mean that they are amendable: it is the eye that chooses in a bi-stable figure, even though it might choose differently at a later time (perhaps due to the thought that I must look for another figure). Then there is an even more important point: there are Gestaltic constants, which doesn't mean they derive from a table of judgments, nor that they make experience possible, nor that they derive from it – so much so that one of the flagships of Gestalt psychology is precisely that its laws often apply in contrast to experience. It would also be wrong to assert that one solution is 'more right' than the other, as conversely you can and should always say of concepts; but that an outcome appears no more correct than the other does not imply that they are both purely subjective.

(b) *It is so and not otherwise, but not because it has to be so.* Here things are much simpler, and can be explained by way of the problem of the names of colours. There is no reason to call 'blue' blue rather than red, apart from the fact that we do. The Maoris have 3,000 names of colours but do not see many more colours than we do: they simply do not separate them from the object with a non-perceptual linguistic operation, like when we say 'salmon pink' or 'mauve'. The fact that a colour is what it is depends on its chromatic wave – i.e. it is its own business.

(c) *It is so and it has to be so.* There is a sphere where the transcendental argument works perfectly: that of soap bubbles, snowflakes, crystals and symmetries. Here it seems that nature weaves a mathematical harmony; however, in light of these few cases, it is hard to claim that optics is corrected by geometry, which means that every fact must comply with a law. Indeed, something can be or appear fully organised without there being any particular reason or external goal: this happens with organisms, so that biology would ultimately fall outside of the transcendental.

3. *Collapse.* Most of the time it is very easy and automatic to insert what we see into our belief systems: antinomical cases, such as perceptual illusions, reveal certain laws that remain unnoticed in normal cases, but fortunately they are nothing more than single cases. In ordinary experience, I see a pen on the table, I believe there is a pen on the table, I'll take if it someone asks me to take it; I think it's raining, I look outside, and I see something that makes my judgment true. Following orders, acting without thinking, understanding a sentence, and experiencing reality before science all depend on how we are made and would be inexplicable if the structure of perceptual experience weren't easy to conceptualise: this does not mean that it is conceptual, but that conceptual structures are genetically and content-wise rooted in perceptual experience, without fully depending on it, because the senses think their own way. One shouldn't give too much credit to the idea that integrations are due to the intelligence of our perceptual systems, failing to note that, as intelligent as they may be, they would hardly work in an antinomic world – that would create the same awkwardness we feel when faced with a text written in esoteric characters. One can argue that the mind always looks beyond what is effectively perceived; nevertheless, we often notice when we are making such integrations – which, after all, do not appear exactly perceptual – and when we are not. Hence my main point: apart from successful integrations, there are cases in which what we see doesn't fit with what we think, or when it goes beyond our current knowledge, which is the final blow to the transcendental argument. If it is so, though, one must look at illusions from a different perspective, considering them neither as a simple deviation nor as a homogeneous phenomenon.

Antinomy between Aesthetics and Logic

Illusions. The inflation of illusions is not generally motivated, and speaking too easily of 'appearances' doesn't seem to be a wise strategy. Rather, one can attribute a different ontological status to things (present and inter-observable), reflections (inter-observable but depending on other things), afterimages (depending on other things but not inter-observable) and phosphenes (non-inter-observable and with no objective counterparts). Let's take the case of the rainbow: I see a rainbow, I point it out to someone and they see it; it is an object, not a ringing in one's ears; it is out there. However, as I walk towards it, it stays where it is, like the horizon, while a chair or a mountain would get closer. Or else: I'm on a plane, I look out the window and see a rainbow, but the person next to me doesn't. For me the rainbow is real and has nothing subjective about it. 'Subjective' would be a fear of mice as opposed to eating them, whereas it would be enough to swap seats for the other person to see the rainbow.

Things are different for reflections, which are inter-observable but have a different status from rainbows, being more like shadows. In fact, they depend on something consistent that can be acknowledged at a phenomenal level. In particular, if the reflection is well defined (say, a mirror image), then we almost forget about it and conclude that the real thing is out there. Things change for phosphenes and afterimages, which are not inter-observable and are present in space but are not encountered in space. Also, a phosphene is not a sort of memory whereas – as I suggested earlier – an afterimage is. Once this is clear, one can speak of 'illusion' in many ways, in particular with respect to what one knows and what one thinks. It is not all the same, and these different ways ought to be distinguished.

1. *Intra-theoretical 'illusions'*. There are cases in which appearance is only such in the light of a theory: what comes about is actually different from what the senses testify. However, saying 'actually' only means that there is some scientific theory able to explain things differently. Therefore, we are dealing with something that is true for perception and false for interpretation, as in the case of heliocentrism: it seems to me that the Sun revolves around the Earth, but cosmology proves that the opposite is true. However, I can spend a whole life thinking in line with geometrical hypotheses, and nothing will change, apart from marginal experiences such as plane trips. So, geocentrism and heliocentrism are merely theories, just like monophysism, with the sole difference that they can be verified through a greater physical accessibility. The verification, though, will generally take place on a very

different level compared to the environment I live in, and therefore doesn't seem so crucial. One can rightly say that it is better to claim that the Earth revolves around the Sun: it does not cost anything, it does not change anything, but it is true. In other cases, however, embracing the epistemological version could raise problems. Take again the argument that the Earth looks flat, but is actually round. You will notice that, despite such an assumption, usually shared, a great number of behaviours are – quite justifiably – driven by the assumption that in reality the Earth is flat: no one builds houses with very slightly arched cellars, no one organises conferences to determine if people in New Zealand are really upside down. The flat Earth thus constitutes a level of reality hardly comparable to an illusion, as it is solid and inter-observable; and to understand that in reality the Earth is round, I need a theory, which leads me to extend the sphere of my environment; for example, trying to go to India following a western route, since observation – on an environmental scale – does not lead me to conclude anything of the sort.

2. *Ecological 'illusions'*. In contrast, some verifications are perfectly feasible at the ecological level. Take the case of a velvet suit that under artificial light seems beige and under natural light appears to be salmon pink. Here, in the first instance, it can simply be argued that, unlike the Emperor's clothes, the suit is real, whereas the two colours represent perceptual renditions affected by the light. Ecologically, what seems truer is salmon pink under natural light; but what if we always lived with artificial lighting? However, we are led to believe that the true colour, unfortunately, is the salmon pink, as this is not a theory, but rather a fact proven at a level accessible to us: we go outside, and the suit looks undoubtedly salmon pink, and if we decided only to wear it inside we'd feel somewhat awkward, as if we had dyed our hair. So, no one would claim that a *trompe l'œil* is real, as Moore once did during a conference, when he pointed to a window recently painted, at the back of the room, and, having been unable to check it from up close, said: 'no one would doubt that there is a window here': the ontological status of a *trompe l'œil* is exactly that of a painting or a picture. It works as an illusion only if we maintain a single viewing angle, where our perception of the environment supposes approaching, distancing, looking from different perspectives, touching, etc., all within a reasonable time. For I certainly cannot rule out that I'll have a better sense of touch tomorrow, or

in a hundred years, with less rough hands after the total disappearance of manual work, etc. However, if a fabric seems too rough to me today I do not expect to change my mind or perception: I simply buy a different one. In short, it is harder to suffer from an illusion than to ascertain the reality of things, which is not a theory, but something observable in the environment.

Things are no different for the stick that appears bent under water when it isn't. The first time it happens one might be tricked, and believe that the stick is truly crooked; however, in a normal ecological situation, one can easily discover that the stick is straight; and, if we are surprised, it is not so much because it is straight, but because it seemed crooked. In other words, I do not need special theories to understand that the stick is actually straight. Its crookedness is an appearance, and it can be revealed not by looking at deeper layers of reality, but rather by keeping to the same level of experience: it's enough to take it out of the water, or touch it under water. Something similar, in an even more explicit form, happens if we cross the index and middle finger and hold a marble between them: we are not surprised that there is only one marble, but that our touch, usually reliable, is deceived and seems to conclude that there are two. These two cases are symmetrical: the stick appears crooked to sight and straight to touch, whereas the marble seems one to sight and two to touch. It doesn't take much – another sense is enough – to establish the truth, just as in the case of the *trompe l'œil* (there it was actually enough to reapply the same sense from a different perspective). Likewise, no one would think that a trapezoid that – due to inclination and perspective – appears square is actually a square. What counts as true is the distal stimulus, not the proximal one, because the former is not an appearance, as you can easily note by touching the source of the stimulus, or looking at it from another perspective, just like the stick under water or the *trompe l'œil*. A fortiori, no one would ever think that the circle you get by rotating a lit cigarette in the dark really exists: that circle corresponds to nothing, both as a distal and as a proximal stimulus, and only manifests itself on our retinas. If one claimed that the circle is real, one would have to conclude that cartoons are real too: which shows that the motion of motion pictures is not apparent, but real.

3. *Actual illusions.* If we want to find authentic illusions, we must look elsewhere. For example, the Müller-Lyer illusion presents many aspects of illusion, and yet, like all true optical illusions, is neither inter-observable – which means that it's not only present

as a retinal stimulation, unlike the circle produced by rotating a cigarette in the dark – nor amendable by, say, changing perspective. The problem with the Müller-Lyer illusion is that if everything visible worked that way, maybe geometry wouldn't have been born.

The eye thinks in its own way. When one sees the properties of a triangle it might appear difficult to distinguish seeing from thinking, leading one to conclude that, at least under optimal conditions, the two functions are equivalent. This is why Aristotle wrote that the intellect recognises the abstract in the concrete, and I think of concavity when I see a nose;[52] likewise, Kant argued that I think of circularity whenever I see a plate. But is this true? Or rather, is it always and necessarily true? The fact that I might think of concavity or circularity doesn't entail that I do so every time I see a nose or a plate, nor that – even if I did – this is a functional and unavoidable interaction. When I see a Latin cross I think of a church, if it is a Greek cross I think of a hospital; but is there a link between seeing the cross and thinking of the church or the hospital? Surely the two processes take place simultaneously. Nevertheless, given some entirely idiosyncratic association of ideas, it may be that every time I see a cross I think of a restaurant. Above all, it may be that when I see a cross I am reminded, without there being any relation with the cross, that I have to go to the bank. If the evidential argument is that everything that happens at the same time interacts, then the bank and the restaurant would have to do with the cross as much as the church and the hospital. But if the argument is that thinking is always constitutive of seeing, it is really too challenging. A well-tempered version of a similar argument could go as follows: the retinal image is incomplete, and it is integrated. With what, though? Is it completed in the same way in which we integrate, thinking and not seeing, a torn manuscript? Mental completions do not seem to be endowed with perceptive reality, whereas we do truly see the Sun get bigger when it touches the horizon; indeed, the phenomenon is so evident that, apart from being acknowledged in common sense, it has given rise to a huge number of physical interpretations. This leads us to think that the term 'integration' is not the right one, especially if used indiscriminately;[53] and mostly that perceptive integrations depend much more on the external world than on the internal world. The distinction appears important: by drawing a divide between mental and perceptive integrations, it prevents a mechanism according to which, given that usually when I see something I also think of it (or better, if I think of it I conclude that I'm thinking of it and I could do so as much as I wanted, if I so wished), I must conclude that there is no vision without thought.

1. *Seeing as.* First of all, let's try to recognise the cases which do not have to do with seeing proper, but rather with an extension by analogy that leads us to attribute functions to seeing that are more typical of thinking. These cases are variations of Wittgenstein's 'seeing as': in his *Philosophical Investigations*, it is argued that interpretations add meaning to a figure, but do not objectively enrich it. However, the ontological difference between 'adding meaning' and 'enriching' is often neglected, just as it is forgotten that, if Wittgenstein's discourse has a meaning, then seeing as is not seeing, but something like it.

(a) *Seeing the invisible.* It isn't hard to note (I could also say: it is not hard to see, but I'd still be seeing my laptop screen rather than what I'm trying to point out) that seeing a university is not like seeing a tree. So, nobody would argue that the fact that we use 'see' even in a context like 'I see a strong resemblance between Belisarius's politics and Badoglio's' implies that one can actually see politics. In general, one cannot see what's invisible, as the latter's very name suggests.

(b) *Seeing and inferring.* A second ambiguity is to attribute to what we see properties inherent to what we think about what we see, thereby mistaking seeing for inferring. However, this is a trivial misunderstanding: I see the Moon as being as big as a coin, but I think that it is actually about one-sixth the size of the Earth, so that there is no real reason to speak of 'seeing' when it comes to the outcome of an inference.

(c) *Seeing and measuring.* A third ambiguity is to mistake 'seeing' and 'measuring' (or, more precisely, to consider vision as the preform of what can more correctly be given as 'measure'); however, the difference is not only a matter of degree, but also of field, and the two levels only meet in rulers.

(d) *Seeing and visualising.* A fourth ambiguity is to mistake what I see with the naked eye for what I can see with a scientific device: that is, seeing and visualising. The confusion, despite appearances, is conceptual rather than factual, and doesn't concern the use of instruments but rather what one means by 'seeing' in normal circumstances: I see with glasses, I visualise with a telescope or a microscope, wherever I am. From my vantage point on Earth, I can see the Moon and visualise Pluto. However, if I were on Uranus it would be the other way round, just as on Jupiter I would be in a position to see Europa and, if I wanted, I could even say 'look what a beautiful Europa there is tonight'.

2. *Seeing full stop.* Now that I have clarified verbal misunderstandings, let's look at a few figures. Faced with something like this:

SHADOW

one could argue that only those who can read and speak English are able to give a coherent outcome to the figure. It is not considered, however, that an illiterate person would still see something. On the other hand, the argument may be inverted. Take the following image:

ONTOL.GY

Here it is very clear that I think 'ontology', but I see a different thing; and there is little one can do about it. It is easy to anticipate the objection that 'pure' seeing is a rather obscure concept, so that the whole distinction, at least in practice, is useless. But it's not true: it might be difficult to define pure seeing, but I find no problem in showing the differences between seeing and thinking; and, in particular, I can very well know something and see another. I refer the reader to the long list of cases gathered by Kanizsa,[54] but I want to add one example that seems rather significant: in the following illustration, I tend to mistake the shadows for the dromedaries. I know that's the case and therefore I can amend my perception – contrary to what happens in the Müller-Lyer illusion – but then I end up making the same mistake, because it is fundamentally easier.

156   Hysteresis

All of this brings seeing to the level of what we encounter and therefore can hardly amend. Take Kanizsa's triangle:

Phenomenally I see two triangles, one of which is lighter than the background. I encounter it, just as I can bump into a person, and the result is also true for animals. But the triangle is not physically present, I know, and I am also aware of being able to make it disappear if I complete the black figures by turning them into spheres. After all, the opposite case is very common, in which I do not phenomenally see what is physically present in my perceptual field, and I am not only talking of masquerades but also of the pen I can't find even when it's right under my nose, or the hiker I finally manage to see after following a friend's indications ('a bit to the left, close to that tall tree', etc.). Now take the following illustration:[55]

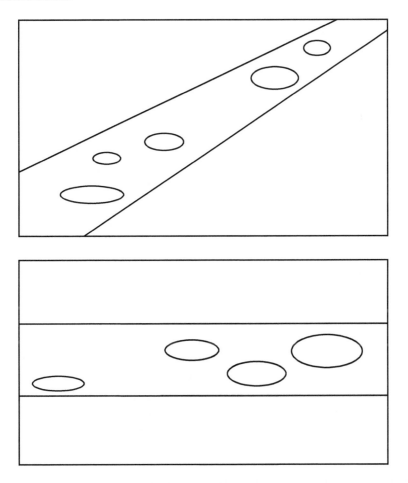

In the first image, I see something that means nothing to me. Then someone might suggest that it's a giraffe's neck: then I would suddenly see a neck, but this could never happen in the case of the second figure.

Autonomy of the World from Conceptual and Perceptual Schemes

Cause and structure. Finally, let's come to the main point of this book. Lucretius wrote:

> Suppose all sprang from all things: any kind
> Might take its origin from any thing,
> No fixed seed required. Men from the sea
> Might rise, and from the land the scaly breed,
> And, fowl full fledged come bursting from the sky;
> The horned cattle, the herds and all the wild
> Would haunt with varying offspring tilth and waste;
> Nor would the same fruits keep their olden trees,
> But each might grow from any stock or limb
> By chance and change.[56]

In simpler terms: how can there be a causal action devoid of a structural effect? There are two possible interpretations.

1. *Matter.* The first, minimalist interpretation is that you really have to recognise the causal role of the external world not only on our intellectual constructions, but also on our perceptual system. Try asking someone what our field of view is shaped like. They will probably reply that it is round or at least round-ish, as they will be thinking of the pupil or the ocular orbit, if not the horizon that – oh, wonder! – happens to coincide with our eyes. Of course it is not so. The field of view is shaped like things, which are not cut by a circle but have blurry sides. If all things truly adapted to the shape of the perceiver, the field of view would have to be round. However, there is a thing called world, resisting the roundness of the pupil and keeping its own shapes, not those of the human eye. On the contrary, the flat projection of a globe is openly distorting, so that Canada and Russia become even bigger than they already are, while the projection does not do justice, in proportion, to the true dimensions of the countries that are at the equator.

2. *Form.* Such an interpretation, then, seems difficult to dissociate from a more challenging hypothesis, namely that the action of the outside is not confused and frantic, but has a clear structural value – which does not mean 'intellectual', as I have tried to show through the antinomy between aesthetics and logic. It is

not guaranteed that unicorns are inadmissible in zoology, and therefore also in logic; likewise, when saying that an affirmative judgment is true I am not saying the same thing as when I claim that the object of the judgment exists (what about negative judgments?). Thanks to the distinction between Truth and Reality, I believe one can look at things differently and without committing too much to the epistemological profile, in a way that is ontologically very useful: conceptual schemes and perceptual systems do not only receive vortices from the external world (besides, vortices would have no reason to offer themselves spontaneously as information) but also forms and structures. Thinking of a cause without structure is as impossible as conceiving a general idea rather than a particular idea with added general properties. So, just as you cannot think of a dog in general, it is unclear how a cause could be exerted in a purely formless manner: if I am stung by a mosquito, it is a mosquito that stings me, exactly at that point and not another; the effect will be different from that of a bee sting or a wasp sting, etc. If I massage my sore calf or stroke a cat there will surely be different outcomes (my calf will not purr), but they will depend on the shape of my hand, the intensity of my touch, the amount of pressure and so on. However, I am not trying to construct an ontology of effects. So what is the external world to which I am referring?

Immanent/transcendent. Take a traditional epistemological thesis: I am sure of what is immanent in my consciousness, while everything else seems doubtful and transcendent. But is this true? Let's look at some counterarguments.

1. *How do you know?* If someone tells us their name and where they are from and we ask them 'how do you know?', we would be very rude indeed. Descartes' doubt is hyperbolic, but our world isn't. I can ask 'how do you know?' if someone tells me 'it's daytime now', but only if we find ourselves in a cave. Taking Descartes' doubt further, some have claimed that maybe I am not the one who is thinking, which really seems unlikely outside of amusing literature. Anyhow, following the immanence/transcendence hypothesis, one ends up facing a number of dilemmas: Should we blindly believe everything we see, including that what we see is out there? Or should we relegate everything in transcendence, and trust only what is within us, as evidence of immanent consciousness, delegating the foundation of certainty to

science? Do we have to trust only logic as a separate kingdom? Or should we seek some certainty in transcendence, too? And if so, how? Here the fallacy lies precisely in the reference to blindness: in what sense is our relationship with objects one of blind faith? We see the objects of experience very well, whereas few would be willing to stake their lives – the existence of which, therefore, they do not doubt – on some theory. So, at least initially and in principle, what we deal with is no science: the table is here; I'm not the table; the table is not in me; only with comically heroic contortions could such a list of truisms qualify as a 'knowledge'.

2. *Notebooks*. Hence the positive argument. It might seem legitimate to claim that we trust what we think (it is here, within us) more than what we see (it's out there), and that the only thing we can truly be certain of is our inner doubting. And yet, we are accustomed to writing down our thoughts in notebooks and marking our appointments on calendars (digital or otherwise). Why? Is this an unjustified habit, a naturalistic weakness, or is it the recognition of a character of reality, which exists before and after us, coherently and independently of our consciousness? Ontologically, the criterion of immanence produces a vain and irreparable scepticism, while also conferring a rather odd status on the images of the world present in our mind (and before that in our retinas: is it the inside or the outside?). In fact, on the one hand they should be certain, as they are manifested in the mind, but on the other they should be dubious as they refer to the world, or at least seem to do so.

'Internal to our mind'/'external to our mind'. One might observe: certainly the internal/external pair reflects the natural attitude more faithfully than the immanent/transcendent one. We believe the things outside us more than those inside us, tables and chairs more than our memories: we often say 'If I remember rightly' but very seldom 'is it really a table?' Nevertheless, it is not easy to say what one means by 'outside' or 'external': it isn't what is 'external to my body', because in that case I could increase, so to speak, the external world by cutting my hair or defecating; nor is it what is external to my mind, given that it is unclear where my mind is located – the idea of 'external' would thus be deprived of meaning.

Consider that defining internal/external in topological terms faces obvious objections – such as those I have just listed – and mostly goes against phenomenological evidence. Such evidence, after all, is precisely what is neglected by theories asserting that the head is in the world and the world is in the head. This approach is manifestly wrong: it is clear what a head in the world is, but what a world in the head is is truly hard to understand. Perception takes place there, in the world, but it occurs 'in me'. Certainly, but where? The two spaces seem hard to define and to separate. Suppose that, in line with Aristotle, the soul is like a hand, grasping entities without identifying itself with them. This seems reasonable, and yet doesn't correspond to real experience, as I don't seem to grasp tables and chairs with my soul: with the soul I understand tables and chairs, while with the hand I grasp them.

'Internal to our schemes'/'external to our schemes'. The difficulties diminish when we switch to a functional definition. Therefore, by 'internal' I mean 'internal to our conceptual schemes', and by 'external' 'external to our conceptual schemes': internal will be what, being graspable in a conceptual form, will be susceptible to infinite amendment; external is what cannot be amended. However, seeing as it is a rule, the criterion can be also applied to invisible entities, like logical and mathematical propositions. Vice versa, the world internal to our conceptual schemes includes everything that can be amended and interpreted: that is, essentially, a posteriori synthetic judgments typical of empirical science. Let's try to sum it up in a table.

1. *Perceptive unamendables.* By this I mean everything that comes from the senses and cannot be changed at will. I would only add to what I've said so far a few considerations on ordinary concepts, which turn out to be strictly related to perceptual characteristics, with reference to the remarks I made earlier on the concept of finger and the names of colours. It makes no sense to wonder if French fries could somehow become more French, just like it isn't legitimate to claim that a boat is bigger than it actually is, while it is legitimate to complain if there is no rum in a rum cake. One can make better pizza, put a new Coca-Cola on the market, produce alcohol-free beer, but betterment doesn't represent infinite progress – it is rather variation. The same goes

Table 9. Internal World/External World

External World: Unamendable	Perceptive
	Non-perceptive
Internal World: Amendable	Objects of scientific research in progress

for coins: it is right to say that 'aureus' coins in the fourth century AD had less gold than those of the first century, but it doesn't make sense to claim that they were not 'aurei' – even if, during Theodosius' reign, people distinguished true aurei from false ones.

2. *Non-perceptive unamendables.* There is an essential distinction between the unamendability of perceptive encountered things and that of non-perceptive ones: the former are such even without conceptual schemes, whereas the latter only exist within them, even though schemes cannot amend them. The unamendability of logical objects is grammatical: changing the rules of a game means changing the game; changing the chemical description of a natural genus does not mean transforming it. Therefore, if perceptions are what concepts do not amend, now I am trying to distinguish two families: that of unamendable concepts (which, as regards the discussion of the concept of concept, are not an eminent form of concept) and that of amendable concepts (which, in that regard, are concepts in the strict or epistemological sense).

(a) *Logical and grammatical propositions.* In general, logical and grammatical propositions presuppose concepts, such as 'proposition', 'implication', 'quantifier', and are necessary conceptual truths, that is, unamendable. However, they do not fall within the world internal to conceptual schemes, as schemes here identify with ontology rather than forming the grid that, applied to experience, will result in epistemology as such. 'No bachelor is married' is an unamendable sentence, unless we choose to use words differently, like saying that 'bachelor' means both 'unmarried man' and 'A person who holds a first degree from a university or other academic institution', who (in Oxford and Cambridge), until the nineteenth century, had to remain unmarried. However, it is clear that these are different meanings of the same word and, when it comes to the bachelors of Oxford and Cambridge, we are dealing with a synthetic proposition disproven by experience. So the propositions on which, for Kant, we can ground the internal world are actually rooted in the external world and can be known as objects just like tables and chairs, albeit not in a perceptive way.

(b) *Proper nouns.* There are parts of language that organise instituted realities; however, they are perfectly homogeneous with the reality they institute, contrary to what happens in the relation between oncology and cancer. A typical case is that of proper nouns: being called 'Roberta', 'Dean' or 'Samantha' is not a property common to all those who are called that way, because each of them could have been called otherwise – which sometimes is not such a bad idea, but not for reasons of truth or reference (a woman can be called 'Faith' regardless of her religious beliefs).

(c) *Institutions*. Another case is that of institutions, which are in part different from simple names. The Department of Philosophy and Educational Science in Turin gathers professors from two old departments: that of Philosophy and that of Hermeneutics. However, when the two merged, the idea wasn't to get closer to a pre-existing state of affairs, but rather to create a new one. Likewise, 'Südtirol' and 'Madagascar' today designate relatively different things to what they referred to in the past (the term 'Südtirol' only appeared in 1839, originally indicating both Trentino and Tyrol; 'Madagascar' didn't refer to the Island in the Indian Ocean, but to the part of the African continent next to it), and post-Yalta Poland is very different from Poland after the Treaty of Versailles, but it cannot be said that the transformation has entailed amendment.

(d) *Units of measurement*. This line of reasoning also applies to units of measurement, which refer to an objective reality but cannot be amended. Would it make sense to claim that my uncle's measuring tape is more precise than mine, or that this metre is more of a metre than the prototype metre bar? At most, one could adopt a different unit and still call it a metre, specifying that it is still made up of 100 cm but that centimetres have changed. However, between the prototype metre bar and the new one there would be a relationship of mere homonymy – therefore, there would have been no amendment. Similarly, it makes no sense to say that, with the change of our paradigms, water will boil at 97 Celsius degrees at sea level. If we change the paradigms, we will say something different, such as 'water boils at 700 Banana degrees'. However, to make water boil at 97 degrees one doesn't have to change paradigms, but rather go to the mountains.

(e) *Literary works*. Another case is that of literary works. No one, apart from Torquato Tasso or Alessandro Manzoni, would dream of amending *Jerusalem Delivered* or *The Betrothed*; just as, with the exception of Conan Doyle, no one can ever question that Sherlock Holmes lived on Baker Street.[57] Nevertheless, seeing as these authors have all passed away, one can easily say that no one, ever, until the end of humankind, will be able to amend those works. Conversely, there was a time when it was claimed that the Bible contained a deluge of cosmological errors, because the validation criterion was not the authorial intention, but rather the reference to a world, so that it was a cosmology for patriarchs, and not a Middle Eastern cosmogony. This, of course, doesn't happen with novels: it is strictly impossible – not for factual reasons but for conceptual ones – to claim that maybe, with further research on the private life of Alfred Agostinelli, we'll find out if Albertine Simonet was faithful or unfaithful to the Narrator of the *Recherche du temps perdu*. We'll never know (while we know that Hans Castorp truly was with Claudia, even though it isn't obvious and some might not notice), just like we'll never be able to say that Albertine Simonet is Alfred Agostinelli. We can, however, easily say that the Narrator is Marcel Proust (it is written in the novel). For the same reason, we know everything we can possibly know about Emma Bovary; we can also claim – albeit not as obviously as for Narrator = Proust – that Emma is actually Gustave Flaubert, who said so openly, though not in the novel. However, we doubtless know a lot less than this not only about our closest friends, but also about ourselves.

(f) *Rules of games*. Likewise, rules of games cannot be amended: they can be changed, and the game changes with them. Here science doesn't have the final word either: if Cuvier had decided to change the rules of Rummy, perhaps they would have let him, but not because he was a naturalist; and anyway, especially if the variations had been conspicuous, they would have renamed the game 'Cuvier'.

(g) *True and complete concepts*. The extreme case in the other direction is provided by the ideal scientific propositions: the True and Complete Concepts, which are no longer subject to science as amendability, and therefore can be regarded as analytical judgments. However, the actual realisation of an absolute knowledge in this field is still dubious.

3. *Objects of scientific research in progress*. These are all the propositions on which research is carried out in the area that, from a certain point onwards, has been called 'science'. The internal world, at least at the level of reflection, is so present and pressing that we can be tempted to believe that there is nothing outside the text. I hope I have sufficiently shown that it is not so and, above all, that the external world is not an iceberg emerging in special circumstances, and that it doesn't exist to keep the world of words together. We are so used to drawing theories from our experiences that we end up forgetting the many experiences from which we can draw nothing at all, for lack of time, will or need, or because

by doing so we'd fall into error. In fact, the idea that facts are only there to ground our theories is a mere hypothesis, disproven by a myriad of circumstances, including the fact that 'sensible experience' is not just a superfluous term used to indicate a process that never really takes place. Put it in these terms, it might sound like the answer we give to children after they've asked us 'why' for the umpteenth time: 'because it is like that'. And yet the opposite is true: if a scientist knows something more than an illiterate person it is precisely because there is a layer of experience (like the banana skin on which you slip) that resists any conceptual amendment. Here's the moral of my story, which I might have drawn subconsciously; it is a quotation from T.S. Eliot inscribed by someone on the door of a toilet at the Philosophisches Seminar at Heidelberg University, on which I meditated a lot:

Oh, do not ask, 'What is it?'
Let us go and make our visit.[58]

Three

Speculation

In 1920, two books came out that seemed to divide the field of knowledge in half. On the one side, this world, i.e. *This Side of Paradise*, F. Scott Fitzgerald's first novel.[1] On the other side, the netherworld, whatever it may be, i.e. *Beyond the Pleasure Principle*, an essay written by a mature and almost elderly Freud.[2] Despite his age, Freud was also making a debut in his own way: no longer as a doctor (albeit of souls) but as a speculative philosopher. I insist on the word 'speculative' because it is crucial and appears at the exact midway point of the book, in the first line of the fourth of seven chapters: 'What follows is speculation.' What does Freud mean by this? Something very similar to what Kant means when he says that there is a fate of reason, a kind of disastrous or beneficial destiny that pushes it to go beyond the boundaries it has set itself.

In a book published the following year – *Tractatus Logico-Philosophicus*,[3] which like Freud's and Fitzgerald's works drew on material from the war (and in this case on imprisonment) – Wittgenstein concluded that on this theme of the limit one simply must remain silent. The philosopher thus inaugurated a sad and paradoxical era in which everyone, from physicists to bloggers, can speculate on the highest and most important systems (as they should) while philosophers have to be content with questions of detail that are mostly devoid of interest (and this is really unfair). This era is now coming to an end after a philosophical century that suffered greatly from this interdiction. *Beyond the Pleasure Principle* can serve as the viaticum for this new season of philosophy – let's not forget that some of the most remarkable philosophical expressions of the past century owe a great deal to Freud's little book. For example, Derrida dedicated a seminar to him which was published in 1980 under the (unsurprising) title 'To Speculate on Freud.'[4]

So what is speculation about? Death, of course, and a secondary effect of death that is particularly evident, pressing, needy, harassing – that is, life. For much of his reflection Freud was, despite himself, a monist and an optimist: drives are essentially linked to Eros, and therefore to life and its perpetuation. Pleasure is the way in which these drives express themselves, chasing us during the day and manifesting themselves in the night in our dreams. A dream is a wish, on this point Cinderella and Freud agree. Freud, however, goes a step further in speculative terms, and asks: but then why do we have so many nightmares? For a long time Freud explained this by saying that nightmares were a horrible punishment for desires that were all-too-pleasant, to the point that we did not even dare to dream about them. But in *Beyond the Pleasure Principle* he puts forward a different and more direct hypothesis: Eros is not the foundation that is repressed through horror, but is rather a cover, the superficial ripple of a deep-seated desire rooted in organic life, which wants to return to its origin like a salmon. This consideration, which can also be found in Schrödinger's *What Is Life?*,[5] lies at the basis of the subsequent discovery of the genetic code, i.e. the alphabet of life, which like any alphabet is also the alphabet of death – a dead letter that repeats ancestral traits in the living. And the origin of life is the inorganic, death, Thanatos.

Freud insisted that he had never read Schopenhauer, so as not to prejudice scientific analysis with philosophical assumptions (we should not forget that Freud was born as a positivist). Most probably he was not sincere in saying this, and one need not be Freud himself to understand the reasons for his denial and resistance. Freud does mention Schopenhauer at least once in *Beyond the Pleasure Principle*, and in a letter to Lou Andreas-Salomé confesses that he did read him, along with many other things, but adds that he did so 'unwillingly'.[6] After all, Schopenhauer's presence in Freud is a bit of a purloined letter, because it could hardly be more obvious. Eros is the surface, the representation, the phenomenon, the deception. The depth, the only truth, is Thanatos: the race that every living person as soon as they are born undertakes towards death. Love's Labour's Lost, the varied art-show that Eros puts on in the world, is also and more profoundly Much Ado About Nothing, a great flight into the nothingness predetermined by Thanatos.

Young Nietzsche also appeared to be mainly attracted to the primitive form of life, as more authentic than the civilised kind. Behind all this there seems to be an assumption, à la Rousseau, which identifies the authentic with the primeval and the original. But that is hardly a given. There are at least as many good (or bad) reasons to see it from the inverse point of view, and to consider that what human beings are, as such, is the result of their history and technical advances, which are therefore the revelation of what we really are and what we really want. What makes the reference to the Dionysian interesting is not so much its manifestation of human authenticity as the attraction it exerts on humans. This is part of a general tendency of life to be attracted by regressive forms, as expressed in the fascination that the inorganic exerts on the organic. Freud called it the death drive, as discussed in *Beyond the Pleasure Principle*.

So, did Freud add anything to Schopenhauer and Nietzsche? Of course he did: the role of repetition. For Schopenhauer, who looks at the world with physical and metaphysical impassivity, what matters is the end (i.e. the purpose), and in this case the end full stop. Freud is more interested in the means, that is, the fact that life develops systems to persist for as long as possible – just like Scheherazade who, thanks to her tales, gives herself an extra thousand and one nights, thus postponing her death by almost three years and in the end obtaining salvation. Life is nothing but this deferred death (Kojève recalls this in his seminars on Hegel of the 1930s).[7] For this deferral to work there must be a structure, a memory, something that allows us to appreciate the passing of time, the days that elapse as we approach death and at the same time draw the course of what we call 'life'. This was very clear to Proust, who in those same crucial years was trying to regain lost time through a work of memory that is not relatively futile literature, but awareness of the fact that without memory, recording, accumulation of traces, there is no life (imagine a being radically devoid of memory: it would be neither living nor dead). This is also very clear to neurotics, hysterics and traumatised people, who keep throwing and pulling their reel and feel a malicious pleasure in repeating their reminiscences and sufferings, because that's life and that's amore.

Is there anything we could add to Freud a hundred years later? I will try to do so. But in those crucial years a century ago, Heidegger pointed out that it is precisely the fact of death that gives meaning to life, especially because it gives it time (more or less long, but never infinite) and therefore gives meaning to promises, aspirations, desires and happiness that would make no sense to an immortal. In times like ours, when a stupid superstition makes us fear artificial intelligence, this circumstance becomes fundamental. A machine can keep turning on/off forever; that's what it's made for. Instead, we like all other organisms are given only two options: on, then off, and that's it. Unlike other organisms, however, we can use machines and enhance our possibilities by giving a purpose to both of these mechanisms, which per se have none, and to ourselves, who as such only have the end of our end, like all organisms. Death is a *Meister aus Deutschland* who might seem to be far away but is actually behind every gesture we make, every item we buy online, every message we post. This might sound like something sad or unfortunate, but it's not: it's what makes up the world of culture and spirit – the gigantic and amusing circus that humans have managed to put on by mixing the skills enabled by technology and the thrill and motivation brought about by death.

Speculative realism. As if that were not enough, there is good reason to believe that the question of reality can only be resolved by appealing to speculative arguments. In other words, it is a question of finding a unitary foundation of reality and reducing it to a single element. Now, this role is traditionally attributed to causality, which however has an epistemological value (it is an explanation), while it is up to us to find an ontological value. In this sense, starting from the Internet and through the thematisation of hysteresis, we can refer to a network that is much older than the Web, but which in the latter manifests itself with a power and evidence that was previously hidden. Indeed, this is anything but a mystery; or more precisely, it is a purloined letter sitting in front of everyone's eyes.

The classical arguments against the possibility of defining reality rely on the difficulty of knowing it. Among the ancients this difficulty was mainly based on the power of the illusions of the senses (a stick immersed in water appears bent, while in reality it is straight), and therefore can easily be overcome through an opposition between reality and appearance. Among us moderns, on the other hand, the difficulty is much more challenging, because science provides access to more fundamental levels of reality, in relation to which it is not possible to resolve the issue by appealing to correct sensible perception. The question about the nature of reality therefore becomes the demand for a unifying principle of the different levels of reality with which we are confronted, both in our ordinary experience and in scientific knowledge.

The conflict between the scientific image of the world and that of common experience appears insoluble at first sight. This is because of the discrepancy between the two dimensions: the table on which I am writing is a little denser – from an atomic point of view – than the surrounding air, yet for me there is an essential difference between the table and the air. What can the principle be that holds these apparently antithetical experiences together and that allows us to speak of one reality, and not of various facets and levels, none of which can aspire to the claim of being ultimately real? Today we are better positioned than ever to find it, precisely because of a macroscopic technological phenomenon, i.e. the Web, consisting of a bonanza of records and recordings. In fact, the Web sheds light on reality both retrospectively and prospectively, and in particular it manifests the function of 'hysteresis', which is literally the survival of an effect once its cause has disappeared, but which lends itself to being elaborated as a general theory of reality. Hysteresis, in fact, grasps the essential dimension of reality (i.e. persistence) but at the same time manifests its productive and evolutionary character.

Hysteresis is a metaphysical notion, where 'metaphysics' is understood as the transcategorial, since reality has the characteristic of applying not only to the sphere of being (ontology) but also to the spheres of doing (technology), of knowledge (epistemology) and of aims and objectives (teleology). In each of these spheres hysteresis manifests itself in a different way, but each of them is characterised by its action and can legitimately be defined as 'real', although with different characteristics in each case. The fundamental question that I will try to answer in the speculation of the following pages is twofold. On the one hand: why has a simple quantitative increase in the recording of reality, as determined by the Internet, produced such a radical change in our forms of life and production? On the other hand, and especially: in the case of organisms, why does recording require the radical alteration that is death? Death is the interruption, the moment when the machine stops, but at the same time it is what gives it meaning, what makes the machine go on and the repetition continue. No machine, not even an automaton (never was a term more deceptive) runs on its own.

0

Where Do We Come From?

Where do we come from? From an evolutionary history that is far longer than philosophers could imagine. Instead, philosophers devised a human being capable either of shaping the world through its ideas or created by God to shape the design of providence. In reality, we come from something that was there before us; which means that any hypothesis based on the anthropic principle is structurally inadequate. That is why we must take a leap of the imagination and try to think of the world without humans. If you will, it is a matter of taking God's point of view: which is certainly not the much deprecated 'view from nowhere', since it is built precisely by following the thread of principles that go beyond human nature. We can see these same principles at work in the ongoing technological revolution, which is not only a revelation of human nature, but also at the same time an indication of what made human nature possible before any humans appeared on Earth. It is primarily in the present that the origin manifests itself.

0.1 In the Beginning Was the Web

The answer to the question 'where do we come from?' is a popular version of the fundamental ontological question, 'what is there?', but declined in the past tense: 'what was there?' Or more precisely: 'what was there in the beginning?' The answer is simpler than it sounds, and it is offered to us by none other than Harlequin: 'C'est partout et toujours comme ici, c'est partout et toujours comme chez nous, aux degrés de grandeur et de perfection près.'[8]

Indeed, in the beginning was the Web: at least if we want to believe Plato's hypothesis, which is anything but far-fetched. In the *Sophist*,[9] Plato speaks of a συμπλοκή, an interweaving or network which can mean both the connection of ideas and that of syllables.

It is not difficult to recognise here the ideal antecedent of the Web, providing that one explains the technological or metaphysical condition which makes it possible. Now, Plato also speaks about this condition: in the *Timaeus*[10] he theorises the χώρα, which literally means 'space', 'place' (it is still a very common name for Greek villages), but which in a metaphysical sense indicates an 'intermediate genus', and which consists of a formidable ability to retain. The Demiurge builds the world from ideas, but it is necessary that these ideas find an extension in space and a position in time, and the χώρα responds to this need. As in the case of atoms, conceived by Democritus and then discovered by modern science, the χώρα was conceived by Plato, and realised by contemporary technology, precisely through the Web.

What is important to note is that the Platonic perspective of the συμπλοκή and the χώρα presents a much more exact conceptual analogy with the Web than it does a generic analogy with the sphere of knowledge, such as the medieval *Summae* or the encyclopaedic ideals of early modernity. In the latter, in fact, the emphasis was placed on knowledge and information, while in the case of the Web the decisive aspect is provided by connection and recording. This difference, as we shall see, is decisive for understanding the true nature and properties of the Internet.

The propulsive force underlying the Web is the same that Plato attributes to the χώρα: the ability to record, and then to connect what has been recorded. In many analyses the centrality of recording often takes second place to the connection aspect, but the transformation made possible by the Web consists not so much in connecting already existing data, but rather in creating data on a platform that also connects them. To clarify this point with an example, if the telephone connects two people who simply transfer information, the Web records actions, behaviours, communications; it transforms them, by recording them, into objects. That is to say, it transforms them into documents, and in so doing it generates an archive. A small portion of this archive is available to individual users, who keep track of some of their actions, and a large portion to the platform itself, which can compare the documents produced by one user with those produced by many others. In addition, the Web has computing machines that can find correlations and determine user profiles; therefore it can capitalise on these documents (store them, exchange them, reuse them).

In an effort to give a single name to the thousand faces of Vishnu, so to speak, the clues collected so far suggest one word: hysteresis. This is a widespread term with many different meanings, but from a metaphysical (i.e., transcategorial) point of view, it designates the circumstance by which an event keeps track of the events that preceded it, so that the effects outlive the causes. The scratch on my mobile phone that reminds me of when it fell off the table, the compound interests of capital, the act of speaking a language after learning it, the genes that predispose us to rheumatism and the neurosis that pushes us to establish relationships by repeating childhood patterns are all examples of this. It may seem like nothing, but it is everything.

0.2 Coming to Light

Sooner or later the truth will come to light, as they say: Brutus stabbed Caesar, water boils at 100 degrees Celsius, Ljubljana is the capital of Slovenia, and then many other things that affect us more intimately. Whatever it may be, we have always presupposed the existence of truth in our everyday behaviour, despite the fact that many philosophers have done their best to set it aside, perhaps telling people and themselves that humans, with their weak powers and uncertain ideas, are those who construct the world. But obviously it is not so: a climatic variation of a few degrees would have made it impossible for Kant ever to write the *Critique of Pure Reason*, and if the Big Bang had occurred 10 million years ago, nothing in the world as we know it would exist (in particular we would not exist, but that would not prevent what there is from being exactly what it is). For a world to exist there is no need of a supernatural God or an 'I think'.

Slowly, since there was no lack of time and material, an accumulation of events has reached a certain threshold and turned into something different: hence organic nature, the mind, the will and taxes. This is the semi-technical sense that the word 'emergence' has among philosophers: it is said that a property emerges from a certain pool of facts when, even though it depends on them, it cannot be fully explained in relation to them – for example, the mind emerges from the brain. Ordinary language uses a very similar word: emergency. We speak of emergency units, emergency exits and (for the more sophisticated) states of emergency. Between the two seemingly unrelated meanings there is a basic continuity: what is an emergency if not an event that reveals the possibility of the impossible? And what is more emergent than reality, which plays with all possibilities and affirms itself with unforeseen sharpness and unimagined resources?

Such emergence follows this direction: Epistemology ← Ontology, going from being to knowledge. Epistemology emerges from ontology, while constructivism and deconstructionism as the fundamental trends of modern philosophy followed the direction Epistemology → Ontology, and the metaphysical realism of ancient philosophy was based on the hypothesis of a mirroring: Epistemology ↔ Ontology. In fact, everything that exists in the world and of which – sooner, later, or never – we get knowledge (the truth comes to light, but we don't know when, and it doesn't necessarily happen when it suits us) existed before us and before our knowledge, and would have existed just as well in the absence of any 'I think' (this holds for everything apart from the 'I think' itself, of course). On the contrary, every 'I think' is the result of things existing before it – which, incidentally, explains why it is so natural for thought to refer to the world. Or at least that's the case when one doesn't play the sceptic and make claims like, say, that this book might have been created by the reader's 'I think' – thereby suggesting, with inadvertent malignity, that authors are the unwitting plagiarists of their readers.

The 'I think' is a late product of evolution and everything that preceded it: as well as most of what has come after it or has been, is, and will be what it is regardless of it. The transcendental in the Kantian sense – the transcendental of knowledge – came about very late. From the Big Bang to dinosaurs, from termites to pyramids, up to and including the Internet, most of what the world gives to us (most of what there is) emerges independently of the self ('the dear self', as Kant called it) and its claustrophilia. Before the self and before us, individuals have crossed space and, at a certain point of evolution, have sensed the passing of time and the alternation of day and night, without there being any 'I think' close at hand or even far away, millions of kilometres or a million years away. How to explain this interaction, if not through the fact that individuals allow for it regardless of conceptual schemes and perceptual apparatuses?

Consciousness, knowledge, values and transcendental philosophers are pieces of reality, just like electricity, photosynthesis and digestion, and they emerge from reality like mushrooms.

The whole world – that is, the totality of individuals – is the result of an emergence that does not depend on thought or on conceptual schemes, even though we may of course use the latter to acquire knowledge of such emergence. Physics and logic, like empiricism and transcendentalism, are mere approximations to the individuals that they designate by general names: elementary particles, dinosaurs, gasometers, gauges and tram tracks. The only existence is that of individuals, and perfect knowledge is knowledge of individuals. Knowledge is always historical, regardless of whether it deals with Komnenoi, gastropods, galaxies or the tubercle bacilli. Ours is neither the best nor the worst of all possible worlds, but it's the only one there is, and it is not a flat and banal surface, an undifferentiated *chora* or a cookie dough, but is formed, robust, independent and endowed with a wealth of space and time larger than that of all possible worlds, made of an immensity of meaningful and meaningless events, of wonders, of memorable lives, of monstrosities and unfathomable stupidity. Among those individuals, at this very moment, there are you and I.

Of course, it is permitted to wonder how this emergence happens. Is it due to a magical gesture, something akin to creation? No, it isn't. As I will try to show, it is due to the slow accumulation of recordings, which in the end produces (albeit not necessarily) something qualitatively different from itself. Recording, the ability to keep track, is the origin of emergence. It is thanks to recording that we have the basic features of the world we live in: the fact that its essential elements are individuals, with internal properties, existing and resisting any conceptual scheme, emerging from other individuals; the fact that between matter and memory, as well as between sensibility and intellect, there is a continuity that makes emergence possible; and finally, the fact that necessity and freedom, automata and souls, are not set one against the other, because what we call 'soul' is nothing but a spiritual automaton – a result of emergence complex enough to generate freedom. Restated in philosophical jargon, recording – with its articulations – constitutes the transcendental, the condition of possibility not only of the experience of the world (without memory there would be no consciousness or progress) but also of its very existence. We live in the transcendental, as a philosopher might say with a degree of self-importance. Only this transcendental is not simply a category of knowledge, but comes before ontology and epistemology: it is recording.

So, all we get to know about the world is history. Neither theory (which concerns predictions that become history if they come true) nor empiricism (which again concerns predictions: the use of experience to formulate laws), but history: a tale of individuals that, unlike myth, does not look at the universal and the necessary, but at the particular and the contingent. A science is closer to truth the more it has authentic knowledge of individuals. Perfect epistemology, therefore, is history, as it doesn't define laws but individuals. In this sense, Big Data bridges the gap between epistemology and ontology, appearing as a decisive step forward on the path to the knowledge of the individual. It is not a process of naturalisation, but of individualisation. The progress of epistemology comes not from an increase in the number of laws, but from a growing knowledge of individuals – that is to say, an increase in history. The essential limit of such knowledge is also historical: no individual has had contact with all other individuals, we are not eternal, and most importantly, the quest for knowledge is not our main activity – quite the opposite. Borges' hypermnesic hero Ireneo Funes, if endowed with eternal life and the Library of Babel, would achieve historical knowledge as the absolute knowledge of the past.[11] Such knowledge, with respect to the future, would then turn into a *divine scientia media* ('middle science') à la Luis de Molina,[12] able to know the contingent future without affecting the autonomy of individuals, who precisely because they are ontological and not epistemological, would not be subjected to knowledge (in this case, to prediction).

The reader might very well ask: How do you know? Who told you that? The question is more than legitimate, as we're among philosophers and not fortune tellers. In the first place, there is evidence coming from history, physics and common sense. However, nobody has absolute certainty of anything and certainly that includes me. Hence the speculative nature of the present section of the book. In my understanding – as in that of most people today – the word 'speculative' is not a compliment. And yet I am not sure that 'What can be said at all can be said clearly; and whereof one cannot speak thereof one must be silent': one can always speculate, so long, of course, as it doesn't become a habit. This book talks about some emergences that are found in the natural history of the world. From the elementary particles, to atoms, to molecules, on up to organisms, the world is made up of individuals, which are what they are regardless of any knowledge one might have of them. Individuals and their interactions are what make up ontology (what there is). Epistemology (what we know) and politics (what we do as free or supposedly free agents) emerge much later, if ever, from ontology.

The risk of speculation is that it might be hard and inconsistent. And yet Schelling,[13] who was both a speculative philosopher and a realist one, suggested an approach suitable to our time and taste: that of narration. Mine will be a collection of notes – *Zettel* (to use Wittgenstein's word) or *Weltalter* (to quote Schelling). Theorising emergence means narrating the ages of the world *per speculum et in aenigmate*,[14] approximately and by examples, which taken in sequence make up the chapters of this book. I'll try to make use of the glimmers of history I have at my disposal to tell the story of some ages of the world in which the interactions between individuals generated new individuals – be they a termite mound or hieroglyphics, truth as an epistemological victory or freedom as an ethical achievement. As I said, they are but glimmers. If we had extremely sharp eyes, a very long life and perfect memory, this story would be obvious. But perhaps this hypothesis isn't so desirable after all.

0.3 Pleroma, Pentecost, Emergence

The conviction we should drop is that there is a pleroma, a totality made up of the human beings and the world, present from the beginning of time and manifested in history. This is not so. What is not manifested is simply not (or at least not yet); appearance is a necessary counterpart of essence, so what is given in the world is not the descent of a spirit, as in the Gospel account in which the Holy Spirit, whatever it may be, descends fifty days after Christ's ascent to heaven to enable the disciples to preach. The merit of the Christian tale is that it explains everything in a very succinct way, but the truth is that humanity has endowed itself with spirit through a much more laborious process than that. It was a slow emergence, a path that starts from our animal past and progressively comes to the present, i.e. to what there is, what we are and what we want. This second story is the one we should pay attention to, and to do so we should look at what happens in the present.

So, the point is to choose emergence over a Pentecostal vision. Let me clarify. The Pentecostal image draws from the hypothesis of a short and finite time and space, and imagines that at some point a spirit descends from the heavens, giving life to the dead and the inert, animating all that is without reason and without movement. It is a soul foreign to this world, one which ends up in the body as in a grave. This view comes from Plato, if you want to name names. The image of emergence follows the reverse path. To name names once again, the forefather of this view is Aristotle. We have plenty of time and plenty of space, and in all this time, this space and this matter, anything can happen. A devil's chaplain could write an endless poem about the waste, aberrations and counter-senses that have taken place throughout this evolution. But, in the end, here we are.

Constructivism, which presupposes activity at the origin of being and ideality at the origin of knowledge, is the result of a conception of the universe and life as limited in time and space, and therefore in need of a demiurgic intervention capable of creating the world from nothing and ordering it according to rational principles. When it becomes clear that we are dealing with a universe much larger and much older than what the constructivists thought, there is no longer any need to presuppose any activity or rationality at the origin of being.

The only ingredient for something to be there is that essential performance of hysteresis which consists of recording, a keeping-track that makes it possible to capitalise on memory by transforming it into matter, and on matter by transforming it into memory. Something happens (the first recording of which we conjecture the existence is the Big Bounce – i.e. a cyclical series of Big Bangs; of many others we have direct experience), and this happening can leave a trace without necessarily doing so. If this happens, a process begins which, if successful, leads from technology to epistemology; if instead all trace were lost, neither being (ontology) nor becoming (technology) nor knowledge (epistemology) would take place. In fact, we would have no discontinuity, but a single presence, not even recognisable as such because it could not be distinguished from the past and the future, which would also make it impossible for us to distinguish between process and object.

1

What Is Hysteresis?

Why is there being rather than nothing? What did God do before creation? All such questions find their answer in the possibility of retaining. In the beginning was hysteresis, or rather what makes hysteresis possible: a force that held together a mass (which was both matter and spirit, or at least what we call by these names) that exploded, and which has been expanding ever since. If it did not vanish at once, it was because of hysteresis, which also allows for the principle of identity (A = A).

1.1 Questions

Why does something remain? The big metaphysical question according to Leibniz is 'why is there something rather than nothing, since nothing is simpler and easier?'[15] The weakness of this question is that it comes *ex post*: there is a philosopher, there is a world, and then one wonders why there is something. The temptation to answer 'just because it is so' is really very strong. The fundamental metaphysical question, which seems to be authorised by conjectures about the origin of the universe, from the Big Bang to the Big Bounce, seems to be rather: Why is there memory rather than oblivion? Why does a very concentrated memory, at a certain point, explode (interrupt, break down), giving life to space, time and everything else?

The fundamental force behind the universe is the fact that a system keeps track of previous events so that every single event presupposes those that preceded it. In simple terms, the final straw (both literally and metaphorically) presupposes all the other straws. Usually, one interprets this circumstance in terms of causality, but talking about causes is no different from talking about ends: it is an anthropologism, useful and legitimate, sure, but an anthropologism nonetheless. A neutral view of the process supposes instead that we refer to this 'powerful force' underlying the universe, which manifests itself to us as a recording and from which causality and finality derive.

So it all began with a recording. But on what does the power of the recording depend? The answer, as mentioned, is anything but a mystery; or, more exactly, it is a letter purloined in front of everyone's eyes. Recording has the metaphysical property of transforming passivity into activity, event into object, case into law. When it is recorded, A is no longer just A, but something different and more free: what is recorded is repeatable, and this changes everything, even from an ontological point of view. As mentioned, hysteresis is the ability to preserve the effect even after the cause has ceased to act, and in a few decisive cases (such as the Big Bounce at the origin of the universe in modern mythology, or the *Chora* in ancient mythology[16]) it is the ability to preserve the effect even without a cause. This chronological inversion may seem paradoxical, but it is not: the ability to retain precedes the events, and constitutes their condition of possibility. The trace of the event will remain after the event itself, thus qualifying itself as an effect, although in reality it was also the cause. The genetic question about the origin is intertwined with the ontological question about what there is, but puts it into a broader context that goes beyond the traditional limits of ontology. The sphere of reality is wider than that of being as presence, and it presents itself as hysteresis, the permanence of the effect even after the cause is gone – that is, as difference and deferral.

As the Web shows, it is the technical ability to perform certain things that determines these things, so that actions derive from the technical instrument in use which, rather paradoxically, is perceived as the executor of a previous independent intentionality: for example, the words you are reading right now would not have been possible without a very long technical evolution rooted in hysteresis, and yet the way you and I are led to interpret them is that these words are the product of my thinking, that they are merely expressing this thinking, and that my computer is a simple tool I use to record and transmit my thoughts. But here's how it actually works. Something happens: for example, my fingers tap on some keys, or the Sun shines on the drying rack, and sometime later, when my fingers have stopped tapping and the Sun has set, what I wrote is still there and the clothes are dry. In other words, the effects have outlasted the causes. We find this normal, and at most we take an interest, when necessary, in the search for causes; perhaps, if we are in the mood for metaphysics, we draw the conclusion that the true glue of the universe is causality. But that is not true: the real glue is the persistence of the effects after the disappearance of the causes, i.e. 'hysteresis'.

This explains why memory loss is such an atrocious phenomenon, why a society without documents is very limited, and why a quantitative increase in hysteresis (which among other things allows a hard disk to work) has not only changed the world, but has revealed its deep essence. Hysteresis guarantees the most relevant function of the universe and of life, i.e. emergence, the fact that with sufficient time and space, complex structures may arise from simpler ones (or if you prefer, the fact that more superficial and recent structures may arise from deeper or older ones). In this sense, thought emerges from action, the world from the Big Bang (or rather, from the infinite series of explosions and contractions that mark the history of the universe), society from animal life forms prior to humanisation, and ideas from the iteration of signs.

So, is it still necessary to postulate the intervention of some *logos* (or, more modestly, of some meaning) to account for the world? No, the world owes its contingent emergence simply to an incalculable wealth of time, matter and energy. And when one uses intelligent design to explain the natural world, and intentionality and construction to explain the social world, one makes the same mistake that Spinoza used to reproach in those who resorted to the spirit by assuming that certain performances exceeded the possibilities of the body. So far – noted Spinoza – no one has truly established what a body can or cannot do. Likewise, no one has established what hysteresis alone can really do. Underestimating its scope has led us to appeal to magical entities that we can easily do without, i.e. benign or evil beings to which we have superstitiously attributed power over our lives. Yet perhaps these deities do not have such power on their own, but only as the hypostasis of a more fundamental function: hysteresis.

Why does everything end? There is an irreversible process of energy loss always going on: energy becomes no longer usable for work such as the creation of structures (life is a very sophisticated structure, from this point of view). This loss of energy is commonly called dissipation. The term has a negative connotation for the obvious reason that it corresponds to a waste of resources – the fact is, however, that without waste of resources no work can be done. Put differently, what produces evolution, i.e. irreversibility, is a negative fact, a dissipation of available resources. Down this road, the risk is that resources will run out and everything will end in stillness. On the other hand, without dissipation no structures can be formed; therefore dissipation is a value that is anything but negative. Exaggerating a bit in extending these notions from thermodynamics to biology, one can say that life is a delicate balance between energy, which is continuously supplied (mainly by the Sun) and which alone would produce a shapeless chaos, and dissipation which alone would lead to stillness.

It is worth noting that Kant himself, at a certain point, stopped referring to the thing in itself and conceived instead of the thing as action: to generalise, he started speaking of nature as *physis*, or genesis. In so doing, Kant returned to his beginnings, to his reflections on the living forces, on the universal history of nature and on the physical monadology that kept him busy between the mid-1740s and mid-1750s. Thus Kant proposed a dynamic view of matter, which would be nothing more than the manifestation of a force that acts outside itself and that, by acting, produces natural objects. With action comes place (*Ort*), with place comes space (*Raum*), and with space comes the world (*Welt*). As is easy to observe, this description of matter, which is compatible with the romantic idea of nature as a horizon that includes both spirit and matter, is also perfectly compatible with contemporary physical theories: subatomic particles are energy, and from energy arises matter – not by analysis, but by synthesis, through an emergence that generates something new. This is reassuring, just as it is reassuring to see that this synthesis, i.e. the idea of constitutive acts, is also recognisable in the world of society and its objects, which is more familiar to us than subatomic physics generally is.

Force is the fundamental basis of the universe. It is the chaotic interaction between forces that generates matter and then, through an ever-ascending complexity made possible by the availability of infinite amounts of force and time, the mind. None of this requires some intelligent design at the origin of the process. Just as a force acts on what is outside of it, so multiple forces act on each other when their fields meet. To understand this circumstance it is enough to throw two stones into a pond and look at the interference between the ripples they produce: first the circles meet at the edge of their radiation, then they modify each other. In this way, the nature of forces is modified by their encounter: think of meteorological phenomena, in which air masses, colliding, influence each other in terms of temperature and pressure.

Dynamic expansion creates space, and reciprocal actions (a notion that we find in the *Critique of Pure Reason*,[17] and which finds its justification in Kant's dissertation) generate structure. This perspective, which explains the whole of reality on the basis of mutual action, expels God from the world, at least as a creator, and transforms him into an architect, or rather a gardener. What is worse, forces can be shaped mathematically. At this point, 'God' is simply the name for the cause of a force.

What happens in the meantime? Everything, everything indeed. At the beginning there was an explosion, at the end there shall be thermal balance, and in the middle there is time, which tells the story of a growing tendency towards disorder and heat loss. The origin of the universe therefore presents itself, if we believe the physical conjectures prevailing today, as yielding and passive, so that the hysteresis that was able to hold being together by depriving it of a spatial and temporal dimension gradually weakened and gave rise to space, time and spatial-temporal objects.

Why is there something rather than nothing? Because of a mixture of contingency (empiricism) and necessity (the transcendental). Following an explosion, some very concentrated matter unfolded and became the world – therefore a contingent fact. But in order for this contingency to emerge, transforming itself into the world, the explosion had to show not only the capacity to expand, but also the capacity to record, to keep track. For something to be there, in nature or in society, first there has to be a recording, otherwise the world would be an eternal beginning, a fleeting glow without coherence and without consequence. The condition of possibility of ontology is thus given by hysteresis, which in this case is specified as recording (the world after the Big Bang, or these words after I've typed them, provided my computer does not crash).

Hysteresis is a general trend that can be seen in society, technology and nature. What deserves particular consideration is that here the metaphysical function is assumed by a principle that does not belong to thought and is intrinsically dynamic. There is no memory without matter, because memory always requires a physical medium on which to deposit itself. But, more radically and decisively, there is no matter without memory, because matter, being persistent in time, requires a recording that defines it as matter.[18] This definition may seem circular, but it is precisely this circularity that underlies the speculative hypothesis commonly accepted by physicists, according to which the universe is the result of the expansion of an original and highly concentrated mass, which at the time was matter and memory. It is animistic to think that beer comes out of a tap in order to respond to the action of some primal activity; it was simply compressed in the tap and as it comes out it expands and cools down. It would be no less animistic to attribute the origin of the universe to an action rather than to the principles of passivity and entropy. What was pure hysteresis, with no extension and no time, turned into space, time, processes, events, objects.

To build a world there is no need to know how to make it, and Absolute Ignorance can easily take the place of Absolute Wisdom – chance can be stronger and more effective than intelligent design.[19] That is why evolution, the biological counterpart of the metaphysical emergence that I defend in this text, could only come forward when we became aware of the temporal immensity that is sedimented in the history of the world. Conversely, the myth of creation is the result of too short a time perspective. Following the Bible, people were convinced that the world was no older than 6,000 years and that no new species could be born (the perfection of the divine plan was at stake), therefore they could not explain the existence of complex structures – whether it was the world, the mind, language or society – other than by resorting to the hypothesis of some supernatural creation. Or else, which is the same, they had to invoke a conceptual construction: a temporal action of providence. Likewise, for constructivism the problem was as follows: without the categories and the I-think, how can this improvised chaos be organised? The idea of a project, a design, a construction was a reasonable way to compensate for the short time it apparently took to create the world.

But if we calculate an infinitely longer time, deep in what Vico called 'endless antiquities',[20] everything changes: 13.7 billion years, i.e. the time that separates us from the birth of time itself, make it pointless to refer to any construction or creator. This sublime abundance of time and space has enabled all sorts of disorders, nonsense and dissipation: the economy, let us not forget, is only for those with limited time. Given enough time and space, interactions between individuals will produce anything: this fact alone explains the omnipotence of imbecility (far from any intelligent design!), the Black Death and the Lisbon earthquake, sodium chloride and Cromwell, the battle of Poltava and the *One Thousand and One Nights*. Is there still any need to postulate the intervention of a *logos*?

This spacetime surplus is the best theodicy, and solves a problem that is as old as Ecclesiastes: if the world is so perfectly ordered, there must be a Creator (God) or a Constructor (the I). But if this order includes evil, we must conclude that either God is not the creator or he is evil; or else that the I is trivially masochistic. But things are otherwise. Perfection (provided it is such, given that we have no terms of comparison) is explained by the availability of endless time and material. This same availability, on the other hand, accounts for evil, since we have by no means reached the end of the process. Strictly speaking, it also accounts for God, but puts him at the end of evolution: God is not yet, and hopefully was not at the beginning, since otherwise he would be responsible for far too much. And it is not excluded that, as with amoebas and Tyrolean choirs, the pyramid of Cheops and VAT, Klee and garden gnomes, the day will come, maybe in a million years, when a highly evolved colony of termites will come across a god.

> As if some You would truly come again
> to judge the living and the dead.
> And how many tears and semen shed in vain.[21]

1.2 Metaphysics

Let's ask ourselves the following: what do the following disciplines, with their respective functions, have in common?

Ontology, recording, matter
Technology, iteration, mechanism
Epistemology, alteration, memory
Teleology, interruption, organism

The answer is: Metaphysics, hysteresis, *transcendit omne genus*.[22]

Metaphysics is not something 'beyond' (unless we mean the location of Aristotle's notes on the subject, which Andronicus of Rhodes placed after the books on physics); it is something that is very much right here, and whose effects we experience at every moment. In this sense, hysteresis is the fundamental metaphysical function. I speak of 'metaphysics' because we are dealing not with something that simply transcends physics, but rather with something that is transversal to the physical and symbolic dimensions, in agreement with the principle that (physical) matter is the basis of repetition and (psychic) memory is the basis of remembrance, where both functions manifest themselves as forms of hysteresis, the survival of the effect after the cause is no longer. This parallelism between the physical and the psychic, as well as between the organic and the mechanic – both governed by hysteresis and the resulting emergence – provides a unitary description of both the natural world and the human world (technical and cultural), or, if you prefer, of the macrocosm and the microcosm.

What is the necessary and sufficient condition for everything to take place? The answer is, after all, a generalisation of the constitutive law of social objects. It is necessary to keep track of events even after their causes are gone, and to produce a circle in which the sedimentation of the past produces new objects, which develop intentions, which in turn sediment into other objects, and so on – in a process that is indefinite but not infinite, since in the end entropy will prevail.

Conceptualising the metaphysical dimension of hysteresis means understanding that what appears as an ontological differentiation is in fact a temporal deferral, one that derives from the survival of a trace after the cause that produced it has disappeared. First of all, we have a recording that is generalised. This recording presides over the three decisive phenomena: iteration, alteration and interruption. By removing the event from its immediate dependence on production, recording is defined as a possibility of indefinite iteration; alteration is the circumstance whereby what is recorded is removed from matter and preserved as a form; however indefinite, iteration is not infinite, and therefore has an internal temporality that plays a decisive role in the social world – hence the inevitable interruption.

Transcategorial. Traditionally, 'metaphysics' and 'transcendental' are taken to be equivalent: metaphysics is what *transcendit omne genus*.[23] That is why the scholastic transcendentals were being, unity and goodness – because they are characters that pertain to everything that exists. According to what I said about 'metaphysics', to define the notion of 'hysteresis' the latter must be considered the common root and condition of possibility of all that is. Metaphysics is the transcategorial, and is represented today by the Web, just as previously it assumed other images, from *Chora* to the System. In general, we are dealing with a great medium that preserves traces and that allows for both genesis (something originates and develops) and structure (what has developed takes a form, relates to other developments, and in a long or short time can give rise to meaning).

When Kant defines the supreme principle of the intellect as the ability of phenomena to re-enter the synthetic unity of apperception, he is referring to the fact that knowledge requires hysteresis. The synthetic unity of apperception expresses a need of the subject: it is necessary that knowledge be recorded by an I-think so that it can give rise to a coherent experience, with a before, an after and the effects of permanence, succession and causality. For my part, I believe that this need of the subject is only the manifestation of a more fundamental need of the universe itself. With respect to this cornerstone of ancient and modern epistemology, I just have to add that hysteresis is not only about gnoseology, but affects all areas of metaphysics. Hysteresis is the transcategorial: the transcendental in the classical sense, the metaphysical structure that, being transversal, undermines the traditional distinctions between *physis* and *nomos*, *physis* and *techne*, and between natural and artificial in general. We are generally willing to see memory as a precondition of knowledge, but we are much more reluctant to admit that what is represented in the mind as memory is only one of the functions of hysteresis which, as such, is not limited to the sphere of epistemology, but invests ontology, technology and teleology.

First of all, in ontology, hysteresis manifests itself as simple recording, as the deposition of something (the more effective the more technically equipped it is: think of writing, which goes beyond the limits of individual memory, transient and localised in a body) which allows the archive to form. Then, in technology, it appears as iteration, allowing what took place once to repeat itself indefinitely, resulting in the creation of mechanisms such as credit, normativity, energy storage, technical enhancement and traditionalisation. Therefore, in epistemology, as an alteration, the process initiated by recording and enhanced by iterability allows for emergence, the coming to light of new formations (be they the growth of capital, culture or consciousness). Finally, in teleology, the disappearance of iteration and alteration as interruption gives a sense (a direction, which comes from entropy) to the whole process of hysteresis.

Hysteresis, then, is a metaphysical principle older and more radical than being itself, which is already a result of hysteresis. It is transversal with respect to the Web, the Mind, Society and Nature, just as it is transversal with respect to Ontology, Technology, Epistemology and Teleology. Therefore, it is metaphysical in the sense of the transcategorial: it is what transcends all genera, including that of being, since it is prior to being itself. It is the recording that constitutes the condition of possibility of being and becoming. In other words, it is the 'common root' that, however, does not unite sensibility and intellect, but being, nothingness and becoming.

Secondness. In this framework, technology embodies the fundamental principle of hysteresis and turns out to be a 'first philosophy', to the extent that it is in fact a 'second philosophy', a philosophy that examines the medium between being (ontology, 'firstness' to borrow Peirce's term) and knowledge (epistemology or 'thirdness', again in Peirce).[24] Going beyond the traditional distinctions between nature and culture, form and content, perception and concept, this philosophy of secondness will be called upon to resolve (with a revival and renewal of dialectics, brought back to its authentically synthetic dimension that is resolved in a tertiary scheme) the traditional impasses of reflection on the relationships between ontology and epistemology, determined by a binary Ontology/Epistemology scheme.

The interesting aspect of technology is precisely that it is a medium, a link, which on the one hand enables contact and action in the ontological sphere, and on the other allows, in certain cases, for competence to be transformed into understanding, thereby accessing the epistemological dimension. These circumstances are not surprising. What has been named in so many ways – schematism, transcendental imagination, dialectic or *différance*[25] – is a technological disposition that manifests itself in the most elementary apparatuses and then evolves into formations of increasing complexity, like a reproductive faculty that transports ontology into epistemology. Reciprocally, technology has to do not only with the remote origins of humanity, but also with the highest intellectual achievements: it is involved in mathematics and logic, in the creation of scientific experiments and artistic works, and in the actions and rituals that accompany our social life.

The real fundamental junction on which inscription and alteration depend is iterability. If there were no iterability (Technology) we would have neither being (Ontology, what there is first of all because it has a very limited duration, and that therefore presupposes a recording), nor knowledge (Epistemology), which even more obviously requires memory, inscription, documents, language – a whole apparatus that could not exist without recording. Finally, we would not have meaning and purpose, which belong to us as organisms (Teleology). So, the first product of hysteresis is ontology. In fact, among its many results, hysteresis created the genetic code. And variations in the genetic code, i.e. variations in the recording, produced organisms, among other things, and among them humans, over a very long expanse of time made possible again by hysteresis (without which, I repeat, the universe would disappear in an instant). The latter produced knowledge, again over a very long expanse of time, which then returned to ontology and began to say things like 'here is a dinosaur, here is a gluon'.

Synthesis. We have thus found a way to place recording before being and thought, and at the same time to respond to the obvious objection that can be made against positive philosophy (and in general against any realism that posits a being free from the action of conceptual schemes): how can you think of being without thought? At this point, one has to understand that technology as dialectics and dialectics as technology are not the common root of ontology and epistemology – as suggested by Kant, asserted by transcendental idealism and repeated by Heidegger. Rather, they are the means (reproductive rather than productive) that allows for the transition from ontology to epistemology. In this sense, technology is completely compatible with a positive philosophy, and it becomes an instrument not of alienation or creation, but of revelation and emergence.

The fundamental character of the inscription lies in the fact that the punctual here and now, once recorded, assumes a different existence. If the proper character of physical reality consists in spatial-temporal localisation, hysteresis allows for an indefinite iteration which is the proper character of ideality. The intermediate term, metaxy, is a metaphysical function that resolves the passage from being to non-being and proposes a triad of being/nothingness/recording. The matter of which the Web is made, in its characteristic function, is therefore memory; to understand this, again, we can refer to both ancient and modern cosmologies.

Everything starts with recording: before analysis there is always synthesis, union, totality. And let us not forget that synthesis is not only what was there before, but also what increases our knowledge: there is little pleasure in knowing (analytically) that no bachelor is married, but one can find much more pleasure (synthetically) in knowing that a certain bachelor is a good friend of Emma Bovary's. This could even give birth to a novel, something that wasn't there before, something that doesn't describe what is given, but creates a new object. But what does this synthesis consist of? As I said above, it is something that encompasses ontology and epistemology, in accordance with the vision of nature as unconscious spirit and of spirit as nature brought to consciousness. Therefore, it has nothing to do with the already analysed nature, understood and reduced by the natural sciences. It is not something objectified, but rather a process, an emergence, which has a dynamic characteristic. For lack of a better expression, let us say that it is a productive force: which, after all, is how Aristotle's *physis* is currently interpreted (just think of Heidegger).

Deduction. This is particularly evident in the so-called 'A Deduction', the one we find in the first edition of the *Critique of Pure Reason*. Here Kant argues that for an object to be known it must be perceived ('synthesis of apprehension'), contained in memory or, as Kant says, in the imagination ('synthesis of reproduction'), and finally conceptualised ('synthesis of recognition'). In his presentation, this is an epistemological argument that isolates the minimal criteria of an experience. But as we know, Kant also – and above all – had an ontological objective, which manifests itself in two ways. The first is through the constructive action of schemes. These are forms of the imagination (i.e., as we shall see, of recording) that define substance as the permanence of something in time and cause as the succession of something in time. The second is through the function of the I-think: the receptacle in which experience manifests itself and which is made of time as the form of the internal sense and of space as the form of external sense. The latter appears as the direct heir of the Platonic *chora*, as it contains everything without having any form.

There is one circumstance still worth looking at, since it is crucial. The operations that Kant speaks of are a priori syntheses.

Synthesis unifies two elements; it is not possible without the primary recording. This is already the case with the 'synopsis of meaning' mentioned by Kant.[26] As he rightly noted, every analysis presupposes a synthesis, since to divide one must first have unified. And synthesis is a gesture, just like those synthetic a priori judgments that Kant exemplifies through mathematics (which in its complex forms requires a tertiary recording, but in its elementary forms requires a secondary recording, e.g. the simple mechanical fact of the mnemonic learning of multiplication tables).

Kant wonders how it is possible to extend this process outside mathematics (which for him is not true knowledge), and deploys the whole complex device of transcendental philosophy. But the real keystone is hidden in a place that Kant had not foreseen or even understood: a priori synthetic judgments are not found at the beginning of the process, in the table of judgments that, for Kant, precede the categories. Instead, it is necessary to look for them further down. They are in the schemes, in those methods of construction that for Kant mediate between concepts and objects, but which in fact, if what I've said so far is true, produce concepts by constructing objects.

1.3 Matter and Memory

Hysteresis, as the transcategorial, is the metaphysical function par excellence. More exactly, what has hitherto been called 'metaphysics' can more correctly be recognised as hysteresis. In order to understand the transcategoriality (and therefore the metaphysical character) of hysteresis it will be sufficient to keep in mind the link between matter and memory: the past is remembered by memory precisely to the extent that it is repeated by matter. And the fact that it is repeated by matter, which keeps track of its previous states, is the basis of the fact that it is remembered by memory, which is never without matter.

The past is indeed recalled by memory, as proven by ordinary experience, and it is also repeated by matter, as testified by all the matter that surrounds us. It is the archive of things past: craters reminiscent of distant explosions, mountains preserving shells dating back to when they were at the bottom of now vanished seas – or more prosaically the cracks on our phone screens and the scars on our bodies, tracking our falls (and those of our devices) with relentless accuracy. Therefore, at the origin of two apparently opposing series we have only one principle, that of hysteresis, which is the condition of possibility of those two forms of repetition that are matter and memory.

Hysteresis, the ability to preserve the effect in the absence of the cause that produced it, is the metaphysical origin of both nature (the past is repeated by matter) and culture (the past is remembered by memory). From this single principle one can draw all the performances that explain the fundamental character of the human being and the world. This circumstance establishes an identity between memory and repetition, as well as between spirit and matter. There is no memory without matter, because memory always requires a physical medium on which to deposit itself. But more radically and decisively, there is no matter without memory, because matter, being persistent in time, requires a recording that defines it as matter.

The past is repeated by matter. Recording is not only in the interiority of the mind; it is not only in the exteriority of the social world: it is also in nature and its objects. Something happens – a summer storm, a fire in the woods, a meteorite crashing on the Moon – and matter remembers it in the form of moisture, ash or a crater, thus starting the process whose ultimate outcome, through other forms of recording, is not only the social world, but the mental universe itself. In fact, thought never takes place without the support of a body, which is not limited to the brain, but is made of skin, senses, hands, feet, pens and notepads. The fact that the past is repeated by matter is even more important than the fact that it is recalled by memory, because without matter and its ability to record there would be no memory and no ability to remember. The ancients did not just see Mnemosyne as the divine mother of all the Muses; they also represented her with the very concrete image of a tabula, the wax tablet used to take notes, which is the ancestor of the iPad.

I have nothing to add to the long tradition of emergentism except that emergence is hysteresis. The Big Bang, thus, is actually a Big Bounce, a return to itself, a recording and an iteration, otherwise matter would always be dissolving, disappearing and starting over again. Without going so far as to hypothesise, as in a famous scam, the 'memory of water' capable of remembering every matter or liquid with which it has come into contact, the fact remains that matter remembers itself, i.e. it persists in being what it is, unless changes occur from the outside. This applies to water as well as to every other component of matter. Hysteresis – keeping track, passive synthesis, the remembrance of memory and the repetition of matter – determines the emergence or birth of something new: the universe, life, society, meaning, intentionality, and all the individuals who furnish our world.

Gluons. 10^{-6} seconds after the Big Bang, quarks joined in threes to form protons and neutrons. It is at this point that the building blocks of the universe appeared. The only prerequisite for this to happen was recording. Physicists believe that one of the elementary particles that make up matter is the gluon, from the English word glue, whose function is to hold the other particles together with an action closely related to memory, i.e. keeping track of a state. The gluons referred to by contemporary physicists are the equivalent of Kant's *Lichtstoff*, the ether, i.e. the medium that he was still looking for in *Opus postumum*, in an attempt to give it a name that was not simply that of a faculty of the human mind, in order to avoid the subjective drift that this entailed.

This is what other physical conjectures call 'strong entropy': the glue of a universe made up of individuals different from each other, if only in terms of location. These individuals are intimately historical, because the fabric of which they are made is spacetime. Remember what Proust says in the final pages of *In Search of Lost Time*?[27] The guests in the Guermantes' living room are magnified, as it were, because the small space they occupy in the room must be integrated by the enormous lifetime embedded in them, which turns them into giants walking on the stilts of years past.

The Big Bounce and gluons make up a new mythical image that adds to many others, all characterised by the presence of recording. All the mythical figures about the origin of the universe through retention (a recording) appeared as dreams or images, but the Web has revealed them and placed them before our eyes. The Web has brought out a great metaphysical dream: the idea of the receptacle of all things, of the foundation – neither material nor immaterial, as it constitutes a 'third genus' – based on which the demiurge draws the world. Between Plato's *chora* and the Web as an archive, and as the indefinite possibility of recording, there is a basic continuity in which the latter sheds light on the former.

From gluons to hard disks. Eddington's two tables[28] – the table of common sense and the table of science, the first with a weight, a colour, a shape, the second with atomic particles slightly denser than the surrounding air – turn out to be the same table from the point of view of hysteresis, which accounts at the same time for the phenomenological characteristics and for what we know, but do not see or directly experience, of the tables of everyday life.

By defining being as permanence I am referring to a macroscopic characteristic linked to our experience. Being is something that exists independently of us, that was there before us and will be there after us, and that resists or supports our manipulations. Philosophy has often endeavoured to conceive the condition of the possibility of being – therefore, being as such as opposed to the being of entities, to borrow Heidegger's expression. In other words, it has endeavoured to imagine, again in Heidegger's terms, the ontological difference.[29] What this notion entails (i.e. the definition of a transcendental, of a transcategorial defining being beyond the phenomenological experience we have of it) is perfectly captured by the notion of hysteresis, because it accounts both for the permanence of being and for its performances (iterating, altering, and of course interrupting and failing, as nothingness), and is fully in line with the physical conjecture about the Big Bang and the Big Bounce.

In current technological terms, hysteresis is represented by the hard disk of a computer, which can be conceived as a device whose fundamental function is to keep track of its previous states: apparently the hard disk exerts a merely passive function, but in fact this systematic keeping-track generates a totality that transforms processes into objects. In ontological terms, hysteresis is the dependence of a system's state on its history, and therefore first of all on the recording that made something like a history possible in the first place. In this sense, hysteresis is a metaphysical (i.e. absolute, as it is both empirical and transcendental) principle, the pure possibility of recording.

At this point it is not surprising that when a technological apparatus capable of maximising the effects of hysteresis was invented, humankind turned its eyes away from the conquest of space (which supposedly was its main objective towards the middle of the twentieth century) in order to capitalise on the profits of the conquest of time, i.e. the advantages of being able to keep track of an enormous number of events that previously disappeared like tears in the rain. The boom of hysteresis – that is, the circumstance that every natural or social event, every behaviour, even the smallest, can be recorded automatically and at a very low cost – has completely changed the world in which we live, revolutionising the very nature of production that characterised the industrial world.

This is not only a quantitative extension of hysteresis, but also an immanent qualitative change from analog to digital. Instead of thinking that hysteresis follows information – misled by the traditional view of writing as the hysteresis of oral expression – we should acknowledge that hysteresis precedes and makes communication possible, since the message has to be recorded before it can be transmitted and unpacked. If prior to the Web and the technologies that made it possible information was the norm and hysteresis the exception, in the sense that it might not even take place, now, for there to be information, hysteresis is necessary. In the analog world hysteresis was both at the beginning (to communicate you need a code, and code requires hysteresis) and at the end of the process (communication is ineffective without memory, and in particular, in the case of performance, without memory you cannot produce social objects). In the digital world, which in this sense reveals the hidden essence of the analog one, hysteresis is the condition of the technical possibility of communication, which occurs through packets of recorded information that are recomposed to generate communication.

The past is remembered by memory. Memory is the technological element of the spirit, that which recalls the past with the same automatic force as any external reminder: this is why, though we hesitate to talk about the spirit of a mobile phone, it seems quite normal to talk about its memory. The role of memory in perception and reasoning is obvious: without retention one would not have the fixation of perception, and hence the subsequent functions of imagination and thought. Moving on to an ontological level, memory is a central element of personal identity.

However, even those who have raised well-founded objections to the hypothesis that all personal identity can be traced back to individual memory have had to resort to a form of retention: the body and its continuity through time. Not to mention the immense form of memory preservation that is offered by the sphere of documents and technical recordings. Memory is not necessarily the property of a living subject: it can be found in an ATM or on a tombstone. One should not be fooled by the transcendental illusion according to which a cat's or a professor's memory comes with some spiritual supplement, a magical property that would be missing in the professor's iPad (which in fact remembers things better than both the cat and the professor).

The boom of hysteresis in the Web manifests the nature and structure of a process that in itself goes beyond conservation and revolution, presenting itself as the deep nature of both the natural and the social world. The technological revolution therefore calls for a conceptual revolution, but this is precisely where the problem lies. As implicit memory or declarative memory, as external and technological memory, then as a dialectical device of passage from being to non-being, and finally as the spatial-temporal foundation of the universe, hysteresis constitutes the real power that bridges the gap between nature and spirit, and provides the fundamental structure not only of subjectivity or capital, but of the universe.

Mneme, anamnesis, hypomnesis. Mneme belongs to the sphere of ordinary experience. It is a primary retention (a fixated sensation), which most of the time does not find conscious expression, but rather takes shape as implicit memory. What seems particularly interesting, from my point of view, is the process by which this implicit fixation can become explicit, conscious, declarative, and therefore eventually give life to the superior functions of intelligence and meaning. As we shall see, this is what happens in anamnesis.

All that is iterable can be recalled in memory (with an anamnestic function) or in the imagination: it is such a strong power that Kant and the idealists conceived it as a transcendental or productive imagination. However, it is obvious that at this level it is rather a reproductive imagination, which appears to be productive because it can count on the capitalisation offered by memory. Aristotle rightly distinguished between mneme and anamnesis, thus indicating the two distinct functions of recording and searching for what has been recorded.[30] This second function, which is active (as opposed to the first, which is passive), is precisely the sphere of secondary recording, which enables operations such as the transmission of technical skills, language, anticipation of the future, and oral culture. Secondary recording is thus the condition of possibility of construction, imagination and social objects.

The Web is the hyperbole of tertiary retention, a squared retention that finds no other limit than the availability of electricity. The inventor of gunpowder was primarily thinking of fireworks, the inventor of the telephone was trying to build a radio, while the inventor of the radio wanted to make a telephone; likewise, those who designed the first personal computers did not in any way foresee that they would transform the life of humankind, and those who made texting possible on mobile phones would never have thought that most telephone traffic would one day occur in writing.

Distinguished from mechanisms because they are organisms, humans have always been oriented towards technology, and the latter finds its best expression in hypomnestic iteration. It is the strengthening of secondary retention that makes it possible to overcome the spatial-temporal finitude of the subject of experience. Technology can take place in humans and in general in organisms (think of the improvement of performance through an iteration called 'exercise'). But the characteristic of hypomnesis is that, in addition to organisms, it can and in principle must simply take place in mechanisms: not on the skin like primary recording, and not in the brain like secondary recording, but, for example, on a piece of paper (i.e. the main example of hypomnestic tertiary recording offered by Plato).

With mechanisms we have the beginning of the spirit as liberation from the here and now of perception and from the spatial-temporal limitedness of secondary recording. The social world seems constructed in comparison to the natural world. In reality, it is only a more dynamic case of emergence: nature typically takes a very long time, whereas society is much faster, also because it follows a Lamarckian and not a Darwinian selection, i.e. it does not proceed by chance, but with a degree of planning. In turn, however, external technology is much faster than humans, which on the one hand explains archaisms (characteristics that have proved successful in a certain generation, but that two generations later can prove catastrophic), but on the other hand makes it clear why technical expertise is always ahead of understanding.

Just like computer memories and the massive archive of the Web, neurons do not 'think', but 'download'. It is only the complication of technology over a very long time that generates abstraction: the premise of reflexive meaning. With hypomnestic hysteresis, which takes place outside the mind, a decisive step is taken by humanity – a step perhaps even more important than the imagination, because one wonders whether the latter would ever have arisen at all in the absence of tertiary retentions, or rather whether the development of anamnesis and hypomnesis did not follow a parallel path.

Hypomnestic hysteresis[31] explains the resources of planning, which is the secret of military effectiveness, but more extensively is the foundation of social action, as demonstrated by the importance of bureaucracy in the formation and management of power. The fact that today we have algorithmic governance, and that decisions on the stock exchange are taken by computers, is only one of the infinite examples of the primacy of documentality over intentionality. In the current representation, bureaucrats should simply implement provisions decided elsewhere.

In fact, owning the means of recording is a power in the same way as owning the means of production, and it allows bureaucracy to bypass or anticipate the areas (be they politics or law) to which it is formally subordinated. The spirit of the laws, in other words, finds its concrete application in the letter of bureaucracy. To resume the Kantian analogy, we are dealing here with the synthesis of recognition in concepts. However, solving a long-standing problem of Kant's, this also explains how the concepts were formed; namely, through a three-phase technology in which the inscription provides the matter, iterability provides the form, i.e. idealisation, and alteration consists in the system of differences between the iterated and idealised traces.

It is no longer necessary to wait for the event to repeat itself. It can be recalled artificially and iterated indefinitely. This is the liberation from nature and necessity that takes place in nature itself (hysteresis takes place in nature and is part of nature). Hysteresis fixates interactions and generates potential meanings: a singularity that has taken place, a here and now that leaves a trace. History records the interactions between individuals that perhaps, over a very long time, will lead to society. This initially sediments itself in the rituals and external media necessary for the fixation of memory in a society without writing. However, some form of hysteresis then emerges very early on and does not merely capture the past, but also acts as a structure for the future: documents coordinate actions and take on a prescriptive role.

1.4. The Common Root

Hysteresis and technology. It is no coincidence that the revelation of hysteresis has found its most obvious manifestation in technology. Technology is a medium, something that stands between two terms and produces the two terms between which it mediates. This often appears as something obscure, as an idealistic hyperbole or as a form of constructivism, almost as if the medium were the Cogito that builds the world. But if, for example, we reflect on the 'plural medium' that plays such a large part in our lives, it is very simple: the media are something technological that comes after individuals (ontology) and defines them through interpretation (epistemology) that retrospectively comes to define them as objects. It doesn't create them, mind you – post-truth will never be truth. It shapes them, gives them a form, just like the metaxy or *Ur-teil* which is the copula that gives shape to judgments: S (a certain subject: ontology) is (copula, medium, third, etc.: technology) P (a certain predicate: epistemology).

Let's keep this point in mind: the copula is not ontology (it doesn't give being to things), it is technology. One of the crucial contributions of twentieth-century philosophy has been the performative theory, i.e. the idea that some acts – endowed, let's not forget, with an illocutionary force – produce objects, and therefore have a synthetic value, creating something that wasn't there before (a husband and wife, for example). When we sign a document of acceptance, or when we say 'I do' at our wedding, we are not describing something that is already there, but building something that begins to exist at that precise moment. Let me give a few examples to clarify what I mean.

First example: The mediation of the Holy Spirit. The difficulty of any theology in explaining what it is about lies precisely in the fact that the Spirit is not, properly speaking, because it has no ontological dimension, nor do we know what it is, because it does not have an epistemological dimension – it is a doing. Montesquieu's *The Spirit of the Laws* is after all an objective spirit, which precedes the idealistic spirit, and informs it of itself by virtue of the thesis that the spirit is historical unfolding, in accordance with the Christian view of revelation. This technical element of the spirit is clearly visible in the religions of the spirit, that is, in the universal religions, which are universalised through books, i.e. through the work of the letter. In this sense the letter, the opposite of the spirit, is but a different or deferred spirit, which is another way of saying that the letter is the condition of possibility of the spirit, and not the inverse, as one may think based on Pentecostal conceptions.

Second example: As an intermediate zone between being (which is neutralised through the *epoché*) and knowledge, phenomenology also presents itself as a technology. Phenomenology is no more knowledge than mathematics is, and indeed it was conceived by a mathematician: neither refers to being. But both, if referred to ontology, can either give rise to an epistemology, or function independently of knowledge (hence the unreasonable effectiveness of mathematics).

Third example: All the rhetoric about bottomlessness or the bottomless bottom, typical of German idealism, must be understood as the ontological hypostatisation of a technological movement. This movement is openly present in Fichte,[32] with the technological call to *Tun*, i.e. to action as the original position. However, for him, according to the norm of transcendental fallacy, action is ontologised and epistemologised, while it is simply a transition between a being that is not set, but precedes, and a knowledge that is not necessarily conquered. It is in Schelling[33] that the position of the *Abgrund* takes on an obvious mystical and ontological dimension. It is the retroflexion in the origin of a procedural element, technology as iterability, which permits the transition from nature as unconscious spirit (ontology) to spirit as conscious nature (epistemology). In Hegel[34] the being/nothing/becoming dialectic is an imprecise prefiguration of the dialectic of ontology (being)/technology (becoming)/epistemology (the nothingness of being, as it is a reference to being). From this point of view, it is interesting to note Trendelenburg's proposal,[35] which outlines a succession of becoming/being/nothing. By placing the technical movement at the beginning, it serves as the prelude to an actualistic reformulation of idealism, which – by neglecting the dimension of technology, radicalising the confusion between ontology and epistemology, and replacing recording with the implausible notion of 'spirit' – was a wild goose chase, to use an expression taken from the sphere of action.

Fourth and last example: Dialectical mediation is technological, and the negative pole plays the same role as it does in a dynamo. The negative is only a functional part of the movement, i.e. it is precisely non-being (and not a real contradiction) that activates the dialectic. This is what Marx failed to understand when he claimed that the contradictions of capitalism would generate communism.[36] Instead, as we are seeing, it is the development of capitalism that produces communism, and the contradiction is only a negative functional to development and movement. It is in this sense that technology functions not as alienation (which would be the negative as a real contradiction), but as revelation (the movement that allows for the development and the manifestation of potential, for better or for worse).

The common root. Hysteresis is a general trend in society, technology and nature. It is therefore the fundamental metaphysical principle, in the sense in which Kant speaks of the first metaphysical principles of natural science. What deserves consideration is that here the metaphysical function is assumed by a principle that does not belong to thought and is intrinsically dynamic. The fundamental meaning of hysteresis is that the notions that make up the furniture of the world, both ontologically and epistemologically (existence, purpose, causality, truth, action . . .), derive from the ontological dependence between matter and memory.

Schopenhauer[37] stated that he could give up all of the Kantian categories except causality. I say that I can give up all the structures of the Kantian transcendental except hysteresis, to which Kant himself refers when he speaks of the syntheses necessary for the constitution of experience and when he describes the imagination (a form of recording) as the common root of sensibility and intellect.

First of all, there is a possibility of repetition that comes from recording. What is recorded can be repeated, and its simple existence is a repetition over time of the being of the universe, which considers objects as occupying not only three dimensions in space, but also a fourth dimension consisting of their temporal persistence. The 'common root' of sensibility and intellect, which Kant and Heidegger sought in the transcendental imagination, thanks to the amplification of the phenomenon generated by the technical increase in recording, can now be recognised in hysteresis. Contrary to the transcendental imagination, this is no longer a faculty of the soul, but a function that lies at the basis of being in general – both spiritual and material – as well as of nature and technology, and which manifests itself with particular evidence in the technological boom of hysteresis determined by the Web.

Plato identifies the χώρα with various metaphors, including, of course, that of writing. These metaphors converge in designating the χώρα as pure recording, an invisible and amorphous medium (just like space) capable of keeping track of everything (an absolute recording). Here it is important to note the fundamental difference between the χώρα and the αρχαί of the Presocratics or the numbers of the Pythagoreans. The αρχαί were in fact physical principles (water, for example, as the principle of all things), or purely intellectual ones, like numbers, called upon to explain the harmony of the world. In contrast, the χώρα is a metaphysical principle (in my definition, an absolute one, since it is both empirical and transcendental), namely the possibility of recording as an absolute power.

From the χώρα, meanings may emerge, although not necessarily, through technologies that are summarised by Kant in §59 of the *Critique of Judgment*, and that are much more persuasive than the schematism of the *Critique of Pure Reason*: schemes, examples and symbols. These are not – as Kant thinks – the ways in which we give sensible form to pure concepts (schemes), empirical concepts (examples) or ideas of reason (symbols), but rather shortcuts by which we humans, who are not Watson the supercomputer, try to give order to multiplicity, or at least to cut out islands of meaning in an ocean of nonsense.

From reproduction to production. Philosophers have often come up against a challenge, namely, to answer the question: how is it possible that activity can emerge from passivity? In Aristotle's *On the Soul* the problem reads as follows: the soul is a passive, i.e. receptive function on which impressions are deposited; this also applies to the highest part of the soul, the intellect. However, since it is not permissible for the intellect to be pure passivity (I imagine because in this case freedom would be lost), Aristotle artificially divides the intellect into two parts: a passive, incarnate and individual intellect, and an active, imperturbable, immortal and universal one. At this point one may wonder where this activity comes from, and the only solution seems to be to embrace the hypothesis of a supernatural infusion from above. But Aristotle rejects it, so the question has no answer and the difficulty remains.

Kant, for his part, goes in search of a 'transcendental imagination' considered as the common root of sensibility and intellect, and characterises it as a 'productive imagination'. This productive imagination, which appears as the analogue of Aristotle's active intellect, is called upon to play a crucial role in Kant's theory of knowledge, because it is the function that provides the schemes through which the intellect refers to intuitions. Kant insists that this imagination is different from reproductive imagination, that is, from a form of memory that recombines images of things, and the reason for this insistence is clear: if the faculty that produces the schemes is reproductive imagination, then the *Critique of Pure*

Reason would become a critique of empirical reason – a theory of the association of ideas, an empirical doctrine in Locke's style that explains how general ideas are formed through the repetition of experience, and not, as is Kant's intention, a theory that explains how the pure intellect can determine experience through concepts and schemes that are foreign to it and precede it. However, all that Kant says to characterise this faculty which is so decisive for his system is that it is different from reproductive imagination, without providing further clarification.

Transcendental imagination. Hysteresis is a solution to the enigma of the transcendental imagination, a productive imagination that arises from the reproductive imagination. Just as passivity, once recorded, becomes a possibility of capitalisation and therefore activity, so imagination from retention becomes production, with a phenomenon that can now be explained precisely through hysteresis. The latter, based on the simple permanence of the effect after the disappearance of the cause (which, after all, has been the classic definition of the imagination since Aristotle), also guarantees technological enhancement (iteration), epistemological transformation (alteration) and teleological finalisation (interruption). Hysteresis can be considered as the common root not of sensibility and intellect (as Kant suggested with a perspective focused on human faculties, identifying this root in the transcendental imagination, and therefore referring to the inner world) but of the inner world (memory) and the outer world (matter).

The role of the imagination in the evolution of the human species has rightly been emphasised. What I would like to point out, however, is that this imagination is not an absolutely creative faculty, a wonder and a mystery laid deep in the human soul,[38] as Kant maintains when he speaks of the transcendental imagination. Indeed, Kant himself, who for structural reasons must hypothesise the independence of the productive or transcendental imagination from experience, is decidedly laconic about the nature of this surplus of creativity, and in fact (in agreement with what has been said so far) characterises the productivity of the imagination as a different or deferred reproductivity. The good question now is why simple reproduction can present itself as production, to the point that, with complete naivety, Kant confesses that the only difference between reproductive and productive imagination is that the latter is different from the former.[39] We can offer two interpretations of this statement. The first is ungenerous (though not necessarily unfair) and suggests that Kant has no serious argument for drawing a difference between productive and reproductive imagination. The second, which is more generous and which I would be willing to embrace in this context, is that between reproductive imagination and productive imagination there is a recording–iteration–alteration system dominated by hysteresis.

Thus, the transcendental imagination is the hysteresis that (in this case) is the process by which from the ox head, which was initially an individual, we came to its representation in the caves of Lascaux, then to the exemplary use of that representation, and finally to its stylisation (and overturning: the head is turned upwards, the horns downwards), whence the letter A you are reading at this moment. Ontology manifests itself in a haecceity: that hunt, that bison, that spear. From haecceity, however, a class can arise, according to the logic of exemplariness: that painted ox serves to find others, to recognise them when they are encountered, to organise the action. At this point we come to epistemology, to knowledge; but note well, we do so through the technical mechanism of iteration. There is no *prius* ('ultimate precedent') in thought, no absolute and separate element, no Pentecostal meaning that descends from the heavens or from the immateriality of a homunculus hidden in one's head. The intention (like the ensuing action) derives from the inscription. There is no intention, idea or spirit prior to expression and inscription. Finally, iteration is at the same time alteration: the ontological uniqueness of the individual is doubled, so that iteration (perfect or not) is also alteration.

1.5 Difference

Différance. From a theoretical point of view, the performance of hysteresis can be summarised in the concept of *différance* as elaborated by Derrida, which refers both to a temporal deferral of something (which therefore requires that it first be fixated and repeated) and to a qualitative differentiation (genetic mutation, linguistic variation . . .) which takes place during the deferral. There is no hiatus between the origins of life and the constructions of culture, or between the passivity of perception and the activity of the intellect (to use a Kantian expression). There is rather a continuity, which Derrida expressed with the difficult concept of *différance* with an a. To simplify: all that appears different (diverse) from an ontological point of view, be it life or death, day or night, activity or passivity, is actually deferred (postponed) from a chronological point of view: now I am alive, but my death is merely being deferred; now it is day, but day is only a deferred night; now I am proposing actively elaborated theses, but as the endnotes show, they are the fruit of passively learned notions. Ontological difference is chronological deferral. In these terms, we are dealing with a speculative thesis that is indebted to the Hegelian dialectic and at the same time with a common-sense consideration, the same that leads us to say that time will always tell and that, sooner or later, the truth will come to the surface.

That which is passive and inert persists and can (though not necessarily must) be altered. To illustrate this process I propose an architectural example: the pyramid. It would be naive to think that some Egyptian architect, to please a pharaoh eager for immortality, conceived the idea of a pyramid out of the blue. The way pyramids came to be, indicating the proximity between spirit and nature under the sign of technology, reminds us instead of the origin of termite mounds and the hexagonal cells of bees. Initially, the pharaoh was placed in a simple underground mortuary. However, since the goods collected in the chamber attracted thieves, the access was protected with a pile of stones, and these piles for obvious structural reasons resembled pyramids. Little by little the attention shifted from the underground chamber to the heap, just as the fetishist's attention shifts from the beloved's body to objects that recall it. Finally the pyramid, which became large, autonomous and recognisable, incorporated the chamber. And only at that moment did the functional building acquire a symbolic meaning – as the ascent of the soul towards the sky, as the ray of the Sun that projects itself onto the Earth, as the tower of Babel coming to confuse the tongues, and so on.

Emergence is the result of difference (deferral and differentiation). A medium preserves the trace of an action, i.e. it temporally defers its presence beyond the here and now of its production. And this deferral is also a differentiation, an entity qualitatively different from the original event (it refers to that event but is not that event). By preserving itself, it can associate itself with other traces and give life to new objects, more complex and qualitatively different, with a process of capitalisation. The birth of the universe, the origin of life, the origin of culture, that of industrial, financial or documedia capital, are from this point of view all expressions of a single principle: that of hysteresis. Even the emergence of meaning has a diachronic aspect. The vowel A alone doesn't mean anything. It means something only together with B and C, but this process of differentiation between arbitrary signs takes time, and therefore recording. Thus, one must imagine a three-term process, in which recording brings about diachrony, and the latter brings about emergence. It is in recording that the three processes of inscription, iteration and alteration lie that make emergence possible. Capital is only one of the many historical names assumed by the power of recording.

Philosophy, like ordinary life, has always felt the need to hypothesise an intermediate term between being and nothing that could justify the process of change, which is very evident but at the same time inexplicable in terms of a two-place Parmenidean ontology (being/not-being). This 'intermediate' element (which Plato defines as metaxy) was then variously recovered in the speculative philosophies of the modern age, generally in the form of 'becoming'. Hence, as we have seen, the being/nothing/becoming triad in Hegel's dialectic, as well as the becoming/being/nothing triad in Trendelenburg's reform of that dialectic, and again the notion of *différance* in Derrida. What these references to an intermediate term have in common is the fact that a temporal movement, be it Hegel's or Trendelenburg's becoming or Derrida's deferring, mediates between pure being and pure nothingness.

The explanation of what happens cannot be ideological, but requires a metaphysical analysis. What emerges is not the devil or human wickedness, but metaphysics. What has made the present possible? And, more exactly, what emerges from the present as its condition of possibility? What essence is revealed in history? Metaphysics is what is revealed through the revolution. It is an essence and a structure that manifests itself in history and in the contingency of the present. That is to say, it is what has also been called 'transcendental empiricism': from what is manifested (and therefore is the object of experience) one goes back to its condition of possibility (the transcendental). Derrida's proposal to read Heidegger's ontological difference as a chronological deferral, i.e. as a possibility of persistence that is more fundamental than the being itself (and that would therefore provide us with the definition of being that is not the being of the entity), lends itself to being translated and specified in terms of hysteresis. The latter, as the transcategorial, also invests aspects that are missing in the traditional (and insufficient) reduction of metaphysics to ontology and in the definition of being as presence. The possibility of deferring is a great metaphysical principle of nature and society. A leaves the trace A', which preserves itself in time and defers the event thereby producing something new (think, typically, of debt: I receive something, and I note down a commitment that binds me to a subsequent action in time).

Deferral and differentiation. That which in the philosophical tradition has been named in many ways – as schematism and transcendental imagination, but also as dialectic or *différance* – is actually hysteresis. What appears as an ontological differentiation is in fact a temporal deferral, one that derives from the survival of a trace after the cause that produced it has disappeared. Hysteresis is the transcategorial (the transcendental in the classical sense, the metaphysical structure, as I said before) which, being transversal, questions the traditional distinctions between *physis* and *nomos*, *physis* and *techne*, and in general between natural and artificial. Ontological difference is but a chronological deferral that finds its foundation in hysteresis.

The effect was passive and bound to the here and now of its production, but the trace is active (it exists independently of the cause) and is independent of the spatial-temporal circumstances of its production. The consequences of this independence and capitalisation – i.e. of this independence without removal – with respect to the original causality are as important as (but much less considered than) the consequences of causality, which has long been considered the only metaphysically relevant function in the understanding of the world. What is recorded is no longer an event, but a being, and as such it can be iterated (I can repeat it at will), altered (recording preserves a form without matter, an *eidos* without time) and interrupted (the repetition, though indefinite, is not infinite). On the simple basis of these four elements, metaphysical hysteresis is able to account for the essential characteristics of the event with which we measure ourselves, and at the same time for the general structures of reality that manifest themselves through history and technology.

Deferral is not only the possibility of guaranteeing the persistence of objects in space and time, but also the possibility of differentiation, i.e. of introducing elements of variation in repetition (think of the variation of species based on random mutations, made possible by an enormous temporal extension and an even greater availability of material). Every deferral implies a possibility of differentiation. A is different from A', just as it is different from B' (the trace of the event B). Different in origin, B' and A' have however the common characteristic of being traces, and of being combinable in ways that were not possible for the original events, giving rise to A'B', B'A', A'B'A', etc.

Beyond the causality principle. Hysteresis has the metaphysical property of transforming passivity into activity, events into objects, cases into law. When it is repeated, A is no longer just A, it is something different and more free: what is repeated is repeatable, and this changes everything, even from an ontological point of view. To understand this means to carry out a Copernican Revolution much more challenging than that proposed by Kant, who merely made knowledge depend on memory (and proposed a spurious collapse of ontology onto epistemology), while in the perspective that I defend, being and knowledge are the result of hysteresis. To understand the ontological importance of hysteresis it is enough to imagine a world without recordings, i.e. a world where causes had no effects.

The survival of an effect without a cause (whether this survival is long or short) involves a radical alteration. As mentioned, the consequences of this independence from original causality are just as important as (but much less considered than) the consequences of causality. Instead, it is in the sphere of alteration that the characteristic of epistemology, i.e. understanding, must be sought. Understanding means transforming passivity into activity, and causing a doubling that is epistemological and not ontological (knowing Rome or the universe does not mean doubling one or the other, but producing something ontologically modest and epistemologically very significant). Recording determines the birth of something new: the universe, life, society, meaning, intentionality and all the individuals that make up our world. This sublime (in a mathematical and ontological sense) overabundance of time and space is what has made the world possible, along with all sorts of unrest, nonsense and dissipation.

Hysteresis is thus a candidate to be the unifying principle of the event with a thousand names and faces with which we have been dealing in recent decades. And let's not forget that, if we look at the analyses of the mid-twentieth century that predicted the imminent disappearance of writing, this principle should never have appeared on the world stage. Instead, the ideological representation of a society in which writing would be replaced by warmer media, such as orality and images, has been contradicted by the technological reality of the boom of hysteresis, which does not descend from the heavens of ideas but rises up from the earth of concrete practices, and for this very reason constitutes a historical contingency that at the same time reveals a metaphysical structure that can now be read, just as the physical structure of the world can be read through mathematisation.

The original delay. It could be argued that hysteresis, as the permanence of an effect after its cause has disappeared, presupposes the notion of cause, as well as that of persistence and that of spacetime. How can a first principle be such if it presupposes other ones? I do not believe this is so. First of all, one can ask whether the presupposition is ontological or epistemological: undoubtedly, I need the notion of causality as well as the notion of persistence to define hysteresis, but this does not imply that cause and persistence pre-exist: it could be an instantaneous genesis (as in the hypothesis of the Big Bang and the *Chora*) or it could be a movement of expansion and contraction (as in the hypothesis of the Big Bounce and the *tzimtzum*).[40]

There's also a second line of defence. Suppose that there really were causation and persistence prior to hysteresis. What would they be? The persistence of an effect beyond the cause, i.e. hysteresis. Questions of this kind always sound like the question 'What did God do before creation?', or the subtle paradoxicality of the traditional definition of God as *causa sui* ('self-caused'). Except that if there is something that deserves to be defined as *causa sui* it is precisely hysteresis, which also has the advantage, compared to God, of being an observable and omnipresent phenomenon even in the most ordinary experience. Obviously, the fact that by adding hysteresis to an enormous amount of space and time one can obtain the world as it is and life as we know it does not exclude the possibility that everything could have taken a different course, giving rise to a very different world. The necessity of hysteresis in no way denies that its concrete effects are contingent.

The principle of sufficient reason. Something is there, it exists and persists, and by the mere fact of being there it produces effects in the present. If the present were to pass without leaving a trace (i.e. without becoming a past) we would have no reason to speak of 'existence' (which in any case entails persisting, even for an instant, and which increases its value in direct proportion to its duration). The sphere of recording is the sphere of ontology, because existence is first of all spatial-temporal permanence, therefore existence depends on recording much more than recording depends on existence.

We could take away any building block of the universe and any physical principle known to us, except hysteresis, and in time a natural and social world like the one in which we now live could still be produced. But if we took away hysteresis, nothing in this world up to the edge of the universe, just as nothing of what I am writing at this moment, could exist. The principle of sufficient reason of the universe as well as of the social world and of individual psychology therefore sounds like *nihil est sine hysteresis* (nothing exists without hysteresis, and nothingness is precisely the absence of hysteresis).

Both at the ontogenetic and at the phylogenetic level, both in matter and in memory, recording constitutes the transcendental of the process, which however is not simply an epistemological transcendental, but an ontological transcendental: a *ratio essendi* ('ground of existence') and not only *cognoscendi* ('of knowledge'). It is necessary for something to remain traceable so that this something can contribute to the process of hysteresis, otherwise it would be as if nothing had happened and we would always start all over again. Without the permanence, in matter or memory, of the previous states, which is guaranteed by the inscription of the trace, we would not have processes, but only a single unrelated event.

Hysteresis therefore has a retrospective value, as the constitution of what there is, and a prospective value as the determination of what we know. As far as its present action is concerned, it simply amounts to the presence of a trace: something happens, and the event leaves a trace, whether it is the modification of a surface, the fixation of an impression, a natural or artificial memory, or the production and permanence of a sensation in an organism. The metaphysically relevant aspect of this process lies in the fact that the event, if recorded, radically changes its nature. Initially transient, it becomes permanent: the effect is preserved even after the cause has gone, and what was matter (the physical components of the event) becomes form (the traces that preserve the memory of the event).

Reason and correlation. Here, too, the Web clarifies something that was there since the dawn of time: it is not necessary to rely on some principle of reason to find correlations. We are not witnessing the death of theory (meaningless expression), but simply the passage from the principle of reason to the principle of correlation. What is sought is correlation, not reason (*principium reddendae rationis*, 'principle of sufficient reason'). But according to a recurrent law of technology, the automaton reveals some essential characteristics of the soul. In the vast majority of our performances, what we call 'understanding' is but correlation. The real stake of the whole ongoing transformation is precisely this automation in the form of artificial intelligence, which is nothing other than the enhancement of the mechanical elements of natural intelligence. What we call 'artificial intelligence' can therefore be considered a process of capitalisation of the documents and acts present in the Web with productive and predictive purposes. All documents and acts are recorded and put in a series, and when the recording devices reach an unprecedented level of complexity it becomes possible to transform all the living labour into dead labour, doing away with the imperfections and uncertainties that arise from understanding, and above all entrusting the production to tireless automata.

The algorithm looks for correlations, and it is correlation that creates meaning, not the other way around. Just as there is no private language, so there is no private meaning. Thought does not remain after the world is taken away, as Frege believed (with an *epoché* that anticipated Husserl and was driven by the same intentions: to avoid the reduction of philosophy to psychology). An old Italian saying goes, 'keep praying, faith will follow' – similarly, one can say: 'keep recording, meaning will follow'. The genesis of meaning takes place only within the framework of a code. We must not forget that the principle of combination underlies the genesis of meaning, which does not precede expression (according to the perspective that I call 'Pentecostal': the meaning precedes the expression and descends from above). Rather – in agreement with the perspective that I call 'emergence' – meaning emerges from the combination of elements that, as such, make no sense. Meaning does not descend from above, but emerges from the interplay of differences and the recordings that make them possible.

Aristotle on machine learning. One possible objection goes like this: is it not risky to universalise the concept of 'hysteresis'? Is it not the same mistake as universalising difference or information? Can we really say that the recording of DNA is the same recording as a digital memory? Isn't it, rather, a juxtaposition that only applies by analogy? It is important to clarify this point, and to do so I would like to begin with an image used by Aristotle, which compares sensible experience to a fleeing army.[41] In the flow of experience, the sensations scatter around like a panicked army, until a soldier stops and reassures his companions, so that the phalanx can get back together. In the same way, the flight of sensations stops when a belief is formed. This then becomes knowledge when we are able to transmit to others the beliefs we (rightly or wrongly) take to be true and justified.

The Aristotelian image is interesting in many respects: it explains the gradual passage from feeling to thought; it suggests that, just as sensations are fixated, so categories are formed precisely through the interaction of experiences – through a 'rhapsodic' process that seems so reasonable yet which Kant disliked so much. Most of all, it compares a natural process (the fixation of sensation, but it could just as well be the way a stream digs ever-deeper furrows in the ground) to an intentional process – the soldier who stops, and the others who imitate him. Between the fixation of sensation and the soldier's decision there are many differences, but there is no real gap: no intervention of some magical property that differentiates the soldier's decision from the way in which the water, looking for its way down, turns right or left. Above all, it illustrates a process of hysteresis that goes beyond the sphere of knowledge, also affecting being, doing and aiming. Apart from the last, crucial aspect, the rest is a description of machine learning. But the purpose is reversed. While Aristotle is interested in the ascending path, the Web is about the descending one, i.e. the passage from understanding to simple actions that are reduced to recording.

Let us therefore proceed to an anatomy of hysteresis in its four phases: recording, which corresponds to ontology, to what there is; iteration, which corresponds to technology, to becoming, both in what we call 'nature' and in what we call 'society'; alteration, which corresponds to epistemology, that is, to the exclusively human specification of technology that corresponds to what we know or believe we know; and interruption, i.e. entropy, which, both in nature and in culture, gives hysteresis its direction and meaning.

2

Recording

As we have seen, recording takes the place of causality. There could be causality without recording, but it would be nothing. If there is something, it is because there is recording, which from the logical, ontological and chronological point of view precedes causality, and moreover spares us the absurdity of the theories of some *causa sui* ('cause of itself'). Recording is the ontological version of hysteresis, the principle of permanence of the substance as presence, resistance, existence. The realism I propose is not limited to believing in the existence of tables, chairs and anti-realist philosophers: as negative realism it recalls that reality resists thought; as positive realism it affirms that meaning comes from the world and its affordances; and as transcendental realism it affirms that the common root of resistance and affordance lies in recording. It is therefore necessary to start from here.

Being equals being recorded. If we follow the physical conjectures prevailing today – the Big Bang and its updated version, the Big Bounce – the origin of the universe presents itself as the weakening of an original recording. This original recording is the same currently found in black holes, which gave rise to space, time and spatial-temporal objects. These objects, after all, are characterised in ordinary experience as permanence and resistance, which find their condition of possibility in recording as the persistence of a state. From this point of view, being (i.e. the object of ontology) is the result of recording. Following an explosion, some very concentrated matter unfolded and became the world, which was a contingent fact. But in order for this contingency to emerge, transforming itself into the world, the explosion had to show not only the capacity to expand, but also the capacity to record, to keep track. At the beginning there was an explosion, at the end there will be thermal balance, and in the middle there is time, which tells the story of a growing tendency towards disorder and heat loss. But in each of these stages there is recording as the possibility of keeping track of the previous conditions, which, in the mesoscopic terms of our ordinary experience, defines the spatial-temporal characteristics of everyday objects (if the library behind me suddenly disappeared, I would have good reason to believe I was the victim of a hallucination, whether positive or negative).

2.1 Ontology

What is there? The answer is not 'everything'. There is what was there before me, exists independently of me, and will be there after me. That is why I myself exist: *ego cogito, ego sum* is the most dubious of principles (*est quod ego non cogito*). Reality is not an indeterminate noumenon: it has positive characteristics that are manifested through the fact that beings endowed with different perceptual apparatuses, as well as different interpretative schemes and conceptual schemes, or even devoid of perceptive apparatuses, concepts and interpretative schemes, can interact. For the negative philosophy of the Cartesian matrix (for which the world is nothing but a malleable dough that is shaped by conceptual schemes) it was a matter of denying all ontological consistency to the world so as to bring everything back to thought and knowledge, proceeding to reconstitute the world through epistemology. With positive realism, instead, it is possible to start from ontology to found an epistemology. The latter, when it enters the social world, can and must become constitutive (it is clear that the laws are made by human beings, not atoms), while it cannot be so in the natural world, as required by the negative philosophy that leads from Descartes to postmodernism.

Transcendental fallacy. There is a very strong tendency, and not only among philosophers, to identify ontology and epistemology, falling into the 'transcendental fallacy' I described in 'Observation'. This fallacy is a very natural confusion, something similar to what psychologists call the 'stimulus error', by which they mean the ease with which we replace an observation with an explanation. In other words, it is the ease with which, when we have our eyes closed, we reply 'nothing' or 'blackness' to the question 'what do you see?', when what we see are really phosphenes and flashes. This is not a description but a naive theory of vision: the eye is like a camera obscura, so when the shutter is closed there is nothing or total darkness.

In fact, if we reflect on the metaphysical implications of this fallacy, we realise that it involves a blind and perhaps unconscious faith in the existence of a spirit independent from matter, capable of producing representations and, through them, things. So, if the transcendental fallacy held, not only would Newton's laws have been untrue prior to their discovery (if existence and knowledge are the same thing, the lack of the subject Newton entails the lack of the object 'universal gravitation'), but the objects to which these laws refer would also have had a highly problematic existence. A very natural objection comes to mind: how can one demonstrate that the objects of knowledge exist independently of the subjects of knowledge? My answer is very simple: how can one demonstrate that the objects of knowledge do not exist independently of the subjects of knowledge? Indeed, we have endless evidence to the contrary, all based on the fact that being equals being recorded.

Existence. Ontology is the doctrine of being, of what is there regardless of what we know or believe. Its only condition of possibility, its principle of reason, is precisely hysteresis, permanence in time and space. Since permanence is the character of being, it is not surprising that the essential ontological function is recording, which keeps natural objects in existence and brings social objects into being. So let's start with some essential distinctions. Ontology, what there is, is different from epistemology, what we know or think we know. This difference entails that knowledge depends on being: something needs to exist for it to be known. Without knowledge there would still be lakes, mountains, epistemologists (understood as living beings) and odd numbers, but without being there would be no form of knowledge – knowledge is always knowledge of something, τι κατὰ τινος. This difference between being and knowledge (and the priority of the former over the latter) is a material a priori, stronger than any conceptual a priori. Indeed, if knowledge didn't refer to something other than and prior to itself, then words like 'subject', 'object', 'epistemology', 'ontology', 'knowledge' and 'reflection' would have no meaning – or, better, they would be inexplicable synonyms.

Reality and truth. Is there a link between reality and truth? I can imagine many cringing faces: 'You mean that truth and reality are the same thing?' Of course not. The truth is to reality what epistemology is to ontology: it is different from it and depends on it. The state of things (ontology) which a proposition refers to is true regardless of any proposition, formulation or knowledge: Brutus greeted Cassius the day before the Battle of Philippi (if indeed Brutus greeted Cassius) regardless of any testimony or knowledge we might have of it. Of course, truth and reality are both children of time, but in two different ways: the truth coming to light is the disclosure of something that was already there unbeknownst to us (discovery), while reality coming to light is part of the real that wasn't there before (emergence).

Individuals and objects. If ontology is made up of individuals, epistemology relates to objects (*objectum*: something placed in front of someone). They can be canonical individuals, i.e. individuals in the strict sense: this is the case with natural objects, which exist in space and time independently of knowing subjects, and with social objects, which also exist in space and time but depend on the knowing subjects. Indeed, social objects are generally but not particularly dependent on knowing subjects, as they do not depend on any one specific subject (a 10 euro note does not cease to be such if I personally ignore its value). However, objects can also be atypical individuals, as in the case of ideal objects, which exist outside of space and time independently of subjects, and therefore have a particular manner of existence. A fourth (and last) family of epistemological objects consists of artifacts, which are dependent on subjects as to their production (like social objects), but which (like natural objects) may continue to exist even in the absence of subjects.

Phenomena and noumena. As I have extensively argued elsewhere, the difference between objects and individuals should not be confused with the difference between the phenomena (things as they appear to us) and noumena (things as they are in themselves) of Kantian philosophy. On the one hand, the very fact that social objects constitutively depend on subjects suggests that they do not possess an 'in itself', so that their true being coincides with their appearance, thereby discarding the distinction between phenomenon and noumenon. On the other hand, the fact that, as we have seen, ideal objects are not individuals complicates the deceptive symmetry of the pairs phenomenon-object and noumenon-individual: the number 5 is certainly not the appearance of a more profound essence. Finally and above all, for what concerns natural objects and artifacts, we have demonstrations of the interaction (between themselves, and with natural objects and artifacts) between beings with different conceptual schemes and perceptual apparatuses. That this interaction can take place suggests that, hard though it may seem to imagine that a wasp and a human being may see a flower or a Wiener Schnitzel differently, this depends on the essential characteristics belonging to the flower or the Wiener Schnitzel, thanks to which the human and the wasp may engage in an uncertain battle to have the former and eat the latter.

Being and ought. There is one last crucial point, which will play a fundamental role in this book. Ethics also has a relationship of difference from, and dependence upon, ontology. On the one hand, it is obvious that ontology (being) is different from ethics (ought); on the other hand, however, ethics would be inconceivable without the world. Moral values are not heaven-sent: they emerge from the world – just think that the first value, the value of all values, is indeed reality as imposing itself and demanding attention. The claim of value is to be valid, and there's nothing better to represent this claim than the presence of something that one cannot get around, and that requires us to deal with it. So, ethics without ontology is not conceivable. Think of a world of values without facts. What kind of world would it be? And above all, would those values be such? I do not think so. This can be better understood with an ethical version of the thought experiment of brains in a vat. Imagine that a mad scientist has put some brains in a vat and is feeding them artificially. By means of electrical stimulation, these brains have the impression of living in a real world, but in fact what they feel is the result of simple electrical stimulations. Imagine that those stimulations depict situations that require moral stances: some snitch and some sacrifice themselves for freedom, some commit embezzlement and some perform acts of holiness. Can we really say that in those circumstances there are moral acts? In my opinion, we cannot: in the best-case scenario, these are imaginary acts, or thoughts, with a moral content – they are not themselves moral. Sentencing to prison a brain that has thought about stealing is just as unfair as sanctifying a brain that has thought about doing good deeds.

2.2 Resistance

The first character of being is resistance: physical objects resist transformation and cannot be changed by the power of thought alone (as constructivists assume); social objects, such as obligations and prohibitions, cannot be changed by simply varying our interests (as assumed by the Mafiosi, who, on the other hand, have to comply with much more inflexible laws than those they try to circumvent). If being could be amended with the pure power of thought, the notion of 'being' (as well as those of 'knowing', 'acting' and 'aiming') would make no sense. Resistance manifests itself first of all as persistence: being is persistence, permanence, capitalisation. This applies as much to the natural world – which as far as we know began precisely with the expansion of a recording that gave rise to spacetime – as to the social world, whose objects are the recordings of our social acts. The thesis of causality claims that everything is connected with everything: forget it, that's not the case.

Singularity. Individuals are external to each other, in a non-topological but rather functional way, as they are independent: a virus can be in my body, but it is an individual different from me because I cannot alter our interaction simply by altering my concept of causality (or my biological/medical/physical theories in general), just as I cannot alter the laws of physics or the capital of Luxembourg. This independence is manifested as unamendability: for what concerns the specific individuals called humans, this consists of the impossibility of correcting, with the sole power of conceptual schemes, other individuals – this table is and remains of this colour, regardless of my conceptual schemes, wishes or intentions. Finally, four-dimensionality refers to the fact that, by virtue of their unamendability, individuals do not only occupy three dimensions in space, but also entail a duration that makes them irrevocable: what happens to an individual – from the oxidation of cells that is responsible for aging up to Wellington's counterattack at Waterloo – is irreversible, and this is the essential character of history. Just like the guests at the Guermantes matinée, individuals carry time with them; they are four-dimensional, occupying three dimensions in space and one in time. Let's now have a closer look at the physiognomy of individuals.

Externality. The first character of individuals is that they are external to other individuals. By 'external' I also mean external to our conceptual schemes; that's why, as I was saying, externality is non-topological but functional independence. This externality is the basic requirement of ontology: there is no entity without externality; there is, at most, the part of an entity, which pertains not to ontology but to mereology (the theory of parts). As I said, when individuals are known they become objects, but this does not always happen – indeed, it is the exception rather than the rule. We are surrounded by separate existences over which we largely have no influence (and which, reciprocally and fortunately, largely have no influence over us).

This may seem like an obvious statement, but it actually contradicts the philosophical mainstream of the past two centuries: what has been defined as 'correlationism'.[42] Its fundamental assumption was the following: the necessary (but not sufficient) condition of the existence of X is its knowability by a subject. Correlationism is based on what has been called 'the worst argument in the world', which amounts to saying: if I eat an oyster, I am the one eating that oyster, therefore I am never eating an oyster in-itself, but always an oyster-for-me. This argument is taken to extremes by what we could call the 'fable of correlation', which was the most widespread commonplace in the philosophy of the past two centuries. It goes: 'there is no subject and no object, there is only their relation'. In other words, there is no such thing as the oyster-eater or the oyster on their plate, but only an impersonal 'oyster-eating'. Against all common sense, the practical impossibility of eating oysters as such has become the theoretical condition of possibility of knowing something, because (so the fable goes) if subjects were separated from objects they would not know anything. The sad character of this position is that no matter how great and wonderful the object, we will only ever deal with ourselves, in the best libraries as well as in the best restaurants.

It has been argued that correlationism cannot account for the existence of a reality that pre-exists the subject, but a correlationist could claim that God created us all just now with all our memories. However, if the correlationist were right, we would have as many mental worlds as there are subjects, and the passage from one mental world to the other would be inexplicable. *De facto*, correlationism posits a subject representing an object within it – this is the world described by Kant in the confutation of idealism, proving that, despite its realist intentions, Kant's is also a version of transcendental idealism (albeit a very sober one). The only consistent way to defend the thesis of the correlation between knowing subject and known object as the sole form of existence (*esse est concipi*, that is) is to embrace an idealism which sees matter as something that does not pre-exist the spirit, for it is clear that the relation takes place in the mind, not in the world.

Unamendability. The indefensibility of correlationist claims is due to the trivial experience that tables and chairs, the Sun and the stars, friends and relatives, traffic and the queue at the post office cannot be changed by my thought alone, although they supposedly only exist in relation to me. Obviously this is not the case, and the relation – when there is one – is much thinner than correlationists think. As you probably remember, I call this principle 'unamendability': if the world were truly the outcome of conceptual construction, it is unclear why objects should resist subjects as they do. Contrary to epistemology, which can always be corrected, ontology is unamendable, and a black swan will never turn white on the grounds of the proposition that all swans are white. I may or may not know that water is H_2O, but I will get wet anyway, and I won't be able to dry up solely through the thought that hydrogen and oxygen as such are not wet. Since the basis of externality is not spatial but rather functional, it is understandable why unamendability is a key concept, often misrepresented as a truism: that the world resists us might be obvious, but it still frustrates the dreams of visionaries and metaphysicians, and shows how the 'great outdoors' that some believe is so hard to find begins long before we cross our doorsteps – it is already there, in every minute obstacle that, as soon as we wake up, the world does not cease to set against our thoughts.

To exist is to resist. This is the basis of negative realism: there are objects in the world that exist independently of our thoughts, and we experience this best whenever these objects are resistant to our thoughts. The fact that, for example, thought is not able to amend perceptual illusions means that knowledge is unable to intervene on the level of being, and therefore that the latter is independent of the former. The underlying argument, here, does not consist in saying that the stick immersed in water is really bent because it appears bent, but rather in pointing out that, despite knowing that the stick immersed in water is not bent, we cannot help but see it as bent. Reality is the negative extreme of knowledge, because it is the inexplicable and the incorrigible, but it is also the positive extreme of being, because it is what is given, which exists and resists interpretation, and yet makes it true (when it is true) and false (when it is false), distinguishing truth and reality from imagination or wishful thinking. *Individuum est inemendabile* for the same reason that it *est ineffabile*: the individual cannot be fully penetrated by thought, it can never be reduced to transparency, and this is precisely the sense of the difference between existence and essence, or in my terms, between ontology and epistemology. In all its declinations, unamendability is an ontological character, not an epistemological one, and it defines the identity of individuals, which are not atoms or amorphous particles.

Here are some other characteristics of being. Regularity. If reality is the result of our conceptual schemes, how do we explain the regularity of the world? Why would humanity, usually so divided on everything, accept a culturally constructed harmony certified by science? How can we prove that regularity is, as Hume would argue, a human inclination and not a property of the world? Surprise. There are some things that do not live up to our expectations. They are much rarer than regularity. This too is a difficult element to justify in the absence of an outside world, however you want to qualify it. Opacity. A world dependent on our conceptual patterns not only fails to explain the existence of surprises, but also the opacity of our knowledge, the frustration of many of our experiences, the vanity and tenacity of many of our hopes. Irrevocability. The fact that I don't see dinosaurs today doesn't change the fact that dinosaurs existed.

Democritus' atoms and the particles of contemporary metaphysicians are all the same and can be arranged in the form of tables, chairs or epic poems. What this perspective does not say, though, is who organised the swarms before the appearance of humans. Mostly what appears evident is that elementary particles are nothing but the atomistic version of the cookie dough that, in other metaphysics, makes up the world – a docile matter shaped by conceptual schemes. Individuals, instead, are haecceities, absolute individualities: elementary particles, living things, people and even suprapersonal entities (animal superorganisms, state organisations, etc.). The road leading to the genesis of Dante's *Divine Comedy* is not different from that which, through collisions between neutrons and protons, generated the deuterium nuclei. Only it is much longer, and marked by countless failures and extenuating delays. Above all, most of the time meaning never comes: there can be (and this is what happens most of the time) existence without meaning, just as there is ontology without epistemology. But there is no existence without resistance.

Four-dimensionality. To exist is to resist, but to resist is to persist. Individuals are made of spacetime and of the recording that makes them possible; hence their four-dimensional nature. Points in space, just like instants of time, are kept together by memory, which ensures the presence in space of points, lines and surfaces, while allowing the present to remember the past and therefore to qualify as present. First, at the ontological level, four-dimensionalism as the inscription of a trace (because, ultimately, four-dimensionalism is the fact that along with length, height and depth there is also the past) ensures evolution, i.e. the development of interactions. Secondly, at the epistemological level, in which memory remembers beyond the simple repetition of matter, four-dimensionalism allows for the *História*: the reconstruction of the temporal development of individuals. Had Proust had the time, he could have written the history of the universe. Let me explain this magnificent statement.

The ontological question 'what is there?' can be articulated into two different questions: on the one hand, 'what is there for us as observers internal to spacetime?', and on the other, 'what is there for a privileged observer looking at spacetime from the outside?' From the inside of spacetime, we find three-dimensional entities that extend into space and persist over time. From the outside, however, they would appear as four-dimensional entities extended in both space and time. Proust's *In Search of Lost Time* tries to look at things from within spacetime as they would appear from outside it. Proust's conclusion is that this absolute gaze sees things not only through sight, but also through memory. Thus observed – in the Guermantes matinée – the Princess's guests ultimately appear to the Narrator as 'giants immersed in time'. From a Proustian perspective, the ontological question 'what is there for us as observers internal to spacetime?' has a three-dimensionalist answer only if we merely observe through perception; the answer is four-dimensionalist when we observe with memory as well. That's why, for Proust, true life is literature: because it is life recorded, fixated in a document and made four-dimensional.[43]

The four-dimensionality of Proust's observer, though, is different from that of the external observer. For the latter there is no past, present or future; there are only temporal relations of precedence and succession. Instead, for the Proustian observer there is a privileged moment in time, the present, i.e. the point of spacetime in which the observation takes place. This makes it so that, for the Proustian viewer, things appear to be divided, with a split that reproduces the distinction between narrating self and narrated self: on the one hand, a three-dimensional appearance that perception presents as present (as still existing); on the other, a four-dimensional depth that memory represents as past (as no longer existing). Therefore, already in perceptual experience, individuals do not appear fully three-dimensional, but rather endowed with a four-dimensional nature, a connection with the past that promotes the integration of perception and memory. However, this element weakens with habit – it loses its sparkle. The past – memory – becomes flat, the repeated and faded mark of a sensation, and it is at this point that another sensation (a madeleine, some uneven ground, the clinking of cutlery) causes the resurrection of the past, that is, makes time appear in space. The past, in its four-dimensional depth, is available to experience insofar as it is recalled by memory, and is recalled by memory insofar as it is repeated by matter.

This may seem counterintuitive, because our representation of individuals is three-dimensional, and Proust's reference to the stilts of time is metaphorical. However, on closer inspection, four-dimensionality belongs to everyday individuals that are part of our most ordinary experience. A bottle of milk or a passport bear an expiration date, antique furniture and fine wines have age as their internal property, we distinguish older people from the sick because we attribute their unsteady gait to the time past, ruins have value only because of the time to which they bear witness, the concentric circles of cut trees are a spatial manifestation of their temporal duration, and so forth. As Proust rightly said, no one could ever mistake the gaze of a young person for that of an old one, because the latter is an archive full of images, desires, temptations and surrenders.

2.3 Resilience

The second character of being is resilience. Being saves itself, and is connected to thought in a much more complex and articulated way than transcendentalists imagine. Recording guarantees the emergence, that is, the qualitative transformation of the universe, the passage from matter to spirit, from repetition to invention, from lower to higher states. Of course, the superiority of a state over the present one only depends on an anthropic hierarchy; it has no absolute value (just think how many living species have taken little advantage of the development of civilisation). But since we are human, it would be a very strange claim – and an unbearable excess of hubris – to assume the point of view of beings that are different from us.

Emergence is certainly not an infinite phenomenon. Bound as it is to the human gaze upon the universe, it will end long before the Sun eats up the Earth after having properly toasted it. Obviously there will be changes in the state of the universe even after that, but then there will be no point in talking about 'emergence'. This suggests one decisive element, which is that emergence has an end (in both senses of the term), and that every recording, iteration and alteration sooner or later face an interruption. This end confers purpose and meaning on the whole process. The hypothesis that underlies speculation, and that differentiates this perspective from idealistic speculation, is that we are dealing with an emergence, and not with a Pentecost or a construction. Emergentism is opposed to constructivism in ontology, to exceptionalism in anthropology and to logocentrism in the theory of meaning.

Before us and after us, being is. This is typically a speculative hypothesis since, for all we know, being could appear and disappear according to whether we are there or not. What I have just said suggests something that is not always given the attention it deserves. We are accustomed to considering speculation as a close relative of vain speech, whereas in this case (and indeed in many others) speculation confirms the intuitions of common sense. Conversely, the claim to go beyond common sense leads to the idea that, since we have no proof, but only speculative hypotheses, of the fact that being is independent of our thought and perception, we must conclude that being is dependent on our thought and perception.

Constructivism. If I am not mistaken, in his autobiography Bertrand Russell says he once dined with a lady who told him: 'Solipsism is a wonderful doctrine. We should establish an association of solipsists.' You can say the same thing of idealism. Not Plato's idealism that – Kant would say – is 'solid and in line with a healthy way of thinking', as it merely claims that there are real objects that are no less true and much more certain than material objects. Rather, you can say it of the idealism born out of Kant's legacy: transcendental idealism. For it, the world is the outcome of the construction of an omnipresent and, at least in theory, omnipotent I-think. Pharisaism,[44] articulated in its theoretical equivalent, constructivism, has been the golden age of Pentecostal meaning.

Every philosopher, by having a system, has thought they could govern the world – and believed that such a system came from pure thought already endowed with meaning. Of course, in the analytic world, the realist intuition that a proposition is true or false regardless of whether we know or are able to know things (that is, the distinction between ontology and epistemology) was strongly revived in the 1970s. Nonetheless, the situation was very different in the continental world, for better or worse. In fact, analytic philosophers were unable to grasp the political and cultural implications of anti-realism and reduced it to an academic matter. In continental philosophy, instead, anti-realism was conceived as a political act. To maintain that reality depends on the actions of subjects meant to enunciate the principle of interpretation of the world as transformation of the world. Nothing of the kind happened in the analytic tradition, born out of a realist and commonsensical reaction against idealism: it never went so far as to claim that 'power' or 'the subject' may constitute reality. In making such far-fetched claims, though, continental philosophy was voicing a deeply true intuition: that realism and anti-realism have political and cultural implications that go way beyond academia.

Idealism is not innocent, as Kant rightly said. Unfortunately, however, between realism and anti-realism continental thinkers chose the latter, and thus nullified any claim to a real transformation of the world, or even simply to a sensible understanding of it. Perhaps by the modest and purely gnoseological formulation 'the I-think must be able to accompany all my representations' (the supreme principle of all synthetic judgments) Kant meant something ontologically much more challenging, like 'The self, the owner of the universe', which we find in the notes of his

Opus postumum. What is certain is that it has been understood in this sense, not only by transcendental idealists, but also by twentieth-century anti-realists. The latter generally claimed to be against idealism and sometimes even transcendentalism, and yet they embraced these doctrines with a blind faith, as we do with ideas we haven't had the time to consider properly.

Kant was a giant, but he paved the way for a crowd of dwarfs, and this generates a slight discomfort, because it seems that time has been going by pointlessly, thereby casting into doubt the very idea of progress in philosophy. In particular, postmodernism has endorsed a sort of 'default idealism' for which being a philosopher essentially meant arguing that things depend on words. This default idealism apparently solves all the problems of philosophy, despite presenting the significant flaw of disagreeing with anything we learn from physics, history and even common sense. Saying that the outside world is constructed by the subject means claiming that it is in a relationship of dependence with respect to the subject (or, even more problematically, to aggregates of individuals). The premise of constructivism is the transcendental fallacy, that is – as we have seen – the identification between ontology and epistemology, which in idealistic constructivism is equivalent to being's dependence on thought. The problem, however, is that this supposed dependence seems to leave no trace whatsoever. If correlationism was forced to turn the correlation into dependence, the problem of constructivism is to clarify what this dependence really amounts to and how strong it is. Now, the most paradoxical aspect of the whole thing is that no default-idealist has ever been able to convincingly prove their thesis.

The only way in which the I-think can truly claim to impose its law on the universe is by causal dependence, for which the sufficient condition for the existence of X is its being caused by a subject. To my knowledge, the only philosopher who truly argued for causal dependence is Giovanni Gentile.[45] Contrary to Berkeley or the contemporary versions of his idealism, Gentile claimed that the cause of representations is not God, but rather the knowing subject. Gentile's thesis is that, since reality can only be thought of in relation to thought, to conceive reality means to conceive thought, and therefore the concept of material reality is absurd. Now, if anything, what is absurd is to posit that only what is present to my thought is real – which reduces to unreality everything that is not, starting from the theory of causal dependence and its inventor. If it were true that there is only what is present to the thought of a thinking subject, there would be no difference between introspection and knowledge of the outside world; all past things, from dinosaurs to the Sumerians, would be present just like the thoughts about them; all future things would be no less present than past things (and therefore there would be no difference between possible and real); all the things that the theoretician of causal dependence ignores (and there is reason to believe that there are quite a few) would be non-existent. On the other hand, all that the theoretician of causal dependence thinks of would exist, but only at the exact moment when he is thinking of it.

To avoid these contradictions, constructivists move on to conceptual dependence, for which the necessary (not sufficient) condition for the existence of X is its being conceptualised by a subject. This thesis is one of the possible outcomes of Kant's statement: 'Intuitions without concepts are blind.' This, though, can be interpreted in two ways. In the weak form, it amounts to saying that – for example – without the concept of 'dinosaur' we wouldn't recognise a dinosaur if we saw one. In the strong form, the idea is that without the concept of 'dinosaur' we wouldn't even see a dinosaur if there were one. When trying to defend Kant, it is usually said that he argued for the weak form: concepts reconstruct experience. However, if that were the case, his philosophy would have only been an epistemology and not also an ontology called upon to found (in an anti-sceptical function) not only the possibility of knowledge, but also the objective certainty of the known.

If transcendental philosophy thought it had convincingly answered sceptical objections, it was because it believed that concepts constitute experience. Defenders of conceptual dependence thus find themselves at a dead end. Strong (ontological) conceptual dependence can be traced back to causal dependence and faces the same criticisms. Weak (epistemological) conceptual dependence is not really dependence. In fact, it is banally false that a Tyrannosaurus rex depends on our conceptual schemes, just as it is banally true that the word Tyrannosaurus rex depends on our conceptual schemes. It is also banally true that the word 'Tyrannosaurus rex' is very useful for our knowledge of a Tyrannosaurus rex. However, it is just as banally true that no T-rex ever knew it was called 'Tyrannosaurus rex', which didn't prevent it from having all the characteristics of a Tyrannosaurus rex.

What is to be done? The only solution is to turn conceptual dependence into representational dependence, that is, into a weak conceptual dependence for which the necessary (but not sufficient) condition for the existence of X is its being represented by a subject. Compared to conceptual dependence, representational dependence is programmatically vague. While conceptual dependence claimed that intuitions depend on concepts, representational dependence suggests that our vocabularies have some influence over the external world. This notwithstanding, the problems of conceptual dependence are still there. In fact, either 'representational dependence' means that the word 'dinosaur' depends on us – which is not a dependence in any serious sense of the word. Or, it means that the being of dinosaurs depends on us. However, given that when dinosaurs were there we didn't yet exist, we should infer that when dinosaurs were there, dinosaurs were not there – which is clearly absurd. If we try to give concrete shape to representational dependence, we'll notice that the technical term – just as in causal and conceptual dependence – hides a confusion between ontology (what there is, which is independent of our representations) and epistemology (what we think we know, and might be independent of our representations, as what makes a proposition true is what the proposition refers to).

Ontological independence. What do we experience? Phenomena, perhaps? No: resistance, and nothing else. Through our contact with the outside world we do not know what the world is (*quid sit*), but that the world is (*quod sit*). If recording is the origin of everything, to exist is to resist: there are objects in the world that exist independently of our thoughts, and we experience this precisely when these objects resist our thoughts. That thought is unable to amend perceptual illusions means that knowledge cannot intervene on the level of being, and that therefore the latter is independent of the former. Right now I am lying on a couch. I perceive the composition of its fabric, I see its colour, but beyond all these perceptive phenomena the couch supports me, just as it would support my cat and as it would not be able to support an elephant. This ability to support things also presents itself phenomenally to me through a kind of variation of the sense of touch, or rather an expression of the two elements that are confused in touch – on the one hand, the possibility of perceiving heat, cold, dampness, roughness, etc., and on the other, the fact of perceiving resistance. This resistance, for example the impossibility of passing through the couch as I can pass through the room, is proof of the couch's separate existence from my perceptual organs and conceptual schemes. The couch would continue to support me even if I were asleep (in fact, that is one of the reasons why I bought it) or if I were dead.

Resistit ergo est ('it resists, therefore it exists'). We experience resistance, and this resistance is proof of a separate existence (something like *ego cogito, ergo sum*, but with more *raison d'être*). Negative realism embodies the necessary common-sense objection to constructivism, and provides a minimal basis for the possibility of philosophical work: reality is first and foremost something that says no to us. Resistance defines how being manifests itself in our experience: as stated, to exist is to resist. The first and most fundamental experience of the world is that it resists our action and our thought. It has a specific friction, which is undoubtedly frustrating because it does not allow us to do anything we want, but at the same time is extremely comforting because it assures us that what we do is real and not purely imaginary. Again, being is first and foremost what says no to us, and its main characteristic is unamendability, which is first and foremost ontological independence that manifests itself through resistance.

Unamendability is something that can be understood without too much study: we cannot correct our sensible experiences with a simple act of thought. If we have lost our keys we won't be able to get inside our home, and if we are dead we won't be able to take out a mortgage. This does not mean in any way that sensible experiences are the measure of truth (in fact I have only talked about actions, such as opening the door, or social objects, such as mortgages) or that only what can be the object of experience exists. Rather, it indicates that reality is independent of the experience we have of it: that is to say, ontology is independent of epistemology.

Just as a proposition that in principle cannot be falsified cannot aspire to be true, so too an entity that does not resist modification cannot aspire to an ontological status. Negative realism has nothing to do with naive realism, for which perception would give us true access to reality. Perception is not an infallible gateway to reality (nor is it a systematically illusory one) – it is simply proof of its resistance. I cannot transform, with the power of thought alone, a white object into a black object; I must at least take the trouble to turn off the light. Without this operation – which is an action, not a thought – the white object will remain so, which confirms the unamendability of the perceptual with respect to the conceptual: i.e. the unamendability of ontology with respect to epistemology. However, there is nothing contradictory in seeing the measure of ontology in a perceptual phenomenon; in fact, this does not positively demonstrate that being depends on perception (as in Berkeley's idealism) but rather falsifies the thesis according to which the 'I think' constitutes the synthetic unity of apperception. There can be thought without being, as well as being without thought, and the two dimensions are so alien to each other that the I-think does not affect at all what is there.

Epistemological independence. The supposed epistemological dependence – the supposed dependence of being on knowledge, which is summed up in postmodern slogans like 'being that can be understood is language', or 'there is nothing outside the text' – arises from the confusion between the axiological relevance of something (language is important, history and the subject are important, and what's even more important is having a roof over one's head) and ontological relevance. Language, thought and history matter with respect to reality (who would ever deny it?), so they are constitutive of reality (which is simply absurd).

Of course this isn't the case. Ontology would be exactly what it is even without knowledge, although one of its outcomes is indeed knowledge. In the perspective that I defend, both being and knowledge are the result of hysteresis, which in being manifests itself as a recording, while in knowledge it manifests itself as an alteration. If being is instead made to depend on knowledge, the matter becomes easy but useless. The enthusiasm with which both philosophy and common sense have embraced quantum physics, seeing it as a scientific bail-out of the principle that there are no facts, only interpretations, depends on the fact that it conforms to the transcendental fallacy, that is, to the reduction of existence to the knowledge we have of it.

Technological dependence. As we have seen, unamendability falsifies the idealistic thesis of the constructive character of thought with respect to reality. On the positive side, however, it turns out that the independence of the world from thought does not inhibit action. It is so untrue that intuitions without concepts are blind, that one can have perfectly formed intuitions in the total absence of thought, but simply within the framework of an action. It is as difficult (for me as for anyone else) to intervene in the world through thought as it is easy for me to make all the changes I want through technological actions that do not require – and this is the most interesting aspect – any understanding, but simply competence. Simply put, it is very easy to change the colour of the table in the kitchen: just get paint and brushes. Things will not change because of my knowledge of the chemical composition of the paint, but rather because on my dexterity or lack thereof in handling the brush.

Interaction. We have endless evidence of the interaction, within the same environment, between individuals who differ greatly from each other in terms of conceptual patterns, perceptual apparatuses, knowledge and skills. This interaction (which is action rather than knowledge) certainly does not depend on the hypothetical epistemologies of the beings included in the environment; since this interaction is not destined to fail (as it should under the hypothesis of a purely negative realism) we must necessarily conclude that reality is endowed with an autonomous positivity which allows for these interactions and, in a process of emergence, for complex performances and knowledge.

For constructivism, ontology is an amorphous mass shaped by conceptual schemes (which in turn would only give us access to phenomena, not things in themselves). For metaphysical realism, epistemology would be the faithful copy of ontology, understood, moreover, only as the natural world, without taking into account social objects, ideal objects and artifacts. Contrary to both, realism affirms that reality is not an indeterminate noumenon: it has positive characteristics which are manifested by the fact that beings endowed with different perceptual apparatuses and conceptual schemes, or even devoid of them altogether, are able to interact with each other.

For our purposes, this means at least two things. First, that ontology is a solid space endowed with form, which does not need forms imposed by epistemology. Second, that in order to interact with others and to live in general, one does not need epistemology or concepts; these serve for that extremely rare and specialised function proper to some living beings which is called 'knowledge' (so that between the sphere of knowledge and that of being there is a disproportion which constructivists seem to dismiss: the former is enormously smaller than the latter). But if we have technological dependence, we do not need epistemological dependence: the latter is an absurd and laborious apparatus, and above all it is false.

Teleological dependence. Having exhausted these three dependencies – ontological, epistemological, technological – of which only the second is truly in place, I wish to add a fourth one – which is not a real dependence either, but at least makes sense. I mean teleological dependence: the fact that being as a whole, having no meaning, receives it from humans. They too, like all other organisms, do not have an end (purpose) other than their end (death), but unlike other organisms they project a sense and a purpose onto technical instruments as well as onto nature in general. Epistemological dependence probably alludes to something like this, which must be understood within the framework of a teleology: the purpose of being is illuminated by language, but being as such has no purpose, nor therefore any dependence on reason as the faculty of purpose.

What humans bring to the system is not intelligence, but need, which interacting with technology generates what I will later describe as 'responsiveness'. For various reasons, the behaviour of a prokaryote and that of a professor have the same origin: the ability to extract energy from the environment and to use it to grow, develop and self-replicate. This gives irreversibility to the events, which in turn determines the genesis of meaning: the latter is born as a direction, and then is specified as sensibility and reason. The passage to higher stages, and in particular to reason, is possible because human organisms are enhanced by mechanical and repeatable performances, both inside and outside themselves: idealisation, an almost indefinite and economic possibility of iteration, since it can be obtained with pen and paper alone; hysteresis, which is the condition of possibility of idealisation; and the consequent formation of language, culture and social institutions, which are born to counter the tendency of the universe to disorder. However, this dependence does not modify being, but simply allows us to evaluate it, and therefore to recognise the meaning of emergence, which without teleological dependence would have none.

2.4 Emergence

The third character of being is emergence.[46] As recording, it lays the foundations for change and transformation. Ontology as such is not simple negativity, as might appear from the definition of being as resistance. The very fact that being resists, and therefore possesses a consistency, is also what allows for existence, which is one of the most remarkable results of hysteresis. Existence does not necessarily have a meaning (on the contrary, in the majority of cases it does not). Nevertheless, there can be a sense of being, which nonetheless does not lie in the past but in the future, in the meaning that being receives from technology (the use we can make of what there is) and from teleology (the end that we can give to entities, starting from ourselves).

Unamendability and interaction characterise reality as something that punches us in the face, escapes us, or comes towards us. This is what I call emergence, which I have tried to sum up in some cardinal concepts: the resistance and persistence characteristic of negative realism, for the unamendability of which individuals do not get out of the way or disappear so easily; and the characteristics of positive realism, variously linked to interaction – the direction of a movement, the fixation of traces, the invitations and the affordances that come from individuals (revising Eco's example: I can use a screwdriver to open a package, but not to have a drink).

Since it is prior to and independent of our knowledge, reality (to which we obviously belong ourselves) is composed of individuals: units that are what they are independently of anything else (senses, concepts, past experiences). Despite the view put forward by Berkeley and his many heirs, there is no need to be known or to know in order to exist. The starting point of realism is not the knowledge of things in themselves, but the independence of the world from the observer; in this sense, ontological empiricism is different from traditional empiricism, which is instead gnoseological and potentially idealistic, bringing experience back to knowledge rather than to existence.

The myth of the given. What has made ontology problematic for empiricism and transcendentalism is the difficulty of reconciling being-in-itself (as independent of knowledge) and being-for-us as we know it. We can simply respond to this difficulty, however, by pointing out that the real problem is not the form in which we come into contact with what there is, but its independence from our conceptual schemes and perceptual apparatuses. That the temporal phase of a process is perceived as an object, or that a certain chromatic wave is perceived as the colour blue does not mean in any way that the object is dependent on the subject. This is the paralogism in which modern idealism has occurred.

Phenomenalism. When in high school they teach us that we only know phenomena and not things in themselves, after our initial perplexity this view seems obvious to us: the table I have under my eyes is white, but if I turned off the light it would turn black; I like what I am eating, but if I were sick I would not like it. In short, we see things only as they appear to us, and we never have total and internal access to them. At this point, there are only phenomena and, as Schopenhauer put it, if a reasonable being reflects a little bit on it, they can come to only one conclusion: that the world is my representation. But the good question is: has this recourse to phenomena and representations really opened our eyes, or has it closed them instead?

Let's consider a trivial but enlightening circumstance. As a paradigmatic representation, Schopenhauer proposes an eye that looks at the Sun, but seems to neglect the fact that a looked-at Sun is different from a merely represented Sun: in particular, you can look at the Sun only for an instant, while you can represent it as much as you want. Once it is clarified (which is not so simple) that the phenomenon of the Sun is not the remembered or imagined representation of it, but the Sun we are looking at right now (and only now!) many problems ensue. In fact, Schopenhauer speaks of an eye that looks at the Sun and a hand that touches the Earth. The use of the singular is not accidental, since if there were two eyes and two hands, as there usually are, the following doubt could arise: the fact that the Sun and the Earth give the same sensation to both eyes and both hands may depend on the fact that the relationship between the two poles of the representation, the subject and the object, is not perfectly balanced but leans towards the object.

This doubt would become even more substantial if the one-eyed observer found themselves not only having two eyes, but in the company of other observers with whom to share their impressions and doubts. Further doubts would come if the immobile observer switched to a dynamic situation, in which the objects (excluding the Sun, of course) were manageable, and even better if these operations had no cognitive purposes but, as happens in most of our lives, were simple interactions with the environment. In fact, the appeal to phenomena and to the world as a representation, which works so well when we are the solitary and immobile observers of inanimate objects, loses much of its persuasive force when we are with others, in motion, and especially when objects are not static or we do not have a purely cognitive relationship with them.

Simply put, the confidence – if not the credulity – with which I accept that the sheet of paper in front of me is a phenomenon changes completely if instead of the sheet there is a hungry tiger, but also, without going too far, if the sheet is a subpoena. Scepticism and contemplation give way to action, and the perspective changes. In fact, we discover that our relationship with the world focuses primarily on interaction with artifacts, social objects and people, with respect to which the notion of 'phenomenon' appears problematic. Is a corkscrew a phenomenon? You may believe it if you wish. Is a court summons a phenomenon? Are our friends and relatives phenomena? Again, you might think so if you wish, but only on the condition that you are able to explain what would change in your attitude and above all in your behaviour if instead of phenomena they were things in themselves.

Correlationism. After leaving high school we go to university, and here we are told about the myth of the given. What underpins the criticism of the myth of the given is the (naively scientistic) idea that, given the impossibility of accessing things in themselves, ontology is reabsorbed by epistemology. The presupposition of the myth of the given is correlationism. This is the idea of philosophies of access, according to which the object is given only in correlation with a knowing subject. In a few moves, reality is thus done away with, without even bothering to enunciate openly immaterialist, sceptical or solipsistic theses. However, this operation is not as immune from the myth as it claims to be.

The strong version of it is represented by continental philosophy, in the line of thought that leads from transcendental idealism to the radical philosophies of the second half of the nineteenth century, and hence to postmodernism. Here we are dealing with an idealism whose basic argument is the following: since there is no being independent of knowledge, the rationality (or irrationality) of the world is the result of the constructive activity of our conceptual schemes and our perceptual apparatuses. The weak version is represented by analytic philosophy, in the line of thought that leads from positivism to logical empiricism, and hence to cognitivism. Here we are dealing with a scientism whose basic argument is the following: philosophy has exhausted its autonomous cognitive role, which is now entirely fulfilled by the natural sciences. With respect to these, philosophy has a purely reconstructive function: it is called upon to reconstruct the logic of scientific research.

United by the transcendental fallacy, these two versions of philosophy share the basic assumption of transcendentalism, according to which the order we find in the world depends on the order that reason gives to the world (or at least to the part of it that is willing to be influenced). It is the basis of Kantian philosophy and even more so of the rationalisms that preceded it since Cartesianism: like the latter, it is a rationalisation of intelligent design. Transcendentalists do not commit themselves to the divine creation of the universe (Kant in particular maintains that we have no proof either for or against creation, the existence of God, the finiteness or the infinity of the world), but they presuppose the creationist perspective when they maintain that the order of phenomena depends on the order of the minds that observe them.

In fact, the world of correlationism is a subject that represents an object within itself. From the ontological point of view a crucial difficulty thus arises, because the only coherent way to defend the thesis of the correlation between knowing and known as the only form of existence is to embrace an idealism that sees matter as something that does not pre-exist the spirit, since it is evident that the relationship takes place in the mind and not in the world. *Esse est concipi* ('being is being thought of'), indeed. The supreme principle of all synthetic judgments, the thesis that the I-think must be able to accompany my representations, can be translated into *cogito ergo est*, or, even better, *in est quia cogito*: there is something only to the extent that I think of it.

Transcendentalism. Kant claims not to speak of ontology out of epistemological concerns (but in fact he is confusing ontology with epistemology). But the fact that things are not necessarily as they appear to us does not mean that things are not, since the effects they produce on us are real and consistent. There is therefore no reason to give up, as Kant proposed, the proud name of 'ontology' in order to fall back on the more modest 'critique of reason' (or at least that is what Kant believed, although it is not clear to me why it would be more modest). We can still build an ontology, which in this case is a theory of the effectiveness of being, i.e. the way in which being manifests itself in our experience, and first of all of its resistance – the fact that it cannot be modified with the sole action of thought (that this is a particular manifestation of being does not take away that there is a being; therefore it is not clear why one should call 'critique of reason' something that is an ontology for all intents and purposes). Knowing and believing that one knows are obviously not the same thing. And we can never be sure that what we call knowledge is actually such. Any relationship with knowledge is therefore speculative, in that it goes beyond the critical norm that would require us to refrain from calling knowledge what might in fact be non-knowledge. Given this circumstance, we will never be able to empirically prove that epistemology has any effect on ontology.

'The I-think must be able to accompany all my representations.' Kant lodged this principle as a critical caveat against the illusion of a knowledge of the world unmediated by our conceptual schemes, but in Kant's legacy the critical caveat turned into dogmatic certainty: we never know the world directly, because it depends on our conceptual schemes. Hence a path whose radicalisation is found in Nietzsche's thesis that 'there are no facts, only interpretations': if there is no being independent of knowledge, then there are only interpretations. The basic misconception of the transcendental fallacy lies in the assumption that we can only relate to the world through conceptual mediation.

For the transcendental fallacy, ontology is identified with epistemology, and with an epistemology that speaks to us not of things themselves, but of how they must be made to be known to us. This fallacy was repeated in the twentieth-century critique of the 'myth of the given',[47] which supports the dependence of ontology on epistemology with this argument: if I want to be able to use data as the basis for a theory, then these data are not independent of theory. If, on the other hand, I claim that data are independent of theory, then I can never use a single piece of data to confirm or disprove a theory. As a result, if I want an ontology to serve as the basis for an epistemology, then epistemology must build the ontology. The argument may seem to flow smoothly but it is intimately inconsistent, because an ontology built by an epistemology is an epistemology and not an ontology, and an epistemology that knows an epistemology (instead of an ontology) is not even an epistemology.

By arguing that the given is a myth, we implicitly introduce an even more insidious myth: if you want an ontology (a field of things that are there) to serve for an epistemology (a field of things that we know), epistemology (our conceptual schemes) must inform the ontology; but an ontology informed by an epistemology is an epistemology – a strange knowledge which, curiously enough, does not correspond to a being, since in this case being and knowing coincide. Put in these terms this sounds absurd, but one need only think of how many philosophers maintain that 'there is no such thing as a subject and an object, there is only the relationship between subject and object'. Well, these philosophers are essentially saying that mushrooms do not exist, and in fact they (the philosophers) do not exist either, but there is only the act of 'eating mushrooms'. And yet it is the philosophers, and not – for example – the mushroom, who will be asked to pay the bill.

Constructivism. The transcendental fallacy, which begins with Descartes' natural doubt and culminates in the Hegelian criticism of sense certainty, lies along a road that for moderns has come to coincide roughly with philosophy: the criticism of naive realism, acquisition of the constructivist perspective, and then a shift to an exclusively critical-deconstructive philosophy, i.e. a purely negative dialectic. For negative philosophy – which, by practising the transcendental fallacy, makes the positive, i.e. being, the simple reflection of knowledge – it would be an unforgivable naivety (or more exactly it would coincide with the renunciation of philosophy) to claim that things work differently. The negativity consists precisely in denying the world in the name of thought, and ontology in the name of epistemology: you cannot have access to things per se, you only have things for yourself, be they phenomena, data of meaning, representations or ideas. What there is, ontology, 'exists' (at this point quotation marks become necessary) only to the extent that it is thought and known by an epistemology, and therefore depends on conceptual schemes: intuitions without concepts are blind, indeed facts are full of theories; or rather there are no facts, only interpretations, and that's it.

Constructivism is easy to posit in theory, but in practice it doesn't work so well. In fact, it is not difficult to observe that my conceptual schemes and perceptual apparatuses (despite apparently mattering a great deal) are unable to change the data, which remain there as they are, unamendable. Moreover, one of the most common experiences is to interact with beings who have conceptual patterns and perceptual apparatuses different from one's own (for example, when playing with one's cat). Again, how is this possible, and what do supporters of the myth of the given have to say about it? Usually nothing. It is on these facts that the passage from phenomenalism to realism, and from phenomena to things in themselves, is based.

The given of the myth. Constructivism is the view that reality depends on our conceptual schemes and perceptual apparatuses. It is the alternative ontological doctrine to emergentism, and has been prevalent over the last two millennia: in fact, it is based on creationism and has been theoretically reworked as transcendental idealism and its postmodern sequels. Emergentism follows the reverse path. For it, the world is the result of an overabundance of matter, space and time that needed a single ingredient in order to work together: 'hysteresis', i.e. the possibility of recording and the resulting performances, right down to the genesis of conscious beings like you and me.

Constructivism makes a fair point about the relevance of action, but makes it depend on a concept or a contract – it cultivates the idea that everything from society to values is produced with a variant of the social contract: we sit at a table and happily agree, provided that bullies and solipsists do not create their own values and rules in the privacy of their homes. If everything were really constructed as suggested by the hypothesis of the myth of the given, answering questions like 'who invented chess?' or 'who came up with jokes?' should be very simple, just as it should be simple to name the inventor of Juno, the Indian castes, Indo-European institutions, or the wheel.

This is not the case, however, and not only for empirical reasons related to the difficulty of going far back in time (some jokes are quite recent), but simply because things didn't happen that way. It is not as if someone, or some group of friends, in order to overcome the boredom of a lazy afternoon in Isfahan, decided to invent chess. First there were battles, then games that imitated them, and finally the setting of rules whose final result was the game of chess. The same is true for the gods, for forms of government, for castes, and of course (going further back) for languages. What this dark genesis presents to us is much more interesting (and important) than the deconstruction of the myth of the given, and it is precisely the given of the myth, the positivities we face in the world, the values we inherit and share long before we understand them, the languages we speak, and the gods we worship, be they Juno, Shiva, or Sapiens Sapiens.

First of all we have a competence without understanding, positions that are not comprehended, rituals whose meaning is ignored and social structures that are inherited. Then sometimes, and more rarely than we think, the spirit manifests itself precisely as intentionality. One will never overestimate the fact that hysteresis causes a qualitative change, the passage from passivity to activity through passivity, itself based on the simple phenomenon that what is inscribed can be iterated. And what can be iterated is no longer passive, but becomes active and animated. This is a crucial point: the birth of intentionality (understood as the basis of representation, consciousness, self-awareness and motivation) from documentality, from a competence without understanding. To put it another way, the birth of the soul from the automaton. The priority of intentionality over documentality is a metaphysical mistake equivalent to the confusion between ontology and epistemology. The world of the Web is no exception. We are immersed in this positivity of the myth, in the given of the myth, which should not therefore be considered as a simple absence of knowledge, as an easy thing that is overcome by the criticism of the myth of the given. If this were so, the Enlightenment would have imposed itself for thousands of years.

2.5 Reference

The fourth character of being is reference. Being is what truth refers to, whether positively or negatively. Ontology is what exists regardless of what we know or believe we know. This realist definition of ontology stands at the antipodes of the idealist ontology, whose archetype is not to be found in Plato – who was an ontological realist – but in Berkeley, who made the existence of objects depend on the knowledge we have of them. Berkeley's error, which is the fundamental characteristic of any idealism in the true sense, has been a feature of modern philosophy ever since Descartes. It starts from the hypothesis that existence is first of all thought, then it makes being depend on thinking, and finally, with Kantian transcendentalism, it turns the conditions of possibility of an object's existence into the conditions of its knowability. Since thought neither precedes nor constitutes being, realism presents itself first and foremost as negative realism. Reality is that which escapes or opposes thought, i.e. that which is different from it. In this negativity, realism manifests itself as the direct antithesis of idealism: *esse non est percipi*, being is what it is even when it is not perceived, and therefore what cannot be changed in its essential properties by perception or thought.

The distinctive character of ontology is the alternative between being and not-being. This may seem like a small matter, but in fact this alternative is the foundation of the three fundamental characteristics of what there is: unamendability, interaction and emergence. The characters of being are the characters of reality, which precedes truth. Between the former and the latter there is an ontological and logical dependence, as well as a chronological difference: if reality is only potentially relational (if there are humans then reality will strike them and tell them 'talk about me'), truth is thematically relational (in the perspective that I defend, we will see, there is truth if and only if there are humans capable of making the truth).

Theories of truth. In the light of what has been said so far I propose three theories of truth: hypotruth, which corresponds to mainstream hermeneutics;[48] hypertruth, which is mainstream analytic theory;[49] and mesotruth, which is what I would like to elaborate in these pages.

Hermeneutic thinkers have developed an epistemic theory of truth which is in fact a hypotruth, i.e. a subordinate truth, since it is detached from ontology and consists rather in the conceptual schemes that mediate and in fact constitute our relationship with the world. In this version, with varying degrees of radicality, 'true' becomes synonymous with 'conforming to a shared belief'. Thus, hermeneutic thinkers rightly note that truth does not go without saying, but requires context and actions. Yet they go too far when they claim that the truth consists only in verification procedures, and that the idea of a world 'out there', independent of our conceptual schemes, is a pre-Kantian naivety. Not only do they provide a theoretical bailout to post-truth (which doesn't know what to do with it), but above all they miss the opportunity to give hermeneutics its proper dimension which – as I will try to argue later – is technological and not ideological.

Most analytic philosophers have developed a very strong notion of truth. I'll call it hypertruth, because it postulates a necessary correlation between ontology and epistemology, in which the proposition '"snow is white" is true (epistemology) if and only if snow is white (ontology)' implies: if snow is white, then it is true that snow is white, so that it would be true that snow is white even if there were (now or ever) no human on the face of the Earth. For the supporters of hypertruth, if it is true that salt is sodium chloride, then this proposition was also true for a Greek of the Homeric age even though he did not have the tools to access that truth. To describe truth as the relationship between the proposition 'snow is white' and the fact that snow is white is an easy thesis to share. From this, however, supporters of hypertruth draw the conclusion that this proposition would be true even if there had never been a human being on Earth capable of formulating it. And this is far from obvious.

This second part of the thesis of hypertruth appears motivated by the concern that, otherwise, hermeneutical and hypotruthist drifts would be given too much room. But this is by no means inevitable. For example, Heidegger's thesis according to which, before Newton, the theories of the motion of the planets he enunciated were not true is not in itself relativistic: Newton's laws (epistemology) did not exist, but the reality to which they referred existed (ontology). Newton's work consisted in revealing something that was already there. To say this does not mean – regardless of Heidegger's conclusions – that the motion of the planets was created by Newton, but that the true conception of the motion of the planets depends on the apparatus (in this case, mathematics) thanks to which Newton was able to elaborate his own laws by applying them to physical reality. Likewise, the true conception of the Medicean Planets depends on the technical apparatus (in this case, a telescope) with which Galilei discovered them, and this conception is not so despotic as to transform into planets what are in fact the four main satellites of Jupiter.

The fact that the salt is sodium chloride or that there once were dinosaurs on Earth does not depend in any way on us and our conceptual schemes. However, it does depend on us that there is such a thing as chemistry (which might very well never have been developed), and that we have studied bones and fossils. So, the planets were there before Newton's laws, and of course they were exactly what they were without the intervention of any conceptual scheme. To claim instead, with the proponents of hypertruth, that these laws were true even before they were discovered is either to formulate a meaningless assertion, or – converging involuntarily with the supporters of hypotruth – to make interactions between planets depend on conceptual schemes.

Hypotruth and hypertruth are opposed by what I call mesotruth. This term is due not so much to the fact that it is halfway between the two, but rather to the fact that it insists on the role of technical mediation between ontology and epistemology. In mesotruth, truth is neither the epistemology that shapes ontology (as claimed by hypotruthists), nor the ontology that is reflected in epistemology (as argued by hypertruthists), but a three-term structure that includes ontology, epistemology and technology. The latter is to be considered as the element, thus far largely underestimated by philosophers, that ensures the transition from ontology to epistemology, and that allows the truth to be made. For mesotruth, truth is the technological result of the relationship between ontology (what there is) and epistemology (what we know).

Verification praxis. Now, what is the link between hysteresis and truth? Let me give you an example. There are twenty-two beans in a can (ontology); I count them (technology); I utter the sentence 'there are twenty-two beans in this can' (epistemology). The sentence is true. The can weighs a certain amount (ontology); I put it on a scale (technology); I utter the phrase 'this can weighs 100 grams' (epistemology). This sentence is also true. If I were in the United States I would say that the can weighs three-and-a-half ounces and it would be equally true, although 3.5 and 100 are two different numbers. Bottom line: the truth is relative to the technical instruments of verification, but absolute with respect to the ontological sphere to which it refers and to the epistemological need to which it responds. 'Relative' and 'absolute' indicate, in the version I propose, two different forms of the dependence of truth, i.e. with respect to ontology and with respect to technology.

According to the view I advocate, there can be reality without truth, but no truth without reality, and the truth is something that is made, i.e. the set of true propositions that emerge from reality. What do I mean by this? A positive theory of verification. 'To verify' comes from the Latin *veritas facere*: to make the truth. This has two sides to it: that of invalidation (if snow is not white) and that of convalidation (if snow is white). In light of my threefold perspective, I propose a further differentiation: instead of understanding the ontological foundation as a 'truthmaker', given that ontology is what provides the material, I would suggest indicating the ontological layer as a 'truth bearer'; the function of 'truthmaker' instead, for what I have said, goes to technology, which indeed is responsible for making the truth; lastly, epistemology has the function of 'truth teller'. Finally, teleology (the end for which truth is made, which is not a natural fact) is the truth user.

To clarify this theory, I therefore propose the following terminological reform. Truth bearers are the states of things with respect to which a proposition is true (the beans in the can). They therefore constitute the ontological element of the process. Truthmakers are the operations necessary to produce true propositions about states of affairs (in this case, counting the beans). They therefore constitute the technological element of the process. Truth tellers are the propositions necessary to communicate the results of the operations carried out by the truthmakers with reference to the truth bearers (in this case, the phrase 'there are twenty-two beans in this can'). They therefore constitute the epistemological element of the process. Finally, truth users are the recipients of the message, because without subjects the truth would make no sense.

3

Iteration

The second manifestation of hysteresis is iteration, to be understood as a property not of being, but of becoming. Consider, by way of example, a natural process such as the transmission of the genetic code; an artifactual process such as the splintering of a flint; and a cultural process such as the formation of a language or ritual. In each of these cases we are dealing with a succession of repeated acts (the copying of the code, the repeated percussion of the flint, the iteration of certain gestures or certain sounds). Little by little, each of these iterations gives rise to a being, both in the form of praxis, i.e. of action (for example, a ritual dance or a conversational exchange), and in that of poiesis, i.e. of production (the genesis of a life form, an arrowhead, a literary work or a legal code). The characteristic of acts, inasmuch as they are repeated, is therefore once again a variant of hysteresis, which in this case is the iteration of an act that is characterised by a competence not necessarily (indeed, only very rarely) accompanied by understanding. Both nature and technology as well as society operate by iteration much more than by understanding, which is why they are emerging structures and not the result of a divine or human construction that follows an intelligent design or some form of intentionality.

Becoming equals being iterated. What is iteration? Hegel wrote[50] that meaning can only arise if something happens at least twice: '*Einmal ist keinmal*', once is the same as never. For example, it could be a message sent by mistake, or containing an error, which is why when we subscribe to some service they ask us to confirm our email address. But, beyond this obvious practical function, iteration hides a metaphysical power that is not always taken into due account, and which acquires particular relevance at a time when technology, which is first of all iteration, has acquired unprecedented evidence, even though of course it has always been both in us and outside us, since we are intrinsically technological animals. Iteration strengthens, just like when you hammer a nail; it facilitates, like a path that becomes more and more open the more it is trodden upon; and it can even destroy, like the drop that digs into the rock, or build, like the drop that creates a stalactite. The problem is that organisms, no matter how much they iterate, sooner or later get tired. Even the most petulant of children will eventually get tired of asking 'why?' Machines, however, iterate without effort – at most, you have to recharge them. Things are different with organisms: a fatally exhausted horse, or an athlete who dies of a heart attack after a race, won't be resurrected.

Here's the common root. Hysteresis (ὑστέρησις), as we said, is an original delay, something that comes later, and which embodies the idea of *différance* in the best possible way: it comes later and records, it iterates by recording, and iteration is the prelude to alteration and interruption. The common root of sensibility and intellect, as well as of passivity and activity, and of reproduction and production, is to be found precisely in these two essential performances of hysteresis. On the one hand, by keeping track, hysteresis enables the repetition of the same; on the other, precisely because the track can and in a certain sense must degrade due to entropy, it ensures alteration, the production of the other, change. Technology doesn't seem to enjoy the same metaphysical nobility that we attribute to ontology and epistemology. But, if we pay attention, technology is not absent from metaphysics: it is simply not noticed. The focus on hysteresis shows precisely that technology plays a role just as crucial as, if not more crucial than, its noble sisters. Iteration allows what once took place to repeat itself indefinitely, enabling the creation of mechanisms such as credit, normativity, energy storage, technical enhancement and traditionalisation. Iteration is the foundation of technology, of the passage from the passivity of the track inscription to the activity of track iteration. Technology is every repeated action, both in nature and outside it (provided that such an externality with respect to nature can be conceived). This repetition leads to a strengthening of the result and a simplification of execution.

Recording, iteration, technology. Recording can be enhanced through iteration, and this enhancement is what we call 'technology', which in its human version is the scope of what we do in a regulated way. Again, we are dealing with a process of hysteresis that affects both what we call 'nature' (a technology that has, literally, all the time and space in the world at its disposal) and what we call 'culture' (a technology with limited times and spaces). The drop digs into the stone or builds stalactites; by practising for a reasonable number of times we become able to tie our shoes or speak a language; by studying, reading, rereading and commenting we can become professors; and if we had sufficient time we could all write *Don Quixote*, like Pierre Menard in Borges's story.[51]

There are three fundamental manifestations of iteration. First we have the cumulative effect, namely enhancement. A sound is enhanced by a rhythm, either by extending and complexifying the original message (and thus strengthening it), or by making it exceed the spatial-temporal limits of its genesis. In this sense, it is not surprising that the Web has acquired so much power and has brought about such important transformations, considering that it is the largest recording-iteration apparatus ever seen in the history of the world. Secondly, there is the effect of deconstruction, such as when a word is repeated over and over until it gradually loses its meaning. Thirdly, iterability ensures the functioning of the technical apparatus. In fact, recording is first of all the condition of possibility of technology, as an intermediate term between ontology (what there is) and epistemology (what we know, and which in turn requires recording, in order to increase and perpetuate itself).

Technology, whose birth must have been contingent like everything else in the universe, gives its protection and at the same time reveals its inadequacy. This is the typical case where teleology reveals archaeology. Only the (contingent) circumstance that humans have at some point equipped themselves with technical supplements has caused them to define the essence of the human being. We have on the one hand a world that exists, ontology, and on the other a world of things that we know or think we know, epistemology. Between these two there is a medium that is not and is not known, but is simply done.

Technology is the becoming that phenomenologically manifests itself to us humans in what we do, in the skills we possess without necessarily being preceded or accompanied by understanding. Realism entrusts the positivity that idealism assigns to the constructive activity of the spirit to an emergence process that exercises a technological function. Technology defines a second process immanent to hysteresis, i.e. the possibility of an indefinite iteration, which is opposed to *tyche*, to chance, to aleatoriness, by means of the only possible resource: the repetition of the identical, both in us and outside of us. Animal, human and technological evolution are all based on the same principle: iterability. We find it in regulated and iterable activities such as breathing; instead, physical processes such as boiling are not technical, although they can become so under certain conditions (controlling breathing to achieve certain purposes, boiling water to cook food).

3.1 Technology

There are many superstitions about *techne* and technology: allegedly it is cold (which is paradoxical, considering that the use of fire is *techne*), it is alienating (one could only wish! Unfortunately, it actually reveals the human being for what it is), and we would be better off without it (which is obviously false: we would die at age thirty at best). But among all these superstitions, the most monumental and false of them is the idea that *techne* and technology are something modern, like plastic or at least stainless steel, as suggested by the expression 'age of technology', with which both philosophers and non-philosophers often define the contemporary world. Of course it's not like that. *Techne* is as old as human beings: it was born when hominids began to turn into humans. And this transformation did not take place through an increase in the brain mass, as the latter is not necessarily advantageous from the evolutionary point of view (the Neanderthals had a brain bigger than ours), but through an externalisation and a strengthening of our abilities by means of *techne*. Since this process took place in a natural context, the alleged distinction between technology and nature must be abandoned.

Technology manifests what we are and what we want. That has been the case since time immemorial, but today it has become completely evident: digital technology is a great archive of what we are as social beings and soon also as biological beings.

Not the creation of values or norms, but the construction of technical apparatus is the first act of the naked ape, whose first concerns consist in eating, arming itself and warming itself (and therefore also dressing). The first norms, as derived from technology, will appear long afterwards. With 'technology' I therefore designate the wide sphere of actions that we perform in a competent manner without having any prior knowledge. These actions are highly varied, and range from lighting a fire without any notion of physics to speaking a language without any grammatical and syntactical knowledge of it, to creating works of art without having the ability to account for how they were made. In this sense, technology has a privileged relationship with gestures (although of course there may be technologies of thought, such as logic, mnemonics or arithmetic).

After being (which does not necessarily make sense) and before knowledge (which necessarily does), there is technology, in which phenomena emerge. These phenomena manifest a sense, a direction from which, in time, a sense as understanding may (but does not necessarily have to) emerge. In the medial stage of technology there does not seem to be any magic. Certain transformations occur and do not seem to require the intervention of a Pentecostal meaning. I pour salt into boiling water and the salt melts. I throw a flower into the same water and it withers. Is it because the salt or the flower were too hot? Claiming this of the salt is bold, of the flowers a little less so – after all, flowers do feel something, they follow the light, and they move away, though slowly, if something bothers them. What do they have that salt does not? Some magical living principle? No, simply more complex functions, which also produce a certain sensitivity. If I throw a monkey into boiling water, it will definitely feel something and will react. It will probably think something unpleasant about me, too.

But what does the monkey have that the flower does not? Is there a qualitative leap between these two beings? Of course, one can ironise about the positivistic obsession with quantity, contrasting it with the authenticity, vitality, spirituality, transcendence of quality, but this seems rhetorical to me. Quantity does not automatically lead to quality, but it is also true that in life, quality, singularity and even feeling and spirit are captured through quantity. The necessary though not sufficient condition of culture is to know many things; the necessary though not sufficient condition of hate or love is that they exceed a certain threshold, manifesting themselves in a certain quantity of hate or love; if Picasso had only painted one painting, I doubt he would have been Picasso. To expect quality and authenticity to descend from heaven (because that's what is implied, like it or not, when you set quantity against quality) is to cultivate a superstitious religion. Instead of a magical qualitative leap we have a complication of functions, particularly as relates to recording and movement, to the point of having goals and dreams and developing a consciousness.

The skin of the flower and that of the monkey are not so different, and are composed of cells that have the principle of external sensitivity (according to Freud's hypothesis, the external surface of the cell is the origin of both the skin, i.e. the place of sense as sensibility, and of grey matter, i.e. the place of sense as intelligence and meaning).[52] The processes and mimetic movements that mark the birth of consciousness – fears, pleasures, aspirations, actions – are activated by a cerebral surface that descends from the skin. In short, there is a link between the hand and consciousness, that is to say also between sense as direction and sense as understanding, and this is paradoxically what Heidegger suggests in a passage where he argues that man alone has a hand, while a monkey only has a limb.[53] I would suggest that the monkey also has a hand, and that's why it has a soul. If we recognise that there is a much stronger link between thought, movement and sensation than we think, then we will add an important piece to the gradualism that sees a common thread, so to speak, running from physics through chemistry to biology to psychology.

Techne and technology. With the word 'technology' I refer to the categorial domain that collects all the different modes of empowerment of doing, just as ontology is the categorial domain that collects all the different ways of being, epistemology the categorial domain that collects all the different ways of knowing, and teleology the categorial domain that collects all the ways of ending (i.e. both the purpose and the end of something). By '*techne*' I mean instead the object of technology, i.e. any type of iterable and regulated action with an external purpose, carried out by an organism or mechanism. This results in either a doing aimed at achieving a purpose (praxis) or a production that generates an artifact, i.e. the objectification of a purpose (poiesis). In this sense, technology manifests its action in those regional spheres of ontology which are ecology (the environment and in particular the human environment), anthropology (the distinctive features of the human animal compared to other organisms) and economy (the distinctive features of the social world).

Action and iteration. Technology is therefore any form of action enhancement through iteration. In this sense, the trained use of one's body, linguistic competence, the codification of social reality, as well as everything that in the animal world goes under the obscure name of 'instinct' is part of technology, which therefore is not governed by the natural/cultural opposition (in both cases there is technology), but by the iterable/not iterable one. What is iterable is technological, what is not iterable is not (the structure of a snowflake is technological in this perspective, a snowfall is not, because it repeats itself in a chaotic and irregular way). Iteration is thus the character of technology (natural and artificial), which is the foundation of ontology itself (the past is repeated by matter), and which, in a particularly conspicuous form, provides an enhancement to the human animal. In humanity, iteration and empowerment are transformed into a supplement.

Epistemology is about what we know, or think we know: it is a form (syntax, judgment, concepts) and its values are true and false. Ontology is about what there is: it is a power (something real, something that acts: resistance, unamendability, etc.) and its values are existent and non-existent. Technology concerns what we do and its values are success or failure (or if one prefers to use Austin's terminology,[54] happiness or unhappiness). It is a becoming, which is no longer a being (which is or is not) and is not yet a knowledge (which is true or false) but a doing, in which a competence takes place that can, although not necessarily, lead to an understanding. (While typing these words I have only a vague idea of the psychophysical mechanisms that regulate this activity, and I would not type any better if I were a neurophysiologist).

Techne and tyche. In the concept of 'hysteresis', *techne* and *tyche*, repetition and chance, go together. But as regards iteration, the specific function of hysteresis that I shall now address, I will focus on the undifferentiated repetition that underlies the functioning of technical devices. So then, the main character of technology is iteration. *Techne* opposes *tyche* (chance, randomness) with its only possible resource: the repetition of the same. Animal, human and technological evolution are all based on the same principle: iteration. The second interesting aspect is that whereas competence is required to perform these acts, understanding is not. Contrary to Kant's vision, it is not 'first the concept, then the scheme'. There is first of all the scheme, the method of construction, and then the object and the concept, if necessary (which often isn't the case – what is the concept of the *Mona Lisa*, for example?).

Compare a termite mound and the Sagrada Familia basilica in Barcelona.[55] They look the same, but how is this possible? Gaudí drew designs, made representations, whereas termites have nothing of the sort. Yet this is precisely the point: even Gaudí's neurons had no representations – they simply 'downloaded', just like termites. After all, the latter have found a shortcut: instead of creating representations, like Gaudí's neurons, they directly create the Sagrada Familia. It is true that the termites building a termite mound identical to the Sagrada Familia are very different from Gaudí designing the actual one. The difference however does not lie at the top, but at the bottom, i.e. in the fact that in Gaudí's case there is a representation (including the representation of an end) that is not given in the case of the termites. The latter, however, compared to Gaudí's neurons, have the advantage of not representing what they produce and the end for which they do it – they just produce it, without even needing to give a reason for it.

Competence is a praxis that can involve a poiesis, a practical attitude that leads to a result: the termite colony makes a mound, Messi scores a goal (which he could never do if he had to calculate the ballistics of the ball every time), Gaudí builds the Sagrada Familia following his design, but also changes it little by little, according to the circumstances and maybe following the advice of a worker who barely knows what the drawings look like but sees a practical problem. Moreover, poiesis, the more or less ritualised action, can also happen without reason, like when people scribble on a piece of paper or tinker with their mobile phones.

Without hands, and without the experience of manipulating and grasping, we would have had no thought; without the competence of manual skill we would have had no understanding, which – let it be said in passing – explains why the distinction between intellectual work and manual labour is always problematic (and more so today than ever before). This aspect is neglected by the conceptions according to which human intelligence is a unique and special system that cannot be reduced to the manipulation of signs, but allegedly adds something magical or ineffable to it – 'understanding'. I do not deny that there is understanding, I simply suggest that there is no discontinuity between the manipulation of signs and understanding, and that consciousness is not a transcendent property, but rather an emerging property arising from an evolutionary process made possible by the most stupid and random of designs: the superabundance of material and time in the universe.

Even in language there can be competence without understanding, since I can correctly identify an object starting from its name (referential competence) without being able to insert it in an epistemological horizon, however minimal (inferential competence). Speaking does not necessarily involve knowing the meaning of the words we use, and it never means knowing it fully. All the more so since even the inferential dimension can be dealt with in terms of a 'competence' that at least in certain cases appears able to do without an 'understanding'. In this sense, the Wittgensteinian motto 'meaning is use'[56] seems to suggest that meaning (both inferential and referential) is primarily a matter of competence (use) rather than understanding. This is demonstrated as much by the effectiveness of well-trained automatic translators as by the way in which we learn our mother tongue, which (unlike studying another language) clearly happens without understanding.

This also applies to mathematics and apparently more abstract forms of thought. Euler argued that the strength of his mathematics lay in the pencil he used, and Turing's great discovery was that in order to calculate, it is not necessary to know what mathematics is, but only to have the technical skills that make the calculation possible. A system of signs is made to interact for practical or ritual reasons. Over time, however, the signs become emancipated and sophisticated, and above all the actions (operations) that are performed with these signs become increasingly refined. In the end, the sphere of mathematics emerges as a collection of true theorems and operations. Thus, among the various products of technology, the most important though underestimated one is the truth (I'll come back to this later).

Art is another canonical sphere of competence without understanding; at the same time, it constitutes a traditional sphere of creativity, that is, it leads to the emergence of something new in a manner analogous to a priori synthetic judgments. The artist does not know why they made the artwork exactly that way (Leibniz's doctrine of *nescio quid*, 'I know not what'); the work of art – since the invocation to the goddess in Homeric incipits – has always been conceived of as inspired, as something that comes from the outside and is not mastered by the author, and most of the time the descriptions of the creative process appeal to unconscious elements or to an automatism that guides the realisation (the characters act as if they were alive; certain words – for example, 'Nevermore' in Poe's 'The Raven' – guide the whole composition). This is why art is technical. In writing *Wilhelm Meister's Lehrjahre*, Goethe did not have the complete picture of what he was aiming to do from the beginning. However, when the work was finished it became the archetype of the *Bildungsroman*, which established the rules of the genre in a dynamic form, taking on an exemplary and canonical function.

This aspect, however, is not restricted to art, but applies to technology in general, which on the one hand appears as the realm of repetition, but on the other is the sphere of inventiveness; this is all the more interesting because it is not animated by any preliminary intentionality. Nobody could have predicted from the outset the many possible uses of the lever and the wheel (not to mention more complex apparatuses), so that the functions that are usually traced back to the human super-faculty of the imagination must rather be attributed to the possibilities of hysteresis, externalisation and accumulation that are immanent to technology.

And let us not forget that social interaction is an eminent example of this competence without understanding. A human group performs a certain initiation rite that is linked to a pre-human past. The rite evolves into more complex and codified forms (scout promise ceremony, consecration, military service . . .). Finally, it takes the legal form of adulthood, and creates a series of rules and laws, determining a sphere of truth. The image of human action as an unconscious praxis that becomes conscious only through historical becoming fully accounts for our intuitions. We do not know the reasons for our actions, and only sometimes can we explain them to ourselves. Reciprocally, knowing the principles of our actions does not make us more efficient (otherwise, professors at military academies would be the greatest strategists, which almost never happens). Social emergence has a performative character that is directly productive, that is, it becomes construction.

'I remember everything, but understand nothing.' This being so, we have to slightly change the order of Freud's famous succession: remember, repeat, re-elaborate (which, after all, described an analytical and not a purely synthetic operation). First we have repetition, i.e. pure iteration, the past repeated by matter; then remembrance, i.e. the past remembered by memory; and finally re-elaboration, i.e. understanding, which, I repeat, may never happen, as Zeno Cosini, Svevo's hero, confesses: 'I remember everything, but understand nothing.'[57]

Most of us live without knowing much about our metabolism, termites produce complex mounds without following any designs, and Homer composed his verses in a state of inspiration. This resource is very important because if understanding were to precede competence (as constructivists suppose) most of us would not survive, termites would not build mounds, and Homer (assuming he understood his own metabolism and therefore did survive) would not have composed the *Iliad* (to do so he would have needed Greek grammar and elements of prosody, criticism and literary history that were inaccessible to him). From this we can understand the centrality of technology in both nature and in society: competence without understanding explains most of our activities and our relationship with the world, the transmission of skills, as well as the fact that these skills can (though not necessarily do) bring understanding by accessing the level of epistemology.

3.2 Repetition

An abacus, a computer and a Kantian scheme are all based on the possibility of iteration, which Kant himself suggests when he says that 5 is the construction method of *****.

Synthesis. As stated, first there is synthesis, the gesture that cannot be understood through the analysis of its components. We act before we think, and by doing so we discover new truths. By contrast, understanding is necessarily linked to the formulation of analytical reasoning, which operates in the sphere of already established knowledge. This action permits the emergence of truth from reality. It is a knowledge that results from doing (unlike analytical judgments, which are a knowledge that emerges from further knowledge, and therefore are not surprising). Competence is a praxis that can result in a poiesis, a practical attitude that leads to a result: the bee makes honey, the termite builds the termite mound, Michelangelo sculpts Moses, Maradona scores a goal, and so forth. But poiesis, i.e. the more or less ritualised action, may also happen with no reason, as shown by people who knit, scribble on a piece of paper or play with their phone. Without hands, without the experience of handling and grasping, we would not have developed thought; without manual competence (prehension) we would not have had understanding (comprehension). Hands are prehensile, they grasp things (as Hegel knew very well, seeing the noun *Begriff*, 'concept', as related to the verb *greifen*, 'to grasp'[58]). Hands indicate and, when they indicate without grasping, making gestures, they initiate the production of symbols.

Speaking a language, lighting a fire, writing a novel, counting, interacting socially: these skills do not rely on conceptual schemes, but on interpretative schemes, which in some cases (for example, finding a four-leaf clover in a meadow) mediate between concept (abstract and general) and perception (concrete and individual), but in many others – indeed, in the vast majority – apply to perceptions or operate in the world independently of concepts. This is not surprising: we have a disposition that manifests itself in the most elementary devices and evolves in increasingly complex formations, like a reproductive faculty that transports ontology into epistemology. Conversely, technology is not only related to the remote origins of humankind, but also to our highest intellectual achievements: it shows itself in mathematics and logic, in the creation of scientific experiments and artistic works, in the actions and rites that accompany our social lives.

Praxis. The gesture can be repeated, and it becomes praxis, which through repetition can generate competence (think of learning to write). Praxis can be imitated, and can itself consist of imitation (mimesis was originally the imitation of the movement of the stars through dance). Practice, moreover, can be enhanced – herein lies the value of training and exercise. The dynamic result of iteration is the strengthening of performance. The dead labour accumulated in the instrument reduces the physical strength necessary for an operation; the repetition of gestures makes them automatic and frees reflection for innovative purposes; the overlapping of traces generates easier paths, both in the mind and in external nature (think of a watercourse).

Technical apparatuses are an eminent example of the power that comes from the automatic iterability of any function. But these apparatuses are only a circumscribed yet very cumbersome manifestation of a more general function of technology, which is exercised in metaphysics (a process such as idealisation derives from the technological fact of the possibility of indefinite iteration), society (think of the constitutive role of ritual) and concepts (the notion of 'meaning' would be inconceivable if one could not rely on the iterability of signs, which is the condition of possibility of meaning). What is recorded can be repeated, with a time delay that generates facilitation and enhancement (hence the benefits of exercise). Technological devices are an eminent example of the power that comes from the automatic iterability of any function. This is of particular interest: the result of iteration is in fact the possibility of the generation of the idea as a possibility of indefinite repetition.

Poiesis. Finally, we have poiesis, i.e. praxis recorded, which can therefore be retained and transmitted. Poiesis can be traditionalised, and this leads to an incalculable increase in hysteresis, which is then transformed into culture and offers a possibility of understanding infinitely simpler than praxis. New generations don't start from scratch every time. 'It is now no longer the laborer that employs the means of production, but the means of production that employ the laborer',[59] lamented Marx. This statement, as the rest of *Das Kapital* shows, suggests that there should be a relationship between man and technology in which the former is not alienated but in control. In truth, any kind of relationship with technology involves a form of submission, which therefore depends on the nature of man and technology, and not on capitalism. Now, anyone who makes a Nespresso must service the machine, and not only use it, and this activity is not labour. Even artisanal work is conditioned by (and receives its purpose from) the tool being used, and this also applies to intellectual performance. Confirming what has been said about 'learning by doing', Proust claimed he was not free in writing his books, but almost followed a script; as mentioned, Euler found his theorems on the tip of his pencil. Now, Marx cultivated the illusion of a free craftsman who was alienated by a cruel world. But if Proust and Euler were not free, then who is? While this is not the same as comparing Werther to an English miner (Goethe was well aware of the difference, as are we), it seems that the relationship between man and technology must be interpreted, as I propose in these pages, as an essential form of revelation.

What is often an emergency tool – something that you find there and then to defend yourself, attack, or lean on, reacting to danger or fatigue – can be philosophically considered as an instrument of emergence, or as a form of preadaptation that ensures the emergence of essential traits of human nature and society. The stick as a universal supplement to humanity remedies our natural imbecility (in the literal sense of the term) and allows for a series of acts of capitalisation. First of all, there is the capitalisation of strength, because the stick can act as a tool, a lever or a club. Then, there is the capitalisation of authority. There is no need to actually use the stick when we can hint that we could use it at any time – here the better stick is the club (the ancestor of the baton and the sceptre) rather than the lever, the ancestor of industrial and artisanal works. And since the pen wounds more than the sword, the club will soon turn to other types of capitalisation: the capitalisation of memory in knowledge, the capitalisation of acts in duty, the capitalisation of traces in power. These are the most important capitalisations in a time like ours, in which recording reveals all its incredible, long overlooked power.

Technology, understood in the broadest sense as the transition from ontology to epistemology, can be conceived of as a science of emergence. Emergence, as an evolutionary phenomenon both in nature and in society, takes a very long time to unfold, showing an intrinsic correlation between emergence and temporality; however, the emergence of knowledge from being can be achieved much more quickly. Consider how quickly one can shift between the shapes of a bi-stable figure, or think of a detective's sudden intuition, the quick understanding that comes with experience, and now the data instantly processed by an algorithm. In this emergence, recording plays a key role. Here we touch on a metaphysical foundation. Emerging means generating a quantitative accumulation of traces, the result of which is a qualitative change. For this to happen it is necessary that the traces are recorded, that is, that the accumulation takes place. As we have seen, hysteresis is the most extensive transcendental, as it makes emergence possible. If we have recording, in fact, we can generate a system of relationships and differences that will lead to the emergence of meaning on the conceptual level, and of temporality on the level of intuition.

And once meaning emerges, that's it. The hand, which is no longer a tool, but a motor and a driving force, will generate a technical system that first takes care of finding energies other than human strength – so that the motor soon becomes the wind or water that moves the mill, and then, at a turning point that will be the basis of the industrial revolution, the pressure of steam. Artificial intelligence is no exception, and is fully part of this transition from tool to motor to driving force. Also in this case, intelligence, which was originally a direct instrument of the human being, has become a motor and a driving force because it provides artificial intelligence with its fuel, i.e. the database on which to run, while also determining the system of purposes and needs to which artificial intelligence is called to respond. Ultimately, however, the aim of the whole process consists in transforming the tool not only into a motor, but above all into a driving force, that is, into the ultimate purpose. This is the situation we are witnessing today. Freed from any productive necessity, the hand is essentially destined to writing, to controlling devices, to opening packages. Completely exempted from production, today the hand (like the human being) finds its *raison d'être* in consumerism.

3.3 Remembrance

The past is remembered by memory. It is not matter that emerges from memory, but memory that emerges from matter through praxis and poiesis. About 120 million years ago, a caste of worker bees without wings originated among termites; it was then, in the Cretaceous, in a process that is not yet completed, that their political and social ascent began. Termite mounds are reminiscent of the Sagrada Familia, but obviously no termite has ever seen Gaudí's projects. All of this has emerged from the depth of time. Similarly, the 'waggle dance' with which bees indicate the distance and position of pollen was not heaven-sent: there must have been a long transition from early warning signals to the highly ritualised contemporary repertoire of honeybees. The entrance of history into nature is manifested through genetic modifications and reinforced by behavioural changes that depend on communication (which in the case of insects is 90 percent chemical and olfactory) and on something that looks like the ancestor of culture: the progressive refinement of the laws governing the operation of a superorganism. An overall sense emerges, generated by individuals who as such have none.

Schemes. Iteration is the ability, which manifests itself in technology, to repeat what has been recorded, with all the consequent strengthening and simplification effects. Technology is the field of action (praxis) and production (poiesis), and as such it is present in both nature and history, if we want to refer to these traditional fields whose opposition is lost in light of hysteresis. It will come as no surprise that the definition of a scheme, as offered by Kant, is that of a technical device. Kant rightly understood that to move from concepts (epistemology) to objects (ontology) it is necessary to use an intermediate term that he called 'scheme', and which he characterised with a strongly technological qualification – he spoke of schematism as a 'hidden technique' (*verborgene Kunst*, which usually translates as 'hidden art', but whose meaning is obviously the same as 'hidden technology'). However, conditioned by his dualism and by his Pentecostal attitude (which in this case amounts to the idea of a priori as opposed to experience), Kant described schematism as a top-down process, although he did not exclude (as is even clearer in the *Critique of Judgment*) a bottom-up process, which for him was the subsumption of the subcategories of the objects of experience.

Imitation. Imitation is iteration in the context of social objects. Leaving collective intentionality aside, we are faced with one of the oldest insights into human nature – and indeed animal nature, given that parrots and monkeys are the paradigms of imitation. Humans grow up by imitating others and continue to imitate others even as adults. This intuition soon received philosophical confirmation: for Plato, imitation explains almost everything, including the relationship between the sensible world and the world of ideas. And if Aristotle (understandably) excludes the possibility that tables and chairs can really imitate ideas, he admits (as is only natural) that one tends to imitate one's parents; this is one of the rare topics on which agreement still reigns today, among psychologists for instance. Even without referring to philosophical authorities, it seems obvious enough that we were born to copy: the fundamental character of every social fact is precisely its imitative nature, as Gabriel Tarde claimed, and it is difficult not to imitate him in this. Here it is not a question of evoking a hidden faculty, but rather of recognising an obvious and trivial behaviour, which can be seen in the stock market as well as the class struggle, in advertising as well as in fashion.

It is not only about acts, but also about knowledge. In fact, mimesis underpins so-called 'social cognition', which involves both understanding the behaviour of others based on the attribution of mental states such as beliefs, desires, emotions and intentions (mindreading), and sharing those states (empathy). The identification of brain areas (so-called mirror neurons) that are activated not only when we perform certain movements or feel certain emotions, but even when we observe others perform the same movements or express the same emotions, has been taken as proof that the understanding of others' behaviours occurs precisely through their mental imitation. Regarding the kinship between mimesis and mirroring, it is worth noting that mirror neurons are particularly sensitive to gestures, which are the genetic site of mimesis. 'Mimesis', for the Greeks, initially designated a set of gestural techniques aimed at making the invisible visible, so to speak: the Bacchic exaltation, the expression of pain at funeral ceremonies and even the movements of the stars reproduced through dance. Thus began the long journey that led to devotional books such as *The Imitation of Christ*, or to sophisticated works of art, which at least for a large portion of the Western canon have also been characterised as imitations of nature or other works; in many cases this has provoked mimetic attitudes in readers, sometimes with extreme consequences, such as the suicides induced by reading *The Sorrows of Young Werther*.

So far so good: indeed, too good. One problem with the thesis presented so far is that it appears inflationary, so to speak: there is mimesis everywhere. Is it to be concluded that everyone imitates, and therefore everyone does the same thing, except perhaps one who is at the origin of the imitative chain? One puts one's hands up and everybody follows? This is clearly not the case, fortunately, and when it happens it is only in highly conditioned contexts: cases of collective psychosis, Nuremberg gatherings and voodoo rituals. Morality, law and common sense rightly assume that we – and not some inscrutable First Imitated Person – are responsible for our actions. So quite sensibly, when some blamed Goethe for the suicides 'caused' by his *Werther*, he replied not only that more people died in English mines, but also that those mimetic suicides fell totally on the shoulders, perhaps weak but completely individual, of those who had taken their own lives.

This consideration is also found in our negative judgments of conformism. Although imitation is the rule of social bonding, conformism is denigrated, plagiarism is prosecuted, and it is considered offensive to imitate people's cadences or movements (at least in cases when they can see us do it). At the opposite pole, creativity is even overrated. Very often the tension between imitation and originality develops a sort of double bind: one must imitate, one must have models, but at the same time one must not imitate, because imitation is a limited and servile attitude. So what can one do? In one of the recurrent controversies about mimesis, concerning the imitation of the classics, a humanist of the early sixteenth century, Paolo Cortese, said that he certainly wanted to resemble the ancient models, but like a son resembles his father and not like a monkey resembles a human being. This essentially seems to suggest as follows: that the son brings something of his own (for example, Oedipal hatred) whereas the monkey does not.

In short, if it is true that imitation is the basis of the social bond, it is also true that this basis gives rise to subjectivity with a strong (though not very strong) degree of autonomy: there are original people and conformists, creatives and non-creatives, strong characters and weak characters. These categories of naive psychology refer to common observational data, and in fact all the examples of the pervasiveness of mimesis contain phenomena of originality: the class struggle involves charismatic leaders, fashion rewards originality (at least in theory), and in the stock market some people actually manage to make money amidst general panic. This is how the financier George Soros could rightly proclaim himself one of the most consistent followers of Popper – whose student he actually was for a few months – for having applied his principle of falsification: in the stock market, those who manage to go against the current (i.e. falsifying the expectations of others), though in a rational way, have a good chance of earning money.

If, as I have said, collective intentionality can be replaced by the more ordinary and less esoteric notion of 'mimesis', the question remains as to how mimetic acts construct social reality. This is where conventions come into play. It has rightly been observed that there is a difference between imitation and convention. Convention is a deliberate and conscious imitation, at least to a certain extent (then, of course, there are conventional people who stand out for their inability to understand that their actions are indeed shaped by conventions). My thesis is that convention is not imitation, or rather, not only imitation. Convention is one of the steps in the process of articulation and complication that leads from mimesis to the construction of social reality. In other words, imitation (and this is the fundamental point I would like to make) is the cause of convention, as well as of social reality as a whole.

Idealisation. Idealisation is iteration within ideal objects. Iterability is the transition from passive to active. It is no longer necessary to wait for the event to repeat itself: you can recall it artificially and iterate it indefinitely. It is the liberation from nature and necessity that takes place in nature (recording takes place in nature and is part of nature) and necessarily so (what is recorded is an event that has all the necessity of contingency). Hysteresis fixates interactions and generates potential meanings.

A singularity took place. A singularity here and now leaves a trace. History records interactions between individuals that perhaps, and in a very long time, will lead to a society. This initially settles in rituals, in external media necessary for the fixation of memory in a society without writing. However, some form of recording emerges very quickly. For example, soon come the first technical acquisitions, such as flint working, which allow for a reification of memory in artifacts; likewise, it does not seem accidental to me that we soon have wall paintings like those in Lascaux. Once again, this is a case of proto-documentality which, as palaeontologists suggest, has a descriptive and prescriptive value, just like our documents today: the paintings show where and how to hunt, for example, or which animals are sacred. With the development of writing, sociality evolves much more rapidly, and the role of documents becomes stronger. In fact, documents set and coordinate actions and take on a prescriptive power.

Indefinite iterability therefore ensures the possibility of idealisation. An idea is not an eternal type that is actualised in a series of copies, but rather an instance that repeats itself, and that precisely in this repetition determines the transition from the example as an occurrence to the example as an archetype. Idealisation transcends the here and now of perception, and enables its iteration and passage outside the genetic sphere. Idealisation is the premise of informatisation. To be effective, my information must be recorded by the receiver (otherwise it would be empty words).

What characterises the digital world is the fact that recording is preliminary to communication. Its necessity, at this point, is not only logically constitutive, but ontologically so. The fundamental character of iterability (and of the recording that precedes it) lies in the fact that the here and now, once recorded, assumes a different existence. The scar I got on my right index finger as a child after tinkering with my father's razor recalls an event that happened more than half a century ago; a photograph fixates an image and turns it into a repeatable representation as long as the medium is preserved, etc. If the character proper to physical reality consists in spatial-temporal localisation, recording allows for a potentially indefinite iteration, which is the character proper to ideality.

This circumstance suggests that what we call 'ideality' (depending precisely on the possibility of indefinite iteration) is a modification of reality, not the reverse.[60]

Iteration is a possible consequence of inscription and is the condition of possibility of idealisation. What's an idea? A number, a relationship, a founding principle, as in the Platonic sense; a faint image, as in the empirical sense; a purpose, a regulatory principle, as in the Kantian sense. What holds these three apparently disparate meanings together is the fact of iterability. What takes place is a process of incalculable importance, a transformation whereby the here and now of sensible presence, by the simple passive fact of inscription, becomes an ideality: being iterable, the trace can be repeated indefinitely, i.e. it accesses the status of ideality. Taking up the analogy with Kant once again, we are dealing with the synthesis of reproduction in the imagination.

If things are as I have tried to illustrate, there are three great theses regarding the relationship between inscriptions and ideal objects. One, of the constructivist type, could be called 'the idealisation thesis', because it asserts that writing lies at the origin of idealisation, and therefore of ideal objects. The other, of a Platonic type, is what I defend; I call it the 'socialisation thesis', because it asserts that writing does not preside over the creation of idealities, which are independent of them, but rather over their socialisation. In between, there is a further aspect of inscription-iteration: its ability to give rise to psychological constructs, i.e. ideas in an empirical sense, in agreement with what I propose to call the 'psychologisation thesis'. It is worth exploring them in depth so as to highlight the basic differences between ideal and social objects.

Idealisation thesis. From this perspective, every form of inscription takes a step forward in idealisation; that is, in emancipating a formulation (of a theorem, for example) from its contingent and subjective character. Oral language, which perfects the idealisation taking place on the basis of perception, frees the object from the subjectivity of the inventor, but limits it to the original community. Only writing – which appears as the most empirical of elements, as an inanimate medium – is able to perfect this ideality, removing it from the spacetime finiteness of the inventor and his contemporaries, thereby achieving that independence of meaning with respect to the present community in which the perfection of ideality consists. In this framework, writing would be the condition of possibility of objectivity, although the idealisation thesis does not specify whether it is a necessary or a sufficient condition – and indeed everything suggests that we are dealing with a necessary but not sufficient condition, even within the idealisation thesis. By this I mean that, even if the inscription was a condition of idealisation, it does not follow that everything inscribed is true; therefore, the Pythagorean theorem possesses sources of truth that are independent of their inscription. Characteristically, in fact, the idealisation-iteration system does not make it true that 2 + 2 = 5. Hence the idealisation-iteration is not Platonic, as it does not refer to true ideas. At most, it can be a way to explain the genesis of ideas as psychological constructs, i.e. in the empirical sense. But in this case we are not dealing with the constitution of ideal objects, but with a psychic process.

Psychologisation thesis. The idealisation thesis can, however, be recovered to account for the psychologisation thesis. The argument runs like this: what is an idea (in the sense of Frege's 'thought'[61])? An entity that, in principle, is independent from the one who thinks it, and that as such continues to exist even after the person who thought it has ceased to think it, for the moment or perhaps forever. Now, in order for such a condition to be realised, it is not enough to assert that the idea is 'spiritual', precisely because then it could depend exclusively on the psychic acts of the individual. Instead of focusing on the spiritual character of the idea, the idealisation thesis invites us to consider the fact that an idea, in order to be such, must be indefinitely iterable (through the sign that fixates it); and that the possibility of repeating it begins at the very moment when a code is established, whose archetypal form (original and not derived) is offered by the written sign, by a trace that can be iterated even (though not necessarily) in the absence of the writer. A written text, be it even a shopping list, best represents the condition of ideality, precisely because, unlike psychic processes without external manifestation, it can access an existence separate from its author. But as we have seen, ideality must be understood here as it was seen by the empiricists; the idealisation thesis is limited to explaining the way in which iteration intervenes both in the psyche (as the psychologisation thesis) and in society, where it presents itself as the socialisation thesis.

Socialisation thesis. The socialisation thesis asserts that what is described by the analysis of the inscription-iteration is not the birth of the Platonic idea, but the socialisation of either an idea that has a previous and separate existence – as in the case of a genuine ideal object such as Pythagoras' theorem – or an act between two parties, as in a shopping list, which did not have an independent existence that was separate or prior to the act, and which therefore constitutes a genuine social object. But to understand how much social objects differ from ideal objects it is enough to consider a simple example. When an autoresponder on the phone tells us that 'the number you have dialled does not exist', this, from the point of view of both numbers and ideal objects, is completely absurd, since there are no non-existing numbers. It is clear that here the number is understood as a social object, as a code, and not as a number in the sense of an ideal object. In fact, numbers as such all exist: it makes no sense to say that, e.g., 011774573 does not exist (or that, as in the messages of American telephone companies, 'it is not a working number' or 'it is not in service': numbers qua ideal objects certainly cannot do any 'work'). Things are different for numbers as social objects, and indeed for social objects as a whole.

3.4 Re-elaboration

We do not understand by analysing, but by making gestures that take place during the continuity and change of time that are preserved and externalised through documents. As for the productive force of human and natural technology, in both cases it is a competence without understanding. One may in fact wonder how it is possible to interact with a world that is not dependent on our conceptual patterns. But this problem only arises if we believe that knowledge must be preliminary to interaction and action. Yet obviously this is not the case. Most of the actions we perform in the world are the result of a doing that does not require knowledge. Therefore, first of all there is a technological development, which is an accumulation of skills without understanding: knowing how to chip a flint without necessarily having words to describe what you are doing, or (at the other end of that story) knowing how to make very complicated calculations by entrusting them to the knowledge placed in the paper, pen and inkwell, in the computer, or in that particularly complicated technical tool that is the human mind.

This, too, is an apparatus made of competence without understanding: the real work of the mind is done by neurons that download without understanding anything; understanding, i.e. the result of the sum of these downloads, comes later if ever. In this sense, it is ontology that forms epistemology through technology, and the myth of the given is transformed into the given of the myth. So technology makes pots, not lids: it offers a competence, but not an understanding. It has been argued that one of the most nefarious illusions produced by the Web is that an increase in data and computation would lead to some clarification of our existence. Now, there is no reason why data couldn't do that. Obviously, they could not do it in themselves, no more than the results of a medical analysis can illuminate the patient without a doctor's diagnosis. Underlying this attitude is the fallacious assumption that the quantitative growth of data should immediately produce knowledge, and the fact that this does not happen is evidence of the cognitive ineffectiveness of data.

What is produced through repetition is a skill that does not require prior understanding, although it can produce it, either immediately or eventually. In all these cases we can verify the enhancement that comes from hysteresis, which explains the omnipresence of technology in both nature and culture. In this sense, iteration is able to produce artificial intelligence, which is in no way different from natural intelligence, since it shares its mechanical processes (counting, using a linguistic code, etc.). This artificial intelligence (like natural intelligence) is not a general intellect, however, because competence is not accompanied by understanding.

Performativity. The fundamental characteristic of technology, from the point of view of results, is performativity. As mentioned, if the ontological alternative is between existence and non-existence, the epistemological alternative is between true and false, and the teleological alternative is with purpose or without purpose, the technological alternative is either success or failure. Success can give rise to an act (and in this case it is praxis) or an object (and in this case it is poiesis). Praxis has, so to speak, hysteresis behind it (it is the iteration of gestures learned and perfected through exercise); poiesis also has hysteresis in front of it, with all the effects deriving from imitation and exemplarity. The relationship between ontology and epistemology guaranteed by technology is not one of construction from top to bottom, but of emergence from bottom to top, so that epistemology emerges from ontology through technology, that is, through competence without understanding. Technology, from this point of view, really acts as a bridge between ontology (a certain set of available entities) and epistemology (the knowledge that can derive from it), not through the superimposition of conceptual schemes over perceptual elements (as in the binary system Epistemology → Ontology), but precisely through the ternary scheme Ontology → Technology → Epistemology.

The relationship between being and knowledge is guaranteed neither by a direct causation of the latter with respect to the former (as in Kantian transcendentalism) nor by a direct causation of the former with respect to the latter (as in metaphysical realism), but by technology as a competence without understanding, i.e. as a doing that can, although will not necessarily, be translated into knowledge. Knowing something means knowing something true (knowing something false equals not knowing) and knowing how to argue because what we know is true. It is therefore possible to collect mushrooms without poisoning oneself, to treat illnesses effectively, to regulate one's life in a sensible way, to make simple or complex calculations, to behave excellently in society, or to compose admirable works of art, without being able to account for what one is doing. If this seems surprising, consider that the reverse is even more so.

If in the case of the natural world the iteration manages the transition from ontology to epistemology, in the case of the social world the iteration takes place, instead, from epistemology to ontology. The idea is very simple: you cannot get married (or stipulate a contract, or perform any social act) in just any way, but always according to a certain form. For example, at your wedding, you must answer 'I do' and not 'certainly' or 'you bet'. The illocutionary force of the act (ontology) is thus dependent on the form (epistemology) and derives from the iteration of a ritual (the 'due forms', the forms that iterate a certain pattern, thereby conforming to it). Note that it derives from iteration, not from understanding: I could be a civil law professor and know everything about marriage, but I could not actually get married unless I repeated the right formula, that is, the codified form of the act. So in social dynamics, there are not just two levels at stake, what we know and what there is, but three: what we know, what we do and what there is. This third and very important level is precisely that of technology as competence (know how) without understanding (know that) reinforced by iteration.

Invention. This process has a synthetic dimension in that it adds something instead of just analysing what is already there. Analytical truths, those that inform us that no bachelor is married, are much less interesting than synthetic truths, which inform us about married women who spend time with bachelors. This search for synthetic truth involves doing without knowing, i.e. an art; for example, Maigret investigates and is unable to explain the logic of his investigations, and Kant reminds us of the mysterious nature of a simple operation such as 7 + 5 = 12, in which the concept of 12 cannot be deduced from the analysis of 7 and 5 because I could get to 12 by summing, for instance, 6 and 6 or 10 and 2.

The technological dimension of truth implies a competence that is not necessarily accompanied by understanding. I can ride a bicycle without knowing the laws of physics, and I can calculate that 7 + 5 = 12 without knowing the fundamentals of arithmetic, just as I can do body weight exercises with extraordinary dexterity without having the slightest notion of the physiology of my body, and just as Homer (deplored for this by Plato) could describe battles with great success without ever having commanded or fought in one. Conversely, I can read all the cookbooks in this world, but nothing guarantees that I will become a chef worthy of the name because of it.

The fundamental question of the *Critique of Pure Reason* is 'how can there be synthetic a priori judgments?', i.e. propositions that broaden our knowledge but precede experience and are independent of it? Kant wonders how it is possible to extend this process outside mathematics (which for him is not true knowledge), and deploys the whole complex device of transcendental philosophy to do so. But the real keystone – at least if we follow the examples given just now – is hidden in a place that Kant had not foreseen or even understood: a priori synthetic judgments are not found at the beginning of the process (precisely in the table of judgments that for Kant precede the categories) but in the schemes. Kant was so interested in a priori synthetic judgments because in his conception they depended on concepts that were independent of experience and were therefore certain. Now, we can easily note that informative a posteriori synthetic judgments come from operations: we get the number of beans by applying the rule 'add one', and many pieces of information (for instance, what time it is or how much we weigh) come from machines that have no concepts, but only mechanisms regulating their functioning.

The true story of schematism. On the one hand Kant offers us a hyper-conceptualist view ('intuitions without concepts are blind') by which even the most distracted of intuitions depends on concepts. And Kant's world is made up of epistemology (conceptual schemes with which we order the world) and ontology (the world that we order, and which we never really know, as it is made of things in themselves that we can only access as phenomena). On the other hand, however, in the chapter on schematism Kant mentions a third term that lies between concepts and intuitions (that is, between epistemology and ontology): the scheme, which as mentioned is defined as a 'hidden technique' (*verborgene Kunst*). The scheme performs operations (Kant defines it as a 'construction method').[62]

But how does re-elaboration work in practice? Simplifying beyond reason while hoping to be clear, I'd say that we have individuals (a chair, which is such regardless of my knowledge), objects ('chair': the individual recognised by a concept) and facts (the fact that there is a chair). I come to this fact with an interpretative scheme that does not consist of concepts, but of procedures: I sit down, for example, without formulating any concept (as would a Kantian, who makes my use of the chair depend on the possession of the concept of 'chair'), but simply exploiting the resources provided by the encounter between the chair and my body (a cat could do something similar).

Later I will formulate the concept of 'chair', which, however, belongs to the sphere of knowledge and not of doing, the latter instead being managed by the intermediate sphere of hermeneutics. In the case of, say, rheumatic pains that I can experience without any concept of 'rheumatism', I will elaborate interpretative schemes that result in the consumption of ibuprofen, which will produce its results even if I do not possess, nor will ever possess, the concepts of 'rheumatism' and 'ibuprofen'. The result of an act that is a valid interpretation is a fact. The constitutive rule of facts follows that of social objects, and it comes down to: Fact = Recorded Act. A fact is the result of an action of an agent on a patient that has the characteristic of being recorded.

In turn, facts may (though they need not) become objects, i.e. conceptually identifiable parts of ontology. But without the mediation of facts and technology, individuals could never become objects (on the other hand, objects are faithful to individuals). Let us suppose that the same football match is seen by someone competent and someone else who is incompetent. Where the latter will only see a bunch of people chasing a ball, the former will see a match, goals, offsides and, of course, a bunch of people chasing a ball. The interpretative scheme is a technological apparatus (a sort of infrared viewer): it is neither epistemological (as believed by analytic thinkers, hypostatising the experience of natural objects) nor ontological (as believed by hermeneutic thinkers, hypostatising the experience of social objects).

Interpretation. Hermes is the messenger of the gods, and the hermeneuticist is a postman, one who exercises the operation of carrying messages (a hieroglyph, a novel in Hungarian, a threatening message or a love letter) that he almost never understands. And all the meanings of hermeneutics, ancient and modern, can easily be traced back to practical operations: expression (the meaning of *hermeneia* in Aristotle) is the act of carrying out, translation is transportation, understanding is grasping – a manual operation – and the very deconstruction typical of nineteenth- and twentieth-century hermeneutics has a clear technical connotation. By proposing interpretation as an operation I want to focus on three aspects.

The first is the pragmatic character of interpretation, the fact that it is perfectly possible without understanding, which we have seen is only one of the traditional functions of hermeneutics. Kant's assumption is that in order to have competence it is necessary to have understanding ('intuitions without concepts are blind'). Yet if one claims to derive competence from understanding one does not get very far: schematism is a mystery; an analysis of what is needed for transcendental schemes is boring, and Kant exempts himself from it with the same lightness (or awkwardness) with which, earlier on, he avoided providing a detailed table of categories, leaving the burden to the reader by way of entertainment or homework.

If the problem with schemes and the problem with categories seem to go hand in hand, it is for an excellent reason: schemes do not follow categories, they precede them, as they are construction methods that are not limited to the bare furnishings of categories (which in turn derive from judgments, i.e. from epistemological functions). Therefore, much more can be done, and, strangely enough, Kant himself, without correcting the chapter on the schematism, reformulated the whole issue in the *Critique of Judgment*, in which he addresses two great cases of competence without understanding. The first is that of the artist who produces works without being guided by a concept – works that will be enjoyed by people who, again, will not need concepts because 'beauty pleases without a concept'. The second is that of nature which, without an intelligent project (Kant came before Darwin, but his critique of teleology already affected the view of Intelligent Design), gives shape to living beings.

The interpretative scheme is not a conceptual scheme (whatever this desperately vague expression may mean) but a practical rule through which we interact with individuals. In most cases the rules are neither known nor explicit (walking, playing with the cat, apologising), in others the rules are explicit, but not 'understood'. What do I understand, really, when I count the beans in the jar? I follow a rule ('add one') that I learned as a child. At the same time, counting is an interpretation not in the sense that it defines some conceptual horizon, but in that it fulfils the practical function that traditionally belongs to hermeneutics, which is unsurprisingly referred to as *hermeneutikè techne*:[63] the technique of transporting messages, capable of performing a mediating function that offers a link between the ontological layer of being and the epistemological layer of knowledge.

The second aspect is the external or mechanical character of interpretation. Are we sure that the schematism and the common root of sensibility and intellect are hidden, as Kant says, in the depths of the human soul? Why inside and not outside? There is nothing in the brain that justifies our difference from non-human animals. Much, instead, can be found outside the brain, in what we do with our hands and using tools. Typically, hypomnestic externalisations of memory are not extraneous to creativity but explain why, apparently, we have more imagination than animals, who are less hypomnestically equipped and therefore have to keep everything inside, so to speak. The process by which I add a horn to a horse has no need to take place in the depths (or surface) of my soul. I can do this without any difficulty using cardboard templates, pen and paper, or a drawing program on my computer. Outsourcing simple functions is one of the crucial features of technology: the handle of a suitcase allows me to carry it without having to clasp it with both arms, wheels reduce effort, etc. This convenience becomes a necessity when it comes to performing complex functions: the only way to make a chiliohorn – an animal with a thousand horns – is to draw it, or rather to assign the task of drawing it to a computer program. We should never overlook the wealth of possibilities offered by the automatic and the inanimate.

The third aspect is that this operation allows for judgments, that is, it can turn into epistemology. An action can repeat itself without generating products, and that is what practice is. An example of this is metabolism, and so are all actions related to metabolism, both in our nature as organisms and in that of social subjects (nutrition, desire, fitness). In this sense there is no difference between human technology and natural technology, since in both cases we are dealing with unconscious production. The DNA, the amoeba that splits in two, the tennis champion who plays a short ball, the idiot savant or the mobile phone that perform a complex arithmetic operation – they all do rather than know. I don't need to have a conceptual notebook telling me that handles are used to open and doors to enter: I simply do it, without knowing and without thinking about it. Hilary Putnam rightly noted that meaning is not in the head, but in the environment. Those who find this view a little esoteric could simply look at a child interacting with a mobile phone, a professor sitting at a table, or (to take Leibniz's example) a donkey going straight to the hay without having read a line of Euclid.

Thus, to invoke the theories of truth described earlier, mesotruth recovers hermeneutics without falling into hypertruth or into the correlationism of hypotruth. The mistake made by postmodernists was twofold: that of making hermeneutics an epistemology (the whole of knowledge would be the result of interpretation) and that of making it an ontology (there are no facts, only interpretations, or more modestly, every fact is subject to interpretation). The hyperbolic (and false) 'there are no facts, only interpretations' must therefore be replaced by the principle that the existence of interpretations does not exclude the existence of facts, individuals and objects. As attractive and radical as the idea of undoing the truth may seem (which unsurprisingly bewitched both philosophers and non-philosophers after Nietzsche), making the truth sounds like a better idea, though is undoubtedly more difficult, since the saying 'criticism is easy, art is difficult' also applies to the art of interpretation.

3.5 Verification

We must answer questions such as: How is ontology conceivable without the mediation of epistemology? How do we manage to circumvent the seemingly unattainable myth of the given, the idea that being always goes hand in hand with the thought of being, since the I-think must accompany all my representations? I would recall what Vico used to say: *Homo non intelligendo fit omnia* ('Man becomes all things without understanding')[64] – humans act before understanding. And understanding, if and when it comes, is not the premise (as Cartesians think) but the result. It depends upon something that is prior to and external to thought, i.e. a know how and not a know that, a *können* and not a *kennen*. This competence may (but need not) become understanding, which means that technology may give birth to islands of epistemology – that is to say, of conceptual knowledge – but the great fundamental force remains unconscious. The strengthening of competence does not happen through clarification (as happens in understanding) but through repetition, exercise, which performs an essential function not only in physical activities, but also in spiritual activities such as speaking a language or performing arithmetical operations. Repetition produces, at the same time, a strengthening and a facilitation of the operation being repeated.

Synthetic a priori acts. Technology carries out synthetic a priori acts, of which the synthetic a priori judgments Kant tells us about are a subspecies. In both cases, in fact, the result cannot in the least be obtained from the analysis of the premises: 12 is not obtained from the analysis of 7 and 5, but derives from their sum; and, *pace* Leibniz, a statue is not obtained from the simple analysis of the marble of which it is composed. The same is true for the outcome of a battle, the taste and texture of a cake, the stipulation of a contract or the formulation of a promise. The synthesis, the result, is a posteriori, but this does not detract from the fact that the conditions that make it possible are a priori, in the sense that they cannot be minimally anticipated and understood through the simple analysis of form, acts or materials.

Action can generate products, and it is poiesis. All the forms of documentality in the social sphere, as well as reproduction in the organic sphere, are examples of this. The boom of recording characteristic of the documedia revolution has had the effect of generalising the poiesis, since every recorded practice accesses the poietic status. The art hidden in the depths of the human soul, schematism as the medium between sensibility and intellect, is in fact the psychological and philosophical transposition of the relevance of gestures and dexterity as the constitutive elements of thought and as distinctive features of the human being. The so-called synthetic a priori judgments, so problematic and at the same time so necessary, actually have to do with the sphere of gesture and competence without understanding – the sphere of a doing that is not yet knowledge.

In the case of social objects (promises, bets, holidays, money . . .), just as in the interpretation of force in both Kant and contemporary physics, there is a force which, manifesting itself through a form (which need not necessarily be understood: how much do we understand about the terms and conditions we mindlessly accept on the Internet?) produces an object. This object is literally a synthesis in the Kantian sense, since the social object, say 'marriage', cannot be deduced from the analysis of its components (the two people who contract it, and who might well not marry) any more than the concept of 12 is already included in the concepts of 7 and 5. This synthesis lies at the basis of natural objects no less than social objects, since the concept of water is not included in that of hydrogen and oxygen.

For Kant, schemes mediate between concepts and objects, but in fact (if what has been said so far is true) they produce concepts by constructing objects: the Sagrada Familia, and probably also the *Critique of Pure Reason* in all that went beyond Kant's initial intentions and pushed him to write a second and then a third *Critique*. In this sense, the genesis of the three Critiques is the best challenge to the fundamental assumption of the first (but not of the third!), namely that understanding systematically precedes competence. This is not true: competence precedes understanding even in works that claim that understanding precedes competence – let alone in areas such as genius, in which inspiration is the result of perspiration, of a great effort, of a *travailler sans demander pourquoi* (to quote Freud, who was very familiar with the unconscious). Technology is doing without knowing, competence without understanding, and is equally found in Raphael, a mobile phone or a community of ants. Analysis is an understanding that can (though need not) follow synthesis.

Making the truth. At some point, in the *Confessions*,[65] Augustine poses an elementary and almost comical question: Why should I confess to God, who knows everything? What is the point of telling one's life to someone who knows more about me than myself? The answer is enlightening: Augustine says he wants to 'make the truth', not only in his heart, but also in writing before many witnesses. Does he mean that one makes the truth just as one makes post-truth? Of course not: one can hardly pass off some fashionable nonsense to an omniscient being. He rather means that truth is not only an inner process, but also a testimony that is made publicly and has a social value, and is above all something that entails an effort, an activity, a technical skill. The truth is the production of conceptual artifacts (usually propositions) about pre-existing objects. It is therefore a poiesis, a generative making of a product.

It has been observed[66] that C.D. Broad uses 'prehend' to designate what Russell means by 'acquaintance'. This should not be understood simply as a parallelism between manual grasping and conceptual grasping; on closer inspection it suggests a link between manuality, the theory of reference and the theory of truth. The direct knowledge to which Russell refers, and which Broad characterises as a form of pressure, is also the correspondence theory of truth (where indirect knowledge, by description, recalls instead the contextualist theory of truth). In this case, therefore, a link is also established between technology and correspondence. What we have described when speaking of the evident and mysterious nature of correspondences recalls an analogous circumstance, that of Augustine's paradox of time, and the way Heidegger explains it can also be applied to the correspondence theory of truth. Many philosophical intuitions militate in this direction.

Consider Vico's perspective on the equivalence between truth (*verum*) and fact (*factum*). This perspective should not be understood in the sense of actualism and postmodernism for which reality is socially constructed (in fact, Vico is talking about epistemology, not ontology), but rather in the sense that truth is the result of an activity. In line with this approach, Vico establishes his other fundamental principle that humans do what they do (including the truth) without knowing it: if the truth is made, then, as we have regularly seen so far, epistemology is the result of technology, which, as a competence without understanding, does not require prior knowledge for conceptual transparency.

This is the intuition underlying the pragmatist 'learning by doing'. Learning a language, painting a picture, but also performing a mathematical calculation, developing a theorem, devising a scientific experiment, etc. – these disparate activities are not the result of an analysis, but rather have to do with a synthetic operation. In other words, doing is not simply the execution of a routine, but plays a decisive role in the invention of the new. Even the most precise painter will sometimes find something unexpected while painting: inventions that do not take place in their mind but outside on the canvas, due to a succession of actions and possibly of corrections (so-called 'repentance'). Much in the same fashion, the great Indian mathematician Srinivasa Ramanujan said he saw the formulae on the tongue of the goddess Namagiri at the temple,[67] and was unable to justify them in a conventional manner: he saw them in an intuitive and synthetic way, as external objects independent of his mind, to the point that some – given that he often wrote down only solutions, not calculations – claimed that he intuited the result but couldn't prove it. To give yet another example, Umberto Eco (a theoretically very conscious narrator) said several times that the novel started, for him, when the characters began to act as if following their own will, giving rise to a narrative that transformed the author into a spectator: the development took place in the text, not in the author's mind.

Finally, all the conceptions that establish a link between truth and practice, from Hegel's reason immanent in history to Marx's view that the most significant production of capital is ultimately knowledge, also go in this direction. All of this has been treated, in the most recent philosophy, as a picturesque, mystical or metaphorical element. On the contrary, I think we should take it into due consideration, especially because it often sounds like a Freudian slip that does not necessarily agree with the ideas of the philosopher who said it. When Hegel argues that the hand is responsible for human happiness and establishes an essential link with truth, and when he emphasises the proximity of manual grasping and conceptual grasping, on the one hand he expresses one of the most widespread insights among philosophers, and on the other he enunciates a perspective that in fact denies the idealistic structure and which could have been adopted by Marx. Rather than bringing Hegel back down to earth, Marx could have advised him to 'speak as he eats',[68] i.e. with his hands. Indeed, this had already happened with Plato, who, after having condemned technology and specifically writing (the place where the link between technology and thought appears more manifest), described thought in the form of writing, which is to say, technology.

Truthmakers. Translating Kant's proposal into my own terms, I suggest that we invert the epistemology/technology/ontology succession (with ontology as such being inaccessible) into ontology/technology/epistemology. First there is ontology, with individuals that are not inaccessible as such, because they manifest clear characteristics in their interaction (among themselves and with us). That is, at first there are individuals (e.g. snow) whose properties are independent of me, of you, of my cat and of whomever: this is the ontology of what we will later recognise as natural objects. Then there are interpretative schemes, namely the operations that generate facts and are not free or subjective. I see the snow with my visual apparatus and note that it is white (the operational aspect appears more clearly if we think of salt, which I have to taste to realise it is salty, or of beans, which I have to count). Finally there are judgments, which constitute objects: snow is white; salt is salty (and, much later, salt is sodium chloride); there are twenty-two beans in this jar. If I said that snow is black, salt is sweet and there are twenty-one beans, this would not be an interpretation but a mistake. What I do when I interpret something – to repeat – is not apply a conceptual scheme to some formless matter ('there are no facts, only interpretations'), but rather note the emergences of ontology (the properties of the snow, the salt, or the beans independently of me), through technological procedures (looking, tasting, counting) that may (though do not necessarily) produce epistemological judgments.

This technological aspect of truth accounts for something that is often neglected. The intuitive definition of truth dictates that it is the correspondence between a proposition and a thing: the phrase 'snow is white' is true if and only if snow is white. So far so good, but the problem starts when it comes to explaining what we mean by 'correspondence': does it mean that words resemble things? This problem reminds us of Augustine's view on time ('What then is time? If no one asks me, I know what it is. If I wish to explain it to him who asks, I do not know'), which is solved precisely by placing the emphasis on the technological dimension of truth, which, just like cycling or lighting a fire, can work perfectly well even if we don't know the reasons for it (as happens with the 'unreasonable effectiveness' of mathematics, which today finds an eminent and disturbing illustration in algorithms).

What does it mean for a proposition to correspond to a thing or a state of affairs? This difficulty is usually the starting point for theories of truth other than the correspondence theory. The fact that no satisfactory alternative has yet been found suggests, however, that the defect does not lie in correspondence, but in conceiving of adaptation as a kind of contemplation, which is obviously not true. If this were the case, the truth would be within everyone's reach and error would be inexplicable, or else could be simply explained as a kind of ocular defect (after all, Plato puts it in precisely these terms). If instead we recognise the intrinsically technological component of truth, the problem is easily solved. In fact, technology (like the sphere of action in general) is a competence without understanding. I don't need to know the laws of physics or biology to walk or to mate, just as I don't need to be familiar with the basics of arithmetic to make a calculation, whether it be basic or complex. This explains why the correspondence theory of truth is both intuitive and obscure.

4

Alteration

Hegel wrote that 'sense' is a wonderful word,[69] because it has two opposite meanings: On the one hand, it indicates the senses – sight, hearing, touch, smell and taste – and all that has to do with sensibility. On the other hand it indicates meaning, as in 'it makes no sense'. This circumstance cannot be considered accidental. The sensible and the intelligible have a common root, as we have seen, and this root is found in the environment, in the interactions and inscriptions that take place within it, and in recording as a metaphysical condition of interactions and the environment: in reproductive imagination instead of productive imagination, in repetition instead of creation. If meaning can be grasped by the senses before the spirit, it is because it is outside before being inside.

How does spiritualisation happen? On the level of technology, Hegel observed that iteration is what ensures the transition from material to spiritual. The technology to which Hegel refers is the practice of embalming corpses in the Egyptian religion, which he interpreted as a first intuition of the immortality of the soul. And he noted that death, as suggested by embalming, occurs twice: first as the death of the natural; then, with embalming, as the birth of the spirit. Without recalling the long tradition that, from Plato to Hegel, sees the body as the material aspect of the sign, Hegel's thesis is that the simple preservation of matter, which makes it iterable, generates the process of alteration that ensures the passage from the material to the spiritual, from passivity to activity, from the pyramid to consciousness.

Perfect repetition is not the norm, but the exception. For example, for the organisms that reproduce asexually (which are evolutionarily older than those that reproduce sexually), mutations, i.e. alterations, take place as errors in the copying of DNA, i.e. in the principle of iteration. From these exceptions come good or bad things, at least if we take the point of view of humans, such as genetic mutations, whether they be useful for the evolution of the species or result in the death of the individual, as in the case of neoplasms. This is how, finally, we have alteration: the rank of soldiers comes together, or, outside the metaphor, perceptions (in the Aristotelian example) turn into meanings. Sedimentation causes transformations in organisms: DNA produces chains that generate more and more complex forms of life; in politics or art external regulation leads to new expressive forms; on the Web simple iteration is organised, resulting in recursion and algorithms that make the archive even more powerful, enabling the collection of Big Data. And then, for the alteration to be saved, more iteration is needed. Think again about mutations, which are a very common phenomenon. Each of them involves the modification of DNA, but for the most part they are neutral (i.e. without effects) or negative, because their carriers become extinct. In order to originate something new, like a species, mutations must be adaptive and not only recorded but also iterated (recording is a necessary but not sufficient condition: neutral mutations are inherited but lead to nothing).

This is not just speculation, but is reflected by evidence that is very close to us. When we sought a semantic Internet, that is, so long as we tried to apply a transcendental to recording, we missed a seemingly simple goal: to create translation machines. But now that the Web has grown to the point of generating Big Data, and a text archive ideally similar to the Library of Babel, we are witnessing the fact that simple inscription and iteration determine the genesis of meaning, producing algorithms that are relatively effective for translation. In alteration, the system formed through iteration can, though will not necessarily, generate knowledge (epistemology).

4.1 Epistemology

When we came into the world the world was already here: not as some inert residue, but rather as a structure from which living beings emerge with their social and ideal worlds. When one comes into the world one is already coming from the world, a world that surrounds us and comes forward with obstacles and resources, with a complex reality; this being-in-the-world makes it implicitly senseless to ask how we access the world. If I were to wake up in an unknown room, the right question wouldn't be 'How can I know this room?' (of course I can know it, I'm in it) but rather, like Jonah and Pinocchio in the whale's belly, 'How did I get here? Why am I here?' The problem is not to explain how the mind refers to the world, but rather how the mind emerges from the world, and the answer to that question comes from technology as iteration. In this framework, the process of idealisation as an outcome of iteration and alteration constitutes a decisive element for the passage from technology to epistemology, from becoming to knowledge (or supposed knowledge): in other terms, from iteration (the same is repeated) to alteration (the same is known and becomes the object of understanding). As soon as we possess ideas, we are also able to formulate statements about something, i.e. to carry out processes in which epistemology is revealed as the result of a cooperation between ontology and technology, where the first offers the matter, the second the process and the third the form (the proposition S is p, where p claims to be true of S).

Epistemology is what we know, or think we know. Philosophers, after attributing to it the gigantic power of building or at least shaping ontology (constructivists), or the huge task of reflecting the whole of natural reality (metaphysical realists), limit themselves to meagre hints as to what it actually is. Epistemology would be Science (without further characterisations), the Space of Reasons, or a set consisting of I-think plus a variable number of categories. Here, in agreement with Hegel and Wolff, it would be better to be more precise: epistemology is the encyclopaedia, i.e. the whole of knowledge, in reference to both natural objects (which exist independently of our conceptual schemes) and social objects (which instead need our conceptual schemes in order to exist, without this meaning that we are the manufacturers of our conceptual schemes).

This encyclopaedia develops through consciousness, language, writing, and the world of laws, politics, science and culture. And when it reaches this stage it becomes capable of two operations. The first is the reconstruction of the natural world, which is the object of natural science. The second is the construction of the social world, which is the object of social science, and in which epistemology has not only a reconstructive but also a constructive role, since it explains the laws of formation of social objects. The combination of these two dimensions constitutes the encyclopaedia, the totality of knowledge. This totality is not a general spirit that wanders without roots or connections, but rather the concrete totality of everything that has been written; that is, the sphere of documentality, which we consider thematically in the practical and social sphere (given the importance of documents in everyday life, and the function of documentality in the construction of social objects), but which underlies the very construction of the encyclopaedia as the totality of knowledge, i.e., as the totality of true things.

More importantly, epistemology depends on ontology to the extent that knowledge is always knowledge of something independent of the knowing subject. The object of epistemology is reality (one has no knowledge except of reality) and the result of the cognitive process is truth, the expression of true propositions with respect to reality. For epistemology (a symbolic sphere) to take place, an alteration of ontology is necessary, a doubling such that a statement is the true equivalent of a state of things. It is necessary for being to be altered, doubling itself into a representation (which in turn finds its condition of possibility in hysteresis). In general, representation is a process of abstraction, which selects certain aspects of the object to the detriment of others (this is why epistemology is always poorer than ontology). The first abstraction, the fundamental one, is the one that takes shape without matter and already takes place in perception.

Epistemological difference. The main characteristic of epistemology is therefore alteration. It is evident that something like an alteration takes place when something is known by someone, when one moves from ontology to epistemology. If instead there were identity between ontology and epistemology, the very meaning of epistemology would be lost, since knowledge is always knowledge of something other than oneself. What the reflection of the twentieth century has defined as an ontological difference, meaning the difference between beings and being, must be defined with greater precision as an epistemological difference, that is, as the difference between the entities and the knowledge we have of them.

Neglecting this difference reduces ontology to a mere noumenal layer and shifts philosophical inquiry to the level of pure phenomenology, with the result of seeing the world as the simple reflection of our conceptual schemes. Thus, both ontology and epistemology are emptied of meaning: the former is reduced to a pure semblance subjected to epistemology, and the latter is deprived of its fundamental character, that of being knowledge of something other than itself. This is why quantum physics creates so many problems in epistemology, generating an anomalous crossing between ontology and epistemology. But quantum phenomena do not allow us to treat the whole of reality as if it were a prosthesis of quantum physics. The world as we experience it does not obey quantum physics, unless we want to take to the letter the Italian proverb 'the master's eye fattens their horse'.

4.2 Truth Bearers

It is important to note that a proposition like 'snow is white' only makes sense for humans, although it is also true regardless of their existence. The formation of meaning is a final process in which the system of iteration and alteration observed in technology and epistemology is lost, and corresponds to the production of a teleology (of a purpose) to be understood as the encounter between an end as final point (the interruption of a process) and an end as a goal (the assignment of meaning to the process). This circumstance is a specific characteristic of organisms, which in the case of humans is expressed as the production of conscious and themed purposes (values, meanings, storytelling).

'What is true and what is false is what human beings say; and it is in their language that human beings agree.'[70] The description of humans as naturally dedicated to knowledge is in fact a grand exaggeration: just think how late knowledge has appeared in the history of humankind, and how sporadic it is in the life of each of us, including professors. Rather than a natural development of some tendency of human nature, knowledge must be considered as an alteration, far more auspicious than a neoplasm but of the same kind. Where there might have been nothing but competence, at a certain point understanding took over, with an alteration that was then maintained and traditionalised in the various forms assumed by knowledge. Two elements played a key role in this. On the one hand, the development of a technical competence, which manifests itself in the process of verification, and on the other the outcome of a function which is mechanical in itself, but which in humans is a response to organic needs: understanding.

Even a machine is capable of making the truth. We can see it very well in the many tools that humanity has been using – scales, the abacus, calculators – which are generally capable of making the truth. The problem is that these truths make no sense; they have no meaning for anyone. In addition to the performative dimension, as truth is a social object, there is also a recorded act: a documental dimension of truth. Even the greatest truth, if discovered by someone with no memory, would fall into oblivion, and if we did not bother to communicate and record our truth, it would perhaps continue to exist in some hyperuranion (where it already existed before we discovered it) but it would disappear from the world of history and humans. That is why the truth needs texts, witnesses and documents.

Truth bearers always come after ontology and technology. This aspect is to be understood in both an ontological and a chronological sense (this may not be evident in 'snow is white' but is very clear in 'salt is sodium chloride'), since knowledge, being knowledge of something, necessarily comes after the known thing. Knowing that snow is white means having the concepts of 'snow' and of 'white', and linking them in a judgment, which is true if and only if snow is white. The sphere in which judgments take place is epistemology which, however, depends not only on ontology but also on technology, which is the way in which epistemology has access to ontology.

So, truth bearers always come third, and their field of reference is therefore thirdness. If ontology is about presence and absence, epistemology is about truth, falsehood and non-knowledge (that which is neither true nor false). It is neither an inert sphere which only mirrors what is there, nor an overactive sphere which fabricates everything there is. Rather, it is the field in which concepts take shape. The concepts of 'number' or 'disabled' do not exist in nature. They are gradually sedimented and culturally selected: concepts like 'calories' and 'phlogiston' survive, but as historical and non-physical notions; over time, new concepts are formed. In the case of social objects, concepts have not only a descriptive but also a performative value, as they highlight ontological layers still unseen: workers will discover that they are victims of surplus value, people of colour will find out they are discriminated against, and the bourgeois gentleman will find that he has spoken in prose for all of his life. But even in this case, the truth refers to an ontological layer that is independent of epistemology, which merely gives it a form.

Homer's salt. It seems strange to suggest that the proposition 'salt is sodium chloride' was true in Homer's world (to be more precise, at Homer's time), yet so many hypertruthists claim that it was rather true of Homer's world (to be more precise, for us today considering Homer's world). Now, if by 'Homer's world' one means planet Earth, that world is neither Homer's nor ours nor anybody else's, so saying that 'salt is sodium chloride' is true of Homer's world' is meaningless. If, however, one means Homer's age, then saying that the proposition 'salt is sodium chloride' is true of Homer's era is simply false. Being true (today) of the world we know – which probably has many characteristics in common with the world in which Homer lived, although we cannot be absolutely certain – does not equal being true (consequently) of an epoch in which, among other things, it was not known that salt is sodium chloride.

It also seems strange to suggest that a proposition like 'salt is sodium chloride' (not to mention 'stalking is a crime', 'practising Christians do not eat meat on Friday', 'Nelson won the Battle of Trafalgar') can have meaning regardless of language, and therefore regardless of humankind. So, some hypertruthists insist on the non-linguistic but logical nature of propositions. However, I do not think that this changes much, both because hypertruthists often themselves speak of propositions as linguistic expressions (and one could hardly do otherwise) but especially because logic, like mathematics and language, is a technology whose existence depends on the existence of humans. We will see this shortly in my own theory, which incidentally is not very original, since it is shared by all non-Platonist philosophers (that is, by most philosophers). Unless one is worryingly anthropocentric and attributes properties of today's age to very ancient times, the proposition 'there were once dinosaurs on Earth' only appeared at a certain point in time: previously, dinosaurs had existed but nobody knew it. And saying that for Homer it was true that salt is sodium chloride is like saying that 'dinosaurs exist' (in the present) is true for us.

Finally, coming to the idea, shared by hypo- and hypertruthists, of a necessary correlation between ontology and epistemology, it is worth observing that this correlation (which in fact is simultaneous) would deprive epistemology of its meaning. In fact, virtually all of the beliefs held true 10,000 years ago, as far as we know, have now changed: Ramses II never suspected that he was dying of tuberculosis, although he did indeed die of it. This is not true only of scientific knowledge. The whiteness of snow is a perceptive datum, which applies to humans but not to bats. The proposition does not express a necessary fact: if there were no humans, snow would have all the properties it has, but the proposition 'snow is white' would not be there, and would seem meaningless to anyone disagreeing with the hypertruthist belief that reality and truth are correlated. Even more so if 'snow is white' stood for 'snow appears to be white to the human perceptual apparatus' or (to complicate things even further) for 'snow has the dispositional property of appearing white to the human perceptual apparatus'.

4.3 Forms of Life

As I said, thirdness is an essential characteristic of truth. Truth comes after reality because it refers to it, differs from it and depends on it. This is clear from a chronological perspective: from the point of view of truth, reality is not a starting point, but a point of arrival, something that only comes later (if all goes well). In this way, truth is not archaeologically founded in reality; it is teleologically oriented towards it. The ontological emergence goes from past to present; the epistemological operation goes from present to past. This – anticipating the point I will deal with in the final part of this section – is the principle of making the truth: finding out how things are, starting from a situation of not knowing. Truth therefore does not take place at the same time as reality, but always comes next. In this sense, truth has a teleological dependence on ontology (its purpose is to enunciate the truth about ontology), and a causal dependence on technology (without some form of technology we would have no truth).

'This is agreement not in opinions, but rather in form of life.'[71] Form of life indeed; I propose three levels of it. The first is the representation of an individual: *história*, the fact that a particular event took place. The second level is exemplification: the individual becomes the representative of a class, *história* becomes *mythos*, the generalisation of the particular, an example, precisely as a form of life. The third level is abstraction: the individual disappears, so that we now have only the class, the abstract. From *mythos* we pass to *logos*.

História. Myths do not descend from some ideal Olympus: they arise from reality. When talking about myths, however, one usually goes back to very ancient times and is forced to adopt a conjectural reasoning. I would like to make a much more concrete example of the relationship between reality, individuality and insurgence: surprise. Indeed, one of the most important aspects of individuality is that it is surprising. Particulars have a fine grain that cannot be anticipated by the generality of the concept ('house' is much less detailed than my home or yours); likewise, they have a capacity to surprise that, once again, far exceeds the conceptual imagination. We can certainly say that *mythos* is more universal than *história*, but that's only because it has already mourned, that is, it has forgotten the dead, the concrete and transient individual. Like mourning, though, universalisation and generalisation are never perfect. What in Homer's Hector is more universal and necessary than the Hector who truly died under those walls, whose corpse was dragged around them with a cruelty we still find in today's wars? After all, universality is a flaw, a lack of determining particulars, as in the difference between idealised and realistic statues. Therefore, *mythos* always comes next. In the Beginning was not *logos* – we have suspected this for a while – nor *mythos*, but *história*: accidental individuals in the real world.

But how do we go from *história* to *mythos*? The role of the imagination in the evolution of humankind has been rightly underlined. What I wish to highlight, though, is that this imagination is not absolutely creative, a wonder and a mystery deposited in the depths of the human soul, as Kant claims when talking about the transcendental imagination. Simply put, the transcendental imagination is iteration. I am not the first to make this point. For example, it was already the core of a 'remote' dispute between Locke and Berkeley about the general idea. If experience is always experience of particulars, Locke asked, how is it that we can have something like the general idea of a triangle? Locke imagined a kind of overlap: you see an equilateral triangle, then a scalene, then a rectangle – and in the end the general idea of triangle comes out. Berkeley mocked him: what kind of triangle would it be: large, small, equilateral, scalene, or all of these and none of them? The alternative proposed by Berkeley is called the diagram: the idea is particular, but refers to something general. Berkeley, in fact, was speaking of instantiation, i.e. the process by which the individual, while remaining such, is generalised by way of example: it proves to be of general interest precisely because it represents a concrete individuality.

So, the example is abstract insofar as it is concrete: it is a part extracted from a (real or virtual) series that, by the virtue of this extraction, allows for an abstraction – the passage to the concrete case of the series it refers to. Which means that every time we are faced with a case, if we take it as an example, we cease to treat it as a simple individual, but we seek the series to which it belongs, the law it refers to, acting as judges, physicians or zoologists in front of a case, a symptom or indeed a specimen. Everything, at this point, can be looked at from two perspectives, one that particularises it as an individual and one that generalises it as an example. The magic, as it were, is that nothing outwardly changes in the individual when, if taken as an example, it passes from individual to general, and from *história* to *mythos*.

Mythos. In order to be normative, something has to be normal, because *ad impossibilia nemo tenetur* ('Nobody is held to the impossible'). However, if something is normative it isn't 'normal', because most things in the world are not normative. Between ordinary and extraordinary, thus, there is a tension that can be schematised as follows: 1) the example has to be ordinary, otherwise it isn't a good example; 2) if it is a good example, though, it participates in the exceptionality of examples; 3) despite deriving its legitimacy from being an ordinary case, it ends up being an extraordinary case (which was typical of TV celebrities a few decades ago: 'he/she is one of us'); 4) therefore, it gets its normativity from its normality.

Exemplification is a very common thing, but it involves a sophisticated operation: you take an individual, you consider them as the specimen of a class, and then you look for other individuals who can be specimens of that same class. When taxonomists think they have found a specimen of a new species, they store that concrete specimen (as an example of the species, precisely); but the fact that it is that organism and not another is accidental: it is simply the one they happened to find, it does not possess exemplary characteristics in itself. An example is 'any case whatsoever'. And yet it triggers a complicated process, a sort of split encompassing both the case and the law, the particular and the general, the accidental and the necessary. The example describes what is normal, but this normal can be exceptional, without contradiction. Much irony has been expressed over the École Normale in Paris or the Scuola Normale in Pisa, where students are anything but 'normal'. However, it should be said that in both cases there is a third term, 'superior', clarifying things, despite fostering the paradox of a superior normality or a normal superiority.

Exemplarity of the example. Exemplarity is a distinctive feature of human action, which must be developed in three directions. The first is the ability to make examples, i.e. to invent objects or actions that can become models of behaviour and action. The second is the ability to take things as examples, to find them in the great repertoire of the humanistic tradition, which as such is nothing more than a great inventory of examples and models. The third, finally, is the capacity to set an example: that is, to carry out coherent action capable of being a source of inspiration for others.

Making an example. Let's start from the process of making an example. An example is something that is made. An example is abstract in that it is concrete: it is a part extracted from a (real or virtual) series that, precisely as a result of this extraction, allows for an abstraction, i.e. the transition from the concrete case to the series it refers to. As stated, this means that every time we are faced with a case, if we consider it as an example, we cease to treat it as a simple individual and instead seek the series to which it belongs.

This intrinsic duplicity of the example struck Kant to the point that he proposed a terminological distinction between *Beispiel* (instance) and *Exempel* (exemplary case).[72] In short, Kant believed that there is no legitimate relationship between the trivial and the exceptional case, between the stereotype and the prototype. This is not surprising, for someone who insisted so much on the difference between the empirical and the transcendental. But it is precisely the reflection on the example – which in the *Critique of Judgment* is the sensibilisation of empirical concepts – that suggests that these two levels are not separate, but rather are characterised by an interweaving of old and new, empirical and transcendental, which reveals the characteristic powers of secondary repetition.

Taking as an example. Let's move on to the case of taking something as an example. In fact, the split between the concrete and the abstract that takes place in the example is the premise of a split between the ordinary and the extraordinary. Caesar or Napoleon are good examples of generals only if their characteristics are typical of all generals. And at this point we realise that Caesar and Napoleon are not good examples of generals, because they were too good. Typically, generals are much worse than these two.

So Caesar or Napoleon are rather examples of an ideal general, something that is more of an example to follow. On the other hand, a good example of a general – in the sense of a typical general – is instead any one of the many generals defeated by Caesar or Napoleon.

This fact suggests that an example, to be such, must not only prove to be exemplary but also indicate, at the same time, an ought, an end, even an unattainable peak: in short, something that is anything but ordinary. There is a very complex logic at work here, where the alternative between being and ought coexists in one exemplary case. The Italian word *campione* clearly expresses this tension. A *campione* (which means sample) can be a specimen, something with no value like a perfume sample. At the same time, though, *campione* also means champion: something extraordinary, like a sports champion or a champion of freedom – a defender.

The word 'model', in contrast, is less restricted to the Italian semantic field. Take a model of a car: it is a car, but much smaller and lacking the essential functions of a car. Unlike the sample/champion, a model has two particularities. On the one hand, it cannot be a fragment ('a sample of fabric', sample case, etc.) but claims to be the reproduction of something that already exists, perhaps aimed at the production of something (like the paper models for clothing, which were used to hand-make clothes in poor economies). On the other hand, following the logic of exemplarity of the example, the model as a typical example can become an ideal, a purpose, a goal, or at least a standard. So, there are model schools and model students. In Mexico there is even a *Cerveceria Modelo*, as if to say the 'model beer', produced by Grupo Modelo with clear ambitions of exemplariness, so much so that it is the leading Mexican beer. And fashion models are anything but ordinary or typical people: they are chosen precisely because they are extraordinary.

This circumstance is particularly evident in the peculiar example we call a masterpiece. What is a masterpiece? In the artisan schools of the past, the masterpiece was the work that the student had to produce to show his competence. We can therefore assume that most of the time it was a fairly ordinary work, a bit like a school essay: in other words, anything but a masterpiece in the current sense of the term. Real masterpieces are called this because they are placed at the beginning of a chain of imitations, and perhaps even invent a new genre. The implicit assumption of these imitations is that they can never become masterpieces, and that if they did, they would cease to belong to the previous series, and would give life to a new one. The opposite of the masterpiece, perhaps the failed masterpiece, is the typical: a minor result of the logic of exemplarity. There is a sense in which 'exemplary' means 'typical', and it is no longer a compliment (except, perhaps, in the expression 'typical cuisine' or similar instances, in which the typicality constitutes a value in itself). Expressions like 'the typical French' or 'the typical bureaucrat' are not flattering. Perhaps a paradoxical compliment can be found in the expression 'typical imbecile': the insult lies in the word 'imbecile', and the word 'typical' perhaps attenuates it; this is not the case with the phrase 'classic jerk', where the banality of evil appears to be aggravating.

Setting an example. To conclude, let's come to the more explicitly teleological manifestation of exemplariness, i.e. the phenomenon of setting an example. There is a sense in which exemplarity is the mystical foundation of authority and the origin of normativity. This is perfectly obvious in common law systems, where the case becomes law. In civil law systems we have a letter at the origin of the spirit (the ten commandments, the twelve tables), which codifies previous customs (and with this we return to exemplarity). What has happened, thanks to recording, can become an example, a norm, and therefore a value. As stated, a good example should always carry an element of 'whateverness'. However, this randomness then becomes something authoritative, important and normative. The example of a father is not an exemplary father if not by chance; if one were an exemplary father, in a sense, one would cease to be a good example of a father. In accordance with this law, it might happen that a case becomes famous – a 'gate' or an *affaire*. In short, something that exceeds the norm or institutes a new one – and therefore a new normality. A case may cease to be typical, becoming exceptional, or it may cease to be exceptional, becoming the norm. So, within the tension between normal, norm and normative there are, in succession: the whatever case, i.e. the accidental; the typical case, i.e. the normal; and the hyperbolic case, i.e. the extraordinary, which for this very reason is the model to follow, or even the idea in the Kantian sense.

4.4 Logos

Verum scire est scire per causas ('to know is to know by means of causes'). In all these forms of life (*história, mythos*, exemplarity . . .) there is a common and unexpressed ideal: *logos*, knowledge, the object of epistemology, which is a rarer and more uncertain good than one is led to believe. Epistemology is composed of statements, which can be true or false. This dependence on truth and falsehood characterises the epistemological role of representation and distinguishes it, for example, from the imagination (this fact of common sense was already underlined by Aristotle, and is only neglected by weak spirits who cannot distinguish imagination from reality). Conceptually, in agreement with the *Theaetetus*, epistemology is defined as true belief accompanied by reason. Contrary to what Kant thought, knowledge does not condition in any way the natural being (which is what Kant referred to). Epistemology does not have a causal role with respect to natural ontology (it may have a role in social ontology, but that is not what Kant was talking about) and precisely for this reason its recognition of causal links does not constitute a tautological function. Knowledge consists in recognising causal links from the operational point of view, but for this very reason, from an ontological point of view, it rests on hysteresis, i.e. the possibility of retention that allows for the recognition of succession and hence the supposition of causality.

The relationship between epistemology and ontology is neither construction nor correspondence, but emergence. There is a first level, that of an ontology of the natural world, in which we pass from the inorganic to the organic and finally to the conscious – without it being necessary to presuppose any 'intelligent design' (after all, not even classic idealists assumed this). At this stage we have the constitution of an ontology that is the premise for an epistemology, for a knowledge of what there is. In an only apparently distinct perspective, this process occurs in the production of knowledge, which takes place when simple competence (iteration) is transformed into understanding (alteration): white snow is a state of affairs, the proposition 'snow is white' is a true proposition (if snow is white) and finds its condition of possibility in the interaction between an ontological layer (snow and its properties, guaranteed by recording), technological verification (the observation of snow as competence without understanding) and epistemological assertions (the proposition 'snow is white'). It is not a miracle, but certainly it is a problem which the multiple performances of hysteresis help to solve. (What is the relationship between the words and the states of things to which they refer? The phrase 'snow is white', for example, is neither cold nor white.)

At the conclusion of his *New Essays on Human Understanding*, Leibniz raises this issue through a combination that, at first, appears surprising.[73] There are two mazes in which human thought gets lost. The first is that of predestination, the second is that of continuity and movement. In both cases, in fact, we deal with conflicting intuitions. We have the impression of being free, and this impression grounds our moral and social lives (hopes, regrets, punishments, rewards . . .), yet we also have the feeling that every action is determined by a previous one and therefore is not free. Similarly, it seems logical to us that Achilles will reach the turtle that's a foot ahead of him, but as soon as logic starts examining the issue one notices that when Achilles catches up that foot, the turtle will already be further away, and so on ad infinitum. For both conflicts, the problem is: how to introduce discontinuity in continuity – freedom in morality and movement in Achilles's case? What I said about the relationship between iteration and alteration should help provide an answer to the dilemma.

Continuity and discontinuity. Alteration, i.e. discontinuity, does not conflict with iteration, but is a possible consequence of it. *Iter*, 'again', and *alter*, 'otherwise', derive from the same Sanskrit root, *itara*.[74] This is no surprise, since here we are dealing with an aspect that is logical and ontological and not just linguistic. Iterating also means altering: the ontological uniqueness of the individual is doubled, so that the iteration (perfect or not) is also an alteration. This may appear to be a futile speculative game, but bear with me. Think of a bar, late in the evening: a client sits in front of his whiskey, drinks it, raises his glass and says to the bartender: 'Give me another one.' This does not mean that he wants a different drink (or even worse, a different glass). He wants the same whiskey: another glass (alteration) of the same (iteration). *Natura non facit saltus* ('nature doesn't make leaps'), and that doesn't just apply to bars. There's no real leap from nature to culture: DNA stops repeating itself regularly and gives rise to an evolution of the species or to a neoplasm; a memory can become corrupted and complicated to the point of becoming an original thought; a long series of data can be simplified to the point of becoming a theory; a series of regulated actions can deliberately treat a part of the world in such a way as to make true statements about that part of the world (I get on the scales, look at the display, and pronounce or think the phrase 'I weigh 86 kilos, I need to lose weight'). The leap takes place between ontology (what there is) and epistemology (what we know or believe we know). On the ontological level, in the case of the whiskey glass, there is iteration (it is still a whiskey glass), but on the epistemological level there is alteration (it is another, one more, a second glass).

Extra hysteresim nulla causa ('there is no cause outside hysteresis'). Realism is an emergentism based on hysteresis, just as idealism is a cognitivism based on the arrogance of the learned. For idealists, existence is subordinate to the knowledge we can have of it, while for realists knowledge emerges from an existence independent of any knowledge. In these terms, the problem of realism arises only after transcendentalism, the modern form of idealism. Epistemologically, being manifests itself as independence from our conceptual schemes (this very independence is the decisive argument against the ontological proof of God's existence and its variants in transcendental idealism). The universe is very old, and in so much time anything can happen, including the transition from inorganic to organic nature, and the various degrees of the latter – perception, apperception, retention, protention, imagination. These performances are variants of inscription: the adventures of a track that is fixated. The impressions are deposited; any change, in behaviour or in DNA, leaves an inscription, which can remain dormant or generate transformations, precisely those on which evolution rests. The layering of traces enabled by recording accounts for a central element of emergence we came across a while ago: competence without understanding, which over a very long time produces meaning, namely the essentially historical process that leads from ontology to epistemology, and sometimes to the attribution of meaning.

Predestination and freedom. Hysteresis as the co-presence of iteration and alteration finds its elective application in the sphere of freedom and predestination, Leibniz's other maze. In this field, the debate on free will has generated enormous confusion. Born at a time when explaining meant identifying the causes of something, the debate necessarily leads to the denial of freedom, since it is obvious that an effect, once it has occurred, could not but follow from the cause that produced it. If we see the scene again, it will become clear that Sam had to play 'As Time Goes By' again and that Blücher could only precede Ney on the fields of Waterloo, and that, for the same reason, we couldn't help but do whatever we did. With this perspective, or more exactly with this retrospective, we only grasp one side of responsibility, which is interesting from the point of view of reward and punishment, that is, answering for what one has done. However, if we can be called to answer for it, it is precisely because we are free – a notion that is denied by the causal perspective. If answering for makes sense, it is therefore necessary to introduce another perspective, that of answering to, which is based on principles that are not causal but final. This is where the last function of hysteresis comes into play, i.e. interruption.

5

Interruption

The three musketeers (recording, iteration, alteration) are actually four, and the system, to be complete, needs a fourth element[75] – interruption, which is the essence of speculation. Teleology, i.e. having an end, is the outcome of interruption: this happens whenever a process stops (typically, a machine breaks down or a living being dies). Interruption equals crisis, i.e. the cessation of a system of recording and iteration, in either a definitive or a transitory form. As such it should not be conceived as mere negativity, because it constitutes the condition of possibility of meaning. We understand what a hammer is when it breaks, and what a human is when they die. It is at this point, at the end (as the final moment), that we recognise the end (as the purpose) of a mechanism or organism, and it is the prediction of this interruption that determines the economic and ethical system of values.

Interruption is the decisive and conclusive element of hysteresis, what stops the machine and at the same time motivates it. The fact that it can be subject to irreversible processes gives meaning to the whole. Teleology sheds light on archaeology. This affair may seem complicated, or like little more than wordplay, but it has a meaning that concerns, precisely, the meaning of history. Who we are as human beings was not written from the beginning – quite the contrary. What we are appears at the moment when we glimpse a direction, the place to which we are going. It is therefore in the future, in becoming, that we recognise the origin. Precisely for this reason it is important to look into the present, into what happens and in the directions it is taking, to recognise the essences of things.

Only that which has an end can have a time endowed with meaning and direction. It is not by chance, therefore, that final causes concern organisms and history, i.e. the two areas in which time and transience are everything. Everything, in nature as well as in technology, has an end, which manifests itself as an interruption. *Alles, was ist, endet.* If alterations are things that sometimes happen and sometimes don't, there is one thing that eventually always happens: the interruption, the end. It may sound bad, but it is the greatest of all goods because it gives meaning to every act of our life. From the point of view of the universe, entropy is the end of all things. From the point of view of organisms destined to end but capable of projecting purposes outside themselves (like humans), it is instead the beginning and the condition of possibility of finality, of teleology. Interruption is the characteristic of every being.

And it is precisely interruption that, achieving hysteresis, i.e. coming to stasis (from the death of the individual to the thermal death of the universe), enables the rise of finality, of *telos*, and that is why interruption corresponds to the sphere of teleology. The origin of this interruption, however, is a temporality that essentially concerns organisms rather than mechanisms. What is the proper characteristic of a fungus compared to an integrated circuit? It is this: iteration, sooner or later, is subject to interruption, but in organisms this interruption is much more significant than in mechanisms, because it is irreversibility without redemption. This irreversibility triggers a process of capital importance: the organism, which has no end in itself, develops a series of teleological attitudes (temporality, urgency, anxiety, boredom) and in the case of the human organism projects them outside of itself in the form of artifacts, rituals, symbols and social structures. Interruption is therefore not something negative, but rather the passage from efficient causes (what there is, which drives the process of emergence) to final causes (what is not there, which orientates the process of emergence, giving it meaning).

5.1 Teleology

Interruption is the teleological version of hysteresis. At a certain point entropy prevails, and that's the end of all things. Precisely this certainty, and the urgency it dictates in the metabolism of organisms, is the origin of sense, direction and overall significance in the world of life. Entropy is therefore the condition of possibility of every sense and meaning. This circumstance, in turn, draws its condition of possibility from hysteresis, and therefore is an effect of hysteresis in the same way as iteration and alteration, because an interruption can take place only within a process. Despite being seemingly uneconomical, interruption gives the general sense to the economy of the whole process of hysteresis. Only the perspective of an interruption, especially if it is irreversible, gives a direction to the process and outlines its meaning, in the theory of meaning as well as in the philosophy of history, in the granting of loans as well as in the life of every one of us.

Like intentionality, consciousness is a simple soul supplement, made to introduce an intrinsic difference between human and non-human animals that in fact can only be based on an extrinsic basis: having a technology. Indeed, this view fails to see that the real supplement is technology. The latter, developing also as culture, capitalisation, normativity and reflection, can lead to that pang of remorse or feeling of being that we call 'soul'. And there is no need to have any awareness of death to develop a teleology. All it takes is the call of hunger, which arouses a sense of irreversibility and urgency that distinguishes between an organism and a mechanism. Being for death is a difficult thing to conceptualise and endure, and humans live most of the time as if they were immortal. If it depended on their consciousness, their behaviour would be very little conditioned by the immanence of the interruption that awaits them. But for the irreversibility to come forward, consciousness is not necessary; all that is needed is hunger, fatigue, boredom, desire – all the characteristics of a mortal body, even if not necessarily provided with a soul conscious of mortality.

The priority of intentionality over documentality is a metaphysical blunder equivalent to the confusion between ontology and epistemology. There is no *prius* ('precedent'), no absolute and separate element, no Pentecostal meaning. The intention (like the ensuing action) derives from inscription. There is no intention, idea or spirit prior to expression and inscription. First there is only life, metabolism, hunger and urgency. Then a circle is created in which the soul nourishes the automaton, with its needs, times and senses, and the automaton strengthens the soul by giving it codes, intentions and purposes that it would never have imagined if it had simply focused on feeding itself.

Humans, compared to other organisms, have the capacity to strengthen the needs dictated by their internal purpose through mechanisms, which are characterised, on the one hand, by an explicit external purpose (a knife is made to cut, a book is made to be read) and on the other hand by the ability to achieve this purpose through the iteration of procedures. The rose has no reason to exist, it blooms because it blooms. Scissors do have a reason to exist, as they are made to cut – for example, they can cut a rose. Sounds have no reason to exist, but language does, such as to give a name to the rose. So on the one hand, mechanisms have a manifest external purpose: they were built for a purpose, and the idea of a useless machine is nothing more than an intellectual provocation. On the other hand, the thing that most resembles a useless machine is an organism, which possesses what is so problematically called 'internal purpose'.

We are used to favouring efficient causes, but in so doing we cast a shadow over final causes, which are omnipresent in technology, history and life. I use scissors in order to cut things, Caesar crossed the Rubicon in order to become a dictator, I dressed up like an old fop in order to impress my date on Valentine's Day. All these purposes would be inconceivable for a mechanism (and in fact scissors are made to cut, but in themselves have no propensity to do so). Speculation means recognising final connections. The quintessence of speculation is the philosophy of history, which takes on the question of the meaning of being. The final laws are the laws of wisdom, which emerge only retrospectively: that is, speculatively, precisely in the form of the philosophy of history.

And this history started long ago. In the Cambrian period, between 540 and 485 million years ago, trilobites stopped going round and round and started moving in one direction. This led them to give meaning to their existence, and to encounter a much wider environment than they knew before. It was not only wider but better equipped, actually, because in turn the animal had senses that, even in the case of trilobites, did not depend on a sense conferred by thought, but rather on the directions, resistances and the invitations of individuals. When speaking of sense as direction I am aware that I am proposing a philosophically anomalous use of this word. Usually by 'sense' philosophers intend something's way of giving itself, how an object appears to a subject. But without sense as movement (which precedes all understanding) we would not have sense as a mode of presentation and then of understanding and meaning. The example of poetry and versification is illuminating in this regard: the meaning is derived from the prosody rather than preceding it, which justifies theories about the poetic origin of language. The same applies to the central role of imitation in the attribution of meaning: unconscious meaning is constituted through inscription, conscious meaning through the – initially senseless – imitation of the actions and attitudes of others.

5.2 Direction

Sense is inconceivable without a doing and a direction. Without time and beings going in one sense (direction), nothing would make sense (meaning), and this is not a simple pun but a serious truth, as I will try to illustrate in these final pages. Individuals follow directions, such as the following:

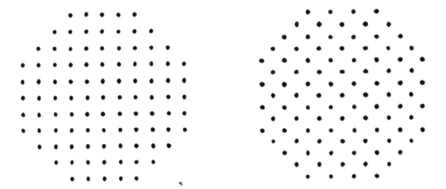

The two patterns are perfectly identical, only the second is inclined by 45 degrees with respect to the first. Directions count in perception, thought and even social interaction; above all, the world is already ordered (it follows directions) before our intentions and our concepts intervene in it. This pre-existing order is what makes it the case, for example, that the life of a tick only requires three stimuli: smell, temperature, touch – in other words, something that is probably a bit less complex than the Kantian system of judgments, categories and schematism. This is the enigmatic 'synopsis of sense' that Kant mentions in the first transcendental deduction: the fact that the world appears organised before we begin our conceptual activity (which is the problem of transcendentalism).

However, it is worth noting that Kant was also an emergentist. For example, he criticised the principle of the identity of indiscernibles[76] (which makes ontology and epistemology collapse onto one another) through the case of incongruent counterparts: a right hand and a left hand are identical in concept, but necessarily occupy different parts of space, since they are non-overlapping. Kant also noted that the division of space strictly depends on our physical constitution, namely, on the fact that we have a head and feet (up/down), a forehead and a neck (front/back), a right and a left side.

This series of determinations of the bodily scheme is what allows us to recognise objects: in a piece of paper we distinguish the top, the bottom, the recto, the verso and the direction of writing (no matter if from left to right or otherwise). This also holds for our judgments on cosmic regions. To orient oneself in space means finding the East (Orient), and then the West, the North and the South. But this is not possible without the feeling of right and left, which is a sensible and bodily intuition that also regulates our astronomical, mathematical and speculative intuitions – our orientation in thought and in the world. This perspective, which posits that sense emerges from the body and the environment, strongly clashes with Kantian constructivism, and is the position that I wish to defend here.

This accounts for the fact that sense (direction) comes before concepts. Millions of years before concepts there was already a shared world of direct experience. Sharing, of course, can be very basic (I can interact with a cat without sharing my intentionality with it). In fact, the world is not a desert organised by concepts, but a place full of directions, invitations, interactions and institutions. This is how interaction and coordination take place in a rich, inviting and sensed environment. When the environment is not like that, we notice, and are filled with boredom and depression – and our concepts are not enough to keep us company.

5.3 Meaning

As stated, the end is intimately connected with the formation of meaning. *Sinn*, to send, *Sendung, sentiero* – all these words recall the fact, represented with extreme coherence in Indo-European languages, that the formation of meaning depends on the existence of a purpose. In short, there can be no sense, significance and scope without paths and directions. The constitution of meanings through entropy works this way in organisms. There is an entropic line that leads all that is organised into disorder. Unlike mechanisms, organisms have an autonomous way of offsetting entropy: metabolism (which, however, is itself subject to a progressive slowdown and a final entropy). In this way, entropy generates behaviours in organisms, and these behaviours are all characterised by a finalism. Finality, therefore, has a very elementary organic component; namely, the fact that organisms are finite.

The genesis of finality, i.e. of sense, can be described as follows. On the one hand organisms, unlike inorganic matter and mechanisms, are aware that they have an end (in both senses of the term). This awareness, which in higher organisms can assume different degrees of consciousness, manifests itself first of all as organic needs dictated by the demands of metabolism (hunger, thirst, heat, cold, tiredness . . .). It is these circumstances that, at different levels, determine the sense of temporality, intentionality, consciousness, and in general the sphere of meaning, which as such belongs only to organisms qua endowed with sense and direction. Only in an organism, characterised by a limited lifespan marked by metabolism, can phenomena such as anxiety, expectation, desire, boredom or hunger take place. And it is precisely these phenomena emerging from organisms that give meaning and purpose to mechanisms, which therefore have a reason to exist only as a result of organisms.

Inscription, in fact, does not only refer to the past, but is also projected towards the future. Indeed, as shown by phenomenology, the diagram of time is insufficient if one understands temporality as a mere outflow from past to present. In order for time to be what it is, i.e. a flow, it is necessary that the diagram also includes protention, the expectation of the future. In this mechanism, which is typical of the living, lies the origin of history and thought, that is, the passage from recording to expectation. That is what I would call the messianic genesis of consciousness, i.e. the fact that retention is transformed into protention, generating expectation, sensibility, imagination and, ultimately, the awaiting of death as the speculative core of reflection. At the origin of both the spirit and technology (and of the spirit as a technology) we therefore find inscription, which underlies thought (which finds its first and fundamental resource in memory) as well as society and nature. Inscription fixates interactions and generates potential meanings. The absolute, therefore, is not opposed either to history or to individuals, who are the fundamental ontological components of the universe. All that is narrated in history is individuality: from the course of an illness to a geopolitical development. At more or less extensive levels of generality, history is the way in which epistemology approaches ontology.

Interactions leave traces: on matter (the glass of my watch got slightly scratched against a wall), and on the specialised form of matter called memory. Usually nothing happens. Sometimes an unpleasant event occurs (the glass of my watch breaks), and sometimes a pleasant event happens (a DNA mutation causes the species to evolve; two memories accidentally meet and spark a passion or an idea). In any case, what happens is an accumulation of information and minimal senses that enrich the interactions (trivially: the game with my cat Cleo becomes 'our usual game', and therefore requires some changes, or is played with greater dexterity on both sides). The mystery of animal instinct is the outcome of an interaction in space that is so stable that it appears miraculous. And the elderly often feel uncomfortable in new places because their usual habitats contain information that instruct their behaviours and interactions.

The interaction between individuals, together with the key feature of matter and spirit I have called recording, allows for the constitution of an environment. It is no coincidence that ontology is open to ecology. To emphasise the importance of recording, I call 'tabula' the environment in which the interaction takes place: the environment is inherently endowed with memory, and there is no substantive difference between the tabula we have in our minds and the tabula-environment where interactions take place. The relationship between organism and mechanism typical of responsiveness is found in the genesis of meaning and sense. We first have traces that if iterated become signs, and if altered become meanings. But these senses acquire meaning only when they are related to a vital process – that is, with the purpose and finiteness of organic life, particularly in relation to that responsive animal which is the human organism.

The genesis of pyramids is a good example of the emergence of meaning. First there is a hypogeum; then a mound is added to protect the hypogeum; finally people begin to give meaning to the mound: stairway to heaven, sun ray, or the like. Here begins the process that will lead Hegel to take the pyramid as the symbol of the sign. The process is the following: inscription (hypogeum), iteration (mound), alteration (sign, symbol). It is the birth of epistemology and the emergence of truth, which obviously existed before epistemology, only it did not have the leading role it has taken on ever since humanity developed an epistemology. In fact, what appears to have happened with a process started

120,000 years ago in the Nile valley – to make one example, as similar events have happened in many places around the Earth – and culminated about 5,500 years ago with the pyramids is not the birth of truth (the fact that salt is NaCl has always been true, even though no one knew or asserted it), but rather its emergence, the fact that something was true for someone. In general, the first meanings (as invitations and as ancestors of truth) must be sought in the sphere of pre-adaptation: the mainland, the hand, the campfire, the division of labour. It seems implausible that – again, for example – what we call 'Egypt', with its gods, its language, the pyramids and the papyri, was built by contract, following a discussion and a decision. In other words, it seems unlikely that it was history as opposed to nature. But it is no coincidence that this world of meaning arose in relation to death, which is precisely what gives meaning to the whole process.

Trace. First there is a trace, a simple differentiation on a homogeneous surface, the persistence of an effect after its cause has disappeared. This hysteresis can remain latent and have no meaning: consider fingerprints before their investigative utility was discovered, organic traces that carry the DNA constituting the identity of the cell, or parietal traces that could indicate a human intervention but also the simple action of natural elements. In the ontology/epistemology/technology/teleology quadripartition, the trace is the ontological element, and therefore in itself it is meaningless, since there is no sense in being as such, but only for us – to suppose the opposite means committing an obvious anthropological fallacy. This is simply the natural basis of signification, which suggests that communication of any kind is impossible in the absence of material bases. To be clear, an angelic language cannot exist for reasons both *de facto* ('of fact') and *de jure* ('of law').

Then the trace, by enduring, acquires meaning little by little: the trace can be recognised by another animal, receiving a sense that at first it did not possess, and then maybe it is conceptualised eventually as a trace by a hunter or an ethologist. The trace will thus be repeated, will receive a name, will generate a ritual, and little by little will take on a meaning, just like in the arc that leads from a childhood echolalia to Joyce's *Portrait of the Artist as a Young Man*, and then back to the echolalia of *Finnegans Wake*. After the pleasure of leaving traces, and after the illustrious struggle against time waged by traces, comes meaning. It is futile to think that meanings arise in nice and ready form. At the beginning there is nonsense: 'Once upon a time and a very good time it was there was a moocow coming down along the road and this moocow that was coming down along the road met a nicens little boy named baby tuckoo ...'.[77] Then – after a period that sometimes lasts longer than a lifetime – meaning emerges: a notch, another notch, Robinson's calendar, the Egyptian dynasties, up to language as a system of differences (and therefore of repetitions).

Sign. Let us try, now, in a purely speculative way, to describe the passage from the sensible to the intelligible and from sense as direction to sense as meaning. Claiming to break the solidarity between these two poles, and to think that art would be the greater the further it departed from sensation, was the first mistake that led to the deadlock of Great Conceptual Art:, i.e. art that would be worthy qua Great (i.e. an exception) and qua the expression of a Concept. But there's more. Just as in Jane Austen, there is Sense and Sensibility: another duplicity similar to that of the marvellous duplicity of the word 'sense'. The idea is very simple. What do we look for when we look at artworks? Feelings, first of all. Otherwise we would read a treatise. It is not truth that is sought in art, and art's reference to beauty (or to the representation of the ugly, the horrid, etc.) is explained in this emotional framework.

Hegel's thesis is that the simple recording of material, which makes it available for iterations, generates the process of alteration that ensures the passage from material to spiritual, from passivity to activity, from pyramid to consciousness.[78] And that is why the senses are doubled, so that the eye is both sight and discernment (having an eye for something), the ear is both hearing and musical taste, touch is both a sense and delicacy in human relationships, and so on. It should come as no surprise that aesthetics, i.e. the science that for centuries has been dealing with art, takes its name from sensibility (*aisthesis* in Greek). This profound and decisive duplicity explains why a place dedicated to 'aesthetics' can indicate both an academic institution devoted to the philosophy of art and a place for tanning and hair removal.[79]

Meaning. The iteration of a sign can generate meaning; a code is formed that can be repeated and used for communicative and documental purposes. A system of signs generates differences. The really crucial thing, as mentioned, is that the sign (and then the meaning) come after the trace, and not before as in the Pentecostal vision. The sign is the necessary though not sufficient condition of meaning. In order to create even minimal meaning it is necessary that the sign is iterated until it generates a code. Fingerprints make sense only when they can be compared with police records; DNA makes sense precisely because it is repeated in the body; and a word makes sense only because it can be repeated (a language made up of words that cannot be repeated, or that constantly changed meaning, would not be a language).

My sight is not thinking when it identifies a random succession of letters, for example XCZW: it is rather manipulating signs. But then again, it is not thinking either when it reads the word POT (you can get to the end of an article without remembering what you've just read). Thinking only intervenes when an obstacle comes up and, for example, we find the word PUT where we would expect POT. At this point, and only at this point, does perplexity lead us to wonder whether the author meant 'put' or 'pot'. Is this the birth of the magic of the spirit? No, it is simply a more complex manipulation of signs. The spontaneity and creativity that we feel in us, or the fact that we possess mental contents and refer to something in the world, contradict the fact that the origin of all this should be sought in recordings and inscriptions.

Let me explain. When I say 'I'm referring to the number 5', I'm saying something like 'I'm referring to what they taught me in school is the number 5'. And when I say 'six times eight is forty-eight' I'm repeating a nursery rhyme learned by heart, which in no way prevents me from understanding '48'. I could get the same result with an abacus or a calculator, and have no reason to postulate some intentional little man behind the scenes. In order for 'C' to refer to 'cat' in a dictionary, or for the dot with the word 'London' on the map to refer to London, there is no need for a little man transcending the dictionary or the map. On closer inspection (and education is nothing more), the spirit that goes from 'C' to 'cat', or which from the sign 'London' refers to the city of London, has been formed precisely through maps, dictionaries, albums of figurines, calendars, poems learned by heart and cartoons.

In the long run, both Siri and a child will have filled in an ideal table in which all the words we have said to them are recorded. It is very possible that they will then use them wrongly, as sometimes happens to us if we are ignorant, if we are speaking another language, or if we are tired or sick. But the process that takes place in Siri, in a child and in each of us is the same: the formation of a system, and therefore of a meaning, through hysteresis. Often meaning is represented as a Pentecost, as a spiritual content already present in the heaven of ideas, whereas it is better to think of meaning in terms of emergence, as the outcome of a hysteresis that generates a system.

There is no intrinsic value in any of the letters that make up the word 'cat', to such an extent that by combining them differently we have 'act': hence the contingency of the sign and the compositional nature of meaning discussed by Saussure – who, however, was convinced that the sign has a spiritual part, while in the version that I propose spirituality (if we want to refer to meaning that way) is the Gestalt outcome of the combination. The words 'got', 'gut' and 'get' mean what they do not because of the intrinsic properties of the letters that make them up, but because of the system of differences of which they are part; in the same way meaning can only take place within a system and thanks to a network of differences, i.e. recordings. Also in this case, recording precedes meaning and makes it possible, thus enabling the system itself to exist (a private language, i.e. a language that does not rest on an iterable code, is not conceivable). Hence there are two consequences.

The first is that, since there is no intrinsic sense, everything taken in isolation can be said to make no sense (whereas two things put together can begin to make sense: means and end, for example, or identity and difference). The passage from occurrence to meaning, from rhyme to reason, from chance to law, from singularity to system reflects this principle based on recording and on the production of differences (both in the sense of 'diversity' and in that of 'deferrals') that derives from it. This principle does not only have a semantic value, since it operates in the transition from singularity to system. In this case we are dealing with well-known phenomena, in which simple enumeration determines a meaning. Think of the power of the list, of the et cetera (to which Husserl rightly drew attention); of the power of the catalogue, even if erroneous or senseless (but which retrospectively constitutes meaning, a circumstance stressed by Borges); of the power of rhapsody, i.e. the way in which according to Kant, Aristotle had erroneously constructed his categories, and which instead is an excellent example of machine learning.

The second is that if someone by metaphysical chance wrote a true book on the meaning of existence, existence would lose all meaning, as meaning does not consist in a hypostasis, but in a system (consider for example the story of 'gobbledygook', a term born to manifest nonsense and that through use has acquired a unique and shared meaning). This circumstance suggests an element of the utmost importance. The machines that we fear will do us all sorts of harm, and above all fear will replace us, are in fact already in us, since intelligence is a mechanical element of the human, and human learning works exactly like machine learning. In both cases, indeed, there are processes in which there is a shift from meaning to meaningless sign and vice versa, from meaningless sign to meaning, as long as there is a capacity to record.

Sense. The peculiarly psychological effect by which something means something to someone, expresses intentions, is conceived and perceived as part of a consciousness, etc., depends on the fact that iteration is not infinite and eventually finds an interruption. This interruption is that of entropy, which in the case of organisms defines the sphere of direction, and in the case of responsive organisms, such as humans, generates meaning. What is sense? It is the mechanism that stops working, the interpretation that ceases its wandering and finds something solid: what was simply iterated now means something for someone, someone who is above all an organism. As said, only in an organism can phenomena such as anxiety, waiting, desire, boredom and hunger take place. And it is these phenomena emerging from the organism that give meaning to what for a machine simply makes sense. To be clearer, the phrase 'in a hundred years we will all be dead' has the same meaning if it appears in a book, if it is repeated by a loudspeaker at the station (sooner or later it could happen), or even if it is said by a lecturer in the mood for jokes. But only for the lecturer and for their listeners does the phrase possess a meaning in addition to a sense. And this is due to the trivial reason that in a hundred years they will indeed all be dead (this, incidentally, is also the reason why the phrase means something to both me and you).

Meaning depends precisely on this circumstance: what was simply iterated by an organism or mechanism can mean something for someone. This someone must be an organism (typically an animal), subject as such to those processes of interruption of which I spoke above. If we reflect for a moment on this decisive difference between organic and mechanical, we can not only give a non-mystical or tautological meaning to the *élan vital*, but also explain where exactly the difference lies between the thought of humans and that of computers. The sense of the end, which depends on the irreversibility of the process in a living person (who therefore has both memory and a sense of the end) can only take place in a living person. It may be objected that many living beings do not have a reflective awareness of the end. But it is not necessary to have read a treatise on metaphysics, or to have practised some form of authentic existence, to feel the pangs of hunger and thirst, which remind us – with a clarity that would be sought in vain in any book – that we are dust. And that is precisely why we are truth users.

5.4 Truth Users

One of the reasons why truth does not exist in nature is that if there were no humans (along with the technical and cultural constructs that make them such), truth would not interest anyone. In other words, an essential ingredient of truth (which, again, is in no way an argument for relativism) is humans as truth users.

Making the truth also means finding out whether Albertine is unfaithful (if you are jealous like Proust), reporting the butler to the police, discovering a new therapy for a disease: truth has a dimension that is not only epistemological (this is completely obvious) and not only technological (this is a little less obvious), but also teleological. The truth does not depend on someone's wishes – as posited by nihilism which thus renders the truth useless by decreeing the triumph of interpretations – but is made in view of something or someone. Since the truth is not a species found in nature such as sodium chloride, it is addressed to someone who is the aim of the research: the patient who has asked for a check-up, the curious user who looks something up on Wikipedia, the child who asks the reason for something and the jealous boyfriend who secretly reads his partner's WhatsApp messages are all part of the truth, as its final cause. They are precisely the truth users, and are no less important than the truth bearers (Albertine) the truth makers (her careless revelations), or the truth tellers ('Albertine is unfaithful'): all these elements receive meaning only in light of an end, which is precisely the user or, more prosaically, the cuckold.

This example obviously indicates the practical genesis of truth, and does not in the least affect its value. The reasons that Rousseau accumulates to discredit the sciences, and which are all attributable to the fact that they respond to human needs, do not in the least constitute a genealogical argument against truth. It is natural and right that truth initially responds to individual needs and practices, given that life is a necessity and speculation a luxury. But it is equally true that the truth can detach itself from this practical genesis (and writing is one of the most foolproof methods in this sense, as it can address completely different recipients from the original user). This is how truth becomes a (virtual) heritage of all humanity, and history presents itself as the story of humanity's infinite tendency towards truth.

Four

Recollection

The fundamental claim of new realism[1] is not that what idealists take to be ideas are actually real things like trees and chairs. In fact, any new realist is perfectly aware of the merits of a coherent idealism and is far from indifferent to the charms of a new and reworked transcendentalism.[2] The point is this: rather than an ontological commitment to the existence of given classes of beings (or as I prefer to say, of objects), new realism is the claim that such ontological commitment shouldn't leave the issue of reality to science, thereby limiting philosophy to a merely educational function. In this sense, the way in which new realism understands philosophy (that is, as a construction and a system, together with a clear ontological commitment) is much closer to nineteenth-century idealism than twentieth-century postmodernism.

I believe this is the right starting point for clarifying the function and scope of new realism in contemporary philosophy (to which I shall limit myself for lack of space, thereby leaving aside its scope in fields such as architecture,[3] literature,[4] pedagogy,[5] art theory,[6] political theory,[7] social sciences,[8] media studies[9] and public discussion).[10]

Nineteenth-century idealism. The twentieth century was a short century not only as far as history is concerned, but also philosophically speaking. At least until the First World War, there were fully coherent and widely accepted idealist systems in the philosophical community (this held true for the English-speaking world and Italy more than Germany, which had been the cradle of transcendental idealism at the beginning of the 1800s). It is against such systems that, as we know, twentieth-century thought went through the birth of what would later be called 'analytic philosophy'. The *raison d'être* of the philosophy brought forward in England by Bertrand Russell and George Edward Moore was the critique of neo-idealist systems, and specifically that of John Ellis McTaggart (1866–1925). It was a call for common sense and the 'robust sense of the real' thanks to which, in response to McTaggart's claim that time doesn't exist, Moore could object 'I've just had breakfast'.

Alongside this rebellious gesture, which paved the way for a very influential philosophical current, something was stirring on the other side of the Atlantic. In the 1910s, six American philosophers joined the trend of 'New Realism'.[11] They were Walter Taylor Marvin, Ralph Barton Perry, Edward Gleason Spaulding, Edwin Bissel Holt, William Pepperell Montague and Walter Boughton Pitkin. These names are unlikely to ring a bell with the reader, which attests to the minimal success of the movement. New Realism had no Bertrand Russell, no Wittgenstein and no Moore. In the successive phase of 'critical realism',[12] it had Lovejoy, Santayana and Sellars (Roy Wood Sellars, father of the more famous Wilfrid), but the philosophical mainstream went along with analytic philosophy, which seemed to envisage a stronger break with idealism and more intriguing new approaches.

However, if we want to understand what brought about New Realism a century ago (along with the realist versions of German neo-Kantianism[13]) as well as early analytic philosophy, we should focus on idealism, against which it was pitted. Such a task cannot be achieved in these pages, of course, also because neo-idealism was very robust and endowed with an argumentative quality that was enviable by post-idealist continental philosophy standards (and a richness of content that was enviable by analytic philosophy standards). I shall limit myself to a small sample that I believe is significant: the opening lines of *The Theory of the Mind as Pure Act* by Giovanni Gentile (1875–1944):

> Berkeley in the beginning of the Eighteenth century expressed very clearly the following concept. Reality is conceivable only in so far as the reality conceived is in relation to the activity which conceives it, and in that relation it is not only a possible object of knowledge, it is a present and actual one. To conceive reality is to conceive, at the same

time and as one with it, the mind in which that reality is represented; and therefore the concept of a material reality is absurd.[14]

We must credit Gentile for the honesty with which he expresses his ontological commitment: only what is present to his thought is real, while everything else falls into the domain of the unreal. If this were true (unless you want to embrace a radically solipsistic credo), there would be serious consequences for our most obvious assumptions: those assumptions on which we all (Giovanni Gentile included) base our lives. In fact, if only our mental representations were real, then there would be no difference between introspection and knowledge of the outside world. All things past, from dinosaurs to the Sumerians, would be present only to the same extent as the thoughts that think them. All things future would be no less present than things past (and therefore there would be no difference between possible and actual). Everything Giovanni Gentile ignored would have been non-existent; on the other hand, anything he thought of would have existed, including Pegasus. However, all of this would have ceased to exist with Gentile's death.[15]

We might wonder how a great thinker like Gentile was unable to see the blatant absurdity of his thesis, and the answer is easy enough. Gentile wrote almost three centuries after the *Meditations on First Philosophy* and 130 years after the *Critique of Pure Reason* and the subsequent Copernican Revolution in which, instead of inquiring into the nature of things, it was posited that we should simply investigate the way in which we humans can know them. In other words, Gentile had deeply interiorised assumptions that were far from obvious. The first is that we only have an immediate relationship with thought, which in turn mediates every relation we have with the world. The second is what I have called the 'transcendental fallacy':[16] that is, the confusion between ontology and epistemology, between what there is and what we know (or think we know) about what there is.

In addition to having the philosophical blessing of Descartes and Kant, this fallacy is also very natural. The psychology of reasoning has shown the theoretical deception due to which we are much more sensitive to the *modus ponens* ('method of affirming') than the *modus tollens* ('method of denying'), and common sense has codified the confusion between what there is and the fact that we have access to it as 'out of sight out of mind'. It is a very natural confusion, something very similar to the 'stimulus error': when we are asked what we see with our eyes closed, we tend to say 'nothing' (while the truth is that we are seeing phosphenes, consecutive images and so on). We are not giving a description, we are proposing a naive theory of vision: the eye is like a camera, so when the lens is closed there is nothing or, at most, perfect darkness. From this point of view, the boutade that Ramses II did not die of TB because Koch isolated the tuberculosis bacillus only in 1882[17] is an ingenious and epistemologically equipped variation of this human tendency to self-deceit and overestimation.

However, if we consider the metaphysical implications of this fallacy, we'll notice that it entails a very strong ontological commitment to the existence of a spirit independent of matter, able to produce representations and, through them, things. This is perfectly coherent with an idealistic framework, but much less so within a postmodernist one.

Twentieth-century postmodernism. For much of the twentieth century, realism was marginal. A regional specialty relegated to Australia, like marsupials,[18] and roaming marginal streets compared to both the analytical and the continental mainstreams,[19] or limited to extra-philosophical areas such as the psychology of perception.[20] Proposals for a realist epistemology, such as Roy Bhaskar's (1944–2014) 'critical realism',[21] appeared far less seductive than the anarchism brought forward by Paul Feyerabend (1924–94),[22] for whom all scientific methods are equally valid, or the fascinating theses expressed by the postmodern American philosopher Richard Rorty (1931–2007), for whom objectivity has no intrinsic value.[23] The idea of a 'descriptive metaphysic' respectful of common sense advanced by the English philosopher Peter Frederick Strawson (1919–2006)[24] seemed a lot less heroic than the 'deconstruction of metaphysics' proposed by post-Heideggerian reflection.

Should we conclude that, in many cases, there has been a continuation of nineteenth-century idealism? In a way, paradoxical as it may seem, we should. Rorty noted the similarities between nineteenth-century idealism and twentieth-century postmodernism.[25] However, between the two idealisms there is a fundamental difference. Nineteenth-century idealism laid its cards on the table: there is no time, there is only what is being thought of, etc. Conversely, postmodernism followed a very different strategy.

With Rorty, it suggested that reality's dependence on thought is 'representational',[26] meaning that it doesn't concern objects but rather the vocabulary we use to designate them. Now, if by 'representational dependence' we mean that the existence of, say, Tyrannosaurus Rex depends on our conceptual schemes, then it follows that when Tyrannosaurus Rex existed, it didn't exist, as we humans didn't yet exist. However, if we mean that the word Tyrannosaurus Rex depends on our conceptual schemes, then this is not dependence in any serious sense of the term.

At this point one has to ask an obvious question: how is it possible that such dependence, which is at most epistemological (our knowledge of dinosaurs is what makes them relevant to us, or we wouldn't have known a thing about them), is passed off as an ontological dependence (so that our knowledge somehow constitutes the dinosaurs' being)? The answer comes from another American philosopher, but a new realist this time: Graham Harman. Harman has noted how the fundamental trick of postmodern idealism consists in claiming to lie beyond both idealism and realism, as well as beyond both subject and object.[27] Formally, postmodernists do not assume an idealist or subjectivist ontological commitment, since they claim to stand beyond the distinctions between subject and object and between idealism and realism. However, by arguing that reality or objectivity are given only in connection with a subject, they surreptitiously introduce an idealist and subjectivist thesis. Harman gives some significant examples of this attitude: for Husserl objects are always the correlates of intentional acts; for Heidegger beings are always related to Dasein; Merleau-Ponty formulated the slogan 'there is for us an in itself'; and Derrida wrote that the difference between signified and signifier is nothing (which, by the way, proves it legitimate to read his cryptic 'there is no outside-text' as 'there is nothing outside the text').

Statements like 'being that can be understood is language' or 'language is the house of being', which have been the catchphrases of twentieth-century continental philosophy, are just so many variations on the existential thesis that there is no subject or object, but only the relation between them. The revival of Nietzsche's thesis 'there are no facts, but only interpretations' proposed by radical hermeneutics appears to be a foreseeable outcome of this mindset: if there are only relations, then there are only interpretations.[28] We would be wrong if we thought that this situation belongs to the past. As rightly noted by Thomas Kuhn, a philosophical dogma persists until the retirement of the last of its proponents. In this light, it is not surprising that in 2015 one could still read as follows:

> Against this new realism I have merely quoted minor characters like Erwin Schrödinger, whom I have already referred to in the past, for instance in my first *Krisis*. The new realists' approach is far from being knowledge of nature. The problem of great contemporary science, as well as of true philosophy, is the overcoming of the subject-object discourse. There is no subject and no object: there is only the relation between them.[29]

This is somewhat like claiming that there is no left hand and no right hand: there are only the two hands joined in prayer – unless you want to embrace a coherently Berkeleyan perspective, which would also entail a formal demonstration of the existence of God.[30] The Australian philosopher David Stove (1927–94) called this 'the worst argument in the world'. To claim that we can only know things if they are in relation to us, and that therefore we cannot know things in themselves, is no different from claiming as follows: since we are the ones eating oysters, when we eat oysters we cannot eat oysters as such, but only in relation to us.[31] This is a radicalisation of the worst argument in the world. In fact, if we are to believe that 'there is no subject and no object, there is only the relation between them', then we must conclude that there is no such thing as a customer in the restaurant, nor is there an oyster on the plate, only an impersonal 'oyster-eating'.

The passage I have just quoted is interesting both as a document and because it sums up several prejudices towards new realism (for instance, it confuses it with a form of naturalism[32]) and in general attributes to it the straw-man thesis according to which the mind mirrors reality as it is. Obviously, new realism has never supported a thesis of this kind, and the reference to naive realism and common sense plays an essentially methodological function in the new realist strategy: we must be able to provide explanations that account for commonsensical intuitions.[33] The price to pay for not considering common sense, in fact, is not giving up a sophisticated and demanding philosophy, but rather philosophical carelessness, an abundance of catchphrases ('there is only the relation'), and an inflation of bad arguments that confirms the continuing validity of Hegel's saying that arguments are as cheap as apples.

For instance, to say (with a bizarre generalisation of quantum mechanics) that the observer modifies the observed in any area and at any level would mean that using scales in shops is useless, as both the client and the owner modify the good's weight by looking at it. This simple consideration says nothing about reality, nor does it claim to assert (with a philosophical primitivism that no realist would ever tolerate) that reality is exactly what it appears to be. Rather, one of the most relevant theses of philosophical realism is that not only is reality not what it appears to be, but also that there are areas of reality we know nothing about. This, however, does not legitimate the change of perspective implemented by Kant, who, noting the difficulty of knowing how things are in themselves, suggested that philosophy should rather focus on how they should be made in order to be known by us. By doing this, Kant took the first step on a slippery slope whose final outcome is the argument that there is no subject or object, but only their relation.

The situation can be summed up as follows. Nineteenth-century idealism was a coherent movement addressing the fundamental problem of philosophy: that is, being a thought accounting for the whole of reality. In order to do this, however, it had to hypothesise some role of thought over reality. This was favoured by the transcendental fallacy, that is, by the confusion between ontology and epistemology. With postmodernism things went differently: there was the 'hermeneutical fallacy', that is, the confusion between the axiological relevance of something (language is important, history and the subject are important, but it is even more important to have a roof over your head and to be able to cook lunch and dinner) and its ontological relevance. Language, thought and history affect reality (who would ever deny it?) therefore they constitute reality (and this is simply absurd).

This is how a group of onomaturges has turned into a bunch of demiurges. If the worst argument in the world were true, not only would Newtonian physics not have been real before Newton[34] (there is only the relation between subject and object, therefore if the subject Newton is missing, the object Newton's Laws is missing too), but the very objects to which Newton's Laws refer would exist only in a very problematic way.[35] Note that this is the same outcome reached by Gentile, only it is far less obvious.

In the analytic world, the realist intuition that a proposition is true or false independently of the fact that we know or can know how things are – in my terms, the distinction between ontology and epistemology – was strongly reasserted in the 1970s by Saul Kripke[36] and Hilary Putnam.[37] However, the situation there was very different from that in the continental world. In continental philosophy, in fact, anti-realism was politically tinged. Claiming that reality decisively depends on the actions of subjects means (as explicitly proposed by Foucault and Vattimo) holding up the principle of interpreting the world and at the same time transforming it. No such thing happened in the analytic tradition which, as we have seen, was born as a realist and commonsensical reaction against idealism, and therefore never supported theses like those that 'power' or 'the subject' can constitute reality.

Twenty-first-century realism. As is now well-known, the term 'new realism' has a precise date and place of birth: it was born on 23 June 2011 in a restaurant in Naples. Markus Gabriel was planning to organise an international conference on the new trends in philosophy, and I suggested he entitle it 'New Realism'. In fact, it was my belief that, after postmodern anti-realism, realism was back to the fore. I summarised my theses on new realism in a short article[38] and a few longer pieces,[39] and a huge debate followed. The first signs of this could be spotted at three major conferences (New York,[40] Turin[41] and Bonn[42]), as well as in my *Manifesto of New Realism*,[43] and the collective volume *Bentornata Realtà*.[44] The international reception was exceptional: suffice it to say that, as early as 2013, it was one of the topics addressed at the World Congress of Philosophy in Athens.[45] This warm welcome shows that the time had come for realism also in continental philosophy. But why did it take so long? To answer this question, I have to provide the reader with a few remarks on the history of new realism.

When, in the early nineties,[46] I first started criticising the hermeneutical and postmodern environment in which I grew up, I started from something that seemed to be unnameable back then: perception. In fact, if being that can be understood is language, and if there is nothing outside the text, then perception proper doesn't exist and has no autonomy: there is nothing but the docile feud of conceptual schemes. So, recovering aesthetics as *aisthesis* was the first step of my realism. The second has been to mark a difference between ontology and epistemology. The third has been to elaborate a realist theory of the social world. The fourth has been to provide a general realist ontology, and this is what I am currently working on.[47]

The first *annus mirabilis* ('marvellous year') in the history of new realism can be found in 1997. That year, together with the pamphlet by Alan Sokal and Jean Bricmont against the postmodernist abuse of science,[48] Umberto Eco's *Kant and the Platypus*[49] came out, surprisingly (we thought)[50] raising some perplexities with regards to Kant that were close to those mentioned in my *Estetica razionale* and in Diego Marconi's *Lexical Competence*.[51] However, the general climate remained deeply anti-realist. Jean Baudrillard had recently declared that the Gulf War was nothing but a media fiction,[52] while Richard Rorty[53] and Joseph Ratzinger[54] argued for solidarity over objectivity. Ian Hacking ironised on the number of objects (including diseases, nature and quarks) that, according to postmodern thinkers, are the outcome of social construction.[55] John McDowell re-proposed a particularly idealist Kantianism,[56] and Karl Rove, counsellor of the President of the United States, George W. Bush Jr., claimed that America, as an empire, could create its own reality.[57]

In the first two decades of the new century, however, many original and theoretically relevant positions have come to the fore, which can be (provisionally) unified under the name 'speculative realism'.[58] In this framework the pioneer was Manuel DeLanda,[59] but one should also mention the realist re-working of Heidegger's philosophy proposed by Harman.[60] Thus we come to a second *annus mirabilis* of new realism, 2006: the date of publication of a number of books introducing topics that would be long discussed. I speak of Quentin Meillassoux's metaphysics,[61] Paul Boghossian's epistemology,[62] Günter Figal's hermeneutics,[63] DeLanda's social theory[64] and Iain Hamilton Grant's philosophy of nature.[65] This presaged the major philosophical event of 2007, when the first meeting of Speculative Realists took place at Goldsmiths College in London, including Harman, Meillassoux, Grant and Ray Brassier.[66] A second such conference took place in Bristol on 24 April 2009. In the same timeframe, there started being talk of 'object-oriented ontology':[67] almost a resurrection of the theory of the object of the Austrian philosopher Alexius Meinong (1853–1920).[68] Finally, an international conference in Paris in 2014 marked the encounter between new realism, speculative realism and the realist elements of phenomenology and analytic philosophy.[69]

The future of realism. But let's return to the present and, if possible, the future. On 20 February 2015 a conference was held in

Amsterdam entitled 'the future of realism'. I was there together with Harman, the French philosopher Tristan Garcia and the Argentinian philosopher Gabriel Catren; during the final round-table we discussed what the next moves of realism would be. The common impression was that there would be many different forms of conflicting realisms, and that at some point idealism would probably come back to the fore, but stronger and better equipped than its twentieth-century ancestor. For now, though, there are three prevailing forms of realism.

The first is negative realism, which embodies the dutiful commonsensical objection to constructivism and offers a minimal basis for philosophical work to take place.[70] It is an essential element of any serious philosophy and I have personally tried to grasp it in my notion of 'unamendability'. If the world truly were the outcome of conceptual construction, if object and subject did not exist separately but there were only their relation, then why would objects resist subjects so much? Of course, one could reply with Fichte's *Science of Knowledge* that an infinite I opposes a finite Not-I to a finite I, and such an answer deserves to be taken into account. However, unfortunately, if there is one thing universally shared by all forms of twentieth-century idealism it is the rejection of infinity – therefore, such a position turns out to be unacceptable.

The second form of realism is neutral realism.[71] This type of reflection is adopted especially by Gabriel: to exist is to exist in a field of sense. For analytic authors such as Putnam, Boghossian and De Caro, this field of sense is traditionally referred to science, understood in a non-reductionist sense. For continental authors like Meillassoux and Gabriel, however, it has a different characterisation. For Meillassoux, sense is conferred with reference to mathematics (in accordance with Meillassoux's master, Alain Badiou). For Gabriel, instead, in what ultimately amounts to a re-launching of the hermeneutic tradition, sense is a character proper to human existence. This point is articulated with a wealth of arguments in his *Why the World Does Not Exist*, signalling Gabriel's fundamental belonging to a Heideggerian reflection.[72] My concern here is that to make existence depend on sense is excessive. There can be existence without any sense, as our own lives can very well demonstrate. For Heidegger, existence and sense coincide: for instance, in his course on the *Fundamental Principles of Metaphysics*, he claims that only man has world and is a world constructor, whereas the animal is poor in world and the stone is worldless. However, Heidegger seems to forget that – leaving aside the wealth of the animal and inanimate worlds – a human being can very well be poor in world (think of the working class during Dickens's age) or worldless (the people exterminated in Auschwitz) without this meaning that they don't exist.

Finally, there is positive realism. This is the direction followed by Harman and myself. The starting point here is a very simple observation. We have infinite proofs of the coexistence, within the same environment, of beings very different in terms of conceptual schemes, perceptual apparatuses and skills. This interaction (in fact, it has more to do with action than knowledge) certainly can't depend on the hypothetical epistemologies of the beings involved. Since this interaction is not (at least not always) doomed to failure – as should be the case according to a purely negative realism – we must necessarily conclude that reality is endowed with its own positivity, thus allowing for these interactions and, through a process of emergence, complex performances and knowledge.

As for me, I am working on the (I believe, legitimate) project of a transcendental realism,[73] which is no less ambitious than transcendental idealism. Synthesising negative and positive realism and overturning transcendental idealism, reality appears as the condition of possibility of knowledge. In this sense, positive realism can recover the tradition of emergentism[74] (thought as emerging from reality, as opposed to constructivism seeing reality as the construction of thought) and ecologism (the environment as the area of interaction of beings endowed with different conceptual schemes and perceptual apparatuses).[75] This transcendental realism appears as a general theory of the process of emergence that, starting from the organisation of animal life,[76] proceeds to address the formation of thought[77] and finally normativity and motivation.[78]

In any case, one thing should be clear by now. Unlike twentieth-century New Realism, which was born too soon, twenty-first-century New Realism has strong reasons to expect a significant flourishing within its domain – indeed, this is already happening. Furthermore, it is historically in a better position. As I mentioned above, twentieth-century New Realism was a less powerful and structured answer to idealism than the one offered by analytic philosophy. A century later, the situation is very different. On the one hand, analytic philosophy is being rethought and renewed,[79] which makes it more open to continental philosophy. On the other hand, continental philosophy is no longer content with commenting on tradition (for which indeed there is nothing outside the text!) and is open to argumentation and ontology.[80]

On 18 January 1895 in Vienna, Franz Brentano delivered his lecture 'The Four Phases of Philosophy and Its Present Condition'.[81] The idea was that philosophy goes through different and recurring stages. The first is rapid progress due to a purely theoretical interest accompanied by a scientific opening to empirical cases. The second is a practical interest, in which the inquiry into nature and the search for truth are motivated by social usefulness and applied philosophy. The third is scepticism. Since human interests are not satisfied by an exclusively practical focalisation, there is a prevailing scepticism about human cognitive possibilities. The fourth stage is mysticism: a hyperbolic reaction to scepticism characterised by the invention of new methods and the discovery of new powers seemingly able to create new types of knowledge (this sounds very much like postmodernism). But the wheel keeps turning and goes back to where it started. Again: realism, praxis, scepticism, mysticism and so forth. One may think that this is a sort of eternal return, but it isn't: everything comes back, but it is not the same as before.

Brentano was the last philosopher before the analytic/continental divide came into being. Things changed with the generation after him: the English philosopher Michael Dummett[82] has written that Frege (a canonical author of analytic philosophy) and Husserl (a canonical author of continental philosophy) were originally very close, just like the sources of the Rhine and the Danube, but their outcomes are as distant as the North Sea and the Black Sea (and, one might add, while the Rhine flows into a quite regular estuary, the Danube bogs down into a marshy delta, which might be a good allegory of many outcomes of continental philosophy). It would not be the first time in the history of philosophy that two philosophical traditions cease to communicate: in the eighteenth century there was a similar situation in many ways, since there was a fracture due to the abandonment of Latin as the common philosophical language. Ultimately, even if the only result of new realism was to overcome this schism, new realists would be very happy with that. And their heirs, be they realists or idealists, will find themselves with a philosophically more stimulating situation than the division that characterised a good part of the twentieth century.

Notes

Series Editor's Preface

1. Maurizio Ferraris, *Documentality: Why It Is Necessary to Leave Traces*, trans. R. Davies, New York: Fordham University Press, 2012.
2. Markus Gabriel, *Fields of Sense: A New Realist Ontology*, Edinburgh: Edinburgh University Press, 2015.
3. Maurizio Ferraris, *Goodbye, Kant! What Still Stands of the* Critique of Pure Reason, trans. R. Davies, Albany: SUNY Press, 2013.
4. Thomas Nagel, 'What Is It Like to Be a Bat?', *The Philosophical Review*, 83/4 (1974): 435–50.
5. See below, p. 182.

Observation

1. A sketch of what follows can be found (in an extended version) in 'Mente e mondo o scienza ed esperienza', *Rivista di estetica*, n.s., 12 (2000): 3–77 and 'Il problema non è l'ornitorinco, è Kant', *Rivista di estetica*, 13 (2000): 110–220. The first essay was about John McDowell, *Mind and World*, Harvard: Harvard University Press, 1999; the second took its cue from Umberto Eco, *Kant and the Platypus*, New York: Harvest Books, 1999. I am very grateful to Tiziana Andina, Marilena Andronico, Carola Barbero, Stefano Caputo, Roberto Casati, Massimo De Carolis, Anna Donise, Nicoletta Giorda, Tonino Griffero, Pietro Kobau, Paolo Legrenzi, Luca Morena, Carlo Nizzo, Roberto Poli, Alessandra Saccon, Achille Varzi and Giovanni Vicario for the productive discussions, criticism and comments (in many cases, such as to dictate new directions to my argument).
2. T. Mann, *Buddenbrooks: The Decline of a Family*, New York: Vintage International, 1993, p. 3.

3. C. Wolff, *Philosophia prima sive Ontologia*, Frankfurt-Leipzig: Renger, 1729.
4. G. Tomasi di Lampedusa, *The Leopard*, New York: Vintage Classics, 2007, p. 184.
5. G.W. Leibniz, *Discourse on Metaphysics and the Monadology*, trans. George R. Montgomery, New York: Prometheus Books, 1992, §19.
6. O. Lipmann and H. Bogen, *Naive Physik. Arbeiten aus dem Institut fur angewandte Psychologie in Berlin. Theoretische und experimentelle Untersuchungen über die Fähigkeit zu intelligentem Handeln*, Leipzig: Barth, 1923. A more mature realisation of this perspective can be found in P. Bozzi, *Fisica ingenua*, Milan: Garzanti, 1990.
7. P. Legrenzi, 'Naive Probability: A Mental Model Theory of Extensional Reasoning', *Psychological Review*, 106/1 (1999): 62–88 (with P.N. Johnson-Laird, Vittorio Girotto, Maria Sonino and Jean-Paul Caverni).
8. 'If I have exhausted the justifications I have reached bedrock, and my spade is turned. Then I am inclined to say: "This is simply what I do."' L. Wittgenstein, *Philosophical Investigations*, Hoboken: Blackwell, 2001, §217.
9. G. Kanizsa, *Vedere e pensare*, Bologna: il Mulino, 1991, pp. 30ff.
10. I. Kant, *Critique of Pure Reason*, trans. Norman Kemp Smith, New York: Palgrave Macmillan, 2007 (A = 1781, B = 1787).
11. I. Kant, *Critique of Judgment*, trans. James Creed Meredith, Oxford: Oxford University Press, 2007, §75.
12. Cf. M. Massironi, 'La via più breve nel pensiero visivo', *Sistemi intelligenti*, a.-VII, 2 (1995): 223–61.
13. M. Massironi, *Fenomenologia della percezione visiva*, Bologna: il Mulino, 1998, p. 152; S. Roncato and R. Ruminati, 'Naive Statics: Current Misconceptions on Equilibrium', *Journal of Experimental Psychology: Learning, Memory and Cognition*, 12 (1986): 361–77.
14. R. Casati, *La scoperta dell'ombra*, Milan: Mondadori, 2000.
15. Cf. C. Becchio, *Ragionamento deduttivo e spazialità. Un'ipotesi sperimentale e alcune considerazioni filosofiche*, Dissertation, Università di Torino, a.y. 1999–2000.
16. In 1768 (in *Of the first ground of the distinction of regions of space*, and then again in *What does it mean to orient oneself in thinking?*, which he wrote thirty years later), Kant had developed an ecological notion of space, defined based on the body (the right and left hand, head and feet, chest and back), which responded to a need of the

Copernican Revolution, but came into conflict with the Newtonian idea of absolute space.
17. J.H. Lambert, *New Organon* (1764), 'Phenomenology or Doctrine of Appearance', sect. l, §§1, 2, 7.
18. Casati, *La scoperta dell'ombra*, pp. 172–4.
19. P. Bozzi, *Fenomenologia sperimentale*, Bologna: il Mulino, 1989, p. 165.
20. Plato, *Philebus* 38e–39a, in *Platonis Opera*, ed. J. Burnet, Oxford: Oxford University Press, 1903. This is an epistemological shift (in that case, legitimate) that is found up to Husserl: the initial sense of *knowledge* is given only as a final sense; we *now* know that the Moon is a satellite made in such and such a way, and that it was such also 10,000 years ago, when people thought differently.
21. Kant, *Critique of Pure Reason*, A 102. Many, starting from Vaihinger, have supposed this was a typo. After all, in the literature Kant draws from, imagination is the retention of sensation, in an Aristotelian sense: 'nihil est in phantasia, quod antea non fuerit in sensu' (A. Baumgarten, *Metaphysics* [1757], London: Bloomsbury Academic, 2014, §559); 'Sine praevia sensatione nullum in anima phantasma oriri potest' (C. Wolff, *Psychologia empirica*, 1730, §106 (Transl.: *Empirical Psychology, Treated According to the Scientific Method*. Prostat in Officina Libraria Rengeriana.).
22. Alfredo Ferrarin, in 'Construction and Mathematical Schematism: Kant on the Exhibition of a Concept in Intuition', *Kant-Studien*, 86 (1995): 131–74, has developed the best analysis I know of in this regard, but has argued for a thesis directly opposite to my own: he thinks there is a crucial difference between Kantian schematism and mathematical constructivism, because Kant doesn't think he can produce an intuition, as instead happens in mathematical construction. However, the point is: if schematism didn't construct anything, if categories merely had a regulatory value and so on, then transcendental philosophy would be pointless, and Kant could not even *hope* to have replied to Hume.
23. Compare B 225 and B 17.
24. And there is nothing wrong with this, seeing as they do have properties, cf. R. Casati and A. Varzi, *Holes and Other Superficialities*, Cambridge: MIT Press, 1994. But for Kant it isn't so.
25. R.M. Chisholm, 'The Loose and Popular and the Strict and Philosophical Senses of Identity', in *Perception and Personal Identity*, ed. N.S. Care and R.H. Grimm, Cleveland: The Press of Case Western Reserve University, 1969, pp. 82–106. The problem is

similar to that of figural qualities in Ehrenfels and founded objects in Meinong. See note 27.

26. Bozzi, *Fenomenologia sperimentale*, p. 52.
27. W. Metzger, *Die Entwicklung ihrer Grundannahmen seit der Einführung des Experiments*, Vienna: Wolfgang Krammer Verlag, 1941. Strictly speaking, this distinction can be traced back to Herbart, worried about the idealistic reduction of Kantism to a representation theory initiated by Reinhold on the basis of a trend that, as we have seen, is widely attested in Kant. For an excellent overview, see G.B. Vicario, *Psicologia generale*, Rome-Bari: Laterza, 2001, pp. 93ff.
28. A. von Meinong, 'Über Gegenstände höherer Ordnung und deren Verhältnis zur inneren Wahrnehmung', in *Zeitschrift für Psychologie und Physiologie der Sinnesorgane*, 21 (1900–2), pp. 187–272, §2.
29. As indeed wrote Augustine (*Confessions*, X, 1.1): 'volo eam [veritatem] facere in corde meo coram te in confessione, in stilo autem coram multis testibus'. He did so rightly, after all: truth is only made in *confession*, because in life we do something else most of the time. And Proust is correct when he claims that when writing we become attentive and scrupulous, whereas when living we let lies ruin us.
30. A. Darling, *Redcoat and Brown Bess*, Bloomfield (Ontario): Museum Restoration Service, 1971, p. 19.
31. F. Nietzsche, *The Will to Power*, New York: Vintage Books, 1968, p. 267.
32. A. Campanile, *Ma che cos'è questo amore*, Milan: Corbaccio, 1998, pp. 197–9.
33. It would make more sense to say it is vague; however, not knowing how many beans make a pile does not mean that there are no piles: it just means that there is no pile-science, because it's enough to take a guess.
34. My son gave me an excellent description of shoe tying, but the operation itself is rather difficult for him; similarly, in general, it is a lot easier to criticise than to do. On the difference between inferential competence (connecting words with other words) and referential competence (connecting words with things), cf. D. Marconi, *Lexical Competence*, Cambridge MA: MIT Press, 1997.
35. E. Lask, *Logik der Philosophie*, in *Gesammelte Schriften*, Tübingen: Mohr, 1923, II, p. 74.
36. E. Husserl, *Experience and Judgment* (1938), Evanston: Northwestern University Press, 1975, §10.
37. Plato, *Theaetetus*, 197b–199c.

38. Marco Tullio Atlan's sentence 'I have thoughts I disagree with' is not an extreme case, nor is it an insignificant hypothesis. When talking about the genesis of a novel or a poem, authors often speak of ideas they got despite or against their will; sometimes we'd happily get rid of guilt feelings we consider irrational, but we don't manage to, and so on.
39. Aristotle, *On the Soul*, trans. J.A. Smith, The Internet Classics Archive, MIT, 432a 10–15.
40. 'The sensible forms of things without the matter (*eidon aneu tes hyles*)', *On the Soul*, 424a 18.
41. E. Husserl, *Logical Investigations* (1900–1), London: Routledge, 2001.
42. After J.J. Gibson, *The Ecological Approach to Visual Perception*, Boston: Houghton Mifflin, 1979, this correspondence between ontology and ecology has no claim to being original. Cf. B. Smith and R. Casati, 'Naive Physics: An Essay in Ontology', *Philosophical Psychology*, 7/2 (1994): 225–44; B. Smith, 'Truth and the Visual Field', in *Naturalizing Phenomenology: Issues in Contemporary Phenomenology and Cognitive Science*, ed. J. Petitot, F.J. Varela, B. Pachoud and J.M. Roy, Stanford: Stanford University Press, 1999; B. Smith, 'Objects and Their Environments: From Aristotle to Ecological Ontology', in *The Life and Motion of Socio-Economic Units*, ed. A. Frank et al., London: Taylor and Francis, 1999; B. Smith, 'Husserlian Ecology', unpublished, 2000 at <http://wings.buffalo.edu/academic/department/philosophy/faculty/smith>; B. Smith and A. C. Varzi, 'The Niche', *Nous*, 33/2 (1999): 214–38.
43. I said so – wrongly – in 'Ontologia come fisica ingenua', *Rivista di estetica*, n.s., 6 (1997): 133–43.
44. L. Wittgenstein, *Tractatus Logico-Philosophicus*, trans. D. Pears and B. McGuinness, London: Routledge, 2001, 5.631. This proposition, which is also found in Scheler in the same years, is taken from Avenarius. I thank Kevin Mulligan for pointing this out to me. I can't find a better theorisation of this notion of 'world' than that given by Derrida in *Voice and Phenomenon* (Evanston: Northwestern University Press, 2011, p. 46): 'What does the "principle of all principles" of phenomenology actually mean? What does the value of originary presence to intuition as the source of sense and evidence, as the a priori of a priori, mean? It means first the certainty, which is itself ideal and absolute, that the universal form of all experience (*Erlebnis*) and therefore of all life, has always been and always will be the present. There is and there will have never been anything but

the present. Being is presence or the modification of presence. The relation to the presence of the present as the ultimate form of being and ideality is the movement by which I transgress empirical existence, factuality, contingency, mundanity, etc. – and first of all *mine*. To think presence as the universal form of transcendental life is to open me to the knowledge that in my absence, beyond my empirical existence, prior to my birth and after my death, *the present is*. I can empty it of all empirical *content*; I can imagine an absolute upheaval of the content of all possible experience, a radical transformation of the world. Doing this will not affect the universal form of presence. It is therefore the relationship to *my death* (to my disappearance in general) that is hidden in this determination of being as presence, ideality, as the absolute possibility of repetition.'

45. Aristotle, *Posterior Analytics*, trans. Octavius Freire Owen, H.G. Bohn, 1853, II, 19.
46. B. Smith, 'Common Sense', in *The Cambridge Companion to Husserl*, ed. B. Smith and D. Woodruff Smith, Cambridge: Cambridge University Press, 1995. More generally, Smith tends to identify common sense and naive physics in the context of a definition of ontology (see B. Smith, 'The Structures of Common-Sense World', *Acta Philosophica Fennica*, 58 (1995): 290–317). Personally, I prefer using naive physics not as the definition of a positive context, but as a reactor to distinguish ontology and epistemology.
47. J.L. Austin, 'A Plea for Excuses', in *Philosophical Papers*, 2nd ed., Oxford: Oxford University Press, 1979, pp. 175–204.
48. Massironi, *Fenomenologia della percezione visiva*, p. 63.
49. As Moore thinks instead. See G.E. Moore, 'Proof of an External World', *Proceedings of the British Academy* 25 (1939): 273–300.
50. J. Barnes, *The Ontological Argument*, London: Macmillan, 1972.
51. Leibniz, *Meditations on Knowledge, Truth and Ideas* (1684), in *Philosophical Papers and Letters*, Vol. 2, ed. L.E. Loemker, Dordrecht: Springer, 1989.
52. *On the Soul*, 431b 13–17.
53. In §14 of the third *Logical Investigation* Husserl rightly says: 'The undetermined expressions "ao *requires integration*" and "ao *is founded at a certain moment*" obviously have the same meaning as the expression "ao *is non-independent*".' Which means, on the other hand, there are quite a lot of independent things, unfounded, nor in need of integration.
54. G. Kanizsa, *Vedere e pensare*; *Grammatica del vedere*, Bologna: il Mulino, 1980.

55. Cf. V. Costa, *L'estetica trascendentale fenomenologica*, Milan: Vita e Pensiero, 1999, p. 151.
56. Lucretius, *De rerum natura*, trans. William Ellery Leonard, 1916, l, 159–66.
57. U. Eco, 'Dove sta Cappuccetto Rosso?', in *Modi dell'oggettività*, ed. G. Usberti, Milan: Bompiani, 2000, pp. 137–57.
58. T.S. Eliot, 'The Love Song of J. Alfred Prufrock', in *Prufrock and Other Observations*, London: The Egoist, 1917, vv. 10–11.

Speculation

1. F.S. Fitzgerald, *This Side of Paradise* (1920), Oxford: Oxford University Press, 2020.
2. S. Freud, *Beyond the Pleasure Principle* (1920), New York: W.W. Norton & Co, 1975.
3. L. Wittgenstein, *Tractatus Logico-Philosophicus* (1921), London: Routledge, 1990.
4. J. Derrida, 'Speculation – on Freud', *Oxford Literary Review*, 3/2 (1978): 78–97.
5. E. Schrödinger, *What Is Life?* (1944), Cambridge MA: Cambridge University Press, 2012.
6. E. Pfeiffer (ed.), *Sigmund Freud and Lou Andreas-Salome: Letters*, New York: W.W. Norton & Co, 1985.
7. A. Kojève, *Introduction à la lecture de Hegel*, Paris, 1947; an abridged English translation was published in 1968 as *Introduction to the Reading of Hegel*, ed. A. Bloom, New York, 1968.
8. G.W. Leibniz, *New Essays on Human Understanding*, 2nd ed., trans. and ed. P. Remnant and J. Bennett, New York: Cambridge University Press, 1996, IV, XVII, §16.
9. Plato, *Sophist*, trans. William Cobb, Savage, MD: Rowman and Littlefield, 1990, pp. 251–9.
10. Plato, *Timaeus*, in *Plato in Twelve Volumes*, Vol. 9, trans. W.R.M. Lamb, Cambridge MA: Harvard University Press, 1925, 49a6 51a5.
11. J.L. Borges, *Fictions*, New York: Penguin, 2000.
12. L. de Molina, *On Divine Foreknowledge (Part IV of the Concordantia)*, Ithaca: Cornell University Press, 1988.
13. M. Ferraris, 'Sum ergo Cogito: Schelling and the Positive Realism', in *Nature and Realism in Schelling's Philosophy*, ed. E.C. Corriero and A. Dezi, Torino: Accademia University Press, 2013, pp. 187–201.
14. 1 Corinthians 13:12: 'in a mirror, in a riddle'.
15. G.W. Leibniz, *Discourse on Metaphysics*, §7.

16. Plato, *Timaeus*, 48e–49a.
17. Kant, *Critique of Pure Reason*, A211–15, B256–6.
18. H. Bergson, *Matter and Memory* (1896), New York: Zone Books, 1988, chapter IV.
19. D.C. Dennett, *From Bacteria to Bach and Back: The Evolution of Minds*, Cambridge MA: MIT Press, 2017.
20. G. Vico, *The New Science of Giambattista Vico*, trans. T.G. Bergin and M.H. Fisch, London: Cornell University Press, 1984, Book I, Annotations to the Chronological Table, A.
21. V. Sereni, *Sopra un'immagine sepolcrale*. Italian original: 'come se un Tu dovesse veramente / ritornare / a liberare i vivi e i morti. / E quante lagrime e seme vanamente sparso'.
22. J. Derrida, *The Beast and the Sovereign*, Chicago: University of Chicago Press, 2011, p. 151, 'does not belong to series or table'.
23. J.-F. Courtine, *Suarez et le système de la métaphysique*, Paris: PUF, 1990.
24. C.S. Peirce, 'On a New List of Categories', *Proceedings of the American Academy of Arts and Sciences*, 7 (1868): 287–98.
25. J. Derrida, 'Différance', in *Margins of Philosophy*, Chicago: University of Chicago Press, 1982.
26. Kant, *Critique of Pure Reason*, A 97.
27. M. Proust, *In Search of Lost Time*, New York: The Modern Library, 1992.
28. A.S. Eddington, *The Nature of the Physical World* (1948), Whitefish: Kessinger Publishing, 2010.
29. M. Heidegger, *Being and Time* (1927), Hoboken: John Wiley and Sons Ltd, 1978.
30. See *On Memory and Recollection*, a part of his *Parva Naturalia*. Aristotle, *Parva Naturalia*, ed. W.D. Ross, Oxford: Oxford University Press, 1955 (repr. 2000).
31. Cf. B. Stiegler, *Technics and Time 1: The Fault of Epimetheus*, Stanford: Stanford University Press, 1998.
32. See his major work, translated in English as *The Science of Knowledge. With the First and Second Introductions*, Cambridge MA: Cambridge University Press, 1982.
33. F.W.J. Schelling, *Philosophical Investigations into the Essence of Human Freedom* (1809), New York: SUNY Press, 2006.
34. G.W.F. Hegel, *Phenomenology of Spirit* (1807), Oxford: Oxford University Press, 1977.
35. F.A. Trendelenburg, *Outlines of Logic: An English Translation of Trendelenburg's Elementa*, Oxford: Shrimpton & Son, 1898.

36. K. Marx, *Capital, Volume 1* (1867), London: Penguin Books, 1990.
37. A. Schopenhauer, *On the Fourfold Root of the Principle of Sufficient Reason and Other Writings*, ed. D.E. Cartwright, Edward E. Erdmann and Christopher Janaway, Cambridge: Cambridge University Press, 2012.
38. Kant, *Critique of Pure Reason*, A 141, B 181.
39. Kant, *Critique of Pure Reason*, B 152.
40. The Big Bounce is a repetition of the *tzimtzum* (צמצום), which in Jewish theology designates God's self-restraint in withdrawing after the creation of the world. The image is particularly significant because it refers to the creation of an empty space (*Khalal/Khalal Hapanoi*, חללהפנוי) – once again, it is a *chora* (*Ha-Makom*, המקום, literally 'the Place', is one of the names of God in rabbinic literature), the work of hysteresis, that gives life to the world: creation, thus, is retraction and hysteresis. The explosion alone would have been a sheer timeless flash. It is only through retention that everything begins, which means that everything begins with retention, and everything proceeds by successive retractions and retentions. This image is in line with the Neo-Platonic doctrine of hypostasis.
41. Aristotle, *Posterior Analytics*, 101a.
42. Q. Meillassoux, *After Finitude: An Essay on the Necessity of Contingency*, trans. Ray Brassier, London: Bloomsbury, 2009.
43. M. Ferraris, *Learning to Live: Six Essays on Marcel Proust*, Leiden: Brill, 2020.
44. M. Ferraris, *Emergenza*, Torino: Einaudi, 2016.
45. G. Gentile, *The Theory of the Mind as Pure Act*, London: Macmillan, 1922.
46. See Ferraris, *Emergenza*.
47. W.S. Sellars, *Empiricism and the Philosophy of Mind* (1956), Cambridge MA: Harvard University Press, 1997.
48. H.G. Gadamer, *Truth and Method* (1960), London: Bloomsbury, 2013.
49. S. Kripke, 'Naming and Necessity', in *Semantics of Natural Language*, ed. G. Harman and D. Davidson, Dordrecht: Reidel, 1972.
50. G.W.F. Hegel, *Encyclopaedia of the Philosophical Sciences in Basic Outline. Part 1: Logic*, Cambridge MA: Cambridge University Press, 2010.
51. Borges, *Fictions*.
52. S. Freud, *The Ego and the Id* (1923), London: The Hogarth Press, 1949.

53. Heidegger, *Being and Time*.
54. J.L. Austin, *How to Do Things with Words*, Cambridge MA: Harvard University Press, 1962.
55. D.C. Dennett, 'Darwin's "Strange Inversion of Reasoning"', *Proceedings of the National Academy of Sciences of the United States of America*, 106, Suppl. 1 (2009): 10061–5.
56. L. Wittgenstein, *Philosophical Investigations*, Oxford: Wiley-Blackwell, 2009.
57. I. Svevo, *Zeno's Conscience* (1923), New York: Penguin, 2002.
58. G.W.F. Hegel, *The Hegel Reader*, London: Wiley-Blackwell, 1998. *Werke in zwanzig Bänden*, 20 vols, Frankfurt: Suhrkamp, 1986, Vol. 6.
59. Marx, *Capital, Volume I*, chapter 11.
60. J. Derrida, *Speech and Phenomenon* (1967), Evanston: Northwestern University Press, 1973.
61. G. Frege, 'On Sense and Reference', *Zeitschrift für Philosophie und philosophische Kritik*, 100 (1892): 25–50.
62. Kant, *Critique of Pure Reason*, A142, B181.
63. M. Ferraris, *History of Hermeneutics* (1988), Atlantic Highlands: Humanities Press, 1996.
64. Vico, *The New Science*, 1.
65. Augustine, *Confessions*, X, 1.1.
66. C. McGinn, *Prehension: The Hand and the Emergence of Humanity*, Cambridge MA: MIT Press, 2015.
67. R. Kanigel, *The Man Who Knew Infinity: A Life of the Genius Ramanujan*, New York: Charles Scribner's Sons, 1991.
68. Translator's note: Italian proverb, which means something along the lines of 'speak in layman's terms', or generally 'keep it simple'.
69. G.W.F. Hegel, *Aesthetics: Lectures on Fine Art*, 2 vols, Oxford: Oxford University Press, 1998.
70. Wittgenstein, *Philosophical Investigations*, §241.
71. Wittgenstein, *Philosophical Investigations*, §241.
72. Kant, *Critique of Judgment*, §18.
73. Leibniz, *New Essays*.
74. *Itara* (adjective); Vedic *itara* (= Lat. *iterum*, 'a second time'): other, second, next, different.
75. R. Brandt, *D'Artagnan und die Urteilstafel. Über ein Ordnungsprinzip der europäischen Kulturgeschichte (1, 2, 3/4)* (1991), Munich: Deutscher Taschenbuch Verlag, 1998.
76. I. Kant, *Dissertatio* (1770), §15. On incongruent opposites as a critique of the principle of the identity of indiscernibles, see also

Prolegomena (1783), §13. Cf. I. Kant, *Del Primo fondamento della distinzione degli oggetti nello spazio* (1768), in *Scritti precritici*, Roma-Bari: Laterza, 2000. I. Kant, *Che cosa significa orientarsi nel pensiero* (1786), Milan: Adelphi, 1996.
77. J. Joyce, *A Portrait of the Artist as a Young Man* (1916), Oxford: Oxford University Press, 2013, incipit.
78. Hegel, *Aesthetics: Lectures on Fine Art*.
79. Translator's note: beauty salons are also known as 'aesthetic centres' in Italy.

Recollection

1. For an exhaustive review, see https://nuovorealismo.wordpress.com. 'A specter is haunting Europe, and not only: the specter of "new realism." The concept of "new realism" was coined by the Italian philosopher Maurizio Ferraris of the University of Turin. [...] The debate on realism is now widespread in different parts of the world, and its promoters include the Argentinian José Luis Jerez, the Mexican Manuel DeLanda, the American Graham Harman, up to the German Markus Gabriel.' (H. Klüver, *Süddeutsche Zeitung*, 3 January 2014). The debate on new realism had triggered almost 1,700 contributions up to 2015: 166 in 2011, 680 in 212, 515 in 2013, 250 in 2014 and 20 in 2015 (see https://nuovorealismo.wordpress.com). For the spread of new realism in Germany see M. Gabriel (ed.), *Der Neue Realismus*, Berlin: Suhrkamp, 2014, including contributions by J. Benoist, P. Boghossian, M. De Caro, U. Eco, M. Ferraris, M. Gabriel, D. Marconi, Q. Meillassoux, H. Putnam and J. Searle.
2. Cf. M. Gabriel, *Das Absolute und die Welt in Schellings Freiheitsschrift*, Bonn: Bonn University Press, 2006. For the proposal of a transcendental realism à la Schelling, see my 'Sum ergo Cogito: Schelling and the Positive Realism'.
3. Cf. the conference 'Neuer Realismus Und Rationalismus Eine Deutsch-Italienischearchitekturdebatee', Italienisches Kultuinstitut, Berlin and Internationale Bauakademie, Berlin, 15 November 2013. Cf. AA.VV., *Architettura e realismo*, Santarcangelo: Maggioli, 2013; N. Kuhnert and A.L. Ngo (eds), *Get Real! Die Wirklichkeit der Architektur/Architectural Realities*, ARCH+, 217, 2014.
4. Cf. the conference 'Les nouveaux réalismes dans la culture italienne à l'aube du troisième millénaire. Définitions et mises en perspective', Université Sorbonne Nouvelle-Paris 3, 12–14 June 2014. Cf. also the

series of conferences 'Realisms New and Old', University of Turin, spring and autumn terms 2015. Cf. also M. Quaglino and R. Scarpa (eds), *Metodi Testo Realtà*, Alessandria: Edizioni dell'Orso, 2014.
5. Cf. E. Corbi and S. Oliverio (eds), *Realtà fra virgolette? Nuovo realismo e pedagogia*, Lecce-Rovato: Pensa MultiMedia, 2013; *Pedagogia e vita*, 71 (2013); *Journal of Educational, Cultural and Psychological Studies (ECPS)*, 9, Special Issue on New Realism and Educational Research, 2014.
6. Cf. the conference 'Speculations on Anonymous Materials' (with M. Ferraris, M. Gabriel, I.H. Grant, R. Mackay, R. Negarestani), Museum Fridericianum, Kassel, 4 January 2014, and the series of conferences 'Phantome des Realen' organised in 2014 by Zürcher Hochschule der Künste, with A. Avanessian, A. Düttmann, M. Ferraris, M. Gabriel, I. Grant, G. Harman, D. Mersch and G. Schiemann.
7. The political relevance of new realism is the focus of the series of conferences held at the Swiss Cultural Institute in Rome in 2012, whose acts have been published in C. Riedweg (ed.), *Discorsi d'attualità. Dal 'postmoderno' ai nuovi orizzonti della cultura*. The text has appeared in Italian (Rome: Carocci, 2013), French (Geneva: Droz, 2014) and German (Bern: Schwabe, 2014).
8. A. Maccarini, E. Morandi and R. Prandini (eds), *Sociological Realism*, London: Routledge, 2011; L. Martignani, *Sociologia e nuovo realismo*, Milan-Udine: Mimesis, 2013.
9. See my 'New Realism and New Media: From Documentality to Normativity', in *Philosophy of Emerging Media, Understanding, Appreciation and Application*, ed. J. Katz and J. Floyd, Oxford: Oxford University Press, 2015.
10. From 3 April to 3 July 2014 the German newspaper *Die Zeit* published a series of articles on new realism in philosophy, art and architecture, with contributions by T.E. Schmidt, U. Schwarz, B. Stegemann, B. Pörksen, M. Gabriel, I. Radisch and M. Seel. Analogous debates have taken place in Italy (*La Repubblica* and *Alfabeta2*), Spain (*Revista de Occidente*) and France (*Philosophie Magazine*).
11. R.B. Perry et al., 'The Program and First Platform of Six Realists', *Journal of Philosophy, Psychology and Scientific Methods*, 7 (1910): 393–401; R.B. Perry et al., *The New Realism: Cooperative Studies in Philosophy*, New York: Macmillan, 1912 (new ed. Ulan Press, 2012). For a reconstruction of the origin of new realism, see D. Marconi, 'Genealogia del nuovo realismo', *Hermeneutica*, Special

Issue 'Quale realismo?' (2014), with papers by M. Alai, E. Baccarini, S. Bignotti, F. Botturi, M. Cangiotti, G. Cotta, G. D'Anna, P. De Vitiis, C. Dotolo, M. Ferraris, V. Fano and S. Matera, M. Giuliani, L. Grion, P. Pagani and C. Zuccaro.

12. D. Drake, A.O. Lovejoy, J.B. Pratt, A.K. Rogers, G. Santayana and R.W. Sellars, *Essays in Critical Realism: A Co-operative Study of the Problem of Knowledge*, London: Macmillan, 1920.

13. In the same years that gave birth to New Realism and analytic philosophy, the neo-Kantian thinker Heinrich Rickert (1863–1936) elaborated a criticism of neo-Kantianism based on realist assumptions. Cf. *Der Gegenstand der Erkenntnis. Einführung in die Transzendentalphilosophie*, Tübingen und Leipzig: J.C.B. Mohr (Paul Siebeck), 1904 and *Die Logik des Prädikats und das Problem der Ontologie*, Heidelberg: Winter, 1930. For an analysis of this path to realism cf. A. Donise, *Il soggetto e l'evidenza. Saggio su Heinrich Rickert*, Napoli: Loffredo, 2002.

14. Gentile, *The Theory of the Mind as Pure Act*, p. 3.

15. '"But everything is mind." The mind is everything, the thought is there, near the stove, and it burns in the stove, it is fire (". . . already Heraclitus, anticipating . . ."), it is solid wall. I'm thinking about all these things – I told myself – and certainly this is part of the mind; I remember the things that happened a while ago, or a long time ago, and this is also part of the mind. I'm almost falling asleep, the stove, the low light, the professor's words always so monotonous . . . this is a surrender of the mind, no doubt. Take my hands, here on the desk, are they part of the mind? You'd have to stretch the meaning of the word quite a bit. But then again, a straight line is a particular type of curve – although nothing evokes the idea of a curve. After all my hands move in obedience to my will, as directly as my thoughts, fantasies and other remnants of my will. The desk can be part of the mind even though it doesn't obey at all, you just have to extend the borders of the word: it is part of the mind, too. The same goes for the most distant and hardest things – let alone those postulated elsewhere and therefore merely thought of.' P. Bozzi, 'Parlare di ciò che si vede', *Versus*, 59–60 (1991): 107–19, p. 110.

16. Cf. my *Goodbye Kant!*

17. B. Latour, 'Ramses II est-il mort de la tuberculose?', *La Recherche*, 307 (March 1998).

18. Think of David Malet Armstrong (1926–2014), professor at the Universities of Melbourne and Sydney.

19. Cf. Gustav Bergmann (1906–87), member of the Vienna Circle and then Professor at the University of Iowa. His main works are *Logic and Reality*, Madison: University of Wisconsin Press, 1964, and *Realism: A Critique of Brentano and Meinong*, Madison: University of Wisconsin Press, 1967.
20. Paolo Bozzi (1930–2003), the last exponent of the *Gestaltpsychologie* rooted in Franz Brentano's thought and in Austrian realism. See in particular P. Bozzi, *Fisica ingenua*; and *Scritti sul realismo*, Milan: Mimesis, 2009. Cf. also *Bozzetti in memoria di Paolo Bozzi*, 'Rivista di estetica', n.s., 24 (3/2003), XLIII, ed. C. Barbero, R. Casati, M. Ferraris and A.C. Varzi.
21. R. Bhaskar, *A Realist Theory of Science* (1975), new edition, London: Routledge, 2008.
22. P.K. Feyerabend, *Against Method* (1975), revised ed., London: Verso, 1988.
23. R. Rorty, *Philosophy and the Mirror of Nature*, Princeton: Princeton University Press, 1979.
24. P.F. Strawson, *Individuals*, London: Methuen, 1959.
25. R. Rorty, 'Nineteenth-Century Idealism and Twentieth-Century Textualism', *The Monist*, 64/2 (1981): 155–74.
26. R. Rorty, 'Charles Taylor on Truth', in R. Rorty, *Philosophical Papers, Vol. 3*, Cambridge: Cambridge University Press, 1998, pp. 84–97.
27. G. Harman, 'Fear of Reality: On Realism and Infra-Realism', *The Monist*, 98/2 (2015): 126–44. For a history of this, cf. L. Braver, *A Thing of This World: A History of Continental Anti-Realism*, Evanston: Northwestern University Press, 2007.
28. For more on the relationship between postmodernism and realism, see my 'From Postmodernism to Realism', in *Bridging the Analytical Continental Divide: A Companion to Contemporary Western Philosophy*, ed. T. Andina, Leiden: Brill, 2014, pp. 1–7.
29. M. Cacciari: 'L'antiberlusconismo? Un antidoto del c . . .', *Il giornale*, 18 February 2015. For an analysis of the language used in the debate on new realism, see R. Scarpa, *Il caso nuovo realismo. La lingua del dibattito filosofico contemporaneo*, Milan-Udine: Mimesis, 2013.
30. To my knowledge, the only philosopher who took some steps in this direction was John Foster (1940–2009). See his excellent *A World for Us: The Case for Phenomenalistic Idealism*, Oxford: Oxford University Press, 2008.
31. D. Stove, 'Idealism: A Victorian Horror Story (Part Two)', in *The Plato Cult and Other Philosophical Follies*, Oxford: Blackwell,

1991, pp. 135–78. I have obviously simplified the argument due to lack of space. An excellent exposition can be found in J. Franklin, 'Stove's Discovery of the Worst Argument in the World', *Philosophy*, 77 (2002): 615–24.

32. The insistence on the distinction between ontology and epistemology is what makes this hypothesis absurd. The relation between ontology and epistemology was the focus of the conference 'New Realism: Ontology and Epistemology', within the International Conference 'Philosophy of Science in the 21st Century. Challenges and Tasks', CFCUL, Faculty of Sciences, University of Lisbon, 5 December 2013.
33. See my 'Ontologia come fisica ingenua', *Rivista di estetica*, n.s., 6, 1998: 133–43.
34. Which, notoriously, is claimed by Heidegger in *Being and Time* (p. 270): 'Before Newton's Laws were discovered they were not "true"; it does not follow that they were false [. . .] To say that before Newton his laws were neither true nor false, cannot signify that before him there were no such entities as have been uncovered and pointed out by those laws. Through Newton the laws became true; and with them, entities became accessible in themselves to Dasein. Once entities have been uncovered, they show themselves precisely as entities which beforehand already were.'
35. Reality can very well be a thing in itself. This does not mean that this thing in itself has no effects, and especially that this thing exists and has its properties independently of our knowledge of it. I develop this point in 'Ding an Sich', *Das neue Bedürfnis nach Metaphysik*, ed. M. Gabriel, W. Hogrebe and A. Speer, Berlin: DeGruyter, 2015.
36. Kripke, 'Naming and Necessity'.
37. H. Putnam, 'The Meaning of "Meaning"', in *Philosophical Papers II*, London: Cambridge University Press, 1975, pp. 215–71.
38. M. Ferraris, 'Il ritorno del pensiero forte', *la Repubblica*, 8 August 2011.
39. M. Ferraris, 'Nuovo realismo', *Rivista di estetica*, 48 (2011): 69–93 and 'Nuovo Realismo FAQ', *Nóema*, 2 (2011).
40. 'On the Ashes of Post-Modernism: A New Realism?', Istituto Italiano di Cultura, 7 November 2011, with Akeel Bilgrami, Ned Block, Paul Boghossian, Petar Bojanić, Giovanna Borradori, Mario De Caro, Umberto Eco, Maurizio Ferraris, Markus Gabriel, Hilary Putnam and Riccardo Viale.
41. 'Nuovo realismo: una discussione aperta', Fondazione Rosselli, 5 December 2011, with Mario De Caro, Paolo Flores d'Arcais, Roberta De Monticelli, Massimo Dell'Utri, Umberto Eco, Costantino

Esposito, Maurizio Ferraris, Miguel Gotor, Andrea Lavazza, Diego Marconi, Armando Massarenti, Massimo Mori, Stefano Rodotà, Riccardo Viale and Alberto Voltolini.

42. 'Prospects for a New Realism', University of Bonn, 26–28 March 2012, with Jovan Babić, Akeel Bilgrami, Paul Boghossian, Petar Bojanić, Mario De Caro, Maurizio Ferraris, Markus Gabriel, Werner Gephart, Lewis Gordon, Andrea Kern, Susan Haack, Diego Marconi, Stefano Poggi, Hilary Putnam, John Searle, Pirmin Stekeler-Weithofer and Dieter Sturma.

43. Translated in Chile (Ariadne), France (Hermann), Germany (Klostermann), Spain (Biblioteca Nueva), United States (SUNY Press) and Sweden (Daidalos). Further developments of my thought can be found in *Positive Realism*, London: Zero Books, 2015 and *Introduction to New Realism*, London: Bloomsbury, 2015.

44. M. De Caro and M. Ferraris (eds), *Bentornata realtà. Il nuovo realismo in discussione*, Torino: Einaudi, 2012, with A. Bilgrami, M. De Caro, U. Eco, M. Ferraris, M. Di Franesco, M. Recalcati, C. Rovane, H. Putnam and J. Searle.

45. 'New Realism: Philosophy in a Cosmopolitan Sense', XXIII World Congress of Philosophy, Athens, 4–10 August 2013. Graham Harman held 68 international lectures in 2014 (and has no intention of doing that again).

46. 'Ferraris [. . .] made the realist turn at an earlier and lonelier date than DeLanda and the Speculative Realists'. G. Harman, foreword to M. Ferraris, *Manifesto of New Realism*, SUNY Press, 2014, p. ix.

47. For the main stages of my path to realism, see *History of Hermeneutics* (1988), English translation by L. Somigli, New Jersey: Humanities Press, 1996, new edition for Brill 2018; *Experimentelle Ästhetik*, Vienna: Thuria und Kant, 2001; *Il mondo esterno*, Milan: Bompiani, 2001 (new ed. 2012); *Documentality: Why It Is Necessary to Leave Traces*. See also 'L'immaginazione come idealizzazione intraestetica nella *Critica della ragion pura*', *Rivista di estetica*, 42 (1993): 55–67; *Analogon rationis*, Milan: Pratica Filosofica, 1994; *L'ermeneutica*, Roma-Bari: Laterza, 1998; *Goodbye Kant!*; *Doc-Humanity*, Tübingen: Mohr Siebeck, 2022.

48. A. Sokal and J. Bricmont, *Fashionable Nonsense*, New York: Picador, 1997.

49. U. Eco, *Kant e l'ornitorinco*, Milan: Bompiani, 1997.

50. U. Eco, M. Ferraris and D. Marconi, 'Lo schema del cane', *Rivista di estetica*, 8 (1998): 3–27; translated as 'The Dog Schema', *Rivista di estetica*, 76 (2021): 10–39.

51. Marconi, *Lexical Competence*.
52. J. Baudrillard, *Le crime parfait*, Paris: Galilée, 1995.
53. R. Rorty, *Objectivity, Relativism, and Truth: Philosophical Papers, Vol. 1*, Cambridge: Cambridge University Press, 1991.
54. J. Ratzinger, *Svolta per l'Europa? Chiesa e modernità nell'Europa dei rivolgimenti*, Milan: Edizioni Paoline, 1992, pp. 76–9.
55. I. Hacking, *The Social Construction of What?*, Cambridge MA: Harvard University Press, 1999.
56. J. McDowell, *Mind and World*, Cambridge MA: Harvard University Press, 1994. For my criticism of McDowell, see 'Mente e mondo o scienza ed esperienza?'
57. R. Suskind, 'Faith, Certainty and the Presidency of George W. Bush', *The New York Times Magazine*, 17 October 2004.
58. Cf. L. Bryant, N. Srnicek and G. Harman (eds), *The Speculative Turn: Continental Materialism and Realism*, Melbourne: re.press, 2011; P. Gratton, *Speculative Realism: Problems and Prospects*, London: Bloomsbury, 2014; S. De Sanctis and V. Santarcangelo, 'The Coral Reef of Reality: New Philosophical Realisms', afterword to Ferraris, *Introduction to New Realism*.
59. M. DeLanda, *Intensive Science and Virtual Philosophy*, London: Continuum, 2002.
60. G. Harman, *Guerrilla Metaphysics: Phenomenology and the Carpentry of Things*, Chicago: Open Court, 2005.
61. Meillassoux, *After Finitude*.
62. P. Boghossian, *Fear of Knowledge*, Oxford: Clarendon Press, 2006. See also D. Marconi, *Per la verità. Relativismo e filosofia*, Torino: Einaudi, 2007.
63. G. Figal, *Gegenständlichkeit. Das Hermeneutische und die Philosophie*, Tübingen: Mohr, 2006.
64. M. DeLanda, *A New Philosophy of Society: Assemblage Theory and Social Complexity*, New York: Continuum, 2006.
65. I.H. Grant, *Philosophies of Nature after Schelling*, New York: Continuum, 2006.
66. Cf. R. Brassier, *Nihil Unbound: Enlightenment and Extinction*, London: Palgrave Macmillan, 2007.
67. G. Harman, *The Quadruple Object*, Alresford: Zero Books, 2011; L.R. Bryant, *The Democracy of Objects*, Ann Arbor: Open Humanities Press, 2011; T. Garcia, *Forme et objet*, Paris: PUF, 2011.
68. A. Meinong, *Untersuchungen über Gegenstandstheorie und Psychologie*, Leipzig: Barth, 1904.

69. 'Nouveaux Réalismes. A partir du Manifesto du nouveau Réalisme de Maurizio Ferraris', Paris, École des hautes études en sciences sociales, 4–6 December 2014. With Armen Avanessian, Andrea Bellantone, Jocelyn Benoist, Petar Bojanić, Barbara Carnevali, Emanuele Coccia, Mario De Caro, Sarah De Sanctis, Raffaele Donnarumma, Pascal Engel, Maurizio Ferraris, Tristan Garcia, Markus Gabriel, Graham Harman, Iain Hamilton Grant, Anna Longo, Cathérine Malabou, Gloria Origgi, Claude Romano and Vincenzo Santarcangelo.
70. Cf. U. Eco, 'Di un realismo negativo', in De Caro and Ferraris (eds), *Bentornata realtà*.
71. Cf. M. Gabriel, 'Neutraler Realismus', in *Philosophisches Jahrbuch*. Gabriel's essay can be found in English in *The Monist*, 98/2 (2015).
72. M. Gabriel, 'Is Heidegger's "Turn" a Realist Project?', *META: Research in Hermeneutics, Phenomenology, and Practical Philosophy* (2014): 44–73. Special issue 'New Realism and Phenomenology', with papers by J. Backman, J. Benoist, M. Bosnic, M. Ferraris, G. Figal, F. Fraisopi, S. Fumagalli, S. Gourdain, I. Kara-Pesic, T. Keily and V. Palette.
73. See my 'Transcendental Realism', *The Monist*, 98/2 (2015): 215–32.
74. Emergentism, i.e. the doctrine that entities arise from more fundamental entities to which they are irreducible (for example, the mind emerges from the brain and is irreducible to it), was theorised at the beginning of the twentieth century by the Australian philosopher Samuel Alexander (1859–1938) in *Space, Time, and Deity*, London: Macmillan, 1920, 2 vols, and by the English philosopher C.D. Broad (1887–1971) in *The Mind and Its Place in Nature*, London: Routledge & Kegan Paul, 1925. It was recovered at the end of the century by many authors, including D.M. Armstrong, 'Emergence and Logical Atomism', in *A World of States of Affairs*, Cambridge: Cambridge University Press, 1997, pp. 152–3.
75. In accordance with the perspective of the American perceptologist J.J. Gibson in *The Ecological Approach to Visual Perception*. Such a perspective was ontologically developed by Barry Smith, cf. his 'Objects and Their Environments: From Aristotle to Ecological Ontology', and 'Toward a Realistic Science of Environments', *Ecological Psychology*, 21/2 (2009): 121–30.
76. B. Hölldobler and E.O. Wilson, *The Superorganism: The Beauty, Elegance, and Strangeness of Insect Societies*, New York: W.W. Norton & Co., 2010.
77. Dennett, 'Darwin's "Strange Inversion of Reasoning"'.
78. See my 'Total Mobilization', *The Monist*, 97/2 (2014): 201–22.

79. P. Unger, *Empty Ideas: A Critique of Analytic Philosophy*, Oxford: Oxford University Press, 2014.
80. New realism has entailed a recovery of ontological commitment in hermeneutics. Cf. M. Beuchot and J.L. Jerez, *Manifiesto del nuevo realismo analógico*, Buenos Aires: Circulo Hermenéutico, 2013, and J.L. Jerez (ed.), *El giro ontológico*, Buenos Aires: Circulo Hermenéutico, 2015, with papers by R. Cadus, N. Conde Gaxiola, S. De Sanctis, F. Arenas-Dolz, M. Beuchot, M. Ferraris, J.A. Gómez García, J. E. Gonzalez, E. M. Gonzalez Lopez, L. E. Primero Prinos and S. Santa Silia. The Décimo Coloquio Internacional de Hermenéutica Analógica held at the Universidad Nacional Autónoma de México (UNAM), 14–16 October 2014, was entitled 'Una nueva hermenéutica para un nuevo realismo'. See my 'Un nuevo enfoque realista a la hermenéutica', *Cuadernos de Epistemología*, n. 6, Editorial de la Universidad del Cauca (2014): 75–91.
81. F. Brentano, 'Die vier Phasen der Philosophie und ihr augenblicklicher Stand', in *Die vier Phasen der Philosophie und ihr augenblicklicher Stand: nebst Abhandlungen über Plotinus, Thomas von Aquin, Kant, Schopenhauer und Auguste Comte*, Hamburg: Meiner, 1968. An English translation of the text, along with an exhaustive commentary, can be found in B.M. Mezei and B. Smith, *The Four Phases of Philosophy*, Amsterdam: Rodopi, 1998.
82. M. Dummett, *Ursprünge der analytischen Philosophie*, Frankfurt/M.: Suhrkamp, 1988.

Bibliography

AA.VV., *Architettura e realismo*, Santarcangelo: Maggioli, 2013.
Alexander, Samuel, *Space, Time, and Deity*, London: Macmillan, 1920.
Aristotle, *On the Soul*, trans. J.A. Smith, Internet Classics Archive, MIT.
Aristotle, *Parva Naturalia*, ed. W.D. Ross, Oxford: Oxford University Press, 1955 (repr. 2000).
Aristotle, *Posterior Analytics*, trans. Octavius Freire Owen, H.G. Bohn, 1853.
Armstrong, David M., 'Emergence and Logical Atomism', in *A World of States of Affairs*, Cambridge: Cambridge University Press, 1997, pp. 152–3.
Augustine, *Confessions*, trans. Vernon J. Bourke, Washington: Catholic University of America Press, 1966.
Austin, John L., 'A Plea for Excuses', in *Philosophical Papers*, 2nd ed., Oxford: Oxford University Press, 1979.
Austin, John L., *How to Do Things with Words*, Cambridge MA: Harvard University Press, 1962.
Barbero, Carola, Roberto Casati, Maurizio Ferraris and Achille C. Varzi, 'Bozzetti in memoria di Paolo Bozzi', *Rivista di estetica*, n.s., 24 (3/2003).
Barnes, Jonathan, *The Ontological Argument*, London: Macmillan, 1972.
Baudrillard, Jean, *Le crime parfait*, Paris: Galilée, 1995.
Baumgarten, Alexander, *Metaphysics* (1757), London: Bloomsbury Academic, 2014.
Becchio, Cristina, *Ragionamento deduttivo e spazialità. Un'ipotesi sperimentale e alcune considerazioni filosofiche*, Dissertation, Università di Torino, a.y. 1999–2000.
Bergmann, Gustav, *Logic and Reality*, Madison: University of Wisconsin Press, 1964.
Bergmann, Gustav, *Realism: A Critique of Brentano and Meinong*, Madison: University of Wisconsin Press, 1967.

Bergson, Henri, *Matter and Memory* (1896), New York: Zone Books, 1988.
Beuchot, Maurizio and Jerez, José Luis, *Manifiesto del nuevo realismo analógico*, Buenos Aires: Circulo Hermenéutico, 2013.
Bhaskar, Roy, *A Realist Theory of Science* (1975), new ed., London: Routledge, 2008.
Bogen, Helmuth, *Naive Physik. Arbeiten aus dem Institut fur angewandte Psychologie in Berlin. Theoretische und experimentelle Untersuchungen über die Fähigkeit zu intelligentem Handeln*, Leipzig: Barth, 1923.
Boghossian, Paul, *Fear of Knowledge*, Oxford: Clarendon Press, 2006.
Borges, Jorge Luis, *Fictions*, New York: Penguin, 2000.
Bozzi, Paolo, *Fenomenologia sperimentale*, Bologna: il Mulino 1989.
Bozzi, Paolo, *Fisica ingenua*, Milan: Garzanti, 1990.
Bozzi, Paolo, 'Parlare di ciò che si vede', *Versus*, 59–60 (1991): 107–19.
Bozzi, Paolo, *Scritti sul realismo*, Milan: Mimesis, 2009.
Brandt, Reinhard, *D'Artagnan und die Urteilstafel. Über ein Ordnungsprinzip der europäischen Kulturgeschichte* (1, 2, 3/4) (1991), Munich: Deutscher Taschenbuch Verlag, 1998.
Brassier, Ray, *Nihil Unbound: Enlightenment and Extinction*, London: Palgrave Macmillan, 2007.
Braver, Lee, *A Thing of This World: A History of Continental Anti-Realism*, Evanston: Northwestern University Press, 2007.
Brentano, Franz, 'Die vier Phasen der Philosophie und ihr augenblicklicher Stand', in *Die vier Phasen der Philosophie und ihr augenblicklicher Stand: nebst Abhandlungen über Plotinus, Thomas von Aquin, Kant, Schopenhauer und Auguste Comte*, Hamburg: Meiner, 1968.
Broad, C.D., *The Mind and Its Place in Nature*, London: Routledge & Kegan Paul, 1925.
Bryant, Levi R., *The Democracy of Objects*, Ann Arbor: Open Humanities Press, 2011.
Bryant, Levi, Nick Srnicek and Graham Harman (eds), *The Speculative Turn: Continental Materialism and Realism*, Melbourne: re.press, 2011.
Cacciari, Massimo, 'L'antiberlusconismo? Un antidoto del c ...', *Il giornale*, 8 February 2015.
Campanile, Achille, *Ma che cos'è questo amore*, Milan: Corbaccio 1998.
Casati, Roberto, *La scoperta dell'ombra*, Milan: Mondadori, 2000.
Casati, Roberto and Achille Varzi, *Holes and Other Superficialities*, Cambridge: MIT Press, 1994.

Chisholm, Roderick Milton, 'The Loose and Popular and the Strict and Philosophical Senses of Identity', in *Perception and Personal Identity*, ed. N.S. Care and R.H. Grimm, Cleveland: The Press of Case Western Reserve University, 1969, pp. 82–106.

Corbi, Enricomaria and Stefano Oliverio (eds), *Realtà fra virgolette? Nuovo realismo e pedagogia*, Lecce-Rovato: Pensa MultiMedia, 2013.

Costa, Vincenzo, *L'estetica trascendentale fenomenologica*, Milan: Vita e Pensiero, 1999.

Courtine, Jean-François, *Suarez et le système de la métaphysique*, Paris: PUF, 1990.

Darling, Anthony, *Redcoat and Brown Bess*, Bloomfield (Ontario): Museum Restoration Service, 1971.

De Caro, Mario and Maurizio Ferraris, (eds), *Bentornata realtà. Il nuovo realismo in discussione*, Torino: Einaudi, 2012.

De Sanctis, Sarah and Vincenzo Santarcangelo, 'The Coral Reef of Reality: New Philosophical Realisms', afterword to M. Ferraris, *Introduction to New Realism*, London: Bloomsbury, 2015.

DeLanda, Manuel, *A New Philosophy of Society: Assemblage Theory and Social Complexity*, New York: Continuum, 2006.

DeLanda, Manuel, *Intensive Science and Virtual Philosophy*, London: Continuum, 2002.

Dennett, Daniel C., 'Darwin's "Strange Inversion of Reasoning"', *Proceedings of the National Academy of Sciences of the United States of America*, 106, Suppl. 1 (2009): 10061–5.

Dennett, Daniel C., *From Bacteria to Bach and Back: The Evolution of Minds*, Cambridge MA: Bradford Books/MIT Press, 2017.

Derrida, Jacques, *The Beast and the Sovereign*, Chicago: University of Chicago Press, 2011.

Derrida, Jacques, 'Différance', in *Margins of Philosophy*, Chicago: University of Chicago Press, 1982.

Derrida, Jacques, 'Speculation – on Freud', *Oxford Literary Review*, 3/2 (1978): 78–97.

Derrida, Jacques, *Speech and Phenomena* (1967), trans. David B. Allison, Evanston: Northwestern University Press, 1973.

Derrida, Jacques, *Voice and Phenomenon*, trans. Leonard Lawlor, Evanston: Northwestern University Press, 2011.

Donise, Anna, *Il soggetto e l'evidenza. Saggio su Heinrich Rickert*, Napoli: Loffredo, 2002.

Drake, Durant (ed.), *Essays in Critical Realism: A Co-operative Study of the Problem of Knowledge*, London: Macmillan & Co., 1920.

Dummett, Michael, *Ursprünge der analytischen Philosophie*, Frankfurt/M.: Suhrkamp, 1988.
Eco, Umberto, 'Dove sta Cappuccetto Rosso?', *Modi dell'oggettività*, ed. G. Usberti, Milan: Bompiani, 2000, pp. 137–57.
Eco, Umberto, *Kant e l'ornitorinco*, Milan: Bompiani, 1997.
Eco, Umberto, Ferraris, Maurizio and Marconi, Diego, 'Lo schema del cane', *Rivista di estetica*, 8 (1998): 3–27; translated as "The Dog Schema", *Rivista di estetica*, 76 (2021): 10-39.
Eddington, Arthur S., *The Nature of the Physical World* (1948), Whitefish: Kessinger Publishing, 2010.
Eliot, T.S., 'The Love Song of J. Alfred Prufrock', in *Prufrock and Other Observations*, London: The Egoist, 1917.
Ferrarin, Alfredo, 'Construction and Mathematical Schematism: Kant on the Exhibition of a Concept in Intuition', *Kant-Studien*, 86 (1995): 131–74.
Ferraris, Maurizio, *Analogon rationis*, Milan: Pratica Filosofica, 1994.
Ferraris, Maurizio, 'Ding an Sich', in *Das neue Bedürfnis nach Metaphysik*, ed. M. Gabriel, W. Hogrebe and A. Speer, Berlin: DeGruyter, 2015.
Ferraris, Maurizio, *Doc-Humanity*, Tübingen: Mohr Siebeck, 2022.
Ferraris, Maurizio, *Documentality: Why It Is Necessary to Leave Traces*, New York: Fordham University Press, 2012.
Ferraris, Maurizio, *Emergenza*, Torino: Einaudi, 2016.
Ferraris, Maurizio, *Estetica razionale*, Milan: Raffaello Cortina, 1997, n. ed. 2011.
Ferraris, Maurizio, *Experimentelle Ästhetik*, Vienna: Thuria und Kant, 2001.
Ferraris, Maurizio, 'From Postmodernism to Realism', in *Bridging the Analytical Continental Divide: A Companion to Contemporary Western Philosophy*, ed. T. Andina, Leiden: Brill, 2014, pp. 1–7.
Ferraris, Maurizio, *Goodbye Kant! What Still Stands of the Critique of Pure Reason*, New York: SUNY Press, 2014.
Ferraris, Maurizio, *History of Hermeneutics* (1988), Atlantic Highlands: Humanities Press, 1996.
Ferraris, Maurizio, *Il mondo esterno*, Milan: Bompiani, 2001 (new ed. 2012).
Ferraris, Maurizio, 'Il problema non è l'ornitorinco, è Kant', *Rivista di estetica*, 13 (2000): 110–220.
Ferraris, Maurizio, 'Il ritorno del pensiero forte', *la Repubblica*, 8 August 2011.

Ferraris, Maurizio, *Introduction to New Realism*, London: Bloomsbury, 2015.
Ferraris, Maurizio, *L'ermeneutica*, Roma-Bari: Laterza, 1998.
Ferraris, Maurizio, *Learning to Live: Six Essays on Marcel Proust*, Leiden: Brill, 2020.
Ferraris, Maurizio, 'L'immaginazione come idealizzazione intraestetica nella Critica della ragion pura', *Rivista di estetica*, 42 (1993): 55–67.
Ferraris, Maurizio, *Manifesto of New Realism*, New York: SUNY Press, 2014.
Ferraris, Maurizio, 'Mente e mondo o scienza ed esperienza?', *Rivista di estetica*, n.s., 12 (2000): 3–77.
Ferraris, Maurizio, 'New Realism and New Media: From Documentality to Normativity', in *Philosophy of Emerging Media, Understanding, Appreciation and Application*, ed. J. Katz and J. Floyd, Oxford: Oxford University Press, 2015.
Ferraris, Maurizio, 'Nuovo realismo', *Rivista di estetica*, 48 (2011): 69–93.
Ferraris, Maurizio, 'Nuovo Realismo FAQ', *Nóema*, 2 (2011).
Ferraris, Maurizio, 'Ontologia come fisica ingenua', *Rivista di estetica*, n.s., 6 (1997): 133–43.
Ferraris, Maurizio, *Positive Realism*, London: Zero Books, 2015.
Ferraris, Maurizio, 'Sum ergo Cogito: Schelling and the Positive Realism', in *Nature and Realism in Schelling's Philosophy*, ed. E.C. Corriero and A. Dezi, Torino: Accademia University Press, 2013, pp. 187–201.
Ferraris, Maurizio, 'Total Mobilization', *The Monist*, 97/2 (2014): 201–22.
Ferraris, Maurizio, 'Transcendental Realism', *The Monist*, 98/2 (2015): 215–32.
Ferraris, Maurizio, 'Un nuevo enfoque realista a la hermenéutica', *Cuadernos de Epistemología*, n. 6, Editorial de la Universidad del Cauca (2014): 75–91.
Feyerabend, Paul K., *Against Method* (1975), rev. ed., London: Verso, 1988.
Fichte, Johann Gottlieb, *The Science of Knowledge. With the First and Second Introductions*, Cambridge MA: Cambridge University Press, 1982.
Figal, Günter, *Gegenständlichkeit. Das Hermeneutische und die Philosophie*, Tübingen: Mohr, 2006.
Fitzgerald, F. Scott, *This Side of Paradise* (1920), Oxford: Oxford University Press, 2020.

Foster, John, *A World for Us: The Case for Phenomenalistic Idealism*, Oxford: Oxford University Press, 2008.
Franklin, James, 'Stove's Discovery of the Worst Argument in the World', *Philosophy*, 77 (2002): 615–24.
Frege, Gottlob, 'On Sense and Reference', in *Zeitschrift für Philosophie und philosophische Kritik*, 100 (1892): 25–50.
Freud, Sigmund, *Beyond the Pleasure Principle* (1920), New York: W.W. Norton & Co, 1975.
Freud, Sigmund, *The Ego and the Id* (1923), London: The Hogarth Press, 1949.
Gabriel, Markus, *Das Absolute und die Welt in Schellings Freiheitsschrift*, Bonn: Bonn University Press, 2006.
Gabriel, Markus, 'Is Heidegger's "Turn" a Realist Project?', *META: Research in Hermeneutics, Phenomenology, and Practical Philosophy* (2014): 44–73.
Gadamer, Hans Georg, *Truth and Method* (1960), London: Bloomsbury, 2013.
Garcia, Tristan, *Forme et objet. Une traité des choses*, Paris: PUF, 2011.
Gentile, Giovanni, *The Theory of the Mind as Pure Act*, London: Macmillan & Co., 1922
Gibson, James J., *The Ecological Approach to Visual Perception*, Boston: Houghton Mifflin, 1979.
Grant, Iain H., *Philosophy of Nature after Schelling*, New York: Continuum, 2006.
Gratton, Peter, *Speculative Realism: Problems and Prospects*, London: Bloomsbury, 2014.
Hacking, Ian, *The Social Construction of What?*, Cambridge MA: Harvard University Press, 1999.
Harman, Graham, 'Fear of Reality: On Realism and Infra-Realism', *The Monist*, 98 (2015): 126–44.
Harman, Graham, *Guerrilla Metaphysics: Phenomenology and the Carpentry of Things*, Chicago: Open Court, 2005.
Harman, Graham, *The Quadruple Object*, Alresford: Zero Books, 2011.
Hegel, Georg W.F., *Aesthetics: Lectures on Fine Art*, 2 vols, Oxford: Oxford University Press, 1998.
Hegel, Georg W.F., *Encyclopaedia of the Philosophical Sciences in Basic Outline, Part 1: Logic*, Cambridge MA: Cambridge University Press, 2010.
Hegel, Georg W.F., *Phenomenology of Spirit* (1807), Oxford: Oxford University Press, 1977.
Hegel, Georg W.F., *The Hegel Reader*, London: Wiley-Blackwell, 1998.

Heidegger, Martin, *Being and Time* (1927), trans. John Macquarrie and Edward Robinson, Hoboken: John Wiley and Sons Ltd, 1978.

Hölldobler, Bert and Wilson, Edward O., *The Superorganism: The Beauty, Elegance, and Strangeness of Insect Societies*, New York: W.W. Norton & Co., 2010.

Husserl, Edmund, *Experience and Judgment* (1938), trans. James S. Churchill and Karl Ameriks, Evanston: Northwestern University Press, 1975.

Husserl, Edmund, *Logical Investigations* (1900–1), trans. J.N. Findlay, London: Routledge, 2001.

Jerez, José Luis (ed.), *El giro ontológico*, Buenos Aires: Circulo Hermenéutico, 2015.

Joyce, James, *A Portrait of the Artist as a Young Man* (1916), Oxford: Oxford University Press, 2013.

Kanigel, Robert, *The Man Who Knew Infinity: A Life of the Genius Ramanujan*, New York: Charles Scribner's Sons, 1991.

Kanizsa, Gaetano, *Grammatica del vedere*, Bologna: il Mulino, 1980.

Kanizsa, Gaetano, *Vedere e pensare*, Bologna: il Mulino, 1991.

Kant, Immanuel, *Che cosa significa orientarsi nel pensiero* (1786), Milan: Adelphi, 1996.

Kant, Immanuel, *Critique of Judgment*, trans. James Creed Meredith, Oxford: Oxford University Press, 2007.

Kant, Immanuel, *Critique of Pure Reason*, trans. Norman Kemp Smith, New York: Palgrave Macmillan, 2007.

Kant, Immanuel, *Del Primo fondamento della distinzione degli oggetti nello spazio* (1768), in *Scritti precritici*, Roma-Bari: Laterza, 2000.

Kojève, Alexandre, *Introduction to the Reading of Hegel*, trans. James K. Nichols, New York: Cornell University Press, 1968.

Kripke, Saul, 'Naming and Necessity', in *Semantics of Natural Language*, ed. G. Harman and D. Davidson, Dordrecht: Reidel, 1972.

Kuhnert, Nikolaus and Ngo, Anh-Linh (eds), *Get Real! Die Wirklichkeit der Architektur / Architectural Realities*, ARCH+, 217, 2014.

Lask, Emil, *Logik der Philosophie* (1911), in *Gesammelte Schriften*, Tübingen: Mohr 1923.

Latour, Bruno, 'Ramses II est-il mort de la tuberculose?', *La Recherche*, 307 (1998).

Legrenzi, Paolo, 'Naive Probability: A Mental Model Theory of Extensional Reasoning', *Psychological Review*, 106/1 (1999): 62–88.

Leibniz, Gottfried Wilhelm, *Discourse on Metaphysics and the Monadology*, trans. George R. Montgomery, Prometheus Books: New York, 1992.

Leibniz, Gottfried Wilhelm, 'Meditations on Knowledge, Truth and Ideas' (1684), in *Philosophical Papers and Letters*, ed. L.E. Loemker, Dordrecht: Springer, 1989.
Leibniz, Gottfried Wilhelm, *New Essays on Human Understanding*, 2nd ed., trans. and ed. P. Remnant and J. Bennett, New York: Cambridge University Press, 1996.
Lucretius, *De rerum natura*, trans. William Ellery Leonard, 1916.
Luis de Molina, *On Divine Foreknowledge*, Ithaca: Cornell University Press, 1988.
Maccarini, Andrea, Morandi, Emmanuele and Prandini, Riccardo (eds), *Sociological Realism*, London: Routledge, 2011.
McDowell, John, *Mind and World*, Cambridge MA: Harvard University Press, 1994.
McGinn, Colin, *Prehension: The Hand and the Emergence of Humanity*, Cambridge MA: MIT Press, 2015.
Mann, Thomas, *Buddenbrooks: The Decline of a Family*, New York: Vintage International, 1993.
Marconi, Diego, *Lexical Competence*, Cambridge MA: The MIT Press, 1997.
Marconi, Diego, *Per la verità. Relativismo e filosofia*, Torino: Einaudi, 2007.
Martignani, Luca, *Sociologia e nuovo realismo*, Milan-Udine: Mimesis, 2013.
Marx, Karl, *Capital, Volume I* (1867), London: Penguin Books, 1990.
Massironi, Manfredo, 'La via più breve nel pensiero visivo', *Sistemi intelligenti*, a.-VII, 2 (1995): 223–61.
Massironi, Manfredo, *Fenomenologia della percezione visiva*, Bologna: il Mulino, 1998.
Meillassoux, Quentin, *After Finitude: An Essay on the Necessity of Contingency*, trans. Ray Brassier, London: Bloomsbury, 2009.
Meinong, Alexius, 'Über Gegenstände höherer Ordnung und deren Verhältnis zur inneren Wahrnehmung', in *Zeitschrift für Psychologie und Physiologie der Sinnesorgane*, 21 (1900–2): 187–272.
Meinong, Alexius, *Untersuchungen über Gegenstandstheorie und Psychologie*, Leipzig: Barth, 1904.
Metzger, Wolfgang, *Die Entwicklung ihrer Grundannahmen seit der Einführung des Experiments*, Vienna: Wolfgang Krammer Verlag, 1941.
Mezei, Balázs and Smith, Barry, *The Four Phases of Philosophy*, Amsterdam: Rodopi, 1998.

Moore, George E., 'Proof of an External World', *Proceedings of the British Academy*, 25 (1939): 273–300.
Nietzsche, Friedrich, *The Will to Power* (1901), New York: Vintage Books, 1968.
Peirce, Charles S., 'On a New List of Categories', *Proceedings of the American Academy of Arts and Sciences*, 7 (1868): 287–98.
Perry, Ralph Barton et al., *The New Realism: Cooperative Studies in Philosophy*, New York: Macmillan & Co., 1912 (new ed. Ulan Press, 2012).
Perry, Ralph Barton et al., 'The Program and First Platform of Six Realists', *Journal of Philosophy, Psychology and Scientific Methods*, 7/15 (1910): 393–401.
Pfeiffer, Ernst (ed.), *Sigmund Freud and Lou Andreas-Salome: Letters*, New York: W.W. Norton & Co, 1985.
Plato, *Philebus*, in *Platonis Opera*, ed. J. Burnet, Oxford: Oxford University Press, 1903.
Plato, *Sophist*, trans. William Cobb, Savage, MD: Rowman and Littlefield, 1990.
Plato, *Theaetetus*, in *Platonis Opera*, ed. J. Burnet, Oxford: Oxford University Press, 1903.
Plato, *Timaeus*, in *Plato in Twelve Volumes*, Vol. 9, trans. W.R.M. Lamb, Cambridge MA: Harvard University Press, 1925.
Proust, Marcel, *In Search of Lost Time*, trans. C.K. Scott Moncrieff and Terence Kilmartin, revised D.J. Enright, New York: The Modern Library, 1992.
Putnam, Hilary, 'The Meaning of "Meaning"', in *Philosophical Papers II*, Cambridge: Cambridge University Press, 1975, pp. 215–71.
Quaglino, Margherita and Scarpa, Raffaella (eds), *Metodi Testo Realtà*, Alessandria: Edizioni dell'Orso, 2014.
Ratzinger, Joseph, *Svolta per l'Europa? Chiesa e modernità nell'Europa dei rivolgimenti*, Milan: Edizioni Paoline, 1992.
Rickert, Heinrich, *Der Gegenstand der Erkenntnis. Einführung in die Transzendentalphilosophie*, Tübingen und Leipzig: J.C.B. Mohr (Paul Siebeck), 1904.
Rickert, Heinrich, *Die Logik des Prädikats und das Problem der Ontologie*, Heidelberg: Winter, 1930.
Riedweg, Christoph (ed.), *Discorsi d'attualità. Dal 'postmoderno' ai nuovi orizzonti della cultura*, Roma: Carocci, 2013.
Roncato, Sergio and Ruminati, Rino, 'Naive Statics: Current Misconceptions on Equilibrium', *Journal of Experimental Psychology: Learning, Memory and Cognition*, 12 (1986): 361–77.

Rorty, Richard, 'Charles Taylor on Truth', in *Truth and Progress: Philosophical Papers, Vol. 3*, Cambridge: Cambridge University Press, 1998, pp. 84–97.
Rorty, Richard, 'Nineteenth-Century Idealism and Twentieth-Century Textualism', *The Monist*, 64/2 (1981): 155–74.
Rorty, Richard, *Objectivity, Relativism, and Truth: Philosophical Papers, Vol. 1*, Cambridge: Cambridge University Press, 1991.
Rorty, Richard, *Philosophy and the Mirror of Nature*, Princeton: Princeton University Press, 1979.
Scarpa, Raffaella, *Il caso nuovo realismo. La lingua del dibattito filosofico contemporaneo*, Milan-Udine: Mimesis, 2013.
Schelling, Friedrich W.J., *Philosophical Investigations into the Essence of Human Freedom* (1809), trans. Jeff Love and Johannes Schmidt, New York: SUNY Press, 2006.
Schopenhauer, Arthur, *On the Fourfold Root of the Principle of Sufficient Reason and Other Writings*, ed. D.E. Cartwright, E.E. Erdmann and C. Janaway, Cambridge: Cambridge University Press, 2012.
Schrödinger, Erwin, *What is Life?* (1944), Cambridge: Cambridge University Press, 2012.
Sellars, Wilfrid S., *Empiricism and the Philosophy of Mind* (1956), Cambridge MA: Harvard University Press, 1997.
Smith, Barry, 'Common Sense', in *Cambridge Companion to Husserl*, ed. B. Smith and D. Woodruff Smith, Cambridge: Cambridge University Press, 1995.
Smith, Barry, 'Husserlian Ecology', unpublished, 2000, at <http://wings.buffalo.edu/academic/department/philosophy/faculty/smith>.
Smith, Barry, 'Objects and Their Environments: From Aristotle to Ecological Ontology', in A. Frank, J. Raper and J.-P. Cheylan (eds), *The Life and Motion of Socio-Economic Units*, London: Taylor and Francis, 2001, pp. 79–97.
Smith, Barry, 'The Structures of Common-Sense World', *Acta Philosophica Fennica*, 58 (1995): 290–317.
Smith, Barry, 'Toward a Realistic Science of Environments', *Ecological Psychology*, 21/2 (2009): 121–30.
Smith, Barry, 'Truth and the Visual Field', in *Naturalizing Phenomenology: Issues in Contemporary Phenomenology and Cognitive Science*, ed. J. Petitot, F.J. Varela, B. Pachoud and J.M. Roy, Stanford: Stanford University Press, 1999.
Smith, Barry and Roberto Casati, 'Naive Physics: An Essay in Ontology', *Philosophical Psychology*, 7/2 (1994): 225–44.
Smith, Barry and Achille C. Varzi, 'The Niche', *Nous*, 33/2 (1999): 214–38.

Sokal, Alan and Bricmont, Jean, *Fashionable Nonsense: Postmodern Intellectuals' Abuse of Science*, New York: Picador, 1997.
Stiegler, Bernard, *Technics and Time 1: The Fault of Epimetheus*, trans. Richard Beardsworth and George Collins, Stanford: Stanford University Press, 1998.
Stove, David and Kimball, Roger, 'Idealism: A Victorian Horror Story (Part Two)', in *The Plato Cult and Other Philosophical Follies*, Oxford: Blackwell, 1991, pp. 135–78.
Strawson, Peter F., *Individuals*, London: Methuen, 1959.
Suskind, Ron, 'Faith, Certainty and the Presidency of George W. Bush', *The New York Times Magazine*, 17 October 2004.
Svevo, Italo, *Zeno's Conscience* (1923), New York: Penguin, 2002.
Tomasi di Lampedusa, Giuseppe, *The Leopard*, New York: Vintage Classics, 2007.
Trendelenburg, Friedrich Adolf, *Outlines of Logic: An English Translation of Trendelenburg's Elementa*, Oxford: Shrimpton & Son, 1898.
Unger, Peter, *Empty Ideas: A Critique of Analytic Philosophy*, Oxford: Oxford University Press, 2014.
Vicario, Giovanni Bruno, *Psicologia generale*, Rome-Bari: Laterza, 2001.
Vico, Giambattista, *The New Science of Giambattista Vico*, trans. T.G. Bergin and M.H. Fisch, Ithaca: Cornell University Press, 1984.
Wittgenstein, Ludwig, *Philosophical Investigations*, trans. P.M.S. Hacker, Oxford: Wiley-Blackwell, 2009.
Wittgenstein, Ludwig, *Tractatus Logico-Philosophicus*, trans. David Pears and Brian McGuinness, London: Routledge, 2001.
Wolff, Christian, *Empirical Psychology, Treated According to the Scientific Method*, Prostat in Officina Libraria Rengeriana.
Wolff, Christian, *Philosophia prima sive Ontologia*, Frankfurt-Leipzig: Renger, 1729.

Index

action, 41, 43–5, 48, 55, 63–4, 80, 89, 109, 112, 119, 128, 158, 183–6, 200, 202, 206–7, 237, 241, 248, 252, 254, 261, 272, 277, 292, 296, 325
aesthetics, 21–3, 33, 36–7, 46, 49, 104, 115, 143–5, 149, 158, 308, 322
analogy, 66, 174, 200
analytic philosophy, 237, 243, 273, 316, 323, 325–6
appearance, 14, 27, 29–30, 33–4, 36, 58–60, 66, 123, 138–9, 149–50, 152, 170, 179, 218, 225
apperception, 28–9, 32, 39, 46, 64, 189, 232, 297
archive, 174, 189, 193, 195, 199, 225, 250, 283
Aristotle, 10, 47, 65, 111, 134, 138, 153, 161, 180, 187, 192, 198, 204–5, 213–14, 262, 273, 295, 310
Artificial Intelligence, 170, 213, 260–1, 269
Augustine, 278, 280
Austen, Jane, 308
automaton, 171, 177, 213, 242, 301
Avicenna, 10

Badiou, Alain, 324
Baudrillard, Jean, 323
Baumgarten, Alexander, 17–18
Berkeley, George, 25, 27, 228, 232, 235, 242, 290, 316, 320
Bhaskar, Roy, 318
body, 20, 56, 104, 160, 183, 194, 197, 271, 282, 301, 304, 309
Bogen, Helmuth, 13
Boghossian, Paul, 323–4
Borges, Luis, 52, 178, 249, 310
Brassier, Ray, 323
Brentano, Franz, 326
Bricmont, Jean, 323
Broad, Charlie Dunbar, 278

capitalisation, 127, 198, 205, 207, 209, 213, 220, 260, 301
capitalism, 202, 259
categories of experience, 37
Catren, Gabriel, 324
causality, 35, 44, 55, 60–4, 170, 181–3, 203, 209–11, 215, 220
Chisholm, Roderick Milton, 58
colour, 31, 34–5, 48, 76, 109, 111–12, 135, 142, 146–8, 220, 230, 235

357

358 Index

common sense, 21, 27, 65, 140–1, 195, 226, 228, 263, 316–18, 320
consciousness, 31, 46–7, 50, 135–6, 159–60, 176, 192, 242, 252, 282, 284, 301, 305, 308, 311
consumerism, 261
continental philosophy, 13, 227, 237, 316, 319, 322, 325–6
Copernican revolution, 19, 21, 38, 55, 61, 210, 317
Critique of Judgment, 52, 66–7, 204, 262, 274, 292
Critique of Pure Reason, 11, 17, 53, 67, 175, 185, 192, 204, 271, 277, 317

Darwin, Charles, 199, 274
De Caro, Mario, 324
death, 36, 76, 168–71, 207, 234, 282–3, 300–2, 305, 307
deduction, 40–3, 46, 54, 192, 303
DeLanda, Manuel, 323
Derrida, Jacques, 168, 206, 208, 319
Descartes, René, 13, 141, 159, 216, 240, 242, 317
desire, 168, 170, 225, 262, 275, 301, 305, 311
dialectic, 17, 20, 67, 190–1, 198, 202, 207–9, 240
documedia revolution, 277
Dummett, Michael, 326

Eco, Umberto, 279
ecology, 21, 70, 130–1, 252, 306
Eddington, Arthur, 195
effect, 35, 63, 101, 159, 171, 182–3, 188, 194, 205, 210–12, 238, 298, 300, 307
emergence, 175–7, 179–80, 183–4, 186, 188–9, 191–2, 194–5, 199, 207–8, 213, 218, 226, 233–5, 243, 249, 255–7, 259–60, 270, 289, 295, 297, 300, 306–7, 310, 325
empiricism, 21, 38, 62, 132, 177–8, 185, 208, 235, 237
entropy, 186, 188, 190, 195, 214, 248, 300, 304, 311
epistemological inflation, 14–15, 84
Euler, Leonhard, 255, 259
exemplification, 289, 291

faculty to play, 42
Feyerabend, Paul, 92, 318
Fichte, Johann Gottlieb, 202, 324
Figal, Günter, 323
Fitzgerald, F. Scott, 167
Foucault, Michel, 322
Frege, Gottlob, 213, 267, 326
Freud, Sigmund, 97, 117, 167–9, 252, 256, 277
future, 30, 122, 178, 180, 200, 225, 229, 235, 305, 317

Gabriel, Markus, 322, 324
Gadamer, Hans Georg, 13
Garcia, Tristan, 324
Gaudí, Salvador, 254, 261
Gentile, Giovanni, 228, 316–17, 321
Gestalt, 13, 49, 53, 148, 310
God, 10, 20, 65, 96, 120, 128, 173, 175, 181, 185, 187, 211, 221, 228, 238, 241, 278, 297, 320
Grant, Iain Hamilton, 323

habit, 21, 25, 35, 43, 60, 62–3, 87–8, 127, 136, 160, 178, 225
Hacking, Ian, 323
Harman, Graham, 319, 323–5
Hegel, Georg Wilhelm Friedrich, 11, 169, 202, 207–8, 240, 247, 257, 279–80, 282, 284, 306, 308, 320
Heidegger, Martin, 9, 12, 169, 191–2, 196, 203, 208, 244, 252, 278, 319, 323–5
Hemingway, Ernst, 62
hermeneutics, 15, 124, 163, 243, 272–5, 319, 323
Holt, Edwin Bissel, 316
Homer, 15, 57, 73, 244, 255, 257, 271, 287–8, 290
homeric age *see* Homer
Hume, David, 32, 55, 223
Husserl, Edmund, 27–8, 103–4, 123, 127, 135–6, 213, 310, 319, 326

illusion, 14, 34–5, 83, 110, 126, 142–3, 149–53, 155, 170, 197, 222, 230, 239
induction, 29, 89, 125, 132, 138, 145
inscription, 121, 191, 200, 206, 208, 212, 224, 248, 266–8, 282–3, 297, 301, 303, 305–6, 309
intellect, 11, 18, 32, 39, 50, 53, 63, 66, 82, 108–11, 113, 153, 177, 189–90, 203–6, 248, 269, 274, 277
intelligent design, 183–4, 186–7, 238, 247, 274, 295
intentionality, 182–3, 195, 200, 210, 242, 247, 256, 262, 264, 301, 304–5
interaction, 34, 63, 68, 153, 184, 219–20, 233, 235, 243, 256, 268, 280, 303–4, 306, 325
Internet, 127, 170–1, 174, 176, 277, 283
interpretative schemes, 73, 85, 216, 258, 272–4, 280
intuition, 18, 21, 25, 27–8, 37, 40, 45–7, 55–6, 58, 67, 98, 101–3, 143, 145, 204, 229–30, 232, 240, 260, 272–3
I-think, 29, 186, 189, 192, 227–8, 232, 238–9, 276, 284

Kanizsa, Gaetano, 107, 131, 155–6
Koffka, Kurt, 60
Kojève, Alexandre, 169
Kripke, Saul, 322
Kuhn, Thomas, 319

language, 87, 115–17, 119–20, 136–7, 140, 162, 186, 191, 232, 234, 247, 255, 284, 302, 309, 319
Lascaux, 206, 265
Lask, Emil, 103–4
Leibniz, Gottfried Wilhelm von, 9, 13, 18, 32, 64, 104, 108, 118, 128, 181, 255, 275–6, 296–7
Lenin, Vladimir Il'ič, 10
Lipmann, Otto, 13
Lovejoy, Arthur Oncken, 316
Löwith, Karl, 9

Mach, Ernst, 10
Marvin, Walter Taylor, 316

Marx, Karl, 97, 202, 259, 279–80
mathematics, 13, 19, 21–2, 28, 37, 43–4, 46–7, 52, 66–7, 86, 119–20, 124–5, 133, 193, 202, 255, 258, 271, 281, 324
McDowell, John, 323
McTaggart, John Ellis, 316
measurement, 54, 125, 163
mediation, 28, 53, 87–9, 202, 239, 245, 273, 276
Meillassoux, Quentin, 323–4
Meinong, Alexius, 323
memory, 38, 118, 169, 177, 180, 185–9, 192–5, 197–8, 200, 203–5, 212, 224–5, 260–1, 265
Merleau–Ponty, Maurice, 319
metaxy, 191, 201, 208
mind, 12, 31–2, 42–3, 46, 105, 149, 160, 175, 195, 238, 268–9, 279, 284, 320
Montague, William Pepperell, 316
Montesquieu, 201
Moore, George E., 124, 142, 151, 316
myth, 30, 186, 237, 239–42, 269, 276, 289–91
mythos *see* myth

nature, 13, 41, 67, 86, 135, 149, 184–5, 190, 192, 198–200, 202–3, 207, 214, 247–50, 260–3, 265, 305
necessity, 61, 66, 108, 122, 177, 185, 200, 264–5, 313
Newton, Isaac, 11, 19–20, 28, 63, 65, 121–2, 138, 217, 244, 321
Nietzsche, Friedrich, 20, 90, 92–3, 95, 97, 169, 239, 275, 319

objectivity, 39, 102–3, 146, 267, 318–19, 323
organism, 40, 149, 170–1, 191, 199, 234, 248, 252, 275, 283, 286, 299–302, 304–6, 311

past, 30, 137, 180, 193–5, 197, 224–5, 253, 256, 261, 289, 305
Peirce, Charles S., 190
perception, 16, 25, 32–4, 36, 43, 55, 61–2, 79, 84–8, 98, 106, 120, 129, 141, 143, 145, 147, 150–2, 155, 197, 206, 225–6, 231–2, 266, 297, 303, 322
permanence, 29, 44, 55–9, 182, 189, 192, 196, 205, 211–12, 215, 217, 220
Perry, Ralph Barton, 316
perspectivism, 90, 123–4
philosophy of history, 10, 13, 301–2
physics, 11–14, 19–21, 54, 86, 115, 124, 138, 142–3, 228, 232, 271, 281, 286, 321
Pitkin, Walter Boughton, 316
Plato, 34, 57, 104, 173–4, 180, 199, 203, 208, 242, 262, 271, 280–2
Popper, Karl, 264
positivism, 90, 135, 237
postmodernism, 216, 228, 237, 278, 315, 318, 321, 326
post-truth, 201, 243, 278
pragmatism, 71–2, 130
pre–comprehension, 63

progress, 82, 121–6, 161, 177–8, 228, 326
Proust, Marcel, 164, 169, 195, 224–5, 259, 312
psychology, 10, 21, 30, 36–7, 131, 137, 213, 252, 264, 318
Putnam, Hilary, 138, 275, 322, 324
Pythagoras, 268

Quine, Willard Van Orman, 13, 57

Ratzinger, Joseph, 323
reciprocal action *see* action
reductionism, 12–14, 130
relativism, 123, 140, 312
repetition, 83, 169, 188, 194–5, 203, 205, 209, 226, 248, 250, 253, 256, 258–9, 269, 276, 282
representation, 28, 31–3, 36, 40, 47, 64, 70, 168, 227, 230, 236, 238–40, 254, 276, 285, 318–19
Rorty, Richard, 318–19, 323
Rousseau, Jean-Jacques, 169, 312
Russell, Bertrand, 57, 227, 278, 316

Santayana, George, 316
Saussure, Ferdinand de, 310
scepticism, 29, 42, 51, 124, 132, 137, 160, 237, 326
Schelling, Friedrich, 179, 202
schematism, 19, 43–5, 47–8, 50, 54–5, 66–7, 190, 204, 209, 262, 272–4, 277, 303
Schopenhauer, Arthur, 168–9, 203, 236

Schrödinger, Erwin, 168, 320
Sellars, Roy Wood, 316
senses, 11, 15, 19, 34, 39, 41, 66, 85, 110–11, 113, 123, 128, 149, 194, 282, 302
sensibility, 42–3, 49, 65–6, 88, 108–9, 113, 177, 190, 203–5, 234, 248, 252, 274, 277, 282, 305
sign, 183, 208, 254–5, 258, 267, 282, 306, 308–11
singularity, 123, 200, 251, 265, 310
Smith, Barry, 136
social object, 188, 197–8, 217–18, 220, 231, 233, 237, 262, 266, 268, 272–3, 277, 284–5, 287
Sokal, Alan, 323
spacetime, 28, 187, 195, 211, 220, 224–5, 266
Spaulding, Edward Gleason, 316
Srinivasa, Ramanujan, 279
stick, 27, 66, 84, 152, 170, 223, 259–60
Stove, David, 320
Strawson, Peter Frederick, 318
Suarez, Francisco, 10, 17–18
substance, 30, 43–5, 48–9, 55–60, 67, 118, 192, 214
subsumption, 47–8, 50, 101, 262
surprise, 72, 105–6, 152, 223, 290
synthetic a priori judgments, 66, 193, 271, 276–7

tabula, 194, 306
Tarde, Gabriel, 262
text, 41, 164, 232, 267, 283, 319, 322, 326
Timaeus, 19, 174

trace, 180, 182, 188, 207,
    209–10, 212, 224, 265–7,
    307, 309
tradition, 9, 54, 82, 121, 126, 292
transcendentalism, 40, 43, 54,
    65, 132, 177, 228, 235, 238,
    242, 270, 297, 303, 315
Trendelenburg, Friedrich, 202,
    208

Vattimo, Gianni, 322
Vico, Giambattista, 186, 276, 278

Web, 170–1, 174, 182, 189–91,
    195, 197–9, 203, 213–14,
    242, 249, 269, 283
Wittgenstein, Ludwig, 76–7, 142,
    154, 167, 179, 255, 316
Wolff, Christian, 10, 18, 284